Rethinking the Vote

Rethinking the Vote

*The Politics and Prospects of
American Election Reform*

Ann N. Crigler
University of Southern California

Marion R. Just
Wellesley College

Edward J. McCaffery
University of Southern California
California Institute of Technology

New York   Oxford
OXFORD UNIVERSITY PRESS
2004

Oxford University Press

Oxford   New York
Auckland   Bangkok   Buenos Aires   Cape Town   Chennai
Dar es Salaam   Delhi   Hong Kong   Istanbul   Karachi   Kolkata
Kuala Lumpar   Madrid   Melbourne   Mexico City   Mumbai
Nairobi   São Paulo   Shanghai   Taipei   Tokyo   Toronto

Published by Oxford University Press, Inc.
198 Madison Avenue, New York, New York 10016
http://www.oup-usa.org

Oxford is a registered trademark of Oxford University Press

Library of Congress Cataloging-in-Publication Data
Rethinking the vote : the politics and prospects of American election reform / edited by
    Ann N. Crigler, Marion R. Just, Edward J. McCaffery.
        p. cm.
    Includes bibliographical references and index.
    ISBN 0-19-515984-5 (alk. paper)—ISBN 0-19-515985-3 (pbk.)
    1. Elections—United States.   2. Election law—United States.   I. Crigler, Ann N. II. Just,
Marion R. III. McCaffery, Edward J.

JK1976.R48 2004
324.6'0973—dc21   2002044964

9 8 7 6 5 4 3 2 1

Printed in the United States of America
on acid-free paper

To the children in our lives,
and their futures

Contents

Tables and Figures

TABLES

FIGURES

Acknowledgments

The University of Southern California (USC)–Caltech Center for the Study of Law and Politics was founded in July 2000 with the generous financial support of USC Provost Lloyd Armstrong and Caltech Provost Steven Koonin. The animating goal of the center is to promote interdisciplinary, quantitative, and empirical research on important issues at the intersections of law and politics. On November 7, 2000, the world offered up a perfect example of the need for such analysis in the disputed presidential election between George W. Bush and Al Gore. In the weeks and months following this striking event, scholars affiliated with the center played major and varying roles in trying to come to an understanding of what had happened and what, if anything, should happen to make the future of electoral democracy better.

Many of the chapters in this book grew out of a conference held at the USC Law School in April 2001, which was cosponsored by the center and USC's Jesse M. Unruh Institute of Politics. We thank the conference sponsors, the Law School, and all the participants at the conference for their support and helpful conversations and input before, during, and after it. We also thank our academic leaders—Dean Joseph Aoun at USC's College of Letters, Arts, and Sciences and Dean Matt Spitzer at USC Law School; chairpersons John Ledyard and Jean Ensminger at Caltech's Division of the Humanities and Social Sciences; and Dean Lee Cuba, of Wellesley College, for his support of the National Science Foundation sponsored social science summer research program.

We editors would like to thank the many contributors who made our tasks both educational and enjoyable. There was a great deal of give and take during the production of this volume—mainly, our giving, and the contributors graciously taking (or wisely declining), our two cents' worth of advice—and we thank all who put up with it. We also thank Peter Labella, Sean Mahoney, and Terry Deal Michelet at Oxford University Press and many anonymous referees for their comments on earlier versions of the manuscript.

Wendy Lopata deserves special thanks for helping in many ways, including coordinating various versions of the manuscript. Christine Yi standardized the figures and tables. Darin Fox provided critical technical support. Joan Huh,

Stephanie Little, and Kathleen Regan helped with research, references, and copyediting. Lesley Harvey assembled the index with Christopher Gaspar's assistance. We are fortunate to work with such talented and dedicated people.
    We thank all of these people for helping us to rethink the vote.

                                                        Ann N. Crigler
                                                        Marion R. Just
                                                        Edward J. McCaffery

Contributors

R. Michael Alvarez is Professor of Political Science at the California Institute of Technology and Associate Director of the USC–Caltech Center for the Study of Law and Politics. Alvarez received his Ph.D. in political science from Duke University. His research interests include American voting behavior, campaigns and elections, American government, macro-political economy, positive theory/public choice, comparative politics, and quantitative methodologies. Selected publications include "Perception and Misperception: Constituent Knowledge of the Persian Gulf War Vote," 1996, with Paul W. Gronke, in *Legislative Studies Quarterly: Issues and Information in Presidential Elections* (University of Michigan Press, 1997); "Method or Madness: Testing the Intentional Models of Ticket-Splitting," 1993, with Matthew M. Schousen, *American Politics Quarterly* 21: 410–438.

Jeb Barnes is Assistant Professor of Political Science at the University of Southern California. After receiving his law degree from the University of Chicago Law School, he practiced as a commercial litigator in Boston and San Francisco. In 1994, he left the practice of law to pursue a doctorate at the University of California, Berkeley. At Berkeley, he won the Peter Odegard Memorial Award for the most promising scholar, an Outstanding Graduate Student Instructor Award for teaching excellence, and numerous fellowships, including the Charles Atwood Kofoid and Henry Braden fellowships and the Phi Beta Kappa Research Fellowship. Barnes's specialties are public law and American politics, with particular emphasis on interbranch relations. He has two books forthcoming: *Overruled? Legislative Overrides, Pluralism, and Court–Congress Relations in the Age of Statutes* (Stanford University Press) and an edited volume with Mark Miller entitled *Putting the Pieces Together: Policy-making from an Inter-branch Perspective* (Georgetown University Press).

Tami Buhr is Research Coordinator at the Joan Shorenstein Center for the Study of Press and Politics at Harvard University, where she has worked closely on the Vanishing Voter Project. Buhr has been involved in the Shorenstein Center studies of the 1992 and 1996 presidential campaigns and was the pollster for Dartmouth College during the 1996 and 2000 New Hampshire primaries. Buhr's Harvard dissertation is on the 1996 New Hampshire primary.

Erwin Chemerinsky holds the Sydney M. Irmas Chair in Public Interest Law, Legal Ethics, and Political Science at the University of Southern California. After receiving his law degree from Harvard Law School, Chemerinsky served in the Attorney General's Program for Honor Law Graduates. From 1979 to 1980 Chemerinsky was an attorney and associate for Dobrovir, Oates, & Gebhardt and has been a Professor of Law since 1980. He has had numerous publications in both academic and professional journals and is the author of *Federal Jurisdiction, 4th ed.* (Aspen Law & Business, 2003) and *Constitutional Law: Principles & Policies*, 2nd ed. (Aspen Law & Business, 2002). His areas of expertise include constitutional law, civil rights, civil liberties, and criminal procedure.

Ann N. Crigler is Associate Professor of Political Science and Director of the Jesse M. Unruh Institute of Politics at the University of Southern California. Crigler received her Ph.D. in political science from the Massachusetts Institute of Technology. Her research examines how people understand and learn about politics from the news media. Selected publications include *The Psychology of Political Communication* (University of Michigan Press, 1996) and the coauthored books *Crosstalk: Citizens, Candidates, and the Media in a Presidential Campaign* (University of Chicago Press, 1996) and *Common Knowledge: News and the Construction of Political Meaning* (University of Chicago Press, 1992).

Susan Estrich holds the Robert Kingsley Professorship in Law and Political Science at the University of Southern California School of Law. She graduated from Harvard Law School and was the first woman president of the *Harvard Law Review*. Estrich was a law clerk for Justice John Paul Stevens of the United States Supreme Court and taught at Harvard Law School from 1980 to 1989. Her publications include *Sex and Power* (Riverhead Books, 2000); *Getting Away with Murder: How Politics Is Destroying the Criminal Justice System* (Harvard University Press, 1998); and *Real Rape* (Harvard University Press, 1987). Her areas of expertise include sexual harassment, rape, gender discrimination, and election law.

Kathleen A. Frankovic is Director of Surveys and Producer for CBS News, where she has major responsibility for the design, analysis, and broadcasting of results from CBS News and CBS News/*New York Times* polls. Frankovic received her Ph.D. in political science from Rutgers University, was a political science professor at the University of Vermont, and directed the Social Science Research Center there. She was a 1997 recipient of the Mary Lepper Award, given by the Women's Caucus for Political Science to a political scientist who has distinguished herself outside of academia. She is a coauthor of *The Election of 1980, The Election of 1992*, and *The Election of 2000* (all published by Chatham House) and has published many articles on elections and public opinion. Frankovic is President of the World Association for Public Opinion Research and is active in numerous other research organizations.

Andrew Gelman is Professor of Statistics and Political Science at Columbia University. He was the founding director of the Quantitative Methods in Social Sciences program at Columbia. His research interests include Bayesian statistics, sample surveys, public health, and political science. He is the author of many methodological studies of public opinion, voting, and elections, including "Enhancing Democracy through Legislative Redistricting," 1994, with Gary King, *American Political Science Review* 88(3): 541–59 and "Why Are American Presidential Election Campaign Polls So Variable When Votes Are So Predictable?," 1993, with Gary King, *British Journal of Political Science* 23(1):409–51. Gelman has coauthored two books: *Bayesian Data Analysis* (Chapman and Hall, 1995) and *Teaching Statistics: A Bag of Tricks* (Oxford, 2002).

Richard L. Hasen is Professor of Law and William M. Rains Fellow at Loyola Law School in Los Angeles. Hasen, who received his Ph.D. in political science and his J.D. from the University of California, Los Angeles, is a nationally recognized expert in election law and campaign finance regulation. He is author of *The Supreme Court and Election Law: Judging Equality from* Baker v. Carr *to* Bush v. Gore (New York University Press, 2003), coauthor of a leading casebook on election law, *Election Law: Cases and Materials* (Carolina Academic Press, 2001), and coeditor of the *Election Law Journal*. Before coming to Loyola, he clerked for the Honorable David R. Thompson of the United States Court of Appeals for the Ninth Circuit, worked as a civil appellate lawyer at the Encino firm of Horvitz and Levy, and taught at the Chicago-Kent College of Law.

Marion R. Just is Professor of Political Science at Wellesley College and Research Associate at the Joan Shorenstein Center on Press, Politics and Public Policy at the John F. Kennedy School of Government, Harvard University. Her major fields of interest are mass media, public opinion, and elections. Just received her Ph.D. in political science at Columbia University. Her current research focuses on emotions and cognition in voting and local television news. Just's selected publications include *Crosstalk: Citizens, Candidates and the Media in a Presidential Campaign* (University of Chicago Press, 1996); *Common Knowledge: News and the Construction of Political Meaning* (University of Chicago Press, 1992); "Leadership Image-Building: After Clinton and Watergate," 2000, *Political Psychology* 21(1):179–198 and articles in the Special Report on Local News, December 2002, 2001, 2000, and 1999, *Columbia Journalism Review*.

Jonathan N. Katz is Associate Professor of Political Science at the California Institute of Technology; he received his Ph.D. from the University of California, San Diego. His research interests are in American politics, formal political theory, and political methodology. He is the coauthor of *Elbridge Gerry's Salamander: The Political Consequences of the Reapportionment Revolution* (Cambridge University Press, 2002). Katz is a member of the editorial boards for the journals *Political Research Quarterly, Electoral Studies*, and *Political Analysis*.

Gary King (Ph.D., University of Wisconsin-Madison, 1984) is the David Florence Professor of Government at Harvard University. He also serves as the Director of the Harvard–MIT Data Center, as Senior Science Advisor to the World Health Organization, and as a member of the steering committee of the Center for Basic Research in the Social Sciences. King was elected President of the Society for Political Methodology and fellow of the American Academy of Arts and Sciences and has been a Guggenheim Fellow and a Visiting Fellow at Oxford University. He has authored and coauthored more than seventy journal articles and four books in political methodology, other fields of political science, and other disciplines, including *A Solution to the Ecological Inference Problem: Reconstructing Individual Behavior from Aggregate Data* (Princeton University Press, 1997); *Unifying Political Methodology: The Likelihood Theory of Statistical Inference* (University of Michigan Press, 1989); and (with Robert Keohane and Sidney Verba) *Designing Social Inquiry: Scientific Inference in Qualitative Research* (Princeton University Press, 1994).

Jon A. Krosnick is Professor of Psychology and Political Science at the Ohio State University and University Fellow at Resources for the Future. A former fellow at the Center for Advanced Study in the Behavioral Sciences at Stanford University, Krosnick has published on methods to maximize the quality of data collected through surveys, on how public attitudes on political issues are formed and changed, and on the social and cognitive forces shaping political activism and voting behavior. Krosnick serves on the Boards of Overseers of the National Election Study and the General Social Survey and has lectured on survey questionnaire design worldwide at such institutions as the U.S. General Accounting Office, the U.S. Census Bureau, the Office of National Statistics of the United Kingdom, the London School of Economics and Political Science, and the U.S. Internal Revenue Service.

Edward J. McCaffery is the Maurice Jones Jr. Professor of Law and Political Science at the University of Southern California, Visiting Professor of Law and Economics at the California Institute of Technology, and Director of the USC–Caltech Center for the Study of Law and Politics. McCaffery received his J.D. from Harvard Law School and an M.A. in economics from the University of Southern California. His research interests include tax, property, law and economics, and law and politics. McCaffery is the author of *Taxing Women* (University of Chicago Press, 1997) and *Fair Not Flat: How to Make the Tax System Simpler and Better* (University of Chicago Press, 2002).

Joanne M. Miller is Assistant Professor of Political Science at the University of Minnesota. She received her Ph.D. in psychology at Ohio State University. Her research interests include the motivators of political activism and the effects of the mass media on political attitudes. Her research has appeared in the *American Journal of Political Science* and *Public Opinion Quarterly*.

Pippa Norris is the McGuire Lecturer in Comparative Politics at the John F. Kennedy School of Government at Harvard University. A political scientist, she compares elections, political communications, and gender politics. She has published over two dozen books, including most recently a quintet for Cambridge University Press, including *A Virtuous Circle* (2000); *Digital Divide* (2001); *Democratic Phoenix* (2002); *Rising Tide* (2003, with Ronald Inglehart); and *Electoral Engineering* (2003). Full details are available at www.pippanorris.com.

Daniel R. Ortiz is the John Allan Love Professor of Law and the Joseph C. Carter Research Professor of Law at the University of Virginia. After graduating from Yale, Ortiz spent two years on a Marshall Scholarship at Oxford University, where he completed a Master of Philosophy degree in English Studies. He then returned to Yale and earned his law degree. Ortiz led the Task Force on Legal and Constitutional Issues for the National Commission on Federal Election Reform in 2001. His areas of expertise include electoral law, constitutional law, administrative law, civil procedure, and legal theory. Recent publications include "The Federal Regulation of Elections," in *To Assure Pride and Confidence in the Electoral Process: Report of The National Commission on Federal Election Reform* (Brookings Institution Press, 2002) (editor and contributor); "Duopoly v. Autonomy: The Status of Major Parties in a Two-Party System," 2000, *Columbia Law Review* 100(3):753–74; "Governing through Intermediaries," 1999, with Samuel Issacharoff, *Virginia Law Review* 85(8): 1627–70; and "From Rights to Arrangements," 1999, *Loyola Law Review* 32(4):1217–26.

Trevor Potter is a former Commissioner and Chairman of the Federal Election Commission. He is a member of the Washington, DC, law firm Caplin & Drysdale and the Founder and General Counsel of the Campaign Legal Center, a not-for-profit litigation center for campaign finance issues. He is also the editor of the campaign finance law Web site (www.Brookings/edu/campaignfinance) at the Brookings Institution, where he is a nonresident Senior Fellow. A frequent speaker on political finance laws and lobbying disclosure issues, Potter has also testified as an expert on election law before Congress and in litigation.

D. E. "Betsy" Sinclair graduated from the University of Redlands in 2002 with a B.S. in mathematics and economics. She is currently a graduate student at the California Institute of Technology, where she is pursuing research interests in economics and political science.

Michael P. Tichy is a Research Associate in the Department of Psychology at Ohio State University. He holds a B.A. degree from Ohio State University and has conducted research on survey methodology, the news media agenda-setting effect, genetic modification of foods, and public opinion on global warming and U.S. energy policy. He has assisted in the design of a number of questionnaires used in national surveys.

Michael W. Traugott is Professor of Communication Studies and Political Science and Chair of the Department of Communication Studies at the University of Michigan. He is also a Senior Research Scientist in the Center for Political Studies in the Institute for Social Research. A political scientist by training, Traugott received his B.A. from Princeton University and his M.A. and Ph.D. from the University of Michigan. Traugott's research interests include politics and the mass media, campaigns and elections, and survey methodology. He is currently extending previous research on voting-by-mail in Oregon, and he was a participant in a 2000 National Science Foundation conference on electronic voting.

Marianne Holt Viray is the Managing Director of the Reform Institute, a not-for-profit educational organization on campaign finance and election reform. She is a former Senior Associate at the Center for Public Integrity. During Viray's time at the center, she directed two research projects focusing on the changing nature of campaigns and campaign finance laws. Viray also conducted research for *The Buying of the President 2000*, by Charles Lewis and the center (Avon Press, 2000). She is the author of "The Surge in Party Money," in *Outside Money: Soft Money and Issue Advocacy in the 1998 Congressional Elections* (Rowman & Littlefield, 2000) and "The Long Shadow of Soft Money," for *Campaigns & Elections* magazine, May 1999, 20(4):22–27. Viray also produced *The Campaign You Don't See*, a 1998 documentary on soft money and interest group activity funded by a PBS educational grant. Viray has a degree in political science from Brigham Young University.

Catherine H. Wilson received her B.A. in art history from the University of Pennsylvania. She is currently a Ph.D. candidate completing a dissertation entitled "Political Information, Institutions and Citizen Participation in American Politics" at Caltech. She has authored numerous papers studying aspects of the voting decision, including the application of behavioral psychology theory to voting, individual vote choice compared across countries and electoral institutions, and the impact of information on the rate of turnout in U.S. elections.

Rethinking the Vote

Introduction

1

A Tale of Two Democracies

EDWARD J. McCAFFERY

ANN N. CRIGLER

MARION R. JUST

Strangely, the major effect of *Bush v. Gore* was to reinvigorate America's interest in democracy itself, partly by producing a more limited judicial role, but much more by ensuring that all votes would be counted, and be counted equally. By discrediting itself, the Supreme Court that decided *Bush v. Gore* helped to draw new attention to the importance of the franchise, and to the ideals of self-government and political equality. *(Sunstein 2001)*

The armchair generals have been busy criticizing the participants in the deadlock drama, notably the judges (especially the Justices of the Supreme Court). . . . These criticisms seem to me largely misplaced. The participants most deserving of criticism, though as yet largely spared it, are the law professors who offered public comments on the unfolding drama. *(Posner 2001)*

What is to be done about voting reform? That is the question for this book. The context is framed—as it must be, now—by the curious events of November 7, 2000, and the days and weeks following. The book proceeds from the understanding that an exploration of what to do next should begin with some sense of what, exactly, is wrong now: of what, exactly, went awry on November 7 and its aftermath. Reasoned thought should precede action: hence the title for this book, *Rethinking the Vote*. But therein lies a considerable rub. It turns out to be surprisingly difficult to reach an understanding of just what, exactly, did go wrong.

THE CURTAIN RISES

It certainly *seemed* as if something was terribly wrong on the day and night of November 7 and in the wee hours of the morning following. As the Yale law professor and constitutional scholar Bruce Ackerman put it, "[A]fter one of the

---

Authors' Note: Book website available at: www.rethinkingthevote.org

most boring campaigns in history, Americans were sleepwalking their way to the ballot box—when crisis hit after it was supposed to be all over" (Ackerman 2001). First, fairly early in the day, the major networks called the closely contested state of Florida for the Democratic presidential candidate, Al Gore. Political pundits quickly calculated that this meant that Gore, who came into election day trailing in most polls, would win the Electoral College and thus become America's next president. The fly in the ointment came later in the day when the networks changed their call, citing erroneous projections from exit poll data, and declared Florida's outcome uncertain. Still later—now into the early hours of November 8 on the East Coast—the networks called Florida for the Republican candidate, George W. Bush, making him the Electoral College victor. Gore called Bush to concede the election in the face of Bush's victory in the Electoral College, despite having won the national popular vote. Gore left his hotel room and was on his way to making a public concession speech when things changed yet again. The networks reversed their decisions, declaring Florida too close to call after all (see Frankovic, this volume for more detail on the media's calls and miscalls).

What was certain was that whoever had won in Florida would be the next president of the United States. What was uncertain was who had won in Florida.

The initial tabulation of Florida's votes (not including late-arriving overseas absentee ballots, which could legally come in and be counted up to November 18) had Bush's lead at 1,784 votes out of a total vote of just about six million. This was far less than the 0.5 percent margin that triggered an automatic recount under Florida law. A quick mechanical recount soon dropped Bush's lead to 327 votes. The "crisis" that Ackerman cited was underway.

Over the next five weeks a sometimes anxious, sometimes bemused, sometimes partisan public watched and waited as lawyers, election officials, politicians, pundits, and judges battled it out. Gore supporters alleged that Bush and his minions were trying to "steal" the election, bullying their way through the recount process, intimidating those performing the recount, and relying on ballots and ballot-counting procedures that systematically disenfranchised members of the Democratic core constituency—racial minorities, the poor, the elderly. Bush supporters alleged in turn that Gore and his minions were trying to "steal" the election, too, in this case by changing the rules on an ad hoc basis, after the fact, and by forum shopping in the law courts. The story of the recounts and judicial decisions has been told, with varying spins, elsewhere (compare Posner 2001 with Gillman 2001; see also Hasen, this volume). The story came to a halt, more or less, with the United States Supreme Court decision of December 12, 2000, in *Bush v. Gore*, overruling the Florida Supreme Court's demand for a recount (see Chemerinsky, this volume). The next day Gore conceded the election to Bush, and within a week the Electoral College had voted Bush the forty-third president of the United States.

WHAT'S THE PROBLEM?

Those are the simple facts of the matter. With them behind us, we return to our initial question: What, if anything, went wrong? Characteristically, most commentary answering this question has clustered on the extremes.

The View from the Trenches

The view of a good many critics of the ultimate outcome, including the most partisan advocates for Al Gore, was that practically everything had gone wrong. The Supreme Court had "discredited" itself in *Bush v. Gore*, as Cass Sunstein of the University of Chicago Law School alleged in the opening epigraph; the whole thing amounted to a "coup," as Ackerman further charged. In addition to the unprincipled and partisan Court decision, plenty of other things looked bad. Faulty ballot design had systematically disfranchised people in several counties. Inadequate registration lists and polling place problems had disfranchised poor and minority voters in particular. Local election officials had rigged the election in various ways. Partisan politicians in Florida had circumvented democracy before, during, and after the fateful day. Democracy's emperor was shown to have no clothes, at best, and scandalous rags, at worst.

But another view, held by a good many noncritics of the ultimate outcome, including the most partisan advocates for George W. Bush—and presented most forcefully and systematically by Richard Posner—was that nothing in particular had gone wrong at all. The vote in Florida was merely a statistical tie; such things are bound to happen once in a while. The tie had to be broken, one way or another, and the Supreme Court engaged in perfectly plausible, pragmatic, and acceptable decision making to do so, averting the only true crisis that might have occurred: a prolonged period of uncertainty over who was in fact the president. The sole problem was the hyperbole of the academics—including Ackerman and Sunstein—which had discredited these scholars alone. In sum and in short, it was the academy, not democracy or the Court, that was shown to be in tatters.

The Search for a Middle Ground

Where does the truth lie? As a preliminary matter, we suggest looking between the extremes, for some kind of reasonable—if not quite golden—mean. Indeed it is possible, after the remove of time, that both sides might in fact be right, albeit for necessarily different reasons.

Posner might be right in the narrow, immediate context of November and December 2000. Late-breaking developments suggested that Bush had, indeed, "won" in Florida, by the standards that Gore's lawyers themselves wanted to apply (Fessenden and Broder 2001; "Vindicating the Court" 2001). While there is room to quibble with this journalistic finding—which came after the events of another date destined for infamy, September 11, 2001, had made Bush a widely popular president—it is hard to argue with Posner's facts of the matter. A difference of one thousand or fewer votes out of six million is indeed a statistical tie.[1] Voting in a real and imperfect world is an imperfect affair. Any way to break the tie would have involved legal judgments about counting and recounting dimpled and damaged ballots that were sure to make one side unhappy. The Supreme Court, operating under intense time pressure, did a reasonably good job of things, and life proceeded without long-lasting crisis.

But it may also be that the critics such as Cass Sunstein and Lani Guinier were right, although not for the reasons that they themselves often proffered, such as Ackerman's dramatic talk of a "coup." Bush in fact probably did "win" the election under the rules in place at the time. Even if the Supreme Court decision did indeed reflect a significant departure from what little precedent, if any, there was on point (see Chemerinsky, this volume; Hasen, this volume; Gillman 2001; contrast Posner 2001), only a naive formalist would deny that court decisions are often, and maybe even always, "political" in some sense. *Bush v. Gore* may have been a bad decision under many lights, but it was hardly a coup d'etat.

Quite apart from these jurisprudential matters, however, there was something unsettling about the events of November 7, creating an unease that lurks deep and lingers still. "What began as judicial overreaching may be a clarion call for major democratic reform," Guinier, now a professor at the Harvard Law School, wrote in a *New York Times* piece in December 2000 (Guinier 2000). Fair enough, but what kind of reform was being called for? And, more fundamentally, to what end?

SETTING A CONTEXT

To understand the case for a broader rethinking of the vote—and to reconcile the views of Posner and his ilk with those of Sunstein and his ilk—we need a wider context than November 7, 2000, and its aftermath.

Looking Backward

Let us go back to 1787, the year of the Constitutional Convention, for starters. Voting in colonial America was of course far from a universal affair (Dahl 2001; Dinkin 1982; Keyssar 2000; Posner 2001; Rakove 1996). For the most part, only white, Protestant, property-owning males could vote. In the face of this limited franchise, the original Constitution was vague, to say the least, about the mechanisms for electing a president. It wasn't just the cumbersome and indirect expedient of the Electoral College, with representatives chosen by state legislatures voting for president and vice president in thirteen isolated meetings. The very subject of voter qualifications was left to the states; nothing remotely approaching a "right to vote" was included in the original Constitution or in the later Bill of Rights.

The entire pattern revealed an undeniable truth: The founding fathers were hardly populists, or even democrats in the contemporary sense of the term (Dahl 2001; Wood 2002). The initial drafters of the U.S. Constitution presumed that presidents would be drawn from a limited, aristocratic pool of politicians, a "natural aristocracy based on virtue and talents," in Thomas Jefferson's words (as quoted in Mueller 1992), selected in turn by another aristocratic pool, the electors. George Washington himself was assured of unanimity in the Electoral College before agreeing to run for president. Failing to anticipate the rise of political parties, the founders seem to have assumed that the Electoral College would often, and perhaps even generally, fail to elect a president, leaving the ultimate choice up to the state delegations in the House of Representatives, as in fact occurred in 1824 (Rakove 1996). The whole scheme was pretty far from the "one person, one vote" mantra of modern democrats.

But since the founding things have changed in America. There has been a steady if not quite constant trend toward universal suffrage. Important constitutional, legislative, and judicial reforms have advanced a participatory project (Potter and Viray, this volume; Traugott, this volume; Norris, this volume).

Property qualifications soon disappeared from state constitutions. By the time Alexis de Tocqueville came to America in 1830 he saw universal free male suffrage (de Tocqueville 1850). In 1870, the Fifteenth Amendment to the Constitution guaranteed the vote to men who had been slaves; fifty years later, the Nineteenth Amendment gave women the vote. The Twenty-fourth Amendment, ratified in 1964, abolished poll taxes that had in practice disenfranchised the poor. The Twenty-sixth Amendment in 1971 lowered the voting age from twenty-one to eighteen.

Congress added important changes, too, most dramatically in the Voting Rights Acts of 1964 and 1965, which expanded the vote to include American Indians living on reservations, members of the armed forces, and residents of the District of Columbia (42 U.S.C.A. §1973.2). The acts also made voting rights more meaningful by strengthening federal protections (see Potter and Viray, this volume, for more detail on these acts of legislation).

Finally, the Supreme Court, in an important series of decisions, articulated a standard of "one person, one vote," meant to ensure that voting schemes did not disenfranchise de facto those given the vote de jure (Hasen, this volume; *Reynolds v. Sims*).

Notwithstanding this impressive march toward greater participation and a fuller, more meaningful equality—a movement played out over some two centuries—we are still a long way from "one person, one vote," or even from figuring out what, exactly, in concrete terms and across a range of cases, this slogan even means. Americans under age eighteen do not have the vote, nor do certain other classes of individuals, such as resident aliens and convicted felons in most states. More to the point, "one person, one vote" lacks a clear theoretical or practical definition. Most adult Americans now do indeed have the formal right to vote, but no guarantee that their vote will matter at all— and some pretty formidable odds suggesting that it will *not*. Critical reflection about voting in America has long been haunted by the paradox, first and most forcefully pressed by Anthony Downs in 1957, that an individual's vote almost never determines an election's outcome. It's pretty much an arational, if not an irrational, act to vote in the first place (see Gelman, Katz, and King, this volume, discussing "voting power" of individuals under alternative voting systems; Downs 1957). While many pundits were quick to point out that November 7, 2000, proved this perspective wrong because the votes were close in so many states, a plausible case can be made for just the *opposite* conclusion. Even in such a close election, no state, not even Florida, was decided by one vote. Further, and in fact, the closer we get to a literal statistical tie, the more discretion is given to the institutions of government, including Congress, state legislatures, the courts, and the local officials who do the counting and recounting, to determine the outcome. These institutions necessarily had more to do with Florida's outcome—and hence with the presidential election—than any one voter did. Downs's voter's paradox has not been solved; indeed, if anything, it has been compounded. For in the extremely rare case where there is a statistical tie, bureaucrats, politicians, lawyers, and judges have the ultimate voting power.

More dramatically, a wider perspective on November 2000 shows just how far we still are from a true, populist democracy where, in Sunstein's words, "all the votes would be counted, and counted equally." Although the Supreme Court's opinion in *Bush v. Gore* purported to rest on counting votes equally—and most virulent critics of that opinion at least implicitly presumed that there was, indeed, some meaningful way to do so—we should first ask why the election had come down to a battle between George Bush and Al Gore in the first place. This very choice was more or less preordained from the moment that Bill Clinton defeated Bob Dole in November 1996. Long before any primary votes were cast, Bush and Gore were amassing preemptive advantages in campaign war chests that pushed most opposition to the sidelines, in each case trading on the power and prestige of a prior presidency: in Gore's case, of his boss, in Bush's case, of his father (see Estrich, this volume, for more discussion of the role of money in politics). In the primary seasons, the brief popular honeymoons with John McCain, Bush's only real persistent rival, and Bill Bradley, Gore's only one, showed that the public was hungry for some choice, any choice. But in the end the public was left with the most likely candidates from the beginning, and there is ample evidence that plenty of people were less than thrilled with the options: Some 64 percent of voters did not support *any* candidate (Ackerman 2001; Kranish 1999; McDonald and Popkin 2000). Yet while these conditions might suggest a viable third-party candidate—and Ralph Nader at times seemed to fit the bill—that did not happen, either. In the end, Nader won less than 5 percent of the national vote, failing to qualify his Green Party for matching funds in subsequent elections (Martelle 2000).

This is so far more a story of the power of the purse and of party politics than of any true expression of popular will, where each individual voter has an equal say in who, in fact, becomes president (see Barnes, this volume, for a brief discussion of alternative choice rules that might better get at a full set of voter preferences).

With all that, the campaign was so close that each major candidate increasingly focused his attention on a relative handful of swing states, including Florida. Gore virtually wrote off California, certain of its large electoral prize; Bush likewise largely ignored New York, certain not to get its electoral votes. Just about one hundred million votes were cast nationwide on November 7, 2000; Gore defeated Bush in the aggregate popular vote tally: 49,244,746 to 49,026,305. Yet the strategic and policy decisions of the candidates about how to win the Electoral College were based on a comparative handful of voters in a comparative handful of states. Where's the "one person, one vote" in that scenario? Put another way, even if there would have been some way to count all the Floridian votes, would all votes, across the nation, truly have counted "equally?"

SEARCHING FOR A DEEPER UNDERSTANDING

It turns out, not surprisingly, that the lingering and often highly partisan debates between supporters of Bush and the U.S. Supreme Court, on the one hand, and supporters of Gore and the Florida Supreme Court, on the other—between proponents of the view that nothing especially untoward happened on November 7, 2000, and those of the view that practically everything went awry— have their roots in competing abstract theories of what, exactly, the vote is supposed to be doing in the first place: that is, in theories of democracy itself. Both schools of thought have a respectable intellectual lineage, and both can point to elements of American history, practice, and popular thought still prevalent today.

Minimal Democracy

In one camp stand the minimalists,[2] generally conservatives and moderates who can trace their heritage back at least as far as Plato and his well-known distrust of democracy, which he derisively called "a pleasant constitution . . . distributing its peculiar kind of equality to equals and unequals alike" (Plato 1957, p. 316). By the time of John Locke (1698), however, theorists were coming to see that a limited democracy at least might be preferable to the alternatives. This hedged skepticism was given fuller expression nearly three centuries later by another Englishman, Winston Churchill:

> Many forms of Government have been tried, and will be tried in this world of sin and woe. No one pretends that democracy is perfect or all-wise. Indeed, it has been said that democracy is the "worst" form of Government except all those others that have been tried from time to time. (quoted in Jenkins 2001)

In a similar spirit, Edmund Burke had lauded the limited British democracy in contrast to the more radical French variant found in their revolution (Burke 1790).

This model of a limited democracy or republic was no doubt in the minds of many if not all of the founding fathers, who were hardly radical populists, as we have seen (Dahl 2001; Wood 1992). Under this minimalist view, the popular vote is no more than a crude but efficacious check on more despotic alternatives. As the contemporary political theorist William Riker (1982) sees it, "popular rule" provides for an "intermittent, sometimes random, even perverse popular veto" that "has at least the potential of preventing tyranny and rendering officials responsive." Riker concludes that this "minimal sort of democracy . . . is the only kind of democracy actually attainable" (244). In an important and particularly striking expression of the minimalist view, the political theorist John Mueller (1992), almost echoing Plato, states that "[d]emocracy's genius in practice is that it can work even if people rarely if ever rise

above the selfishness and ignorance with which they have been so richly en-
dowed by their Creator" (991). Under Mueller's view, the "minimal human being," generally apathetic and selfish, works to check the potential excesses of
government, allowing for a limited form of democracy that importantly protects property rights and individual freedoms and ensures relatively stable,
consistent governance over time. Minimal human beings coming together under conditions of minimal democracy lead to minimal governments and—so
the story goes—maximal wealth and well-being.

Richard Posner shares this minimalist view. Indeed, it is the central or-
ganizing theoretical framework in his extended commentary on *Bush v. Gore*.
Posner writes:

> American democracy is structured, formal, practical, realistic, and both sup-
> portive of and supported by commercial values. It is not starry-eyed, carniva-
> lesque, or insurrectionary. *It is not pure or participatory democracy,* and it does
> not consider political chaos a price worth paying to actualize the popular will.
> Its spirit is closer to that of Burke than to that of Rousseau. The populism of
> a Jefferson or a Jackson remains a part of our democratic ideology, but a smaller
> part than in the days of yore. These summary reflections, too, will turn out to
> be relevant to evaluating the Supreme Court's performance in *Bush v. Gore*.
> (Posner 2001, emphasis added)

It is no surprise, then, that Posner saw nothing particularly disturbing about
the outcome of the 2000 presidential election. Under the minimalist view, popular elections are mainly beneficial as protective devices against the possibility of extreme and tyrannical governments that would disrespect "commercial
values." Voting is an act designed to foster stability—to avert "political
chaos"—not to "actualize" some amorphous "political will." Democracy in this
sense was working well in offering up two relative moderates, Bush and Gore,
to an electorate that was predictably—and quite rationally—largely apathetic
to the choice between them. Then the electorate—again not irrationally—left
us with a statistical tie that the Supreme Court pragmatically broke. Into this
comfortable and perhaps comforting view, Posner is only troubled by the
Court's hasty interjection of "equal protection" into its rationale for breaking
the deadlock (Posner 2001). Other than this disturbing (to Posner) note, America can take a few moderate steps to improve the technology of voting, of counting and recounting ballots, and then get back to business as usual.

Participatory Democracy

One of the many ironies of the commentary on *Bush v. Gore* is that what has
troubled Posner and other conservatives in victory has given some cheer to liberals in defeat: the Court's invocation of "equal protection," a legal and Constitutional principle responsible for much of the expansion of civil rights and
freedoms under the Warren Court (see Hasen, this volume; Karlan 2001). Pro-
gressives and liberals such as Pam Karlan, Lani Guinier, Cass Sunstein, and
Bruce Ackerman stand in a camp apart from Posner's, one with a different view

of democracy and the democratic project. These theorists uphold a model directly at odds with the minimalist view, a model of participatory democracy, whose ultimate end is the attainment of a rich and meaningful equality among individuals. This view can trace its intellectual roots back to Rousseau and Immanuel Kant. Andrew Jackson and, even more importantly, Abraham Lincoln developed the participatory model historically and politically in the U.S. context. Under this model, voting, far from being a mere check on excessive government power meant to protect commercial interests, is the very expression of government power. Hence America has, in Lincoln's marvelous phrase, a "government of the people, by the people, and for the people."

This participatory view of democracy and the vote animated the great liberationist movements of the twentieth century in America: the feminist effort to get women the vote and the civil rights drive to make the black vote a reality. Its spirit is alive today in the calls made by Guinier and others for "major democratic reform" in the wake of election 2000 and in Sunstein's talk of making the "ideals of self-government and political equality" more meaningful. What makes this set of commentaries consistent—or at least compatible—with the moderate defenses of the Supreme Court opinion in *Bush v. Gore* is that even the most "starry-eyed" (Posner's word) advocate of "pure and participatory democracy" can accept that the statistical tie from November 7, 2000, had to be broken. But while adherents of the participatory theory of democracy and the vote can also accept the need for technological change and improvement at the ballot box (see Alvarez, Sinclair, and Wilson, this volume; Krosnick, Miller, and Tichy, this volume), they cannot happily stop there.

At the most profound level, the U.S. presidential election of 2000 called attention to the fact that our laws are out of step with the greater promise of a truly participatory democracy. What was so unsettling to the many yearning for "all the votes to count, and to count equally" was the invocation of technocratic and legalistic language—mumbo jumbo about dimpled chads and conflicting courts—in response to their cry: Commentators were talking minimalism to groups hungering for participation. To the participatory democrats, accepting—let alone celebrating—voter ignorance and apathy, in the manner of Mueller and the minimalists, is not an option. More needs to be done to educate and empower voters, to make democracy "real."

Challenges Ahead

The challenge for participatory democrats is great, and it ought not be understated. The minimalists, feeling that nothing particularly untoward happened in November and December 2000, can satisfy themselves with comparatively minor, technological changes—better vote-counting machines here, clearer ballot design there, and so on. But what will bring satisfaction to those who believe in participatory democracy?

Participatory democrats need both to articulate and defend an attractive set of ends, and then to find somehow the means to achieve these ends. How? In the persistent face of Downs's voter's paradox—in a country of millions of voters with more millions of dollars at work—how can we get the act of voting to be more inclusive, more meaningful? The pages ahead give many reasons to be skeptical of the quest. There are concerns that changing the voting, registration, or electoral rules will not matter, or will not matter much, in the end (Gelman, Katz, and King, this volume; Norris, this volume; Traugott, this volume). There are even concerns that any changes that might be effected may move things in the *wrong* direction (Ortiz, this volume; Traugott, this volume)—giving too much power to the uninformed, continuing to overrepresent the overrepresented—diminishing the hopes of the most ardent participatory theorists. In the gloomy light of this academic skepticism, however, the enduring dream of somehow finding a government truly "of the people, by the people, and for the people" animates the participatory project. Hope endures.

Clearly the United States and other Western democracies began with a far more minimalist, limited democracy than they have today. The government laid down in the U.S. Constitution has proven over time to be a remarkably stable and yet flexible design, protecting commercial interests while making for a general pattern of internal peace and stability. At the same time, the franchise has indeed steadily expanded, and more people have been allowed to participate in the process of governing, all without catastrophic results. There has been a persistent evolution toward a fuller, more meaningful democracy and vision of equality. The challenge today—the challenge of rethinking the vote—is to see where to go next, now that the obvious steps of obtaining nearly universal suffrage and striking down offensive barriers such as poll taxes have been taken. To participatory theorists at least, there is no compelling reason to stand still; the great American experiment in democracy never has for very long.

THE PAGES AHEAD

The essays in this volume grapple with the issues we have just described in summary fashion, trying to come to terms with what happened in 2000 and why, and with what can and should be learned from it. The problems are interdisciplinary, and so is our lineup of authors, drawn from the disciplines of law, political science, and communications, and from government practice, journalism, and the academy. Many of these authors were firsthand participants in the story of Bush versus Gore; all of them are keen and interested observers of the democratic project.

Part I wrestles with getting a sense of the problems that might need to be fixed. Kathleen Frankovic, a player in the drama of election night 2000 from her post at CBS News, sheds light on a particular and a particularly dark chapter from that fateful eve: the problems of polling and the impact of media coverage and projections on election outcomes. Calls and miscalls stood at the center of the saga of Bush versus Gore. Greater or at least better participation would seem to depend on better or at least more accurate information, but the press of the media's business makes this a challenging goal. Frankovic wrestles with these issues.

Michael Alvarez, Betsy Sinclair, and Catherine Wilson, drawing on personal experience with the Caltech/MIT voting reform project, analyze voting machines and various methods for counting and recounting ballots. Most dramatically, these authors find a racial and ethnic bias in the pattern of voting machines and vote-counting errors in California's elections in 2000. Here seems to be some direct confirmation of the worst nightmares of those who favor participatory democracy—that systematic technical errors and biases made a difference, effectively disenfranchising groups of voters. The result is tentative; the fear is real.

Jon Krosnick, Joanne Miller, and Michael Tichy's chapter suggests that bias in voting results can occur simply because of how the candidates are listed on the ballot. But then who controls the ballot? And what does this bias say about voter rationality? These are themes that later chapters—especially Richard Hasen's and Daniel Ortiz's—pick up. Interestingly, the research that Krosnick and others have done on just this point turned out to play an important role in a real-life legal drama in Compton, California, that unfolded as this book was being finalized; Richard Hasen's later chapter comments on this fascinating turn of events. Krosnick, Miller, and Tichy, while noting that the ballot order effect is likely to be highest in low salient elections, offer a tantalizing hint that even Bush versus Gore itself might have been decided because of Bush's prior placement on the Florida ballot.

Finally in Part I, Andrew Gelman, Jonathan Katz, and Gary King, important quantitatively oriented political scientists, take an analytic look at how voting in the Electoral College in fact works, comparing and contrasting it with direct popular elections. Perhaps counterintuitively, the chapter finds that, in actual practice, abandoning the Electoral College is unlikely to matter much, and most likely would decrease the voting power of the average individual citizen. In other words, greater or more powerful participation may not come as a result of more direct participation.

Part II turns to ways to fix the problems. There are many possible players, at different levels (federal, state, local) and branches (executive, legislative, judicial) of government and a wide array of strategies to pursue, creating a matrix of options. Erwin Chemerinsky begins this part by taking a hard look at *Bush v. Gore*, the legal case. Rather than celebrate its possible opening of an equal protection door, as Richard Hasen is later to consider, Chemerinsky castigates the Court for its radical departure from principles of federalism—principles for which this, the Rehnquist, Court has become best known. By turning its back on its own cherished doctrine of states' rights, the Supreme Court majority showed the narrowly political bases of its reasoning. Where does this leave hope for fair voting and electoral practices? Can the judiciary be trusted? Where does the ultimate power over elections lie, with the states or the feds? With the courts or the Congress? The law is not clear on these points.

Trevor Potter, a former Federal Election Commission (FEC) chairman, and Marianne Holt Viray explore some of the possibilities, hoping to keep or maintain a federal role in the electoral process, but at an administrative level. Along the way, Potter and Viray well describe the lay of the current legal land, and note—as Susan Estrich's chapter will later do, too—the severe limitations of the FEC as currently constituted and funded. To get to a more participatory place for this important federal agency, more needs to be done. But where will the will—not to mention the money—come from?

On a clearly related note, Jeb Barnes focuses on what Congress can and should do. Lending some support to the minimalist school, Barnes speculates that congressional *inaction* might be the wisest course of all. Barnes also notes that what is most likely to be done—technocratic changes to the formal mechanisms of voting—is apt to matter least; more sweeping changes, such as repealing the Electoral College, are remote possibilities indeed. Most striking, the changes that might matter the most of all—to the rules of choice, the ways that voters are allowed to express their preferences—will most likely never even make it on to any legislative agenda. Barnes includes some simple but thought-provoking examples of how outcomes may be skewed by the limited abilities voters have under American voting procedures to signal their true preferences.

Pippa Norris offers important perspectives from abroad. As the world offers surprisingly diverse models of election and electoral systems, Norris's analysis shows what kind of electoral mechanisms have increased participation in other countries. Unfortunately for participatory theorists, Norris finds much the same lesson from other countries that Michael Traugott's later chapter sees in the United States: Most reforms have little if any real, demonstrable impact, and the normative evaluation of what impact the reforms do have is unclear at best. But hope at least endures for participatory theorists, as voting reform continues to proliferate around the globe.

Part III's chapters address what might be the hardest question of all: What, if anything, should be done about the problems of voting and electoral reform, even if we can agree on what these problems are? Ann Crigler, Marion Just, and Tami Buhr begin this exploration by offering some important notes from the real world of flesh-and-blood citizens. The authors look to public opinion about voting and electoral reform and discover that the hope for greater participation runs wide and deep. There is a broad, bipartisan consensus that something ought to be done, that voting ought to be made easier and better representative of the body politic. A significant majority of Americans seem to believe in the power of the vote, and in the participatory project, that "all the votes should count, and count equally." One would think—and hope?—that politicians ignore this popular platform at their peril.

Michael Traugott's chapter, however, begins what turns out to be a series of skeptical notes. Traugott, a leading academic expert in the field, surveys scores of studies and real-world experiments with attempts to increase voter registration and turnout, including such celebrated means as "motor voter," same-day registration, and mail-in voting. Unfortunately, Traugott finds, the results hold little promise for participatory theorists: The effects are small, and more often than not point in a troubling direction—whatever increases in registration and turnout occur seem to come from the already overrepresented demographic groups, namely, the white, the better educated, the more affluent. Those who favor participatory democracy have their work cut out for them.

Richard Hasen's chapter picks up the prospect of an invigorated Equal Protection Clause playing a role in actual voting reform cases. After first noting how the Supreme Court's opinion in *Bush v. Gore* was a significant departure from precedent on this (and other) scores, Hasen proceeds to speculate about what, exactly, an emboldened equal protection analysis might mean in the voting context. In particular, Hasen reflects on the role that social scientists—such as Jon Krosnick and his coauthors and Michael Alvarez and his—might play in this brave new world. As noted earlier, speculation became reality as this book was coming together; a California judge did rely on Krosnick's social science to invalidate an election. But are academics the last best hope for the participatory project, or somehow its enemy? Hasen isn't sure which way it will come out in the end. Indeed, he frets that social science created chaos in the Compton case. In light of the uncertainty, Hasen concludes that "murkiness" in the Supreme Court's equal protection analysis isn't such a bad thing and that the Court ought indeed to "hike slowly in the political thicket," allowing pragmatic possibilities and consensus to emerge.

Susan Estrich's chapter sounds a deep, skeptical note throughout. Drawing from her own experience in the corporate and political worlds, Estrich compares and contrasts the two realms. She notes that there is little real democracy—and, in particular, little free speech—in corporate boardrooms. But the very same First Amendment that is impotent in the corporate context virtually eviscerates the ability to regulate the role of money in the political context. A stark contrast masks a deep similarity—the "old boys" with money win in both cases, remaining in corporate *and* political power. Estrich's one nod at hope—a nod seemingly born as much out of frustration as anything else—is that one day women can come to exercise the political power that their growing economic power suggests, and that maybe they will thereafter change the terms of debates and fair play in both worlds.

Daniel Ortiz ends this final part with perhaps the deepest, darkest, most skeptical note of all for the participatory project: It might just be that greater, wider participation is not a good thing at all. If the marginal voter brought into the process by heightened efforts at voter turnout is as ill-informed and almost random in her or his approach to voting as some of the earlier chapters (most strikingly, Krosnick, Miller, and Tichy) suggest, should we even try to make voting easier and more participatory? Ortiz, a high-ranking advisor to the Ford-Carter Commission on electoral reform, does not offer any definitive answers, although he speculates on some intriguing options, such as empowering small groups of voters to engage in deeper deliberative democracy. Mainly, however, Ortiz poses some haunting questions for participatory theorists in particular.

We editors return to the scene with a brief postscript, hoping to make at least some sense of the whole and trying to show or find a way through the minimalist and participatory tensions in electoral reform. Perhaps because we are editors after all, we also hope to leave the readers with some hope for better days ahead.

NOTES

1. "You had the perfect tie," said Walter Dean Burnham, a professor of government at the University of Texas at Austin, making a statistical point that many scholars have fastened on to. "When you've got an election this close, the most sensible way to determine the outcome is to flip a coin" (Burnham 1982).
2. Barnes, this volume, uses "Madisonian" to get at the same concept as our "minimalist" model of democracy. At the price of some inconsistency among chapters, we retain our preferred label, in part to avoid disputes over the proper interpretation of Madison's own historical ideas and opinions (Wills 2002).

Part I

Problems That Might Need To Be Fixed

2

Election Reform

The U.S. News Media's Response to the Mistakes of Election 2000

KATHLEEN A. FRANKOVIC

> The craft [of journalism] has no more exacting, exasperating task than to formulate on imperfect information at midnight or thereabouts, remarks that must go to the press hours before conclusive news arrives and that will be read in the light of statistics yet unknown or events impossible of prevision. (*Mitchell 1924, 260*)

Reporting results quickly has always been important to the media. Elections feed the needs of news organizations to outshine the competition, but they also give such organizations the opportunity to provide a public service by reducing electoral uncertainty. In 1896, the *Chicago Record* justified its straw poll of Midwestern states as one that would provide information even before the election. Its editor wrote that the pre-election poll results would "give business the opportunity to secure to new [business] lines before the election" (cited in Frankovic 1998). As election reporting shifted from print to radio to television to the Internet—shortening the time of uncertainty—the potential for mischief remained along with an opening for spreading false information. Candidates and businesses each act on early and partial results.

By 2000 only one service—Voter News Service (VNS)—both conducted exit polls and collected vote totals. On the afternoon of November 7, 2000, Internet sites not affiliated with VNS members or subscribers claimed to have the latest exit poll information, "leaked" by those with access. Some of the information was accurate. Some was premature. Some was just plain wrong.

What happened in Florida in 2000—when television networks and wire services first mistakenly called Al Gore the winner of the state's twenty-five electoral votes, and the networks then later declared those electoral votes the property of George W. Bush, only to retract that call as well—was in part the result of journalists' desires to transmit election information as soon as possible. Of course, there was also the fact of a breathtakingly close election, marred by voter confusion and vote-counting difficulties.

A version of this chapter has been published in *Public Opinion Quarterly* (67) 1, Spring 2003.

American journalists have called elections since at least the early 1800s by telling the story of who won and why, and by doing so scoring a beat on the opposition, both political and journalistic. Use of all available tools, from carrier pigeons to the Internet, to tell the story of the election has long been standard journalistic behavior. More than a century ago, one journalist described election reporting this way: "The highest state of fever attends the excitement and strain of the most intense work that falls to the lot of any men, except soldiers in war" (cited in Littlewood 1998, 39).

There is a value in speedy election night reporting. It can at the very least dispel rumors and wrong decisions made because of them. On Election Day 2000, drug company shares slid as news and rumors were spread of a Gore victory online and on talk radio. Despite polls that suggest that Americans would favor news organizations withholding any results until all polls are closed, behaviorally many people seek out the results. Asking "who's ahead" or "who won" is the first question—"why" comes later.

A NEWS TRADITION

Of course, journalists are proud to note that they have beaten the competition by reporting election outcomes more quickly. From the 1950s through the 1970s, television networks routinely took out full-page ads in newspapers touting how frequently they were the "first" to call an election. That practice actually dates to a much earlier time, as noted by Littlewood (1998). In 1896, the *New York Times* boasted that with its stereopticon projections it was able to report results of the New York City election *four minutes* ahead of its competitors. In 1824, the *New York Post* experimented with carrier pigeons to get election results from Washington, D.C. Although the experiment failed, it certainly indicated the length news organizations would go to collect data and quickly transmit it to the public. In the 1840s the telegraph brought results of the national election, which by law would now be held on a single day, to news editors one precinct at a time, although often in a jumble of unrelated numbers. As the *Chicago Tribune* reported in 1858: "Returns from the election held in this state yesterday are presented to our readers as we have received them by telegraph—in a confused mass." The Associated Press, founded in 1847, took advantage of telegraph accessibility, allowing member organizations to receive election news, although the telegraph did not span the continent until nearly two decades later.

Newspapers also experimented with different ways of disseminating results. The *New York Times* stereopticon projections of the 1890s were part of an ongoing trend. In 1860, the *New York Herald* used gaslight to project "Magic Lantern" images onto nearby buildings. These projections became more common with the development of electricity in the 1880s, and newspapers even interspersed entertainment slides with those conveying election results.

The competition to get the results first and present them to as many people as possible (even beyond the thousands who stood outside the newspaper offices) led to complicated schemes of presentation. In 1892, the *New York Herald* used a high-powered searchlight beam that was to take a different path depending on the outcome. It would move south if Grover Cleveland carried New York, north if Benjamin Harrison won. The *San Francisco Chronicle* claimed its colored searchlights could transmit results for fifteen miles. In 1896, the *New York Journal* had a large map of the United States: One color would light for a state when it was declared for the Democratic candidate and another when declared for the Republican. And the *Chicago Tribune* shot up fireworks: different colors for William McKinley and William Jennings Bryan, and a different number of bursts for city, state, and nation.

Progress in interpreting the results also took place near the end of the nineteenth century. "Colonel" Charles H. Taylor, the editor and publisher of the *Boston Globe*, instituted in 1883 what one historian has labeled "the single most important methodological advance in the history of electoral journalism" (Littlewood 1998, 13). The "advance" was the use of key precinct analysis. Reporters sought out voting precincts that were representative of certain social and ethnic characteristics, collected previous voting patterns from these precincts, and then on election night projected the statewide vote from the early reporting precincts. Television networks replicated the technique in the 1950s and 1960s, before the adoption of probability sampling for election night projections.

RADIO AND TELEVISION: SPEEDING UP RETURNS

As early as 1916, election results were broadcast to ships at sea, and the first commercial radio station, KDKA in Pittsburgh, kicked off its official transmission with 1920 election coverage. The early part of the twentieth century was not without its reporting errors: In 1916, based on early returns from eastern states, afternoon papers in western states and the next day's *San Francisco Chronicle* inaccurately reported the defeat of Woodrow Wilson.

By 1952, like their radio predecessors, the television networks reported results as they were received and took advantage of nascent computer technologies to process results and make predictions. Martin Plissner, the former executive political director at CBS News, reported that the network partnered with the Univac Corporation on election night, and by 9 P.M. eastern time, on the basis of just partial results, was able to project Dwight Eisenhower's Electoral College victory (Plissner 1999). NBC, using something dubbed "Mike Mono-Robot," did the same. Networks were willing to use new technology to make calls, even though four years earlier pollsters and some newspapers had been embarrassed by their conviction that Thomas Dewey would defeat Harry Truman.

In the 1960s, television networks went even further, with a methodology reminiscent of "Colonel" Taylor's and a breathtakingly early call that prefigured the reaction to the problems of the 2000 election. Pollster Lou Harris and statistician David Neft, hired as consultants for CBS News at the start of 1964, used a set of "key precincts" to project election outcomes. On June 2, the night of the California Republican primary, Harris called Barry Goldwater the winner at 7:22 P.M. pacific time, after polls had closed in southern California, but before they closed in the San Francisco bay area. Goldwater did carry the state and its eighty-six Republican delegates. The final margin was very close, and the primary effectively gave Goldwater the Republican nomination.

CBS was criticized for calling a state before all its polls closed, potentially affecting the outcome there. An internal review of the network's election policies, procedures, and language followed. The network's president, Frank Stanton, promised: "No forecasting gimmicks will be used on election night and reports of the election outcomes will be based on judgments and perceptions of experienced newsmen, proven statistical methods, and advanced data processing systems, all based on actual vote results" (Stanton 1964).

Lyndon Johnson won the 1964 general election in a landslide, and most networks were able to assign him enough electoral votes shortly after 9 P.M. eastern time, before polls closed in the Pacific and mountain states. After that election, network heads testified before Congress, armed with studies they had commissioned to measure the impact of any early call (CBS, Inc. 1964, for a summary of early social science literature on bandwagon effects; Clausen 1966; Lang and Lang 1968; Mendelsohn 1966; Miller 1967). All of the studies suggested minimal, if any, impact on California voters of the presidential call. The rules for coverage that other news organizations adopted were similar to the internal rules adopted by CBS News in 1964. Bill Leonard, then the head of the CBS News Election Unit, wrote: "Obviously, CBS News *does not* 'elect' anyone. *We report,* however, when someone has been, or apparently has been, elected. A [checkmark] next to the name of the winning candidate indicates that in the judgment of CBS News the particular candidate is the winner" (Leonard 1964, emphasis in the original). The process was to be visible to the viewers. Leonard continued, "In Vote Profile Analysis, we have an important and swift new tool. It is imperative that we use it for what it is and that we share its meaning with our viewers and our listeners."

The networks sought linguistic clarity. CBS News division president Fred Friendly told the *New York Times*: "We will not use the word 'declare' on November 3—we will speak of 'indicated winners,' 'apparent winners,' or 'probable winners' until both our analysis of the vote and the vote itself leave no doubt of the result." The proper language was to be something like: "CBS News estimates that when all the votes are counted, Lyndon Johnson will carry Illinois." Correspondents were warned in many of the following elections: "The CBS News estimate should be so described—as an estimate. Winners should be described as 'estimated winners.' Avoid any reference to 'calling' races or 'declaring' winners" (see Mason, Frankovic, and Jamieson 2001, 52–61, for a summary of the history of television election night calls and language). Similar discussions were taking place at other networks (see Plissner 1999, for descriptions of some of those discussions and an embarrassing error in the 1960 election).

LEADING UP TO 2000: THE CREATION OF VNS

In their coverage of the 1964 California primary, the broadcast networks not only declared winners at different times but also reported different vote totals. Each organization collected data on its own, individually staffing the three hundred polling places in New Hampshire and twenty-three thousand in California. The cost was astronomical, and no two sets of vote totals were the same.

In the summer of 1964, ABC, CBS, NBC, the Associated Press, and United Press International formed the News Election Service (NES) to provide a single source of vote totals that would be consistent across news organizations and would cost each organization significantly less than operating on their own. The news organizations promised to compete in other aspects of election coverage. In fact, by the end of the decade, the television networks began collecting election day information before the polls closed, polling voters on their actions and reasons as they left the polls.

The exit poll, however, was used primarily as an analytical tool, at least until 1980, when NBC News, using exit polls in a number of states, was able to announce that Ronald Reagan had captured enough electoral votes to win the presidency at 8:15 P.M. eastern time, hours before the polls closed on the West Coast. Then-president Jimmy Carter conceded the election in a speech that was also delivered before West Coast poll closings. Even though the early call triggered a new round of congressional hearings and extensive criticism of the use of exit polls to call races, all the television networks were using such polls by 1982.

In 1985, the networks, now with the ability to view likely results throughout the voting day, volunteered to Congress that they would not call or characterize on the air the outcome in a state until the vast majority of polls in that state were closed. That would still, however, make it possible to declare a winner in presidential elections before the polls closed on the West Coast. In return for the networks' promise, congressional committee leaders agreed to try to adopt a uniform poll closing bill, which would shut the polls in the continental U.S. at the same time.[1]

After the 1988 election—another contest called before polls closed in the West—news organizations began another cooperative venture partly as a result of budget cutting. This time the networks decided to cooperate in collecting exit poll data and formed a consortium, to be known as Voter Research and Surveys (VRS). VRS was founded by ABC, CBS, CNN, and NBC. After the 1992 election, VRS and NES were merged to create a single election day newsgathering organization, Voter News Service (VNS). ABC, CBS, CNN, NBC, and the Associated Press would contribute equally to the consortium and each would have one vote on the governing board. FOX News joined the organization for the 1996 election (Mason, Frankovic, and Jamieson 2001, 62–63). VRS had cut down the competition to make calls first. But the spirit of cooperation did not last in the larger configuration of VNS. In the 1994 election, ABC News, using a team of outside researchers, called elections such as the U.S. Senate race in Virginia and the governor's race in New York well before the consortium and its other members did. For the 1996 election and those that followed, all VNS member news organizations had their own "decision teams." The decision teams were sometimes in the newsroom, sometimes in rooms away from the studio. Their role was to study the exit poll data and the voting results provided by VNS and to "call" a race when they believed the winner was clear.

THE 2000 ELECTION AND THE FLORIDA MISTAKES

The close 2000 election tested the VNS models, the network decision rules, and the American electoral system itself in ways that they had never been tested before. By the early morning after election day, every television network had made *two* wrong calls in Florida and had prematurely awarded New Mexico to Democrat Al Gore and the U.S Senate seat from Washington to Democrat Maria Cantwell. In three of these four cases, the errors were at least partly due to bad information from election officials.

Just over 95 percent of Florida polling places closed at 7 P.M. eastern standard time, thereby meeting the criterion that a "vast majority" of polling places in a state be closed prior to the networks' making a call, as the networks had promised Congress. In fact, many previous Florida election calls had been made by the networks at that first poll closing time, including George H. W. Bush's win in 1988, Bill Clinton's in 1996, and Jeb Bush's in the 1998 gubernatorial contest. While the estimates from exit polls suggested a Gore lead, no news organization made the call at poll closing.

The exit poll's methodology through 2000 was straightforward: a two-stage probability selection of precincts within each state, precincts selected proportionate to size, with stratification by geographic location in the state and past vote by precinct. A single past vote was used in establishing both the size and the direction of the past vote. Interviewers, hired and trained by VNS, were stationed at the selected precinct and were instructed to offer an exit poll questionnaire to a sample of voters (every *nth* voter, with *n* determined ahead of time depending on the expected size of the precinct's turnout) and to keep a record of the sex, race, and apparent age (under 30, 30–60, and over 60) of selected respondents who refused to be interviewed or were missed during busy voting periods. Interviewers worked fifty-minute hours; three times during the day they called the input location to report totals and to read the individual responses to the exit poll.[2]

On November 7, 2000, NBC News called Gore the Florida winner at 7:49 P.M. eastern time. CBS News made its call for Gore at 7:50 P.M., with calls by Fox, ABC News, the Associated Press, and VNS itself shortly thereafter. All calls came approximately ten minutes before the last 5 percent of Florida polls closed. The news organizations began retracting their calls at 9:54 P.M., when the models clearly indicated that the election was still up in the air.

At the time the call was first made, network election decision makers had access to the results of more than forty-three hundred interviews conducted throughout the day at 44 of the 45 precincts that had been selected for exit poll coverage (one sample precinct never reported). In addition, 12 of the 120 sample precincts had reported their actual results, and six of those precincts were part of the exit poll sample. Four percent of all the precincts statewide had reported actual votes. By 7:50 P.M., all of the estimation models indicated a Gore victory, and the estimates met the tests of significance.

There were several problems with the data, all discovered after the fact. First, the precincts selected for the exit poll were not a true reflection of the state results. There was a difference between the estimates using actual votes (not just the exit poll results) in the sample of precincts used for the exit poll and the final state totals, with the difference just within the outer limit of the poll's sampling error.

Second, the ratio estimation model was flawed. It relied on past vote results and chose a past race for comparison based on the highest correlation between the vote for the current Republican candidate in that night's election and the Republican candidate in one of three previous elections stored in the computer system for real-time comparison on election night. In the case of Florida, the best Republican vote correlation was with the 1998 gubernatorial election. The correlation between the (Jeb) Bush vote in 1998 and the (George W.) Bush vote in 2000 was .91. But by choosing this race, the size of the absentee vote was underestimated to be only 8 percent of the total. As it turned out, the correlation of the 2000 Bush vote and the 1996 vote for Bob Dole was nearly as high (.88). Selecting that election would have provided a higher and therefore better estimate of the size of the 2000 absentee vote.

Third, the correlation of the Democratic vote in the 1996–2000 comparison was significantly higher than for the 1998–2000 comparison (.81 vs. .71). Had the 1996 presidential race (or even the most recent Senate race) been chosen for use by the ratio estimate, the absentee vote would not have been so underestimated.[3] In Florida, the absentee vote is traditionally over twenty points more Republican than the in-polling place Election Day vote.

Finally, at the time the call was made, the information provided by the six precincts that had both exit poll and actual vote totals was deceptive. Overlaying survey results with the final vote tallies from the exact same precincts (which were collected at poll-closing time precinct-by-precinct) provides a measure of within-precinct survey error and adjusts for any difference in voting behavior between those who respond to the exit poll and those who don't. In past years, this difference has been attributed to many things, including variations in levels of enthusiasm for each candidate.[4] The computation at 7:50 P.M. indicated that, if anything, the exit poll was understating the vote for Gore and overstating the vote for Bush. The network analysts had also seen that pattern in the only state that had a large number of overlaid precincts—Kentucky. However, while the overestimate of the Bush vote in the exit poll remained true for Kentucky at the end of the night, it did not remain true in Florida. At the end of the evening, neither candidate had a significant overrepresentation among exit poll respondents in Florida.

The miscall for Gore, therefore, was the result of simple sampling error, coverage error (although VNS conducted polls of absentee voters in West Coast states, VNS conducted no absentee polling in Florida), and misleading partial information. Shortly before 10 P.M. eastern time, it was clear that the Gore call was not supported by the greater amount of information available, and it was withdrawn.

The Florida election remained close all night long. By 2:10 A.M. more than 96 percent of all Florida precincts had reported their vote totals to their respective counties. George W. Bush had a 51,000 vote lead. A total of 5,575,730 votes had been counted from the precincts that had reported, and it appeared that there were less than 180,000 votes left to count. Gore would have had to receive 63 percent of those uncounted votes to catch Bush. Even though many of the outstanding votes were from the generally Democratic counties of Dade, Palm Beach, and Broward and were expected to reduce Bush's lead, it seemed impossible for the lead to shrink below 20,000 votes. The television networks called Bush the winner of Florida (and therefore of the election) beginning at 2:16 A.M. eastern time. Neither the Associated Press nor VNS itself made the Bush call.

The premature Bush call was made because of two factors: a simplistic model of calculating the outstanding vote when few votes remained to be counted and actual miscounts by Florida counties themselves. VNS computed the outstanding votes by doing several calculations at the county level, taking the average vote totals of all the precincts reporting in the county and assuming that the outstanding precincts would have the same average size. It then took the candidate vote distribution within each county and projected that distribution when all the estimated remaining votes were in. At 2:10 A.M., VNS estimated that there were fewer than 180,000 votes remaining to be counted. However, some of the outstanding precincts were significantly larger than average, and there were still absentee votes left uncounted. The yet-to-be-counted votes totaled more than 350,000, nearly twice as many as estimated. In addition, counting errors remained in the totals, including one significant error in Volusia County. In Volusia County ballots were counted in a single central location, and there had been problems with their computer's memory card. At one point that night, adding a single precinct increased Bush's county total and at the same time *decreased* Gore's total by 16,022 votes.

The Volusia County error eventually was caught, but it was not corrected in the VNS system until 2:49 A.M., long after the Bush calls were made. That counting error as well as an input error in entering votes from Brevard County eliminated the 20,000 Bush statewide vote cushion expected when the call was made. By 3:57 A.M., the Bush call was retracted.[5]

THE POST-ELECTION REFORMS

Soon after the election, each major news organization commissioned a report on its election night errors, and, jointly, the members of VNS commissioned an external review of VNS operations. U.S. Representative W. J. "Billy" Tauzin (R-LA) announced that he would hold oversight and investigatory hearings into the networks' wrong calls. Once again, the media was criticized for calling elections before all the votes were counted. Tauzin went so far as to accuse the news organizations first of "probable bias" and later "incontrovertible bias" favoring the Democrats in the timing of their calls.[6] All of this was taking place while there were still many questions about which candidate had actually won Florida's twenty-five electoral votes and hence the election.

As early as the Friday after the election, Fox News announced that it would no longer announce winners in a state with two poll closing times until *all* polling places were scheduled to close, no matter how few those were. That would delay the possibility of calls in eight states—Indiana, Kentucky, Texas, New Hampshire, Michigan, Alaska, Idaho, and Florida—including three (Texas, Michigan, and Alaska) where just 3 percent or fewer polling places had a later closing time.

Beginning the following week, several news organizations appointed panels to investigate election night. The panels typically included the organization's vice president in charge of standards and practices and at least one outside academic. CNN's panel was comprised *only* of outsiders. The Associated Press did not create a formal panel, as it had never made the early morning Bush call (neither had VNS itself) and could not face regulation from the Commerce Committee since congressional jurisdiction does not reach the print press. Recommendations and reports were made public at various times, beginning with Fox's November promise and ending in early February, when ABC issued its complete report. The VNS technical investigation was conducted by the Research Triangle Institute (RTI) and presented to the VNS Board of Managers on January 22, 2001. On February 14, Tauzin's committee held its hearing (cablecast on C-SPAN) and took testimony from the heads of the Associated Press, the five network news divisions' VNS members, and VNS itself.[7]

THE TECHNICAL REPORT

RTI's technical report for VNS addressed some of the reasons that the mistaken calls were made and suggested a number of improvements that could be made to VNS's methodology. The main suggestions were for:

1. Improving the methodology for estimating the impact of absentee voters,
2. Improving the methodology for estimating outstanding votes in close races,
3. Improving the measures of uncertainty for election estimates,
4. Improving quality control, and
5. Developing better decision rules and exploring new approaches.

The first two suggestions dealt directly with the Florida mistakes. The ratio estimate that indicated a lower absentee share of the vote and the lack of a telephone among absentee voters was addressed in the first suggestion, and the second dealt with what was clearly too simplistic a method for accounting for the last few precincts to report.

The other suggestions related to more general improvements to the VNS estimation system, parts of which dated back more than three decades to work beginning in 1968. In the intervening years the gains in computer power and advancements in statistics had produced new ways of looking at data and permitted more complex manipulations with an increased number of data checkpoints. The recommendation for improved quality control was also directed at the acceptance of the flawed Volusia County results. While RTI proposed these improvements, the report also noted that the overall system of sampling and estimation was "well-designed for estimating the election day vote and generally follows standard statistical practices" (Research Triangle Institute 2001, ii).

THE NETWORK REPORTS

The network reports examined not only the system itself, but also how the network journalists used the information available on election night. The CNN report was written by three outside reviewers: syndicated columnist Ben Wattenberg; Joan Konner, former dean of the Columbia School of Journalism; and James Risser of the University of Missouri. It used the harshest language in describing election night. Wattenberg had already written a column castigating the network coverage and opposing calling elections at all even before the CNN panel was announced. It appears that nothing in discussions leading up to the CNN report altered any of his opinions. The CNN panel's report was rhetorically extreme: In one short section, it characterized CNN and other television news organizations as "excessive," behaving "recklessly," staging a "drag race," and creating a "news disaster." Four times in one paragraph the panel described the networks as "foolish."

CNN issued its own set of recommendations separate from those in the CNN panel's report, which also urged extreme remedial measures. The outside panel had urged that exit polls never be used to call races, but CNN's statement said only that it would not use exit polls to call *close* races. The outside panel also urged CNN not to use sample precincts to call races or to make *any* calls until all the polls across the country had closed.

CBS and NBC brought in outsiders, too. Kathleen Hall Jamieson, dean of the Annenberg School of Communication at the University of Pennsylvania, reviewed CBS's election night transcript; Tom Goldstein, the dean of the Columbia School of Journalism, served on NBC's panel. The public reports ranged from an eighty-seven-page CBS document to a three-page NBC statement. Some reports included sections on topics such as the history of VNS; some were simply summaries of recommendations.

Taken together, the network recommendations fall into five categories:

1. Gathering more and better data,
2. Setting different rules for calling elections,
3. Making changes in the timing of election night calls,
4. Reporting results more clearly, and
5. Managing VNS.

The networks agreed in most of these areas, and some promises matched with the less controversial proposals of the CNN panel.

More and Better Data

Several networks proposed gathering more data to allow for better information in calling races. For example, NBC proposed using more precincts for exit polls, which would reduce the size of sampling error on the estimates produced by the polls. CNN suggested a double set of sample precincts: Votes could be collected from both sets, providing more assurance of the correctness of a call.

All organizations noted the importance of using multiple sources for the tabulated vote (which became so important in making a Florida call in the early morning hours after the election). In fact, there was evidence that had the networks used two sources of the tabulated vote, the second Florida call might not have been made. The Associated Press conducts its own count of the tabulated vote. Although the Associated Press too had the Volusia County error in its count beginning shortly after midnight, it had corrected that error at 2:16 A.M., one minute before the CBS call for Bush. The component of the 2000 VNS system that had been redesigned to accommodate the Associated Press information along with the VNS vote count was not working on election night. The Associated Press decision team, which had access to a second vote tabulation, did not make the premature Bush call.

New Rules for Calling Races

The rules proposed by the networks in this area would mean tougher standards and greater caution. CBS proposed not calling the closest races, but instead using a "leading" status to designate how a state is likely to end up, keeping a step shy of calling a winner.

CNN went the furthest by stating it would not use exit poll tabulations in calling any but the most obvious races. If a race could not be called at poll closing time from exit poll data, CNN said that it would rely solely on the vote from sample precincts to make the call. In addition, CNN said it would not call any race where the margin of victory—the tabulated vote difference—between the two candidates was less than 1 percentage point. This was a response to one of the problems in the Florida analysis: Several networks did not quickly point out to viewers that Florida state law would require an automatic recount of an election that close.

The other rules for calling races involved the relationship between decision makers and the networks' news operations. CBS promised to add a member of senior news management to its decision team, who would have the authority to overrule the team and the stature to prevent demands from producers and correspondents for quick calls. It also said it would place its own reporters in close states to provide additional information about the vote-counting process.

Networks disagreed on where the calls should be made, in each case reversing their practice in 2000. NBC, whose decision desk was in its election night studio, vowed to isolate decision makers from the news operation. ABC promised to isolate its decision desk from access to calls made by other news organizations by removing television monitors from the decision desk's location. On the other hand, CBS, whose decision desk was located two floors above the election night studio, said it would move it into the newsroom, as its post-election analysis suggested that information coming into the studio from reporters in the field (but not provided to the decision desk) might have prevented the premature call for Bush.

The Timing of Election Night Calls

There was uniformity in network recommendations in this area: No calls would be made before the scheduled closing time for all precincts within a state, and Congress was urged to pass legislation providing for a uniform poll closing time for national elections. This type of legislation had passed the House of Representatives in 1985, but languished in the Senate. There had been, however, significant network support for such a rule, beginning with Frank Stanton (then CBS president) in 1965 (see Mason, Frankovic, and Jamieson 2001, 79).

After the 2000 election, a uniform poll closing bill was cosponsored by Representative Tauzin and the ranking Democrat on the Commerce Committee, John Dingell (D-MI), among others. The representatives suggested that the increase in absentee and early voting, with a third or more of voters casting ballots in some states long before election day, might make the notion of uniform poll closing more palatable to voters and to legislators. However, the bill has not yet passed the U.S. House (see Barnes, this volume).

Better Reporting

The networks all noted weaknesses in their coverage, weaknesses that went beyond the mistakes in calls. Both external and internal observers questioned the news organizations' on-air language, which indicated complete confidence in the reported outcomes. Perhaps the most-often quoted of these statements of confidence was Dan Rather's claim early in the CBS broadcast that when CBS called a race, "You can take it to the bank." At the Commerce Committee hearing, David Westin, the president of ABC News, reminded the committee that in many ways, the networks were the victims of their own success, that prior to the 2000 election the method used to call elections had resulted in only six mistakes in their several decades of use (Westin 2001). Only one of those mistakes had occurred during the ten years that VRS and VNS had been in existence. In 1996, VNS and all its members miscalled the New Hampshire Senate election for Democrat Dick Swett, instead of for the incumbent Republican, Bob Smith.

The promises of the networks for improved reporting included two general areas: reminders that calls were estimates or projections and better explanations of how the calls were made. While all election night graphics included an indication that a call was an estimate or a projection, CBS, CNN, and NBC vowed to label them more clearly, even to the point of using bigger type to do so. During election night, reporters often used shorthand in describing the estimates. For example, "Bush won" became a substitute for "CBS estimates that Bush will win."

The process of explaining what reporters knew and how they knew it got short shrift. For example, in the twelve hours CBS News was on the air, VNS (which had provided all the election data) was never mentioned. The other networks were only a little better. Whether a call was based on an exit poll, on sample precincts, or on tabulated votes was rarely made clear. When a call was *not* made, reporters often failed to indicate whether this was because a race was close or because there was not enough information to judge. These problems were acknowledged in the network reviews. CBS and CNN specifically indicated that in the future they would assign a correspondent to the decision desk to explain the process of making some calls and not making others. These explanations would also be supplied before election day.

Networks promised to spend more time explaining the electoral system. CNN vowed to explain recount requirements better, and CBS indicated it would expand its practice of reminding voters that polls could still be open in some parts of the country and would continue to encourage turnout.

Managing VNS

In the days immediately following the election, some organizations suggested that they would cease being part of VNS. Participation in VNS is renewable after each presidential election, and the deadline for withdrawal was pushed back to June 1, 2001, in order to give members the opportunity for formal review.

The recommendations for VNS in the networks' post-election reports followed those suggested in the RTI technical report. The networks urged a review and rewrite of the statistical models, upgrade of the computer system, more absentee coverage and research on exit poll nonresponse and error, and greater quality control in the tabulated vote-counting operation. In addition, CBS and CNN urged that the VNS board representatives (one from each news organization) be members of senior news management instead of technical representatives. With a complete review of the statistical models and a massive computer rewrite underway, as well as a review of quality control procedures, all members in fact renewed their membership in VNS in mid-2001. The VNS board was to consist only of members of the news organizations' senior management. Work on the planned reforms was expected to continue throughout the 2004 election cycle; at that point the changes and the commitment to VNS itself would be evaluated.

CONCLUSION: THE FUTURE OF ELECTION COVERAGE

Despite the wishes of some post-election pundits (and the CNN outside panel), news organizations will continue to call elections. Each organization will likely have its own decision desk personnel and go beyond the calls made by any pool. In this area at least, there will be little change, as there will continue to be network competition to report the results first, long the practice of American media.

But there will likely be change in other ways. The demand for better quality control at VNS, the review of the statistical models, and the requirement that there be multiple sources of vote data suggest that there can be improvement in the *quality* of the information provided to the public on election night. The networks' desire not to make the 2000 mistakes again, as well as their expressed desire to have more information before making a call, will mean that there should be greater deliberation before vote calls. Some calls will certainly be made later, since delaying calls until all polling places in a state are closed will certainly add one hour to the earliest time eight states' results can be called, and that presumably will slow down a news organization's ability to call the national presidential winner as well.

These proposed and adopted changes have one more important implication. At least in the short term, with the system redesign, VNS members have committed to spend more on their election night *costs*. Rewriting the computer system and reconsidering the statistical models from scratch impose a significant expense and can be considered a real investment in election coverage, especially since it would be incurred at a time of economic downturn when all organizations are facing budgetary limits. However, the additional expenditure could not guarantee a working system. The new system, built by Battelle Memorial Institute, crashed on election night 2002, unable to support the election day load of data. VNS itself was dissolved the following January. But exit polls and election night estimates of outcomes by the news media will continue in one form or another.

But perhaps the most hopeful promise made by the people who erred on Election Night 2000 is the promise to lift the veil on the mystery of election night coverage. It is not only the networks that have had a mistaken belief in their own predictive abilities; the candidates and their staff do, too. So do politicians and the pundits, Internet scribes, and radio hosts who fuel election day rumors. Why else would Al Gore have phoned George W. Bush to tell his opponent he was planning to deliver a concession speech after the Florida call for Bush? Why else was the national post-election reaction to the mistakes so strong? The networks' promises to better explain what is happening and why they are calling races should provide all viewers with a better understanding not just of network calls but of the overall electoral process itself.

NOTES

1. The bill, reintroduced in nearly every Congress, would close eastern time zone states at 9 P.M. local time, central zone polls at 8 P.M., and mountain polls at 7 P.M. It would also delay the return to standard time in the pacific time zone for several weeks, so that the Pacific state polls would also close at 7 P.M. local time. There was extensive opposition from airlines and other entities engaged in interstate commerce. See U.S. House of Representatives, Subcommittee on Elections of the Committee on House Administration, Hearings, May 9, 1985; Letters cited in 132 Congressional Record House 158, January 29, 1986.

2. A state's exit polling precincts were a subsample of the precincts that were included in the sample used for collecting precinct votes (the modern-day version of "Colonel" Taylor's and Lou Harris's key precincts). Several estimates of outcomes were made from the sample precincts and exit poll reports. The precinct tallies were weighted by size and their probabilities of selection, a nonresponse adjustment was made following a quality control check, and the results were entered into several estimation models—stratified by geography or past vote, including simple estimates and ratio estimates using the past vote. The models included tests for significance.

3. In fact, had the standard for choosing a past race for comparison been the best *average* correlation for both candidates, the error would not have been made. The system could have chosen the 1996 presidential election.

4. The 1992 Republican presidential primary in New Hampshire provided an instructive example of this. The exit poll indicated that Pat Buchanan might receive as much as 40 percent of the total vote against then President George H. W. Bush. He did not. According to the exit poll, Buchanan voters were more enthusiastic about their candidate than Bush voters were.

5. The premature New Mexico call for Gore was also based on information supplied by election officials in Bernalillo County, who first reported that all but 2,000 absentee votes had been counted. The next day, the county found software problems in its counting program and removed 67,000 absentee and early ballots for recounting. In the Washington state Senate race, misinformation about how much of the vote had been counted caused a too-early call for Cantwell.

6. He later changed the charge to one of "unintentional bias."

7. *Statement from ABC News*, November 22, 2000; *Statement of ABC News Concerning the 2000 Election Projections*, February 8, 2001; *NBC News Summary of Election Night Review* (Tom Goldstein, David McCormick, Maya Windholtz), January 4, 2001; *Statement of CNN Regarding Future Election Coverage*, February 2, 2001; Konner, Risser, and Wattenberg 2001.

3

Counting Ballots and the 2000 Election
What Went Wrong?

R. MICHAEL ALVAREZ

D. E. "BETSY" SINCLAIR

CATHERINE H. WILSON*

INTRODUCTION

Imagine a high school evaluating the results of a comprehensive test adminis-
tered to students to assess the school's performance relative to statewide standards. The school allocates its educational resources according to the results of
this test. Some students answer their tests using pencil and paper, some using
a standard "fill in the bubble" form, some with a computer card where they
"punch out" their answers, and others using computer terminals. After tabu-
lating the answers, the school principal announces that because of errors made
by the students and the grading machines, some of the student tests were not
tabulated. Specifically, she announces that because of the errors 3 percent of
the "punch out" tests were not tabulated whereas only 1.5 percent of the other
types of tests were not tabulated. That the particular way in which a student
took a test was related to the likelihood that his or her test was tabulated deeply
troubled school administrators, parents, students, and people throughout the
community.

Imagine also a scenario where different types of students use each type of
answer sheet. Many more high school students with purple hair use the "punch

*Authors' Note: We thank Tara Butterfield for her assistance with the data used in this
chapter, Mary King Sikora for her administrative help, Conny McCormack and John Mott
Smith for insight and information, and Steve Ansolabehere and Melanie Goodrich for their
comments. This research was supported by the Caltech/MIT Voting Technology Project
with a research grant from the Carnegie Corporation; however, the conclusions reached
here reflect the views of the authors and not necessarily the Caltech/MIT Voting Technology Project. This research was also supported by a grant to Alvarez from the IBM Corporation through the University Matching Grants Program.

out" answer system, while students with orange hair use the other test answering systems. Or, in another scenario, many of the students with purple
hair had never taken a "punch out" style test before, or for other reasons found
the test style confusing, complicated, and difficult to use. Each of these problems produced many more uncounted tests for students with purple hair than
for students with orange hair, even when students with both purple and orange hair used the "punch out" system. Given that the school's educational
policy was determined by the test results, the students with the purple hair
might easily be disadvantaged. These scenarios would be quite troubling because allegations that students with purple hair were harmed by this testing
situation would be difficult to discount.

To many observers, the deadlocked 2000 presidential election seems strikingly similar to these fanciful scenarios. Many analyses of the 2000 presidential election have shown that certain voting systems are associated with higher
rates of uncounted ballots than other voting systems.[1] In particular, studies conducted by Caltech/MIT (2001a, b), the Government Accounting Office (2001),
the U.S. House Committee on Government Reform (2001), and various scholars (see especially Ansolabehere 2001; Knack and Kropf 2001a, b; Posner 2001)
have all demonstrated with a variety of databases and statistical methodologies that punchcard voting systems clearly have high rates of uncounted
ballots, typically higher than other voting technologies.[2] This recent work,
moreover, essentially reaffirms the conclusions of a large body of earlier studies focusing on transitions from paper ballots to punchcards or other types of
voting systems decades ago (Fraser 1985; Mather 1964; Thomas 1968; White
1960), as well as more recent research focusing on the transition to electronic
voting machines (Nichols and Strizek 1995; Shocket, Heighberger, and Brown
1992).

Many observers have also worried that some voters might be more likely
than others to cast ballots that go uncounted. In this regard, most of these same
studies agree: Uncounted ballots are cast more in areas with high concentra-
tions of nonwhite, poor, and poorly educated residents (General Accounting
Office 2001; Herron and Sekhon 2001; Knack and Kropf 2001a, b; Posner 2001;
U.S. House Committee on Government Reform 2001). This same general pattern was confirmed in media analyses of two large, and largely nonwhite, counties (Cook County, Illinois, and Fulton County, Georgia), as well as in a
prominent media consortium's study of the uncounted ballots in the Florida
2000 presidential election ("Bush Still Had Votes to Win in a Recount, Study
Finds" 2001; "A Racial Gap in Voided Votes" 2000). The same patterns have
been found in earlier academic studies from previous elections and in many
different geographic locations (Bullock and Dunn 1996; Clubb and Traugott
1972; Darcy and Schneider 1989; Nichols and Strizek 1995; Vanderleeuw and
Engstrom 1987; Walker 1963, 1966).

Researchers, however, disagree about whether nonwhite, poor, and poorly
educated voters have higher uncounted ballot rates within counties employing voting systems with higher baseline rates of uncounted ballots—especially
punchcard voting systems. Researchers do not find higher rates of uncounted

ballots for nonwhite than white voters using punchcard voting systems (Ansolabehere 2001). Among the earlier studies, Montgomery (1985) reports null results; more recently, the GAO (2001) report on voting systems and uncounted ballots found no relationship between voting systems, race, and uncounted ballots.

The statistical analyses that have shown that higher rates of uncounted ballots occur where punchcard voting systems are used, especially the Votomatic system, have led to calls for the elimination or phasing out of punchcard voting. The more troubling allegations, that nonwhite voters might be more likely both to use punchcard voting systems *and* to cast uncounted ballots when using punchcard systems, have spawned a series of law suits arguing that inequities in voting systems violate Section 2 of the Voting Rights Act and the Fourteenth Amendment to the United States Constitution (see Hasen, this volume, predicting such lawsuits; Potter and Viray, this volume, discussing the laws). Cases making these voting rights claims have been filed in Georgia (*Andrews v. Cox*), Florida (*NAACP v. Harris*), Illinois (*Black v. McGuffage*), and California (*Common Cause v. Jones*).

This chapter begins with an examination of the voting problems uncovered in studies of the 2000 election. It focuses on the concept of "lost votes" and discusses the different places where votes went missing in this closely contested presidential election. The chapter then turns to a case study of the 2000 presidential election and election administration from the state of California. California makes an especially good case for this analysis for four reasons. First, elections data, including overvote and undervote information, as well as elections administration data, are easily available for California's fifty-eight counties. Second, California counties use punchcard, optical scan, and touchscreen voting systems. Third, California's political, social, and economic diversity makes it possible to test important hypotheses about the causes for the rates of uncounted ballots across California counties. Fourth, the focus on California allows us to contribute to the ongoing debate about the use of punchcard voting systems and their eventual decertification in California. Our analysis of the California elections data highlights places where significant election reform is necessary, something discussed in detail in the conclusion to this chapter.

THE 2000 PRESIDENTIAL ELECTION AND
THE CALTECH/MIT VOTING PROJECT

The 2000 presidential election led to a focus on voting systems unprecedented in American history. Never before had the public, press, and politicians looked at the wide variety of ways in which Americans cast their ballots. In general, there are six basic types of voting systems that are currently used in the United States:

1. The oldest voting system is the *simple paper ballot*—voters make their mark on a piece of paper, counted by hand.

2. Another old voting system is the *lever machine,* a large mechanical device that lets voters indicate their preferences by throwing levers and recording votes in a (nonelectronic) mechanical fashion.

3. *Punchcards,* a voting system introduced about thirty years ago, allows voters to indicate their preferences by punching out holes, or "chads," in computer-readable cards. There are three punchcard voting systems in wide use today: two, Votomatic and Pollstar, use cards with many small, usually numbered and prescored, "chads"; the third, Datavote, uses cards with larger "chads," and typically has the names of candidates or ballot measures printed on the punchcard itself.

4. In the last two decades *optical scanning* technology has been introduced; this system works by allowing voters to indicate their vote by connecting broken lines or filling in ovals with machine readable ink. Importantly, optical scanning machines can tabulate these votes either in a central location or can scan ballots for errors and tabulate votes locally in each precinct.

5. Electronics, either in the form of *"direct-recording electronic"* or the newer *"touchscreen"* devices, have been used in the past decade or so.

6. Finally, some election jurisdictions use a combination of these voting systems and hence are called "mixed" voting systems.

Immediately in the aftermath of the Florida vote recount, many groups initiated studies of the 2000 presidential election and issued multiple policy proposals. A unique research group was the Caltech/MIT Voting Technology Project (the Project), a collaborative effort between the social science and technology faculties on both university campuses. The Project was asked by their respective university presidents to identify the technological challenges associated with counting ballots in American elections and to determine ways to fix whatever problems were discovered.

The Project began by gathering as much data as possible on voting systems, their use, and measures of the rate at which each system rejected or did not count ballots. It issued a report on March 30, 2001, entitled "Residual Votes Attributable to Technology: An Assessment of the Reliability of Existing Voting Equipment." This report generated much publicity and widespread interest, largely because it was the first systematic study of voting systems conducted in the wake of the 2000 elections—and because it produced some striking conclusions.

The report focused solely on the "residual vote rate," or the total number of uncounted ballots. Ballots may not be counted for at least three reasons: (1) Voters may not indicate a preference on the ballot (undervotes); (2) voters may make more indications of a preference than are allowed (overvotes); and (3) voters may mark their ballots in a way that is uncountable. The Project focused on the residual vote rate because it is the only yardstick that could compare voting systems across counties, systems, and elections. What the Project found in data collected from 1988 through 2000 were two clusters of voting systems. One cluster, paper ballots, lever machines, and optically scanned ballots, were shown to have the lowest rate of residual votes throughout this period. On both average and median residual vote rate, these three voting systems had lower residual vote rates than the second cluster, consisting of punchcard and electronic voting equipment. The first cluster averaged residual vote rates of around 2 percent; the second cluster around 3 percent.

No one was terribly surprised to find that punchcard systems had high residual vote rates. Initial reports from Florida, and an examination of previous academic research on this topic, led to a hypothesis that punchcard systems would have high residual vote rates. What was surprising was that electronic voting systems—the so-called direct recording devices and newer automated teller machine (ATM)–style voting systems—had residual vote rates roughly comparable to those of punchcard systems. These differences remained even when controlling for a variety of other factors that might influence the residual vote rate.

Why did the electronic systems fare so poorly in the Caltech/MIT study? There are a number of reasons. First, many of the electronic systems that have been used since 1988 have poor user interfaces and bad ballot designs. Second, as electronic systems have only been used in recent elections, there is likely to be a technology learning curve among those who make and administer such systems, and thus a corresponding reduction in residual vote rates over time (the report cites some evidence of this). Third, there might be a similar voter learning curve, as the electorate adapts to a new voting technology. Fourth, electronic voting systems may require more administration in polling places, and thus are potentially more error-prone than other voting systems. Fifth, the electronic technology might be more sensitive to maintenance and reliability problems than other mechanical technologies. And sixth, there might be simple differences in how humans interact with electronic versus mechanical technologies.[3]

The next section of this chapter explores how a single, large, and politically powerful state (California) fared in terms of uncounted ballots in the 2000 presidential election. If there are differences in uncounted ballot rates across technologies and counties, do these differences impact some kinds of voters more than others? In particular, how do minority voters interact with the most error-prone technology, punchcard voting?

VOTING SYSTEM USE AND RESIDUAL RATES

This section discusses the relative uses of different voting systems in the United States and in California. This sets the stage for an analysis of the relative rates of uncounted ballots for each voting system and how these correlate with the racial complexion of each county in California.

The rate of use of the major voting systems in both the United States and California is given in Table 3.1. The first two columns list the distribution of voting systems across the United States, first expressed in terms of the per-

TABLE 3.1 U.S. and California Use of Voting Systems

	Percent of U.S. Counties	Percent of Population	Number of CA Counties	Percent of CA Counties	Percent of CA Population
Paper	12.5	1.3	0	0	0
Lever	14.7	17.8	0	0	0
Punchcard	19.2	34.4	30	51.7	74.0
Datavote	1.7	3.5	21	36.2	38.6
Votomatic	17.5	30.9	6	10.3	42.6
Pollstar	NA	NA	3	5.2	13.6
Optical scan	40.2	27.5	27	46.6	21.4
Central	NA	NA	11	19.0	9.0
Precinct	NA	NA	16	27.6	12.4
Mixed	4.4	8.1	0	0	0
Electronic	9.0	10.7	1	1.7	4.6

Note: Statistics for the United States are from Caltech/MIT Voting Technology Project (2001a, b). Statistics for California were compiled by the authors from data provided by the California Secretary of State and the U.S. Census.

centages of counties using each system and then in terms of the percentage of the U.S. population using each system.[4] The remaining three columns give similar information for California.[5]

In terms of counties, Table 3.1 shows that the most prevalent voting system in the United States in 2000 is the optical scan,[6] with over 40 percent of U.S. counties. Punchcard systems are the next most common, with 19 percent, mostly using the Votomatic system (17.5 percent).

The picture changes, however, when one turns to the percent of the population that uses each type of voting system. In the U.S. population, the most widely used voting system is punchcards. Optical scans are second, followed by lever machines and direct-recording electronic or touchscreen systems. In population terms, paper ballots are hardly used at all.

Punchcards are even more prevalent in California than in the rest of the United States, in terms of both the percentage of counties (52 percent) and the population (74 percent). In terms of both number of counties and statewide population, the use of punchcard ballots is over twice as extensive in California than in the United States as a whole. In California, the Datavote punchcard system is most widespread among counties, while the Votomatic system is the most widespread among the population. Optical scanning voting systems are currently employed by almost 47 percent of California counties, but only by 21 percent of the state's population. Almost 28 percent of counties (sixteen counties in total) use a precinct-based optical scan system, while 19 percent of counties (eleven in total) use a centrally based optical scanning system. In population terms, precinct-based scanning is more prevalent than centrally scanned ballots in California. Only one county in California—Riverside (4.6 percent of the state population)—uses an electronic, touchscreen voting system. Unlike in the rest of the United States, paper, lever, and mixed voting systems are not employed in California.

We now turn to an analysis of the apparent differences across voting systems in their relative rates of uncounted ballots (see Table 3.2). One way to examine the uncounted ballot rate is to study the "residual" vote rate, which is simply the difference between the number of ballots cast (usually for top-of-the-ticket races like president) and the number of ballots counted in the same race.[7]

The first two columns of Table 3.2 give baseline data for the United States. The first column provides the national average residual vote, by the major voting systems, from 1988 through 2000. Note that the same two clusters of voting systems are apparent in the 2000 election alone, as was found by the Caltech/MIT report for the whole 1988–2000 period. There is one cluster of systems with high residual vote rates (punchcards and electronic) and one cluster with lower residual vote rates (optical scan, paper, and lever).

The residual vote rate, undervotes, and overvotes are reported for California counties in the remaining three columns of Table 3.2. In 2000, California counties using punchcard systems recorded higher rates of residual votes than did counties using optical scan or electronic, touchscreen systems. In particular, the Votomatic system stands out with a statewide 2.4 percent residual vote rate, compared to residual vote rates for other punchcard systems (1.8 percent for Pollstar and 0.8 percent for Datavote). Overall, counties using optical scanning systems averaged residual vote rates that were half the size or less than counties using punchcard systems; also, precinct-based optical scanning counties had slightly lower residual vote rates than centrally based optical scanning

TABLE 3.2 Residual Votes, Undervotes, and Overvotes by Voting System

	U.S. Average Residual Vote, 1988–2000 (%)	U.S. Average Residual Vote, 2000 (%)	CA Average Residual Vote, 2000 (%)	CA Percent Reported Undervote	CA Percent Reported Overvote
Paper	1.9	1.3	NA	NA	NA
Lever	1.9	1.7	NA	NA	NA
Punchcard	NA	NA	1.9	2.7	0.4
Datavote	2.9	1.0	0.8	0.5	0.3
Votomatic	3.0	3.0	2.4	3.6	0.4
Pollstar	NA	NA	1.8	1.5	0.3
Optical scan	2.1	1.2	0.9	0.6	0.2
Central	NA	NA	0.9	0.7	0.2
Precinct	NA	NA	0.8	0.5	0.2
Mixed	2.2	2.7	NA	NA	NA
Electronic	2.9	1.6	0.9	0.4	0

Note: Statistics for the United States are from Caltech/MIT Voting Technology Project (2001a, b). Statistics for California were compiled by the authors from data provided by the California Secretary of State.

counties. These rates are consistent with the national figures from the Caltech/MIT report.

The last two columns of Table 3.2 give undervote and overvote rates, by voting systems, in California. Undervote rates are high for punchcard systems, but the rate is driven primarily by the high undervote in the Votomatic counties (3.6 percent). Optical scanning has much lower undervote rates, and precinct-based optical scanning has a lower rate of undervoting than central optical scanning has; precinct-based optical scanning systems usually check for voter mistakes in the polling place and thus the voter can often correct his or her mistakes. Touchscreen voting, in Riverside County, had a rate of undervotes close to zero.[8] On the whole, overvote rates are much lower than undervote rates, but punchcard systems have slightly higher overvote rates than optical scanning systems do. As is the case with undervotes, within the set of punchcard systems, Votomatic has the highest overvote rate. Also, precinct-based optical scanning has a very low overvote rate (0.198 percent), with centrally scanned ballots having a higher overvote rate (0.227 percent).[9] Since the electronic touchscreen system in Riverside County does not allow overvoting, the overvote rate in Riverside County is necessarily zero.

THE ROLE OF RACE IN BALLOT COUNTING

To begin assessing the relationship between race and uncounted ballots in California, Table 3.3 shows the percentages of nonwhites, blacks, Asians, and Hispanics in California in the counties using the various voting systems. The race data we use here and in the subsequent analyses were obtained from the U.S. Census Bureau and measure the number of persons in each racial category.[10]

The first column in Table 3.3 shows that counties using punchcard systems have greater populations of nonwhite residents (43 percent) than counties that

TABLE 3.3   Race and Voting System Use, California 2000

	Percent Nonwhites in Counties Using System	Percent Blacks in Counties Using System	Percent Asian in Counties Using System	Percent Hispanic in Counties Using System
Punchcard	43.2	7.3	11.6	34.3
Datavote	33.8	2.4	8.7	32.7
Votomatic	47.6	9.5	12.0	37.2
Pollstar	41.6	7.0	14.0	27.5
Optical scan	33.7	4.5	10.0	24.9
Central	30.4	5.1	7.4	22.7
Precinct	36.0	4.1	12.0	26.4
Electronic	34.4	6.2	3.7	36.2

Note: Statistics were compiled by the authors from data produced by the California Secretary of State and the U.S. Census.

use optical scanning systems (34 percent). Also, Riverside County's percent of nonwhite population is almost identical to the percent for optical scanning counties. Furthermore, notice that counties using the Votomatic system—which produces the highest residual vote (see Table 3.2) and the highest rate of undervoting and overvoting in California—have the highest nonwhite populations, almost 48 percent. Counties using the other punchcard system with relatively high rates of uncounted ballots, Pollstar, also have relatively high populations of nonwhites (42 percent). Interestingly, when we look at the differences within the optical scanning category, we see that counties that use precinct-based optical scanning, a system that has lower rates of undervotes and overvotes, have greater nonwhite populations than counties that use centrally located optical scanning systems.

The next three columns of Table 3.3 provide detailed breakdowns of the nonwhite population into blacks, Asians, and Hispanics and show the same pattern for nonwhites as a group, except that the one county in California where touchscreen voting is used had a large Hispanic population in 2000. (Note that the numbers do not sum up within each row; there are white and nonwhite Hispanics.)

Our analysis of race and residual voting rate begins with a simple correlation in each county between the percentage of the population that is nonwhite and the uncounted ballots, the overvote rate, and the undervote rate.[11] Then we turn to a multivariate statistical analysis of our data to provide separate confirmation of the relationship between racial composition and uncounted ballots in a county.

Table 3.4 gives the correlation between the nonwhite population and the residual vote, overvotes, and undervotes, broken down by county voting system.[12]

First note the correlations between nonwhite population and residual vote rate for punchcard counties compared to optically scanned ones: These correlations are moderately strong and positive in the case of the punchcard counties (0.44) and weakly negative in the optically scanned ones (−0.15). When we

TABLE 3.4 Correlation Between Race, Residual Vote, Undervotes, and Overvotes

	Correlation between Nonwhites and Residual Votes	Correlation between Nonwhites and Undervotes	Correlation between Nonwhites and Overvotes
Punchcard	0.44	0.53	0.06
Datavote	0.16	−0.05	0.17
Votomatic	0.17	0.43	0.70
Pollstar	0.23	0.14	0.52
Optical scan	−0.15	0.10	−0.03
Central	−0.22	−0.35	−0.26
Precinct	−0.11	−0.28	0.27
Electronic	NA	NA	NA

Note: Table entries are bivariate correlation coefficients.

look at the specific types of punchcard systems, we see positive but modest correlations for each of the three different punchcard systems. The correlations for precinct-scanned and centrally scanned counties are negative, although it is important to point out that the correlation is much closer to zero in precinct-based than in central-based optical scanning.

The second column of Table 3.4 presents the correlation analysis for undervotes. Comparing the correlations for all punchcard and all optically scanned counties, we again see a strong positive correlation in the case of punchcard counties, but now a weakly positive one for optically scanned counties. The strongest positive correlation is for the Votomatic punchcard counties. While the overall correlation between the nonwhite population and undervotes is weakly positive across all optically scanned counties, we do see negative correlations when we break the two optical scan systems into central- and precinct-based optical scanning.

The third column of Table 3.4 provides the correlations for overvotes. Here we see correlations between the nonwhite population and overvotes that are very close to zero for all punchcard and all optically scanned counties. Broken down by type, however, note the high positive correlations for Votomatic and Pollstar punchcards. However, the positive correlation for punchcard counties and the negative correlation for optically scanned counties is in the same direction as the residual vote rate.

This analysis, based on simple bivariate correlations between the nonwhite population, the rate of uncounted ballots, and the rate of overvoting and undervoting, leads us to three important conclusions. First, there is consistently a positive correlation between the nonwhite population and each measure of uncounted ballots across punchcard counties. Second, the Votomatic punchcard system in particular, and to some extent the Pollstar system, have positive and usually strong correlations between the nonwhite population and each measure of uncounted ballots. Third, we also see a general pattern for optical scanning that indicates a negative correlation between nonwhite population and uncounted ballot rates for counties using either types of optical scanning systems.

MULTIVARIATE ANALYSIS

The basic bivariate analysis just presented does not take account of factors that might intervene between race and voting system that might lead to incorrect conclusions.[13] For example, it is plausible to hypothesize that what appears to be a correlation between race and uncounted ballots really is the result of education or income differences between whites and nonwhites in California. To incorporate the possibility of intervening variables, we now turn to a multivariate statistical analysis.[14]

For this we have gathered data on other demographic and economic attributes of the California counties. In particular, in addition to the data from the U.S. Census Bureau on race, the analysis includes measures of the median age in each county; the amount of money each county spent on primary and secondary public education; and the county's unemployment rate, obtained from the California Department of Finance (2001). These variables are included in a multivariate statistical analysis along with measures for the percent of the population that is nonwhite, whether or not the county used a punchcard system; whether or not the county employed technology for local precinct counting of ballots, and the interaction between the nonwhite population of the county and whether the county uses a punchcard voting system.[15] This specification yields a strong test of the impact of race and technology on uncounted ballots, controlling for age, education, and unemployment.

We use two different methods to produce our estimates. First we use simple linear regression. Such a technique in this application might not be appropriate, however, because of the nature of the dependent variable, as all three are percentages—residual, overvote, and undervote rates. Linear regression works best when the dependent variable is continuous and the relationships between independent variables and the dependent variable are linear; in a situation in which the dependent variable is bounded (like a percentage) neither property is necessarily present. For this reason we also estimate the multivariate models using grouped logit, a statistical technique appropriate for the analysis of data that are not continuous, such as percentages.[16] A complete discussion of the results is contained in a methodological appendix for this chapter, which can be found at http://www.rethinkingthevote.org.

Three figures help to interpret these results. Figure 3.1 provides an analysis for residual votes, Figure 3.2 gives the results for overvotes, and Figure 3.3 shows the same results for undervotes. Each figure depicts the rate of uncounted

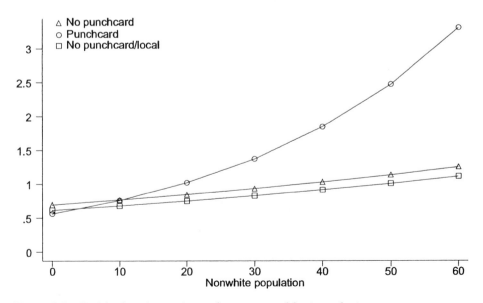

Figure 3.1   Residual voting estimate from grouped logit analysis

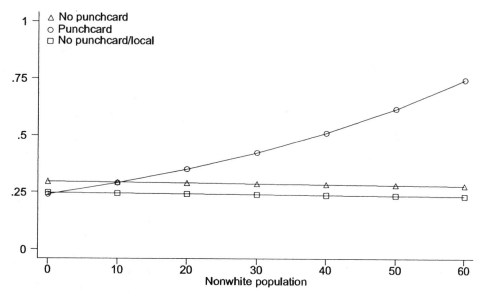

Figure 3.2   Overvoting estimate from grouped logit analysis

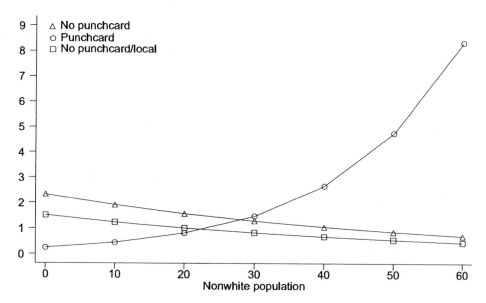

Figure 3.3   Undervoting estimate from grouped logit analysis

ballots for successive population sizes of nonwhites, depending on whether the county uses a punchcard system (graphed with circles), no punchcard and no precinct-based error-checking devices (graphed with triangles), and no punch-card but precinct-based error-checking (graphed with squares). Each of these graphs shows the estimated relationship between the size of the nonwhite population and uncounted ballot rates, for certain types of voting systems, holding the other variables in the model constant at their mean values.

Beginning with Figure 3.1, we see that the estimated rate of uncounted ballots, here measured by the residual vote rate, is low for counties with small, nonwhite populations, no matter what type of voting system is employed by the county. However, in counties with high nonwhite populations—for example, where 50 percent of the county's population is nonwhite—the story is quite different. The residual vote rate for counties that have a 50 percent nonwhite population is almost 2.5 percent in punchcard systems, whereas the residual vote rate is less than 1 percent for counties using other voting systems. The differences between punchcard and non-punchcard counties are stark, and the positive and strong relationship between the size of the nonwhite population and the residual vote rate in punchcard counties is easily seen in Figure 3.1.

The basic conclusion is the same for overvotes, as shown in Figure 3.2 (note that the scale on the vertical axis is different in each figure; overvotes are lower in magnitude than undervotes). The rate of overvoting is quite low for counties with small nonwhite populations, and the divergence between counties with large nonwhite populations using punchcard voting systems and counties with large nonwhite populations using other types of voting systems is stark. To continue the example of looking at counties with nonwhite populations of 50 percent, we see in Figure 3.2 that their overvote rate is twice as high in counties using punchcard systems relative to counties using other voting systems.

Figure 3.3 provides the same analysis applied to undervotes. We again see the same patterns. When there are small nonwhite populations, the undervote rate is low; when there are large nonwhite populations, the undervote rate is extremely high in punchcard counties but very low in non-punchcard counties. With specific regard to undervotes, the estimated difference in undervote rates for counties with 50 percent nonwhite populations is an almost eightfold increase in undervotes for counties using punchcard systems relative to counties not using punchcard systems.

In this section we have examined the relationship between race and uncounted ballots in California's 2000 presidential election. Using a variety of statistical techniques, ranging from simple bivariate correlation analyses to two different multivariate models, we have repeatedly found the same basic patterns. First, nonwhite voters have higher rates of uncounted ballots, overvotes, and undervotes than white voters. Second, this same pattern is most apparent in counties using punchcard voting systems.

CONCLUSION

In a democratic society, the act of casting a ballot on election day is perhaps the most important type of political expression. The translation of voters' opinions and preferences into the ballots they cast should occur ideally without any error, and the technology used to register and tabulate the vote should not impact the vote in any way. Only when the translation of preferences to counted ballots is transparent—and when the process is neutral, does not favor any particular party or candidate, and does not harm the voting process for certain classes of voters—is the voting system operating as it should.

This chapter shows that fundamental fairness in the voting system may not have existed in the 2000 presidential election in California. Substantial evidence, examined from a number of methodological perspectives, documents higher rates of uncounted ballots in counties with large nonwhite populations. This effect is particularly noticeable in California counties that employ punchcard voting systems. Furthermore, there is an interactive relationship between such counties and the size of their nonwhite population.

Why nonwhites in California—and in other election jurisdictions—have higher rates of uncounted ballots than other voters is an open question. As shown by many recent studies, including ours, there is a correlation between nonwhite population and uncounted ballot rates even while controlling for income and education differences of the counties (General Accounting Office 2001; Posner 2001). Clearly these other factors cannot account for the observed correlations. Instead, the differences might be caused by differing levels of political information and involvement, differences in familiarity with voting system technologies, higher levels of newly mobilized voters in nonwhite communities, or other factors. Our focus in this chapter has been on documenting the differences by race, since nonwhite voters are a legally protected class. Future research must study the underlying question of why nonwhite voters have higher levels of uncounted ballots.

There is no doubt—as previous studies have shown—that punchcard voting systems have higher rates of uncounted ballots than other voting systems do. One implication of our study and other similar studies is that there is the possibility of a constitutional equal protection issue in electoral jurisdictions within which voters use different (so-called mixed) voting systems (see Hasen, this volume). Voters within a larger jurisdiction, like a state, might encounter the same issue if they reside in a county using one of the punchcard voting systems that have high rates of uncounted ballots and if other voters in other counties in the same state use different voting systems that produce lower rates of uncounted ballots. Furthermore, this study indicates that in California counties using punchcard voting systems, the rate of uncounted ballots increases with the size of the nonwhite population. The same does not appear to be true in counties using other voting systems. This raises the possibility that Section 2 of the Voting Rights Act might be used as the basis for additional litigation in other election jurisdictions using punchcard voting systems, where similar patterns can be observed. There are many other states in which heavily nonwhite counties use punchcard voting systems, especially the Votomatic system. Unless significant action is taken to provide resources to states and local election officials to replace punchcard voting systems quickly, it is possible that a new area of voting rights litigation might arise focusing on whether nonwhite voters have higher uncounted ballot rates where punchcard voting systems are employed.

NOTES

1. In this study the term "voting system" refers to the method used by each county in the polling place for voters to mark their ballots. In the next section we discuss in more detail the various types of voting systems and their usage in both the United States and California.
2. Disagreement exists over whether punchcard voting systems have higher rates of uncounted ballots than all other systems. For example, the Caltech/MIT report found that electronic voting equipment had roughly similar rates and data did not find that electronic voting systems had such high levels of uncounted ballots. Nonetheless, all these recent studies agree with the basic point that punchcard voting systems are associated with high rates of uncounted ballots.
3. The Project first looked into the heterogeneity in voting systems and the vast differences that can be attributed to different voting systems in the rates of uncounted ballots across counties and states. But as it evolved, the Project discovered that this was only a piece of a bigger puzzle. As the Project held workshops, attended public forums and conferences, interviewed election administrators, and researched the entire process of election administration, the participants became aware of the fact that in any election, many votes go uncounted for reasons other than voting system problems.

   These uncounted votes, or "lost votes," figured prominently in the Project's second report issued in July 2001, "Voting: What Is, What Could Be." Based on research conducted using a variety of sources, the Project found that at least 4 million to 6 million votes were lost in the 2000 presidential election. Approximately 1.5 million to 2 million votes were lost because of voting system problems—faulty voting equipment, confusing ballots, or other problems with voting technology. Even more votes, between 1.5 million and 3 million, were lost because of problems in the voter registration system. Many of these belonged to individuals who showed up to vote but were denied the opportunity to cast a ballot because of some type of error in their voter registration. Finally, up to 1 million votes were lost because problems in polling places, in particular, mix-ups of polling place locations and long lines on election day.

   While the Caltech/MIT Voting Technology Project was initiated to study and fix problems associated with voting systems technology, it quickly learned that voting systems technologies were only part of the problem with elections in the United States. Fixing the problems with voting systems technologies, while obviously important, also would require fixing voter registration systems, polling place practices, and various issues associated with election administration. The next phase of the Project is devoted to more detailed, and in-depth, analyses of voting systems problems.
4. These figures were compiled and reported in the Caltech/MIT Voting Technology Project's report (2001a, b).
5. This data was obtained from the California Secretary of State's Office, http://www.ss.ca.gov/elections/sov/2000_general/vs.pdf.
6. Unfortunately, the national data obtained from the Caltech-MIT report do not break down optical scan systems into precinct- or central-based systems.
7. This is the measure used in the Caltech/MIT report (2001a, b). The second way to study uncounted ballots is to look at the rate of spoiled ballots (Alvarez, Butterfield, and Wilson 2001); unfortunately, ballot spoilage (ballots that are rendered uncountable by voters, by accident, or by machine error) rates are not widely reported. Third, one can decompose the uncounted ballot rates into the overvote and under-

vote rates, where overvotes are ballots that have more marks than allowed for a particular race and undervotes are ballots that have no discernible mark for a particular race. The undervote and overvote rates, unfortunately, are not universally available, although we have the undervote and overvote rates for forty-three of the fifty-eight California counties.

8. The difference between the residual vote rate of 0.9 percent for Riverside County and the 0.4 percent undervote rate is that the residual vote is computed for all ballots counted, which in Riverside includes optically scanned absentee ballots. The undervotes are solely for precinct voters, and in Riverside County precinct voters all used touchscreen systems.

9. As most of the counties that employ precinct-based optical scanning employ error-checking in the precincts, note that overvoting in precinct-based optical scanning counties might indicate intentional overvoting. Of the counties that responded to our query for information about how their precinct-based optical scanning systems were configured in the 2000 presidential election, two, Humboldt and Amador, did not enable error-checking in their precinct scanning systems. Placer County stated that their system rejected only undervotes, or blank ballots. Of the remaining counties that provided us information (only San Luis Obispo and San Francisco did not respond to our requests for information), their systems indicated overvoting on ballots in the precincts.

10. These data come from the "Profiles of General Demographic Characteristics, California" publication of the U.S. Census Bureau. The county-level measures of race we use are for the entire population, not the voting-age population or the population of registered voters. The latter quantities are not measured by the Census, and could only be estimated from these data. We prefer to focus on the known population statistics, rather than use estimated values for voter registration or voter turnout by racial category. Producing estimates of voter registration or turnout for multiple racial categories would necessitate the use of multistage ecological inference estimation, which would be difficult if not impossible in this context; furthermore, ecological estimation of demographic data for county electorates would be quite imprecise and would therefore introduce substantial uncertainty into our estimates. The use of population data in this analysis, rather than demographic data about the electorate, should not be problematic as there is a strong correlation between the population and electoral data. For example, California counties with larger black populations have larger black electorates, and so on.

11. Our focus in the statistical analyses that follow is on nonwhites, rather than the more specific categories of blacks, nonwhite Hispanics, and Asians. First, the broader category of nonwhites is traditionally the category that has been considered the legally protected group. Second, in this data, where we only have a limited number of observations, statistical analyses may become very sensitive to specifications like the relative sizes of these different racial groups. However, to the extent that, for example, blacks and nonwhite Hispanics do not have similar patterns of political behavior, our decision to include both in one measure of the nonwhite population could bias our estimates for the impact of the nonwhite population on uncounted ballots.

12. The correlation coefficient potentially ranges from positive 1 to negative 1. A positive correlation close to 1 indicates a strong positive relationship between the percent nonwhite and the uncounted ballot rate, a negative correlation indicates an inverse relationship, and a correlation close to zero indicates no real relationship between the two variables. Thus, a strong positive correlation for a particular vot-

ing system indicates that as the nonwhite population within counties using that voting system increases, so do the uncounted ballot rates. Furthermore is the question of aggregation bias and whether we are making incorrect ecological inferences (King 1997). In other work using this same data, we conducted an ecological analysis of this data. We did not find results that are qualitatively different from those reported here.

13. Multivariate statistical analysis uses several descriptive variables in a statistical model to explain the variation in the dependent variable. Multivariate analysis is particularly useful because it allows the user to study the impact of one descriptive or independent variable on the dependent variable, holding all of the other descriptive variables constant. For more discussion, see Tufte (1974).

14. By setting up the voting system variables in this way, we can include Riverside County in the analyses, as the touchscreen system is considered to be a local precinct counting system.

15. One important problem that arises with linear regression models in situations such as the one we are studying is that the linear regression estimates can often produce predictions that are outside the zero to 100 percent interval. For example, two of the linear regression specifications we report in Table 3.6 on the book website produce predictions for uncounted ballots for certain ranges of the independent variables that are below zero. This is an important indication that the linearity assumption necessary for the linear regression model to produce accurate estimates of the effects of the independent variables is a poor assumption to make in this context.

16. For more discussion of the grouped logit model see Greene (2000). For an application of the grouped logit model that is very similar to that which we present here, see Alvarez and Nagler (2001). In this application, we used the weighted least squares approach for estimating the grouped logit model, rather than the maximum likelihood approach.

4

An Unrecognized Need for Ballot Reform

*The Effects of Candidate Name Order
on Election Outcomes*

JON A. KROSNICK

JOANNE M. MILLER

MICHAEL P. TICHY

Since the firestorm that erupted nationwide on November 7th, 2000, election technologies in the United States have come under close scrutiny. A commission headed by former presidents (National Commission on Election Reform, 2001), an interuniversity consortium of academic scholars (CaltechMIT Voting Technology Project, 2001b. See Alvarez et al., this volume.), and a good many ordinary citizens have recognized and thought hard about the potentially disastrous consequences of a voting system that falls prey to errors and biases. To be sure, elections like the presidential contest of 2000, with a margin slim enough both within a state and across states to make even the smallest discrepancies in vote counts consequential, are rare indeed. So the substantial expense entailed by changing voting technology to improve accuracy may seem unjustified on financial grounds alone. But such improvement seems more clearly worthwhile in light of its potential to enhance public trust in the electoral process in America and to promote the principle of fairness at the center of American values.

Yet there is a paradox inherent in our nation's approach to the debacle of 2000. While a tremendous amount of energy is being devoted to considering and implementing costly voting reform, lurking in the shadows is another systematic bias that has been altering and will continue to alter the outcomes of many electoral contests, unchecked and unacknowledged in all the debates sparked by the debacle of 2000.

In this chapter, we focus on that source of bias in an effort to pull it out of the shadows, to characterize its operation and consequences, and, we hope, to inspire people who care deeply about electoral fairness in the United States to end it. This source of bias has its roots in the basics of human psychology: The choices people make among alternatives are routinely influenced by the order in which the choosers consider their various options. It ought to come as no surprise that this bias influences election outcomes from a cognitive perspective. And it is surely no surprise to politicians that this bias influences election outcomes, as they have shown an awareness of it for at least a century. Yet election laws around the country nonetheless reinforce and perpetuate the bias rather than attenuate it.

The bias has a simple cause: the order of candidates' names on the ballot. For at least a century, politicians have speculated that name order matters, and most social scientists who have studied the phenomenon concluded that it is real, but state legislators and courts have rarely acted to remove this source of electoral bias.

After reviewing both the speculations about name order effects and the variations in state laws and court decisions, we offer a psychological theory to explain why name order matters and present data from analyses of the 1992 Ohio elections to show that there are indeed substantial name order effects. We then report new findings on the 2000 election in three major states. Most strikingly, we find that even in the highly-publicized and hotly-contested presidential race, name order mattered.

EARLY SPECULATIONS

At least since the beginning of the last century, seasoned political observers have believed that the ordering of candidates' names on ballots has some influence on the outcomes of elections (see Darcy and McAllister 1990). For example, Woodrow Wilson (1910, p. 593) asserted:

> I have seen a ballot which contained several hundred names. It was bigger than a page of newspaper and was printed in close columns as a newspaper would be. Of course, no voter who is not a trained politician, who does not know a great deal about the derivation and character and association of every nominee it contains, can vote a ticket like that with intelligence. In nine out of ten cases, he will simply mark the first name under each office, and the candidates whose names come highest in the order will be elected.

Some years later, Joseph Harris (1934, p. 181) asserted:

> Much more important than the order of offices on an election ballot is the order in which the names of the candidates appear in office group ballots. This is particularly true in direct primary and nonpartisan elections, and is of most importance in cases where several persons are to be elected to the same office. The position at the top of a list of candidates is of material help to the candidate thus favored, especially for minor positions.

These experienced observers speculated that being listed first helps a candidate to win an election, especially when thoughtful decision-making is costly to voters: When ballots are long, many candidates are competing for the same office, voters are not well informed, or party affiliation cannot facilitate voters selections. Under these circumstances, proposed these observers, voters may be affected by name order when making their decisions.

NAME ORDER LAWS

If the early observers were correct and name order does indeed affect the balance of votes cast, and if legislators want to see to it that election outcomes are fair and unbiased, then state laws could prescribe a system of name ordering that advantages no particular candidate. In fact, this is just what is done in Ohio.[1] State law requires that the order of candidate names be rotated from precinct to precinct, such that each candidate is listed first in an equal number of precincts. No candidate has the privilege of a first-place listing more often than any other candidate.

Ohio is not alone in this regard.[2] North Dakota, Montana, and Idaho carry out similar procedures, rotating from precinct to precinct or across paper ballots or counties. In races run in all counties in California, name order is rotated across assembly districts in a similar fashion.[3] In Kansas, name order rotation is done either by precinct or by county. In all nonpartisan races in Iowa, candidates are rotated by precinct, and candidates in nonpartisan races in Arizona are rotated from paper ballot to paper ballot. Michigan rotates candidate names across precincts for nonpartisan races, and Minnesota and Nebraska rotate candidate names across ballots or precincts. Some additional states have procedures that mimic the effect of rotating candidate names, such as Arkansas, where a separate random order of candidate names is created in each county.

But that's it. Only twelve states in the United States rotate name order fully in some or all of their elections. The vast majority of states do not take any such steps to eliminate any advantage of one candidate over another in this regard. The diversity of alternative systems used is startling, as shown in Table 4.1.

One might guess that some of the approaches not entailing name rotation are mandated by very old laws, put in place before the possibility of name order bias was recognized. In fact, some such laws were put in place very recently. Alaska required prior to 1995, for example, that candidate names be rotated on the ballot to give all candidates placement in the first position equally often. But in 1995, the state legislature amended this rule to require instead that one single randomly-determined name order be used for each race. The recommendation to make this change came from the lieutenant governor's Election Policy Transition team, which asserted that "research indicates that the order of candidates' names on American ballots does not significantly influence voters" and that using a single name order would save money and reduce the potential for voter confusion (see *Sonneman v. State of Alaska* 1998).

What could account for this diversity of approaches? Perhaps name order doesn't actually affect election outcomes, and so no system is any better than any other system. Another possibility is that many politicians, parties, special

TABLE 4.1   Procedure for Ordering Candidate Names in General Election

Procedure for Ordering Names	State(s) Using That Procedure
Rotation of candidate names across ballots, across precincts, across counties, or across assembly districts.	Ohio, North Dakota, Montana, Idaho, Kansas, California,* Iowa,* Arizona,* Michigan,* Minnesota,* Nebraska,* Wyoming*
All candidates are listed in one order, determined randomly by a random alphabet.	Alaska,* California*
Democratic Party and Republican Party candidates are listed before all other candidates, in a random order generated separately by each county. Listed next are all candidates affiliated with other parties, in an order determined by the date on which the candidate filed to be on the ballot in the county. Finally, all candidates not affiliated with a party are listed, again in an order determined by the candidate's filing date in each county.	Illinois
Democratic Party candidates are listed first; Republican Party candidates are listed second; candidates affiliated with other parties are listed next (in alphabetical order by party name); candidates unaffiliated with parties are listed last (in alphabetical order by candidate surnames).	Delaware,* Tennessee*
All candidates are listed in one order, determined randomly, either for the entire state or for each county separately.	Oregon, California,* District of Columbia, Florida,* Missouri,* New Mexico,* Oklahoma,* Rhode Island,* South Dakota,* Texas,* Utah,* Washington,* West Virginia,* Wisconsin,* Arkansas
Candidates from the major parties are listed first in a random order, followed by the remaining candidates listed in a random order, done either statewide or separately by county.	New Mexico,* Oklahoma,* New Jersey,* Rhode Island,* South Dakota*
Candidates are listed alphabetically by candidate surnames.	Vermont, Hawaii, Maine, Nevada, Louisiana, Florida,* Georgia,* Indiana,* Maryland,* New Hampshire,* North Carolina,* Rhode Island,* Wyoming,* South Carolina,* Delaware,* Tennessee*
Candidates from "major" parties are listed in a random order first, followed by all other candidates in alphabetical order by candidate surname.	Virginia
In the race for president, candidates from "major" parties (Democratic and Republican) are listed first in alphabetical order by party name, followed by all candidates affiliated with other parties, listed alphabetically by party name. Candidates must be affiliated with a party to be listed.	Louisiana*

(continued)

TABLE 4.1 *(continued)*

Procedure for Ordering Names	State(s) Using That Procedure
In each election held in November of an even-numbered year, the recognized political parties are placed in an order that applies to all races, and candidates not affiliated with a party are grouped together (ordered alphabetically by surname) somewhere in the midst of that list of parties. That order applies to all elections for the next two years. For the elections held in November two years later, the party at the top of the order is moved to the bottom of the party ordering list, and that new order is used for all elections during the next two years.	South Carolina*
The incumbent running for reelection is listed first, followed by candidates affiliated with other recognized parties, in alphabetical order by surname, followed by other candidates, ordered alphabetically by candidate surname.	Massachusetts
Candidates affiliated with major parties are listed in descending order of the number of votes cast statewide for their party in the most recent race for governor. The remaining candidates are listed either in the order in which they were certified to be on the ballot or in a single random order or alphabetically or in descending order of the largest number of residents to be represented by the offices for which candidates from a party are running.	Pennsylvania, Georgia,* New York, Connecticut, Nebraska, Texas,* Florida,* Missouri*
Each county lists the candidates in descending order of the number of votes cast in the county in the most recent race for governor. Other parties are then listed alphabetically by party name, and then candidates not affiliated with parties are listed alphabetically by surname.	Arizona*
Candidates are listed in descending order of the number of votes cast statewide for their party in the most recent race for president of the United States. The remaining candidates are listed in the order in which they filed to be listed on the ballot.	Washington,* West Virginia*
Candidates are listed in descending order of the number of votes cast in the primary election for that race.	Oklahoma,* Washington,* Utah*
Candidates are listed in descending order of the number of votes received by their parties in the most recent election for U.S. congressional representative in the county. Candidates affiliated with parties that did not run candidates in that race are listed next, in a random order. And candidates not affiliated with any parties are listed next, in alphabetical order by candidate surname.	Wyoming*

(continued)

TABLE 4.1   Procedure for Ordering Candidate Names in General Election *(continued)*

Procedure for Ordering Names	State(s) Using That Procedure
Candidates are listed in descending order of the number of votes cast statewide for their party in the most recent race for secretary of state. Parties that did not have a candidate in that race have their candidates listed next in the order in which they filed to be listed on the ballot. Candidates not affiliated with parties are listed next, in the order in which they filed to be listed on the ballot.	Michigan
Major party candidates are listed in a county in descending order of the number of votes cast in the county for their party in the most recent race for secretary of state. Next are listed candidates affiliated with other parties in the order in which they filed to be on the ballot. Candidates not affiliated with any party are listed next in the order in which they filed to be on the ballot.	Indiana
Candidates are listed in descending order of the number of votes cast statewide for their party in the most recent race for governor or president of the United States (whichever race occurred more recently). Candidates not affiliated with parties that ran candidates in that race are listed in a random order.	Wisconsin*
Candidates are listed in descending order of the number of voters registered as a member of their party who participated in the most recent state general election. Following these candidates are all other candidates, listed in the order in which they qualified to be on the ballot.	New Hampshire*
Ordering of candidate names in nonpartisan races is left to the discretion of the elections official in each county.	New Jersey*
Candidates affiliated with the current governor's party are listed first, followed by candidates affiliated with other parties (listed in descending order of the number of registered voters registered to that party in the state), followed by candidates not affiliated with a party (listed in alphabetical order by candidate surname).	Maryland*
Candidates from the Democratic and Republican parties are listed first in a single randomly determined order by party name, followed by candidates affiliated with "minor" parties (listed in a different single randomly determined order by party name), followed by the remaining candidates (listed in a different single randomly determined order by candidate name).	Colorado*

(continued)

TABLE 4.1   *(continued)*

Procedure for Ordering Names	State(s) Using That Procedure
In the race for President, the Democratic and Republican candidates are listed first in alphabetical order by candidate surname. Then the candidates affiliated with minor parties are listed in alphabetical order by candidate surname. And finally, candidates not affiliated with major or minor parties are listed in alphabetical order by candidate surname.	Colorado*
Partisan races: Candidates from the Democratic, Libertarian, and Republican parties are listed first (in alphabetical order by party name), followed by candidates not affiliated with those parties (in alphabetical order by candidate surname). *Nonpartisan races*: The probate judge in each county has the discretion to order names in any way.	Alabama
Candidates affiliated with the party of the incumbent president of the United States are listed first, followed by the candidates affiliated with the other major party, followed by other candidates in a single randomly determined order.	Kentucky
Candidates from parties with whom 5 percent or more voters are registered are listed first, alphabetically by party name. Candidates affiliated with other parties are listed next, alphabetically by party name. Candidates not affiliated with any party are listed next, alphabetically by candidate surname.	North Carolina*
Candidates are listed in the order in which they filed to be on the ballot, with the earliest filers listed first.	Missouri*
Candidates affiliated with major political parties are listed first (in whatever order the county auditor of each county chooses), followed by candidates affiliated with other parties (in whichever order the county auditor chooses), followed by candidates not affiliated with any party (in whichever order the county auditor chooses).	Iowa*
Candidates of the four "major parties" are listed in ascending order of the average number of votes cast for a candidate affiliated with their party in all of the most recent statewide elections.	Minnesota
Candidates not affiliated with the major parties are listed in a random order determined separately for each county or municipality.	
Each county clerk may order candidate names however he or she likes.	Utah*

(continued)

TABLE 4.1   Procedure for Ordering Candidate Names in General Election *(continued)*

Procedure for Ordering Names	State(s) Using That Procedure
The State Board of Elections sends a sample ballot to the County Boards of Elections, and many of them use that sample ballot (although they are permitted to order names however they wish). On the sample ballot, candidates of the Democratic and Republican parties are listed first, alphabetically by party name. Next, candidates affiliated with other parties are listed alphabetically by party name. Finally, candidates not affiliated with any party are listed alphabetically by surname.	Mississippi

*Some (but not all) races run in this state use this procedure.

interests, and incumbents believe that name order does affect election outcomes, and the states vary in terms of whether they want to ensure fairness or protect certain interests or whether they want to expend resources to do so. States that require name rotation invest resources to print and distribute multiple different versions of ballots, and counting of ballots is a bit more complex when varying name orders are used. These resources are more substantial when different precincts use different voting methods (i.e., some use paper ballots and others use punch cards). States that use one random or alphabetical ordering expend considerably fewer resources and take a step in the direction of fairness but nonetheless systematically advantage some candidates over others. And states that advantage incumbent parties or office-holders perpetuate these partisan biases.[4]

DISPUTES IN COURT

In addition to Wilson (1910) and Harris (1934), mentioned earlier, another group of observers has registered concern: candidates who lost elections by small margins and candidates whose names were or would be listed on a ballot in a position other than first and who took their complaints to court (see, e.g., *Bolin v. Superior Court* 1958, *Culliton v. DuPage County Board of Election Commissioners* 1976; *Elliott v. Secretary of State* 1940; *Gould v. Grubb* 1975; *Kautenburger v. Jackson* 1958; *Ulland v. Growe* 1978; *Weisberg v. Powell* 1969). It is instructive to consider the evidence presented in these cases and the court findings themselves.

Experts have testified that being first on the ballot gives an advantage of anywhere from 2.5 to 25% of the vote.[5] Not all expert testimony on this issue has shared this perspective. One expert testified that name order effects do not influence the outcome of political races that receive a large amount of public attention.[6] Yet another expert argued that there was not enough evidence on which to base an opinion about name order effects.[7]

In many cases, courts have written opinions clearly stating that candidate name order does matter. For example, the Supreme Court of Arizona wrote: "It is a commonly known and accepted fact that where there are a number of candidates for the same office, names appearing at the head of the list have a distinct advantage." (*Kautenburger v. Jackson* 1958).

In response to such testimony, courts have sometimes ruled that biased election procedures must be remedied. For example, in *Culliton v. DuPage County Board of Election Commissioners*, 1976, the United States District Court for the Northern District of Illinois, Eastern Division, ruled that DuPage County, Illinois, must devise a system for rotating candidates' names in order to remove any bias advantaging any one candidate or party, for use in future elections. In other cases, courts acknowledged that it was possible that name order might have biased an election outcome, but based a decision not to overturn the election on direct evidence showing that the presence and magnitude of a name order effect on the election in question was probably not large enough to have altered the outcome.[8]

Even more strikingly, in February 2002 Los Angeles Superior Court Judge Judith Chirlin ruled that the City Clerk in Compton (California) had violated California's name ordering law in that city's 2001 race for Mayor, incorrectly listing Eric Perrodin first and incumbent Omar Bradley second. Based upon testimony about the likely magnitude of the name order effect in that race, Judge Cherlin ruled that Bradley would have won if the candidates' names had been ordered properly. She therefore overturned the election result and ordered that Bradley be installed in office. California's 2nd District Court of Appeal overturned Judge Chirlin's ruling on the grounds that California law did not require reversing name order, highlighting potential legal ambiguity.

In rare instances, courts have written opinions denying the existence of name order effects, but not on the basis of any evidence. For example, in *New Jersey Conservative Party et al. v. John J. Farmer et al.* (1999), the court wrote:

> That there is voter apathy and a malaise creeping in our electoral process may be assumed for the moment. The expected consequence of such a condition, however, would be an increasing number of registered voters staying home on election day. The poor turnout in the Republican and Democratic primaries in 1999 referred to in the earlier proceeding appears to support the existence of growing voter indifference. But it is an odd act of indifference for a voter to take the trouble of going to the polls only to then cast a vote without thought; this court, in the absence of clear proof, prefers to believe—perhaps naively—this windfall vote simply does not exist. The apathetic or indifferent may, and no doubt do, stay away from the polls—lately in droves—but nothing before the court suggests they do show up at the polls in order to vote in an unguided fashion.

Despite such exceptions, many people in legal settings, including plaintiffs, experts, and judges, have believed that name order effects could well affect election outcomes. But are these observers correct? Why would a citizen take the trouble of going to the polls but then cast a vote without much thought?

WHY MIGHT NAME ORDER EFFECTS APPEAR?

Name order effects are in fact easy to imagine in light of a variety of findings from past psychological research. Understanding these effects must begin by acknowledging that contemporary American elections often confront voters with tremendously challenging tasks. Voters have routinely been asked to make choices in well over two dozen races, ranging from highly visibile contests to races for offices so obscure that many voters probably could not describe the job responsibilities associated with them. In 1911, for instance, Cleveland, Ohio, voters were confronted with 74 candidates for city offices, 12 candidates for Board of Education, 14 candidates for Municipal Court Judges, and 32 candidates for Constitutional Convention (Davies 1992). Matters were no better in 1992: Cleveland voters were asked to cast ballots in over forty county and statewide races, plus a number of districtwide races.

Because races for highly visible offices (e.g., for U. S. president and congress) receive a great deal of news media attention, often involve well-known incumbents, and usually involve explicit endorsements of candidates by political parties, voters who wish to make substance-based choices can do so in principle. However, candidates in such races rarely take clear and divergent stands on specific policy issues (Berelson, Lazarsfeld, and McPhee 1954; p. 1978), and media coverage of such contests usually focuses on the horserace rather than on the candidates' records and policy positions (Patterson 1994). The cognitive demands of sifting through lots of such media coverage and extracting useful, substantive information about candidates' positions are therefore probably so substantial as to outstrip most voters' incentives to do the work (Downs 1957). So people rely on only a small subset of substantive information to make vote choices, pursuing what Popkin (1991) called "low information rationality."

Media coverage of races for less visible offices (e.g. Attorney General, Auditor, Judge, Sheriff, Coroner, and Board of Education) is often much more limited, making it even more difficult for voters to make choices based on substance (e.g. Graber 1991). People pursuing low information rationality can sometimes rely on cues, such as party affiliation, that can help them identify candidates with whom they are likely to agree on policy issues (Campbell, Converse, Miller, and Stokes 1960; Miller and Shanks 1996). But party affiliations are often not listed on the ballot for the very races that receive the least media coverage. Alternatively, people can rely on name recognition: The candidate whose name sparks a stronger sense of familiarity may be seen as most likely to be the incumbent, who by virtue of his or her presumed experience may be considered the safer choice (e.g. Jacobson 1987; Mann and Wolfinger 1980). But because holders of low-visibility offices probably get very little media attention during their tenures, voters may only rarely recognize their names.

What do people do when no such cues are present at all to guide their choices? If someone knows nothing about any of the races being run on a particular election day, he or she may stay home rather than cast a ballot (Delli Carpini and Keeter 1996), in line with political theorists' notion that democratic governance should be carried out only by those citizens who are able to do so responsibly (see Dahl 1989; Pennock 1979). However, well-intentioned get-out-the-vote efforts may sometimes provide transportation to and press minimally informed and minimally motivated citizens into casting votes when they are completely uninformed about the candidates. And sometimes, more informed citizens go to the polls to vote in a few highly visible contests, yet they are asked to vote in minimally publicized races for relatively obscure offices as well. The higher "roll-off" rates (i.e., the proportion of people who went into the voting booth but failed to cast a vote in a particular race) typical of such races presumably reflect some voters' choices to abstain on the less visible races because they lack sufficient knowledge to make a choice (Burnham 1965; Robinson and Standing 1960; Vanderleeuw and Engstrom 1987). However, other people may feel that to be responsible democratic citizens they must not only go to the polls but must also cast votes in all listed races, even when they know only a little about the candidates and have not made a firm choice among them before entering the voting booth. New technologies—such as blinking lights on machines calling attention to races in which a person has not yet voted—may encourage people to cast votes in these cases.

How do people vote under such circumstances? One psychological theory suggests that people may be inclined to select the first name they see in a list of candidates, creating a "primacy effect" (Krosnick 1991). People tend to evaluate objects with a confirmatory bias. Specifically, people usually begin a search of memory for information about an object by looking for reasons to select answer choices, rather than reasons not to select them (Klayman and Ha 1987; Koriat, Lichtenstein, and Fischhoff 1980). In considering a list of political candidates, voters probably search memory primarily for reasons to vote for each contender rather than reasons to vote against him or her. When working through a list, people think less and less about each subsequent alternative because they become increasingly fatigued and short-term memory becomes increasingly clogged with thoughts. Therefore, people may be more likely to generate supportive thoughts about candidates listed initially and less likely to do so for later-listed candidates, biasing them toward voting for the former.

This theory is consistent with dozens of experiments that presented objects visually and nearly always found bias toward selecting initially offered options (for a review, see Krosnick and Fabrigar, forthcoming). For example, when students take multiple-choice knowledge tests, they are biased toward selecting answers offered early in a list, so they tend to answer items correctly more often when the correct answer is listed first than when it is listed last (e.g., Cronbach 1950; Mathews 1927). When people are told that an experimenter will imagine a series of questions and they should guess which of a set of offered response choices is the correct answer, people tend to select the first ones listed (Berg and Rapaport 1954). When people are asked to taste a set of beverages or foods (e.g., four brands of beer) and select their favorite, they are biased toward choosing the first one they consider (e.g., Coney 1977; Dean 1980). Voters may well manifest the same sort of bias in elections.

People attempting to retrieve reasons to vote for a candidate may occasionally fail completely, however, retrieving instead only reasons to vote against him or her. If this happens for all candidates in a given race, cognitive fatigue and short-term memory congestion would presumably bias a citizen toward generating more reasons to vote against the first-listed candidate than reasons to vote against later-listed candidates. This would induce a "recency effect," that is, a bias toward selecting candidates listed last (see Schwarz, Hippler, and Noelle-Neumann 1993; Sudman, Bradburn, and Schwarz 1996).

Name order might also influence the votes cast by people who have no information at all about the candidates in a race but nonetheless feel compelled to vote in all races in order to be "good citizens." According to Herbert Simon's (1957) notion of satisficing, people are inclined to settle for the first acceptable solution to a problem they confront, especially when the costs of making a mistake will be minimal. If citizens feel compelled to vote in races regarding which they have no information, they may settle for the first name listed, because they have no reason to think that the candidate is not acceptable.

There is one other possible reason for primacy effects: ambivalence. If a voter has paid close attention to a well-publicized race and learned both favorable and unfavorable information about all competing candidates, the voter may feel substantial ambivalence, finding it difficult to choose between the competitors. In this situation, people may settle for the first name they see because they cannot make a choice on substantive grounds, despite having plenty of information about the competitors.

There is abundant theoretical justification for the hypothesis that the order of candidates' names on ballots may influence voters' choices in some races. If people simply settle for the first listed contender when they have no information at all about a race or feel deeply ambivalent, primacy effects will occur. Primacy effects would also be expected in races about which voters do have some information when they can generate at least some reasons to vote for each of the candidates. But when voters can only retrieve reasons to vote against competitors, recency effects would be expected.

Order-based choice should be less likely when voters are more knowledgeable about candidates and have made substance-based choices before election day (Lodge, McGraw, and Stroh 1989). Name order effects should, therefore, be strongest in races that have received little news media coverage and among voters who are exposed to little or none of such coverage. Order-based choice should also be most common in races that do not offer voters heuristic cues, such as party affiliations of the candidates or incumbency-based name recognition. Cognitive fatigue is likely to build as a voter considers race after race on a long ballot, which may increase the likelihood of name order effects. Also, races listed toward the end of a ballot may be perceived as less important than those near the beginning, so voters may be less motivated to cast votes carefully in the former and may therefore be more influenced by name order.

THE STATE OF THE EVIDENCE

During the last 50 years, many studies have been published exploring the impact of candidate name order on election outcomes. These studies have produced evidence suggesting more primacy effects (candidates receiving more votes when listed first) than recency effects (candidates receiving more votes when listed last) or what we call "middle" effects (in races of three of more candidates, candidates receiving more votes when listed in the middle). So it is understandable that scholars might have looked at this evidence and viewed it as supporting the primacy claim.

In fact, we think that Smolka (1977) had it just right in saying that nothing had been proven by this literature, even as of 1990, because of two major design flaws in the approaches taken: inadequate tests of statistical significance and failure to randomly assign groups of voters to different name orders.

Many studies of candidate name order effects failed to report statistical significance tests of differences between the voting patterns of people who saw candidates' names in different orders (e.g., Brooks 1921; Byrne and Pueschel 1974; Hughes 1970; Mackerras 1968; Mueller 1969; Nanda 1975; Scott 1972; White 1950). We therefore cannot assess the likelihood that the differences observed in these studies were due to name order effects or were only illusory, due to chance variation. And among the studies that did report statistical significance tests, some computed them improperly, yielding the same uncertainty of meaning (e.g., Bain and Hecock 1957; Nanda 1975).[9]

Even more problematic, many studies did not involve assignment of voters to different name orders at all. Rather, these studies simply looked at whether, when combining across a large number of elections, candidates listed in different positions typically do better or worse on average (Bagley 1966; Bakker and Lijphart 1980; Brook and Upton 1974; Brooks 1921; Byrne and Pueschel 1974; Hughes 1970; Kelley and McAllister 1984; Lijphart and Pintor 1988; Mackerras 1968; Masterman 1964; Mueller 1970; Nanda 1975; Robson and Walsh 1974; Upton and Brook 1974; Upton and Brook 1975; Volcansek 1981). Obviously, if such differences are observed, they might be due to some factor other than candidate name order effects, such as alphabetic-based preferences.[10]

Only two studies (Darcy 1986; Gold 1952) did not have at least one significant design flaw that precludes making reasonable inferences, and neither found statistically significant name order effects, nor did they explore the impact of such potential mitigating factors as party affiliations or incumbency. Therefore, no conclusions can be drawn from this literature with confidence; whatever conclusions one draws should be reached extremely cautiously and tentatively based upon only these two studies (see also Darcy and McAllister 1990).

OUR FIRST INVESTIGATION: OHIO, 1992

We undertook the first sizable investigation of name order effects that avoided many of the pitfalls that plagued past work in the area. To do so, we took advantage of the fact that Ohio rotates candidate names from precinct to precinct (Miller and Krosnick 1998). Because this constitutes the essence of a true experiment, we were able to test whether candidates received more votes when listed first or last or in some other position.

We gathered precinct-by-precinct vote returns for the three largest counties in Ohio in 1992: Franklin (which contains Columbus), Cuyahoga (which contains Cleveland), and Hamilton (which contains Cincinnati). There were 879 precincts in Franklin County, 2,036 in Cuyahoga County, and 1,041 in Hamilton County. These constituted the units of analysis with which our tests were computed. Analyses of variance conducted on the mean vote totals received by the candidates in the precincts for 118 races in 1992 indicated that statistically significant name order effects appeared in 48% of the races, nearly always advantaging candidates listed first, by an average of 2.5 percentage points.

The tendency for primacy effects to dominate was apparent even in races with nonsignificant name order effects. In races involving two candidates, 75% of the races with nonsignificant name order effects were in the direction of primacy effects. Moreover, the average magnitude of the nonsignificant two-candidate primacy effects (1.14%) was more than 50% greater than that of the nonsignificant two-candidate recency effects (.74%). Likewise, in races involving three or more candidates, 81% of the candidates who had nonsignificant name order effects manifested trends toward primacy, whereas only 19% manifested trends toward recency effects. If there were truly no name order effects present in these races, we would expect to see an even balance of trends toward primacy and recency. The clear prevalence of primacy effects suggests that when compared to the variation between precincts in election outcomes, many name order effects are sufficiently small to go undetected by significance tests, even with this many precincts involved.

In the 1992 study, name order effects were most common when voters lacked substantive information with which to choose between the competitors. One substantive basis for choice is party identification: When voter knows the party affiliations of the candidates, he or she can easily vote for the member of his or her own party. When races are well publicized by the news media, voters presumably know a great deal about the candidates' personal and political histories, positions on policy issues, and more considerations with which to evaluate them. And when an incumbent is running for reelection, voters have presumably learned a great deal about him or her while in office. Not surprisingly, name order effects were less likely to appear when candidates' party affiliations were listed on the ballot, when a race had been well publicized, and when an incumbent was running for reelection. We also found that name order effects were especially likely to occur among voters who were less educated, presumably because they were less attentive to political affairs and accumulated less knowledge about politics in general and candidates running for office in particular. Interestingly, controlling for other race characteristics, name order effects were *more* likely to appear in races listed near the top of the ballot (in which voters feel more compelled to vote) than in races lower down (where voters more readily roll off if they lack information or feel ambivalent).[11] Taken together, this evidence paints a convincing portrait of name order effects as robust and startlingly common in contemporary elections.[12]

The results we reported (Miller and Krosnick 1998) may at first appear to be inconsistent with the two previous studies of this phenomenon that did not suffer from serious design flaws that found no reliable name order effects (Darcy 1986; Gold 1952). However, these studies were different from ours in ways that probably account for the differences in results.[13]

A NEW INVESTIGATION: NAME ORDER EFFECTS IN 2000 IN OHIO, NORTH DAKOTA, AND CALIFORNIA

To further fill out the body of available evidence on name order effects, we conducted new analyses of vote returns in Ohio, North Dakota, and California in 2000. We begin by describing the races selected and the methods used to rotate name order in those races. Then we outline our findings.

Contests Analyzed

In order to be included in our analyses, a contest had to meet a number of criteria. We eliminated all races that involved only one candidate running for an office or where a voter could cast a vote for more than one of the competitors running for a single office. We eliminated races in which the order of the candidates' names was not rotated across voters in a random or quasi-random (e.g., sequential assignment of precincts to name orders) fashion. We eliminated races run in a relatively small number of precincts (in Ohio or North Dakota) or assembly districts (in California) because we would have limited statistical power to detect a name order effect if one had in fact occurred. Specifically, in Ohio and North Dakota, we only analyzed races in which all voters in at least one entire county voted, thus eliminating races that were run in only a subset of precincts in a county. We also did not analyze races run in counties in Ohio that had less than 50 precincts per rotation order.[14] In California, we analyzed data from all statewide races in which candidates' name rotation was done by assembly district and the vote returns were published separately for each assembly district.

Name Rotation

In Ohio, name orders were rotated as described fully by Miller and Krosnick (1998). The process started with listing all of the precincts in the county in an order determined by size of city, date of precinct creation, and the spelling of the precinct names. Then, for each race, a series of different name orders were developed, beginning first with an alphabetical ordering of the candidates. Each additional name order was created by moving the first listed candidate to the end of the list until each candidate had been listed first in one and only one order. The number of name orders created therefore equaled the number of candidates in the race. The first name order was assigned to the first listed precinct; the second name order was assigned to the second precinct; and this assignment procedure continued, rotating repeatedly through the name orders, until every precinct had been assigned to a name order. This was done independently for each race, without regard to the rotation scheme used for the other races on the ballot.

In North Dakota, name rotation was conducted independently by each county. The process began by listing the precincts in descending order according to the total number of votes cast for governor in the last election, starting with the precinct with the largest number of total votes cast and ending with the precinct with the smallest number of total votes cast. The name order assigned to the first precinct on the list was determined by lot. Each subsequent name order was created by moving the first-listed candidate to the end of the list. The first name order was assigned to the first listed precinct; the second name order was assigned to the second precinct; and this assignment procedure continued, rotating repeatedly through the name orders, until every precinct had been assigned to a name order. This was done independently for each race, without regard to the rotation scheme used for the other races on the ballot.

The rotation process for statewide races in California began by first listing all 80 assembly districts in an order beginning with the assembly district at the northwest corner of the state and then working inland and south to end with the assembly district in the southeast corner of the state. The name order assigned to the first assembly district on the list was determined randomly. The name order assigned to the second district on the list was created by moving the first-listed candidate to the end of the list. Additional name orders were created by repeating this process of moving the first-listed candidate to the end. The assignment procedure continued, rotating repeatedly through the name orders, until every assembly district had been assigned to a name order. This was done independently for each race, without regard to the rotation scheme used for the other races on the ballot.

Analysis Strategy

The data were analyzed using the same method employed by Miller and Krosnick (1998). We conducted analyses of variance and regressions to test the significance of linear and nonlinear effects of name order.

RESULTS

Two-Candidate Races

Of the 170 two-candidate races run in Ohio and North Dakota, 39, or 23%, showed statistically significant or marginally significant name order effects. All but two of the statistically significant or marginally significant effects were primacy effects. The percentage point difference between the votes obtained in first and last positions in the races that showed significant or marginally significant primacy effects ranged from 1.41% to 6.32% and averaged 2.88%.[15]

Races with More Than Two Candidates[16]

Of the 136 candidates who ran in races with more than 2 candidates, 50, or 37%, showed statistically significant or marginally significant name order effects. Of the significant or marginally significant effects, 74% were primacy effects, 2% were recency effects, 18% were middle effects, and 6% were primacy and recency effects. The average magnitude of the difference between the first and last positions was notably greater for the significant or marginally significant primacy effects (1.36%) than for the significant or marginally significant recency effect (.40%), suggesting that the primacy effects were more robust.[17]

Perhaps our most interesting finding relates to the presidential election (see Table 4.2). Being listed first on the ballot was an advantage for some candidates. George W. Bush received more votes when he was listed first than when he was listed last in all three states. This difference was marginally statistically significant in California and of a strikingly large magnitude: 9.45 percentage points. Although nonsignificant, the trends in North Dakota and Ohio were in the same direction—1.69 percentage points in North Dakota and .76 percentage points in

TABLE 4.2 Name Order Effects in Races for U.S President and U.S. Senate

Race	California		North Dakota		Ohio	
	Direction of Effect	Percent Difference between First and Last Position	Direction of Effect	Percent Difference between First and Last Position	Direction of Effect	Percent Difference between First and Last Position
U.S. President						
Brown	Primacy	.09	Primacy	.02	Primacy***	.08
Buchanan	Primacy	.06	Primacy†	.41	Primacy***	.18
Bush	Primacy†	9.45	Primacy	1.69	Primacy	.76
Gore	Recency	−4.47	Primacy	.13	Primacy	.67
Hagelin	Primacy***	.06	Primacy	.12	Primacy*	.02
Nader	Primacy	.03	Recency	−.14	Primacy*	.10
Phillips	Primacy†	.11	Primacy	.03	Primacy***	.06
N	80		367		12,142	
U.S. Senate						
Benjamin	Primacy*	1.47				
Camahart	Primacy*	.28				
Campbell	Middle†	−4.57				
Feinstein	Primacy	6.24				
Lightfoot	Primacy**	.35				
Rees	Primacy and Recency*	2.05				
Templin	Primacy	.40				
N	80					
U.S. Senate						
Celeste					Primacy***	1.80
Dewine					Primacy***	1.66
Eastman					Primacy***	.20
McAlister					Primacy***	.60
N					12,142	

Note: For California, N = number of assembly districts; for North Dakota and Ohio, N = number of precincts.
†p < .10 *p < .05 ***p < .001.

Ohio. These percentage point differences each correspond to thousands of votes. Pat Buchanan manifested statistically significant primacy effects in North Dakota and in Ohio, and Ralph Nader manifested a significant primacy effect in Ohio.

Al Gore's regressions revealed nonsignificant trends in the direction of primacy effects in all three states. The percentages of votes Gore received when listed first, second, third, fourth, fifth, sixth, and seventh were 53%, 58%, 64%, 55%, 52%, 52%, and 57%, respectively. Thus, he gained more votes on average when listed first, second, or third (mean = 58.33%) than he did on average when listed fifth, sixth, or seventh (mean = 53.67). Interestingly, he gained about 4 percentage points fewer votes when listed first than when listed last, which yields the negative 4.47 in Table 4.2. But that difference does not accurately represent the overall trend and was not significant, nor was the difference between the 53% of votes Gore earned when listed first and the 58% of votes he earned when listed second.

To summarize, of the 21 tests of name order effects for the seven presidential candidates in the three states, 19 manifested trends toward primacy effects, 9 of them being significant or marginally significant. No significant or marginally significant effects in other directions appeared. This clearly suggests that the presidential race was not immune to name order effects. Although this may have occurred because some voters lacked sufficient information about the candidates to make informed choices, it seems more likely to be attributable to ambivalence.

Elections of representatives to the U.S. Senate were similarly susceptible to name order effects in 2000 (see Table 4.2). The race for U.S. Senate in California manifested plenty of significant name order effects: Five of the seven candidates manifested trends toward primacy effects, three of them significant. One significant primacy and recency effect appeared, and one marginally significant middle effect appeared as well. Likewise, the race for U.S. Senate in Ohio manifested significant primacy effects for all four candidates, even for the Republican incumbent (Dewine, 1.66%) and well-known Democratic challenger (Celeste, 1.8%).[18]

IMPLICATIONS

Our results indicate that there is more than a slim chance that name order could affect the outcome of a close election—even in a major, highly salient race—so it seems worthwhile for all states to assign positions to all candidates equally often across precincts. Indeed, 4 of the 188 races we examined previously (Miller and Krosnick 1998) would have had different results if only one name order had been used, depending on which was chosen (the Franklin County races for County Commissioner I, Supreme Court Justice I, and Court of Appeals Judge IV and the Cuyahoga County Commissioner I race). These four races represent only 3% of the races we examined then, but they nonetheless suggest that effort should be spent to balance name orders in future elections and that states without statutes requiring name rotation should consider adopting them.

One interesting implication of this evidence involves incumbents' well-documented advantage in winning elections. This phenomenon has been explained by a number of factors, including the ability of incumbents to amass greater stores of campaign funds, but little attention has been paid to the fact that name order effects may be partly responsible as well. In a number of states that do not require name rotation, the ordering schemes that were used gave advantages to incumbents. For example, in Massachusetts, the incumbent running for reelection is always listed first. And in various other states, the first candidate listed in a race is specified to be from the party that most recently won that race. Such schemes not only advantage incumbent candidates and parties and enhance the likelihood of stability of governmental personnel from election to election, but they also discourage divided government by consistently according a small advantage to all members of a single party. Some courts have recognized this bias and overturned such laws (e.g., *Gould v. Grubb* 1975; *Holtzman v. Power* 1970; *McLain v. Meier* 1980).

Our findings also have implications regarding the efficacy of democratic electoral systems. Name order effects are instances in which nonsubstantive factors affect election outcomes. As V. O. Key (1957, iii) put it, "A basic condition for the health of a democratic order is the existence of procedures and machinery for the conduct of elections in whose fairness and neutrality a general confidence prevails." Evidence of the impact of name order on election outcomes, he said, would suggest that, "In earthly practice the majority will may be both influenced and distorted by the most humdrum minutiae of election procedure and administration" (ibid., iii). This sort of concern is articulated especially well by Ortiz (this volume).

Rather than viewing our evidence as bad news, as Key might have, we see it as encouraging. Although name order effects in the 1992 Ohio elections and in the 2000 election in Ohio, North Dakota, and California were prevalent, they were also quite small and concentrated among a subset of election contests. Furthermore, had name rotation not been done, the majority will could have been distorted in only 3% of the races of the 1992 Ohio races we examined. Given the magnitude of the name order effects we did observe, it appears that only a very small minority of voters made what Key (1966) would presumably call "irresponsible" choices in this sense. In close elections, however, these few irresponsible voters may determine who wins and who loses.

Our evidence suggests that President George W. Bush acquired more votes when listed first than when listed later in all three states we examined, marginally significantly so in one. Because his brother (a Republican) was governor of Florida, that state's law required that the Republican candidate for President be listed first on all of Florida's ballots. If the name order effects we saw in other states were present in this race in Florida, the number of votes President Bush gained as a result of this law would most likely have been substantial enough to affect the outcome of the 2000 presidential election. In that light, it seems all the more important for states to remove the bias in name ordering prevalent around the country so that Americans can have full confidence in the outcomes of its electoral contests.

Some readers will no doubt be surprised that George W. Bush's vote total would have been so substantially affected by name order in California because some conditions of that race generally discourage such effects. In particular, party affiliations of the candidates were listed on the ballot, and the race was tremendously publicized, through the news media generally and through the voter information booklets distributed to all Californians. On the other hand, no incumbent was running for reelection, and the race was at the top of the ballot, both factors encouraging name order effects. More importantly, the nature of the race was such that many voters may well have been very ambivalent about the candidates. Indeed, seasoned scholar Kathleen Frankovic called the American public the "Ambivalent Electorate" in 2000 (Frankovic and McDermott 2001). Such ambivalence is likely to have contributed to the appearance of name order effects in that race.

It is also important to note that changing laws and rotating the ordering of candidate names is not the only way to minimize name order effects. Evidence that such effects occur less often when races are well publicized, when candidates are listed with political party affiliations, and when voters are especially engaged in politics (Miller and Krosnick 1998) points to other intervention tools. Enhancing publicity to allow the public to make informed choices among candidates, enhancing public motivation to acquire and process such information, increasing the number of candidates whose names are listed with political party affiliations on ballots, and increasing the extent to which members of the public identify with particular parties should reduce the magnitude of name order effects as well.

But the appearance of the marginally significant name order effect in votes for President Bush is an important reason to hesitate before concluding that such interventions can eliminate all name order effects. The presidential race involved candidates labeled with party affiliations and a great deal of publicity, yet a name order effect appeared nonetheless. It is therefore clear that publicity, engagement, and party affiliations do not eliminate all chances of a name order effect appearing. The theory we offered here suggests that when name order effects occur under such circumstances, they are likely to be the result of voters' deep ambivalence about two equally appealing or equally unappealing candidates. Because such ambivalence may happen frequently in the future, the best technique for preventing name order effects from biasing election outcomes appears to be rotation.

Not all rotation methods are equally effective. Among the eight states that do currently rotate at least some candidate names, each one uses a different approach. The more populated each unit used for rotation is, the fewer such units will exist in a state. And rotating across fewer units allows random chance variation in unit population size a greater opportunity to distort election outcome. We therefore recommend rotating from precinct to precinct, as Ohio does. That way, many smaller units are used, which permit more effective rotation statewide and also permit rotation of names for races run within single counties or assembly districts. In addition, Ohio rotates candidate names across absentee ballots from ballot to ballot, a procedure we also recommend. If all this were to be done in every state across the country, the expense of conducting elections would be greater, and the potential for mistakes in implementation would rise as well, but the most important outcomes of our nation's democratic governance process would certainly be fairer, and perceptions of the legitimacy of our governments would be commensurably enhanced.

NOTES

1. Our discussion from here on focuses on ballots cast on election day in general elections; laws regarding primaries are substantially more complex and are not discussed. Absentee ballots are also not discussed.
2. Our description of name ordering procedures is based upon the published name ordering statutes for the States and upon telephone conversations with elections officials in the various states. It proved to be very difficult to confirm all elections procedures with confidence by these methods, so what we offer here are our best assessments of the procedures implemented as of 2002.
3. A variety of procedures are used in California races not run in the entire state. Names of candidates competing for Congressional Representative and the State Board of Equalization are rotated by Assembly districts. State Senators and members of the State Assembly are not rotated unless the districts in which they are running encompass more than one county, in which case each county draws its own random order of the letters of the alphabet and orders candidate names according to that random alphabet. For offices voted on throughout a county, candidates' names are rotated by Assembly district if there are five or more Assembly districts within the county. If there are four or fewer Assembly districts within a county, candidate names are rotated by supervisorial districts. If a race is run in only a portion of one county, candidate names are listed according to the random alphabet drawn by the Secretary of State. Candidates for Justice of the Supreme Court and Court of Appeals of California are arranged according to the random alphabet and are not rotated at all.
4. States may also vary in the credibility they attribute to the argument that name order rotation limits the value of sample ballots distributed to voters during a campaign. If citizens mark a desired candidate on the sample ballot while at home and then vote for the candidate listed in that position on the ballot (not checking to see whether the names match), differences between candidate name orders on sample ballots and actual ballots on election day may cause voting errors.
5. See, for example, *Bohus v. Board of Education Commissioners*, (1971) where the advantage was estimated to be from 2.5 to 25% of the vote; and *Sangmeister v. Woodard* 1977, where being listed first was reported to garner "3.3% more votes than second place" (463). In *McLain v. Meier* (1980), the advantage was "at least 5 percent" (1166). In *Koppel et al. v. New York State Board of Elections et al.* 2000, a name order effect of 4.7% was found in a particular election. Testimony in *Clough v. Guzzi* 1976 reported a 5% to 15% increase in the first candidates' total vote.
6. Professor Robert Darcy has testified a number of times (e.g., *Graves et al. v. McElderry et al.* 1996; *Koppell et al. v. New York State Board of Elections et al.*, 2000), asserting, for example, that, "Position bias is certainty not a factor which affects the outcome of any political races for public office in those partisan elections that receive a large amount of public attention" (*Graves et al. v. McElderry et al.* 1996). Darcy's testimony was based primarily on his own studies of name order effects and his critiques of the methods used in other previous studies.
7. Professor Richard Smolka said, "There has virtually nothing at all been done on the subject and much less anything been shown. There is no evidence upon which to base an opinion" (*Sangmeister v. Woodward* 1977, 463).

8. For example, in a 1972 Ohio State Senate race between Robin Turner and Gene Slagle, Turner lost by 155 votes. Due to improper implementation of the name rotation required by Ohio law, Slagle's name appeared first on 15,289 ballots in Marion County, whereas Turner's name appeared first on 7,629 ballots in that county. In *Turner v. Slagle* (1972), the parties stipulated that when Slagle was listed first, Slagle got 44.2% of the votes, whereas when Turner's name was listed first, Slagle got 42.0% of the votes, a pattern consistent with a primacy effect. Adjusting the vote totals to simulate the numbers of votes that would have been cast for the candidates had name order been rotated properly indicates that Slagle would have received 76 fewer votes and Turner would have received 76 more votes, yielding totals of 57,472 for Slagle and 57,469 for Turner. There is no basis in these numbers to overturn the election outcome, and the Supreme Court of Ohio did not do so.

In a similar case (*Pfeifer v. Fisher* 1991), the Ohio Supreme Court ruled that although Paul Pfeifer was not listed first as often as Lee Fisher was in their race for attorney general of Ohio because the name order rotation required by Ohio law was improperly implemented in Mahoning County, statistical analysis of the election returns showed that Pfeifer and Fisher did not in fact get statistically significantly more votes when listed first than when listed second and that the difference in number of votes obtained was not large enough to have affected the election outcome. Noting this evidence, the court let the election result stand.

9. In name order effect studies, when each voter is *individually* assigned to a name order independently of all other voters, the number of observations on which a statistical test should be computed is the total number of voters participating in the study. This would be the case if a coin were to be flipped for each voter to determine the order he or she is to receive.

However, in some studies, voters were not individually assigned to name orders. Rather, groups of voters (i.e., all those in the same precinct) were assigned to name orders, so that all members of a group received the same order. If this is done, it is inappropriate to use the total number of voters as the basis for computing the statistical significance of observed differences (see Darcy and McAllister 1990, p. 8; Judd and Kenny 1981, pp. 55–57). Such an approach will yield statistical tests that are too liberal, thus making observed differences seem less likely to have occurred by chance alone than is actually the case. Statistical tests in such studies must instead be based on the number of *groups* of voters (in most cases, precincts). Because various studies should have computed their significance tests in this fashion but did not, their results overestimate the level of statistical significance of the differences they observed.

10. In many studies, candidates were listed alphabetically on the ballots (Bagley 1966; Bakker and Lijphart 1980; Brook and Upton 1974; Brooks 1921; Hughes 1970; Kelley and McAllister 1984; Lijphart and Pintor 1988; Mackerras 1968; Masterman 1964; Mueller 1970; Nanda 1975; Robson and Walsh 1974; Upton and Brook 1974, 1975; the basis for ordering was not specified by Byrne and Pueschel 1974 or Volcansek 1981, and it may well have been alphabetical). The question being asked in these studies, then, is whether candidates whose last initials come early in the alphabet do better or worse than candidates whose last initials are in the middle of or late in the alphabet. If such differences are observed, it is impossible to know whether they are due to candidate name order effects or voters' preferences for certain last initials.

There is good reason to believe that voters are probably biased toward candidates whose last initials come early in the alphabet. Two arguments can be made in support of this proposition, both of which follow from the fact that the general population has last initials concentrated primarily in the first half of the alphabet, a phenomenon documented in the United States, Ireland, and Australia (see, e.g., Masterman 1964; Miller and Krosnick 1998; Robson and Walsh 1974). It is well documented that people tend to like the letters in their own names, especially their initials, better than they like letters not in their names (e.g., Johnson 1986; Nuttin 1985). This preference will probably lead people to have a special positive regard for political candidates who share their own initials, since similarity enhances attraction (see Byrne 1971). Because there are more people in the general public with last initials early in the alphabet, this would lead to a bias in an electorate as a whole toward electing candidates whose initials are early in the alphabet.

A second reason why elections could be biased toward candidates with last initials early in the alphabet involves the *mere exposure effect*. Simply being repeatedly exposed to an object typically increases one's liking of that object (Zajonc 1968). Therefore, because many more people in the general population have last initials early in the alphabet, all members of the population are likely to be exposed to such names more often than they are to names with last initials late in the alphabet. As a result, the general population should have a slight tendency to like last names early in the alphabet more than last names late in the alphabet. This slight preference may then lead some voters to prefer candidates whose last initials are early in the alphabet. Clearly, then, studies involving only alphabetical listings of candidates on ballots cannot be used to make inferences about candidate name order effects.

11. We tested the impact of circumstantial factors in regressions predicting the magnitude of the name order effect in the races using an array of variables describing the races' characteristics. We explored the impact of voter education by comparing name order effects in different regions of the state that differed in the average education level of voters.

12. Confidence in these findings is bolstered by their consistency with three previous studies of name order effects in experimental simulations of elections (Coombs, Peters, and Strom 1974; Kamin 1958; Taebel 1975). In two of these studies, respondents were asked to vote in hypothetical elections, were assigned to receive candidates' names in different orders, and were given little or no information about the candidates (Kamin 1958; Taebel 1975). Both studies found significant primacy effects, in line with our results. In a third study, respondents were asked to vote for one of two candidates about whom they had no information; a strong bias toward voting for the first candidate listed was apparent (Coombs et al. 1974). This primacy effect weakened considerably when respondents were told about the party affiliations of the candidates and were told about their standings in public opinion polls (Coombs et al. 1974), reinforcing our evidence regarding partisanship and voter knowledge. Thus, our evidence about the 1992 Ohio elections dovetails reassuringly with evidence from experimental studies of hypothetical elections.

13. Darcy (1986) examined only partisan races held in Colorado, and we found that name order effects are much less likely to occur in partisan than nonpartisan races. In addition, the Colorado counties Darcy (1986) examined used party-block ballots, in which all the Democratic Party candidates for all offices were listed in one column (labeled "Democratic"), and all the Republican Party candidates were listed in another column (labeled "Republican"). In half of the precincts, the Democratic column preceded the Republican column, and in the other half, the Republican column preceded the Democratic column. This type of ballot layout presumably encouraged voters to cast ballots based upon candidates' party affiliations, because this information was very salient. Our results suggest that this minimized or eliminated name order effects.

Gold (1952) examined the effect of name order in the 1951 American Anthropological Association elections, conducted by mail and giving voters all the time they needed to gather information about the candidates before making choices. This presumably decreased the likelihood of order-based voting.

14. Given that many counties in North Dakota contained fewer than fifteen precincts, that we had to obtain vote returns separately from the counties' Boards of Elections, and that many counties failed to cooperate with our requests for vote returns, we worked to obtain data from enough counties to yield at least fifty precincts for each of the seven rotation orders for the race for U.S. president. Of the fifty-three counties in the state, we ended up with data from fourteen of the sixteen largest (excluding one county that did not rotate name order and one county that was unresponsive to repeated requests for vote returns).

15. The prevalence of primacy effects also appears if we examine the direction of the nonsignificant effects. Of the 131 nonsignificant order effects, 90, or 69%, of them were in the direction of primacy effects, and 31% were in the direction of recency effects. A sign test indicates that this is highly unlikely ($p < .001$) to have occurred by chance alone. Moreover, the average magnitude of the nonsignificant two-candidate primacy effects (.90%) was 24% greater than that of the nonsignificant two-candidate recency effects (.73%). This leaning toward primacy effects among the nonsignificant differences is unlikely to have occurred by chance alone and therefore suggests that there were more real primacy effects in these races than we had statistical power to detect.

16. Characterizing the directions of name order effects in these races is a bit complex because the effect may not be monotonic. Although simple primacy or recency effects could certainly occur, a candidate could get more votes when listed either first or last than when listed in the middle of an array. This would be what we will refer to as a "primacy and recency" effect. It is also conceivable that a candidate might get more votes when listed in the middle of an array than when listed either first or last. This is what we will refer to as a "middle" effect.

17. This trend toward primacy effects was apparent even in the instances in which differences between name orders were not statistically significant or marginally so. Of the 86 nonsignificant order effects in races involving more than two candidates, 63 (or 73%) were in the direction of primacy effects, and only 23 (or 27%) were in the direction of recency effects. A sign test again indicates that this is extremely unlikely ($p < .001$) to have occurred by chance alone. The average magnitude of the difference between the first and last positions was larger for the nonsignificant primacy effects (.65%) than the nonsignificant recency effects (.54%).

18. Significant name order effects appeared in these analyses less often than in those reported by Miller and Krosnick (1998). This is most likely attributable importantly to the greater prevalence of partisan races among the set examined here (listing party affiliations of candidates on ballots reduces the likelihood of primacy effects; see Miller and Krosnick 1998) and to the smaller sample sizes examined here for most races. For example, whereas 79% of the two-candidate races in Ohio analyzed here were partisan, only 57% of the two-candidate races analyzed by Miller and Krosnick (1998) were partisan. And whereas the average sample size for the two-candidate races analyzed here (excluding the two statewide races) was 443, the average sample size was 1,132 for the two-candidate races analyzed by Miller and Krosnick (1998).

5

Empirically Evaluating the Electoral College

ANDREW GELMAN

JONATHAN N. KATZ

GARY KING

INTRODUCTION

The 2000 U.S. presidential election rekindled interest in possible electoral reform. While most of the popular and academic accounts focused on balloting irregularities in Florida, such as the now infamous "butterfly" ballot and mishandled absentee ballots, some also noted that this election marked only the fourth time in history that the candidate with a plurality of the popular vote did not also win the Electoral College (Posner 2001). This "anti-democratic" outcome has fueled desire for reform or even outright elimination of the Electoral College (Barnes, this volume; Crigler, Just, and Buhr, this volume; Ortiz, this volume).

This is not the first time that controversy has surrounded the Electoral College system. Perhaps the most scandalous presidential election in U.S. history was the 1876 race between Samuel J. Tilden, a Democrat, and Rutherford B. Hayes, a Republican. The nation was deeply divided; the rifts were caused partly by a deep economic recession and partly by a seemingly endless number of scandals involving graft and corruption in the incumbent Republican administration of Ulysses S. Grant. Making matters even more divisive were a number of third parties that contested the election. Similar to the 2000 elections, the outcome hinged on resolving potential vote count problems in Florida, Louisiana, and South Carolina. These states were so divided, as was the rest of the country, that they sent two slates each of electors to Congress— one set for Tilden and one set for Hayes. Congressional procedures for resolving disputed sets of electors had expired; Congress therefore established a fifteen-member commission to decide the issue of which set of electors to use. After much intrigue, the commission narrowly voted to use the electors for Hayes from all three disputed states, thus giving him the election. Hayes won the election despite the consensus that Tilden had won 51 percent of the popular vote to Hayes's 48 percent.

The Electoral College vote also went contrary to the popular vote in the 1888 election between the incumbent President Grover Cleveland and his Republican challenger, Benjamin Harrison. Cleveland garnered huge majorities in the eighteen states that supported him, whereas Harrison won slender majorities in some of the larger states that supported him. In the end, Cleveland won the popular vote by about 110,000 votes—constituting less than 1 percent of the total vote—but lost the Electoral College.

The other election in which the popular vote leader did not become president was in 1824, when Andrew Jackson won a plurality of both the popular and electoral votes. But because Jackson did not win an electoral vote majority, the election was decided by the House of Representatives, which voted for John Quincy Adams.

The popular vote was even closer in the 2000 election than in the 1888 election. Gore won the popular vote by approximately 541,000 votes—or about half a percentage point of the total vote cast—but, as with both Cleveland and Tilden before him, lost the Electoral College.

Most arguments against the Electoral College have either been based on these particular elections or on highly stylized formal models (see, for example, Banzhaf 1968). We take a different approach here. We develop a set of statistical models based on historical election results to evaluate the Electoral College as it has performed in practice. While we do not directly address the normative question of the value of the U.S. Electoral College, this chapter does provide the necessary tools and evidence to make such an evaluation.

There are two fundamental ways that the Electoral College could be flawed. First, it may be biased in favor of one party. That is, the distribution of votes could have a party's candidate systematically winning the popular vote but losing the Electoral College. For example, if it is likely that the Democratic candidate is to win with overwhelming majorities in a few states, then this will boost the overall Democratic vote share but not necessarily the odds of his or her winning the Electoral College. This is essentially what happened in the elections of 1876, 1888, and 2000. In order to know if this is a general problem, we need to ascertain the relationship between the *average vote share* a party's candidate receives and the likelihood of winning a majority of the Electoral College. Here we develop a statistical model based on an extension of Gelman and King's (1994) model of legislative elections to the case of the Electoral College.

The second possible effect of the Electoral College is on the *voting power* of individual citizens—that is, their influence on the outcome. A natural measure of voting power is the probability that a vote will be pivotal in determining the outcome of an election. This is the basis for almost all of the voting power measures considered in the literature (see Felsenthal and Machover 1998; Straffin 1978, for reviews). If the president were elected by straight popular vote, this measure would be the probability that one's vote would break a tie in favor of a candidate. Under the popular vote system every voter (*ex ante*) has an equal, but small, chance of casting the deciding vote and therefore has equal voting power.

Further, the popular vote system maximizes the average voting power across the electorate (see e.g., Felsenthal and Machover 1998; Gelman and Katz 2001). The Electoral College, on the other hand, divides the electorate into predetermined groups or coalitions by state. The states give all of their electoral votes to a given candidate based on majority vote in the state.[1] Thus, a vote is pivotal *both* if it determines how the state's electoral votes are cast *and* if those electoral votes determine the winner in the Electoral College. Since states vary both in their sizes and in the likelihood of ties, voters in different states will, in general, have different voting power, and as a result the average voting power can be less than under plurality rule. In fact, this is the central critique raised by Banzhaf (1968). Again using the statistical model of presidential elections that we develop here, we can examine the empirical probability that an average voter is pivotal under both popular vote and Electoral College systems.

We show that after appropriate statistical analysis of the available historical electoral data, there is little basis to argue for reforming the Electoral College. We first show that while the Electoral College may once have been biased against the Democrats, the current distribution of voters advantages neither party. Further, the electoral vote will differ from the popular vote only when the average vote shares of the two major candidates are extremely close to 50 percent. As for individual voting power, we show that while there has been much temporal variation in relative voting power over the last several decades, the voting power of individual citizens would not likely increase under a popular vote system of electing the president.

The chapter proceeds as follows. In the next section we consider the partisan impact of the Electoral College. The following section examines the impact on average voting power, including what voting power would have been if electoral votes were allocated by congressional district or by a popular vote system. The final section concludes the chapter.

MEASURING THE PARTISAN IMPACT OF THE ELECTORAL COLLEGE

Most of the popular critiques of the Electoral College have focused on the possibility that the winner of the popular vote will not win the electoral vote, such as occurred in the elections of 1876, 1888, and 2000. That this discrepancy occurred is not surprising because the Electoral College and the popular vote are different electoral systems. In fact, the Constitutional Convention considered several alternative methods for electing the president, including direct popular vote, and rejected them all in favor of the Electoral College. The Convention delegates were concerned that elections would be dictated by the most populous states with little regard for the smaller ones (see also Madison 1788, Federalist No. 69, for further arguments in favor of the Electoral College system). This was thought particularly likely to occur if one of the presidential candidates was a "favorite son" from one of the larger states, who would thus draw large support from only one state or region but would still be able to win the popular vote.

If a primary rationale for eliminating the Electoral College is that the results may be contrary to the outcome of the popular vote, we ought to know how likely this is to happen. We cannot answer this question directly (except in the general sense that this has happened four times in about forty-five elections). However, we can investigate the relationship between popular vote and the probability that a party's candidate wins the Electoral College. We can, for example, examine what popular vote share would be needed for the Democratic candidate to win the Electoral College 50 percent of the time, or even 95 percent of the time. If the vote needed to win 50 percent of the time were substantially greater than half of the popular vote, we would know that the distribution of votes across the states disadvantaged the Democrats. The Electoral College would be biased in favor of the Republicans in this case.

How might the Electoral College favor one of the parties? Think of the Electoral College as a legislative district map. A central concern about any districting is how it affects the translation of votes into seats. The study of this translation in political science is based on the idea of a seats-votes curve, which has appeared in the academic literature for almost a century (see, e.g., Kendall and Stuart 1950). A seats-votes curve is a mapping, stating for a given party's average district vote what fraction of the seats they will receive. The Electoral College represents just a slightly more complicated seats-votes curve. We are interested in knowing the relationship between average popular vote and electoral vote. The complication is that the districts in our case—that is, the states—have different numbers of seats—that is, electoral votes.

As is well known, a legislative districting map may be a gerrymander in favor of a particular party (Cox and Katz 2002). The classic way to engineer such a partisan gerrymander is to pack as many of the other party's supporters in as few districts as possible, thereby creating inefficiently safe districts, while spreading one's own supporters across as many districts as possible, thereby creating winnable but not inefficiently safe districts (see Cox and Katz 1999, 2002, for detailed discussion of this and other methods of partisan gerrymandering). Opposition voters in these districts are wasting their votes: They are contributing to increasing the statewide vote share for their party but are not increasing the number of seats they win. In the case of legislative maps, this gerrymander is often intentional. With the Electoral College, such gerrymandering is not likely intentional because the allocation was set in the Constitution, not by partisan state governments, as is the case with legislative maps. Nevertheless, it could be the case that the distribution of voters across states could create the conditions for a gerrymander favoring one of the parties in the presidential election. If, for example, many Southern states vote overwhelmingly for the Democrat, then the Democratic candidate may do well in the popular vote but still may not win the Electoral College.

If we look at the 2000 election, the distribution of the popular vote was problematic for Gore. Consider New York, the second most populous state, where Gore won with over 60 percent of the votes to Bush's 35 percent. Many of these Democratic voters in New York in essence wasted their votes. If they could have been transferred to another state, Gore could have easily won the Electoral College. On the other hand, Bush "wasted" a large number of votes in Texas. But California went strongly for Gore. And so on (see Barnes, this volume). Clearly, a systematic approach is needed to go beyond anecdotal reasoning.

In order to know if this partisan skew in the popular versus electoral vote gap is a problem in general, we need to estimate the seats-votes curve. The methodology we use is an extension of a model developed by Gelman and King (1994), where the full details can be found.

The procedure consists of two parts. First, using historical elections results, we generate a statistical forecasting model that relates the observable characteristics of a state to the presidential vote. That is, the forecasting model tells us our best estimate for the expected Democratic candidate's vote in a state for a given set of characteristics. We also get an estimate of how variable elections are over time.[2]

The variables we used to forecast the presidential vote are from Campbell's (1992) study. They include each state's deviation from the previous average national presidential vote in the last two elections, indicators for presidential and vice presidential nominees' home states, the partisan breakdown in the lower chamber of the state's legislature, the economic growth rate in the state, and the liberalness of the state's congressional delegation based on Americans for Democratic Action (ADA) and Americans for Constitutional Action (ACA) ratings (see Campbell 1992 for the complete descriptions).

Once we have the forecasting model, we can then consider what would happen as electoral conditions change. For example, we could consider hypothetical partisan swings such that the average vote share varied from the actual election results. By letting these swings vary we can map out the seats-votes curve.[3]

In our case, we are interested in evaluating actual election results, so we will keep the forecasting values equal to the original values for the state. However, by appropriately choosing the partisan swing we can see what the vote distribution would be like as the national average vote varies. This will in turn allow us to calculate the probability that a given state will be won by the democrats for a given statewide vote.

We can then estimate quantities of interest—namely, what total vote shares are necessary for the Democrats to have a 50 percent or a 95 percent chance of winning the Electoral College. These results are presented in Figure 5.1. As we can see from the Figure 5.1, if the total vote share is near 50 percent, the Democrats almost always have about even odds of winning the Electoral College. If their total vote share were over 51 percent, the Democratic candidate would almost surely win. The only election that appears to be different at all is the 1968 election. Under conditions in 1968, the Democrats seem slightly disadvantaged by the Electoral College, but otherwise the results of the Electoral College seems relatively "fair" in the sense of matching the popular vote. Most important, as long as the winner of the popular vote does so by winning on

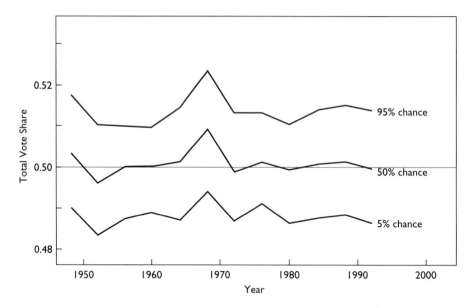

Figure 5.1   Total vote share and odds of winning Electoral College

average 51 percent of the two-party vote, the results from the Electoral College and popular vote will agree.

There is, however, a potential problem with the analysis presented in Figure 5.1. Implicitly, we are conditioning the findings presented there on turnout because the total vote is just the simple average across the states. However, if there are wide turnout differentials between states, this may mask some findings. As an alternative, we also ran the analysis constructing a national average by weighting state vote shares according to their actual population. These results appear in Figure 5.2.

We see some differences between the two figures. Most notably, early on the Electoral College seems somewhat biased against the Democrats, especially during the 1950s. At that time, a Democratic candidate needed larger popular vote shares to guarantee high chances of winning the election. This happened because the Democrats were winning Southern states with huge margins, and so they had lots of "wasted votes." The effect has reduced over time because the Republicans have started to win Southern states. This was not as obvious in Figure 5.1 because turnout was also much lower in the South, counteracting the wasted votes.

Thus, we see some evidence that in the 1940s and 1950s, the Electoral College could have led to results contrary to the popular vote, although it in fact did not. Under current conditions, this gap could only plausibly happen if the popular vote is extremely close, as it was in the 2000 election. In the 1980s, commentators talked about a Republican "lock" on the Electoral College, but really what was happening was that Republicans were winning presidential elections by getting many more popular votes than the Democrats. The Elec-

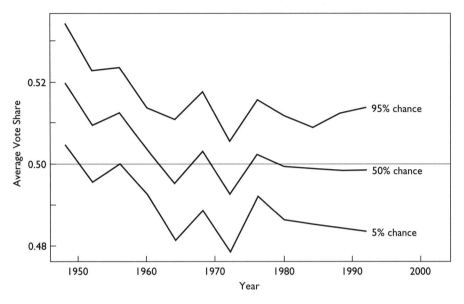

Figure 5.2 Weighted average total vote share and odds of winning Electoral College

toral College per se had nothing to do with it, as is clear from the segments of the graphs in Figures 5.1 and 5.2 showing the 1980s.

ELECTORAL COLLEGE AND VOTING POWER

In this section we explore how coalitional behavior induced by the Electoral College affects the probability that a given voter is decisive in an election, a natural measure to evaluate an electoral system.

The probability of a vote's being decisive is important directly because it represents a voter's influence on the electoral outcome, and this influence is crucial in a democracy, and also indirectly because it could influence campaigning. For example, one might expect campaign efforts to be proportional to the probability of a vote being decisive, multiplied by the expected number of votes changed per unit of campaign expense, although there are likely strategic complications since both sides are making campaign decisions (Brams and Davis 1974). The probability that a single vote is decisive in an election is also relevant in determining the utility of voting, the responsiveness of an electoral system to voter preferences, the efficacy of campaigning efforts, and comparisons of voting power (Aldrich 1993; Brams and Davis 1975; Ferejohn and Fiorina 1974; Riker and Ordeshook 1986; Norris, this volume).

Perhaps the simplest measure of decisiveness is the (absolute) Banzhaf (1965) index, which is the probability that an individual vote is decisive under the assumption that all voters are deciding their votes independently and at random, with probabilities 0.5 for each of two candidates. We shall refer to this assumption as the *random voting model*. While clearly an unrealistic assumption, it does provide a benchmark to evaluate competing electoral rules and thereby make the problem theoretically tractable. The random voting model is, of course, a gross oversimplification, and in fact its implications for voting power in U.S. elections have been extremely misleading in the political science literature, as has been discussed by Gelman, King, and Boscardin (1998) and Gelman, Katz, and Bafumi (2002).

We offer an alternative approach here based on the empirical analysis of U.S. presidential elections. We use results from every election since 1960 as the basis for a set of simulations to calculate the average probability that a given voter is decisive under the popular vote, the Electoral College, and an alternative system in which each congressional district is worth one electoral vote.

How the Electoral College Might Affect Voting Power

Before continuing on it is probably best to consider how the Electoral College might affect voting power. In order to do this we need to consider a couple of different electoral systems. The simplest electoral system is the *popular vote* or *majority rule*, under which the candidate receiving the largest number of votes wins. On the other hand, the U.S. presidential system is an *electoral vote* or *local winner-take-all rule*, in which voters are grouped into several coalitions and the winner in each coalition gets a fixed number of "electoral votes" (with these electoral votes split or randomly assigned in the event of an exact tie within the coalition); the candidate with the most electoral votes is declared the winner.

In a popular vote system, the probability of one's vote being decisive can be approximated with standard statistical techniques, given n, the number of voters, and assuming that the random voting model holds.[4] It is just the chance that exactly half the electorate is voting for one candidate and the other half is voting for the other candidate. This probability declines as the number of voters gets larger.

Now consider the Electoral College system, in which the members of a state separately vote to allocate all of their electoral votes to the candidate that wins the majority of the state's vote.

Under the random voting model, it is best to be in a large state. At one extreme, suppose a single state controlled a majority of the electoral votes. Then this state determines the election outcome, and if one is in that state, then her vote is decisive with approximate probability

$$\frac{2\sqrt{2}}{\pi} \times \left(\frac{n}{2}\right)^{-1/2},$$

which is approximately $\sqrt{2}$ times the probability of being decisive under the popular vote system. However, the $n - 1/2$ voters from other states have zero voting power. Therefore, it can be shown that the *average* probability of a decisive vote, averaging over all voters, is smaller than that under the popular vote system.[5]

To see this further, consider some elections with a small number of voters so that we can exactly calculate the probabilities under various hypothetical electoral rules. Consider an election with nine voters under different electoral rules as depicted in Figure 5.3. Under the popular vote system in the figure, any voter's chance of being decisive is $842^{-8} = 0.273$. Now suppose that three voters are in a coalition (such as a state) and the other six vote independently. Then how likely is your vote to be decisive? If you are in the coalition, it is first necessary that the other two voters in the coalition be split; this happens with probability $1/2$. Next, your coalition's three votes are decisive in the entire election, which occurs if the remaining six voters are divided 3-3 or 4-2; this has probability $50/64$. The voting power of any of the three voters in the coalition is then $1/2 \cdot 50/64 = 0.391$. What if you are not in the coalition? Then your vote will be decisive if the remaining votes are split 4-4, which occurs if the five unaffiliated voters (other than you) are split 4-1 in the direction opposite to the three voters in the coalition. The probability of this happening is $512^{-5} = 0.156$. Compared to the popular vote system, you have more voting power if you are in the coalition and less if you are outside. The average voting power is $3/9 \, (0.391) + 6/9 \, (0.156) = 0.234$, which is lower than under the popular vote system (see A in Figure 5.3).[6]

These examples indicate that under the random voting model, it is to your benefit to be from a larger state. If you are in a state of size m, the probability that your state is tied is approximately proportional to $m - 1/2$, and the probability that your state is itself required to determine the election winner is approximately proportional to m; the product of these two probabilities thus increases with m, at least for $m < n$ (see Banzhaf 1968; Mann and Shapley 1960; Rabinowitz and Macdonald 1986).

This comparison of voting power by state size, however, is only valid given that the random voting model holds. Departures for the random voting model may alter this conclusion (Gelman et al. 2002; see Margolis 1983). We consider empirical estimates of voting power in the next subsection.

Estimating Voting Power Empirically

As has been noted by many researchers (e.g., Beck 1975; Chamberlain and Rothchild 1981; Margolis 1977; Merrill 1978), there are theoretical and practical problems with a model that treats votes as independent coin flips (or, equivalently, that counts all possible arrangements of preferences equally). The simplest model extension is to assume that votes are independent but with probability p of voting for one of the candidates, say, the Democrat, with some uncertainty about p (for example, p could have a normal distribution with mean 0.50 and standard deviation 0.05). However, this model is still too limited to describe actual electoral systems. In particular, the parameter p must realistically be allowed to vary, and modeling this varying p is no easier than modeling vote outcomes directly. Following Gelman et al. (1998), one might try to construct a hierarchical model, as they did for U.S. presidential elections with uncertainty at the national, regional, and state levels.

A. No Coalitions

A voter is decisive if the others are split 4-4:

$$\Pr(\text{Voter is decisive}) = \binom{8}{4} 2^{-8} = 0.273$$

Average $\Pr(\text{Voter is decisive}) = 0.273$

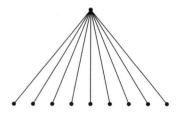

B. A Single Coalition of Three Voters

A voter in the coalition is decisive if others in the coalition are split 1-1 and the coalition is decisive:

$$\Pr(\text{decisive}) = \frac{1}{2} \cdot \frac{50}{64} = 0.391$$

A voter not in the coalition is decisive:

$$\Pr(\text{decisive}) = \binom{5}{1} 2^{-5} = 0.156$$

Avg. $\Pr(\text{decisive}) = \frac{3}{9}(0.391) + \frac{6}{9}(0.156) = 0.234$

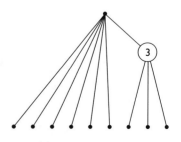

C. A Single Coalition of Five Voters

A voter in the coalition is decisive if others in the coalition are split 2-2:

$$\Pr(\text{decisive}) = \binom{4}{2} 2^{-4} = 0.375$$

A voter not in the coalition can never be decisive:

$$\Pr(\text{decisive}) = 0$$

Avg. $\Pr(\text{decisive}) = \frac{5}{9}(0.375) + \frac{4}{9}(0) = 0.208$

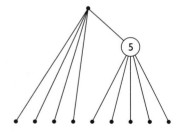

D. Three Coalitions of Three Voters Each

A voter is decisive if his coalition is split 1-1 and the other two coalitions are split 1-1:

$$\Pr(\text{decisive}) = \frac{1}{2} \cdot \frac{1}{2} = 0.250$$

Avg. $\Pr(\text{decisive}) = 0.250$

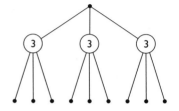

Figure 5.3 Coalitions and individual voting power

We consider a different approach to modeling whether a single vote is decisive. Consider a two-candidate election with majority rule in any given jurisdiction. Let V be the proportional vote differential (that is, the difference between the Democrat's and Republican's vote totals, divided by the number of voters, n). If a particular voter votes, that will add $+1/n$ or $-1/n$ to V; the decisiveness of this vote is 0 if $|V| > 1/n$, $1/2$ if $|V| = 1/n$, or 1 if $V = 0$.

Now suppose that the proportional vote differential has an approximate continuous probability distribution, $p(V)$. This distribution can come from a theoretical model of voting (for example, the random voting model) or from empirical models based on election results or forecasts. Gelman et al. (1998) argue that, for modeling voting decisions, it is appropriate to use probabilities from forecasts, since these represent the information available to the voter before the election occurs. For retrospective analysis, it may also be interesting to use models based on perturbations of actual elections, as in Gelman and King (1994). In any case, all that is needed here is some probability distribution.

For any reasonably sized election, we can approximate the distribution $p(V)$ of the proportional vote differential by a continuous function. In that case, the expected probability of decisiveness is simply $2p(V)/n$ evaluated at the point $V = 0$.[7] For example, in a two-candidate election with ten thousand voters, if one candidate is forecast to get 54 percent of the vote with a standard error of 3 percent, then the vote differential is forecast at 8 percent with a standard error of 6 percent. The probability that an individual vote is decisive is then:

$$2 \frac{1}{\sqrt{2\pi(0.06)}} \exp\left(-\frac{1}{2}(0.08/0.06)^2\right)/10000 = 0.0055$$

using the statistical formula for the normal distribution.

The same ideas apply to more complicated elections, such as multicandidate contests, runoffs, and multistage systems (e.g., the Electoral College in the United States or the British parliamentary system, in which the goal is to win a majority of individually elected seats). In more complicated elections, it is simply necessary to specify a probability model for the entire range of possible outcomes and then work out the probability of the requisite combination events under which a vote is decisive. For example, in the Electoral College, one's vote is decisive if her state is tied (or within one vote of being tied) and if, *conditional on this state being tied*, no candidate has a majority based on the other states. Estimating the probability of this event requires a model for the joint distribution of the vote outcomes in all the states.

In order to estimate probabilities of close elections and decisiveness, it is therefore necessary to set up a probability model for vote outcomes. We want to go beyond the random voting model to set up a more realistic descriptor of vote outcomes. Gelman et al. (1998) fit a state-by-state election-forecasting model, with probabilities corresponding to the predictive uncertainty two months before the election. Here we use a simpler approach: We take the actual election outcome and perturb it, to represent possible alternative outcomes.

We label v_i as the observed outcome (the Democratic candidate's share of the two-party vote) in congressional district i in a given election year and obtain a probability distribution of hypothetical election outcomes y_i by adding normally distributed random errors at the national, regional, state, and congressional district levels, with a standard deviation of 2 percent at each level. We label n_i as the turnout in each district i and consider these as fixed—this is reasonable since uncertainty about election outcomes is driven by uncertainty about v, not n.

For any given election year, we use the multivariate normal distribution of the vector v of vote outcomes to compute the probability of a single vote's being decisive in the election. For the popular vote system, we determine this probability for any voter; for the electoral vote and congressional district vote systems, we determine the probability within each state or district and then compute national average probabilities, weighing by turnouts within states or districts. The actual probability calculations are done using the multivariate normal distribution described by Gelman et al. (1998).

Our results appear in Figure 5.4. The most striking feature of the figure is that the average probability of decisiveness changes dramatically from year to year but is virtually unaffected by changes in the electoral system. This may come as a surprise—given the theoretical results from the prior section, one might expect the average probability of decisiveness to be much higher for the popular vote system.

The results in Figure 5.4 are only approximate, not just because of the specific modeling choices made, but also because of the implicit assumption that the patterns of voting would not be affected by changes in the electoral sys-

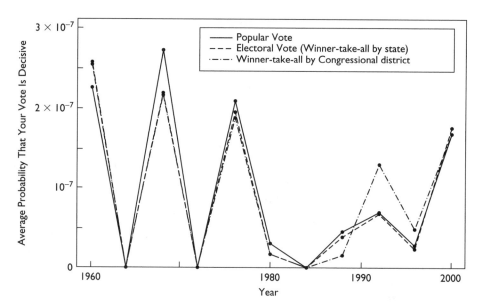

Figure 5.4 Average probability of vote decisiveness under alternative electoral systems

tem. For example, states such as California and Texas that were not close in the 2000 election might have had higher turnout under a popular vote system in which all votes counted equally. Thus, our results compare different electoral systems as applied to the actual observed votes and do not directly address counterfactual questions about what would happen if the electoral system were changed.

However, given these caveats, there does not seem to be strong evidence from Figure 5.4 to argue for moving from the Electoral College to a popular vote system. The average voter is not likely to affect the outcome of the presidential election under any of the proposed methods. Even in close elections, such as in 2000, a voter is more likely to win his or her state's lottery—or be struck by lightning—than to cast the deciding ballot. Further, there is not even that much difference in the voting power across the systems, even if the magnitudes were substantial.

CONCLUSIONS

We have presented statistical methodology to evaluate the two most common complaints against the Electoral College. When subjected to proper empirical analysis, neither of the complaints seem well justified.

With regard to the potential partisan bias in the Electoral College, we find no systematic effect, at least not in current elections (that is, those after the 1950s). We did find that it is possible for the Electoral College system to lead to different outcomes than the popular vote, but only when the nationwide vote is *very* close, say within half a percentage point, for the two top candidates. As we now know from the election of 2000, when elections are that close slight differences in electoral procedure can and will lead to different outcomes.

Our results about voting power and the Electoral College are perhaps a bit more surprising. There is a fairly significant theoretical literature suggesting that the Electoral College was unfair to certain voters. However, these claims are based on the random voting model, which is a highly stylized model of elections. When we looked at the empirical voting behavior, we do not find much difference between voting power under the Electoral College or popular vote systems. But these results are more tentative because in making our analysis we assumed that neither voters nor candidates would have behaved differently under a popular vote system. This is a suspect assumption, but less so than the random voting model that underlies the critique.

Of course, our empirical findings do not directly address normative questions, such as which electoral system should be used. However, our findings can be used to evaluate the positive claims that underlie the normative arguments.

NOTES

1. Actually two states, Nebraska and Maine, allocate Electoral College votes by congressional district.

2. A bit more formally, our probability model comes from a random components linear regression of democratic vote in state i in year t, $v_{i,t}$, on a set of observable regressors, $X_{i,t}$,

$$v_{i,t} = X_{i,t}\beta_t + \gamma_i + \varepsilon_{i,t}$$

where β_t is a vector of k parameters that must be estimated from the data and γ_i and $\varepsilon_{i,t}$ are independent error terms. We further assume that both error terms are normally distributed with mean zero and variances that are estimated from the data. This implies that the vote shares themselves are also normally distributed around the expected conditional mean defined in the equation 1.

3. Formally, the probability model of the hypothetical vote proportions, $v^{hyp}{}_{i,t}$ is determined by the analogous probability model:

$$v^{hyp}{}_{i,t} = X^{hyp}{}_{i,t}\beta_t + \delta^{hyp}{}_t + \gamma_i + \varepsilon^{hyp}{}_{i,t}$$

where $\delta^{hyp}{}_t$ is a known constant used to model statewide partisan swings. If we want to have the average vote equal to some value, $\bar{v}$, then this constant can be calculated by:

$$\delta^{hyp}{}_t = \bar{v} - \sum_{i=1}^{N} (X^{hyp}{}_{i,t}\,\beta_t)T_{i,t}/\sum_{i=1}^{N} T_{i,t}$$

where N is the number of states and $T_{i,t}$ is the voter turnout in state i in year t.

4. Formally, in a popular vote system with n voters, the probability that your vote is decisive is $(n - 1(n - 1)/2)\,2^{-(n-1)}$; that is, the probability that $x = n - 1/2$ where x has a binomial distribution with parameters $n - 1$ and $1/2$. For large (or even moderate) n, this can be well approximated using the normal distribution as $\sqrt{2/\pi}n^{-1/2}$, a standard result in probability (c.f. Woodroofe 1975).

5. Formally, the probability that an average voter is decisive under the Electoral College is $\sqrt{1/\pi n}\,n^{-1/2}$, which a factor of $\sqrt{2}$ less than under the popular vote system.

6. We could also consider more eloborate cases. For example, suppose there are $n = 3^d$ voters, where d is some integer, who are divided into three equal-sized coalitions, each of which is itself divided into three coalitions, and so forth, in a tree structure. Then all the n voters are symmetrically situated, and a given voter is decisive if the other two voters in his or her local coalition are split—this happens with probability $1/2$—and then the next two local coalitions must have opposite preferences—again, with a probability of $1/2$—and so on up to the top. The probability that all these splits happen, and thus the individual voter is decisive, is $1/2d = n^- \log_3 2 = n^{-0.63}$, which is lower than the probability under the popular vote system (for large n, that probability is approximately $0.8n^{-0.5}$). For example, if $n = 3^8 = 6561$, then the probability of a decisive vote is $1/256$ with the tree-structure of coalitions, compared to about $1/102$ with majority rule.

7. If the number of voters n is odd, this approximates $\Pr(V = 0)$; if n is even, it approximates $1/2\Pr(V = -1/n) + 1/2\Pr(V = 1/n)$

Part II

Ways to Fix the Problems

6

Bush v. Gore and Federalism

ERWIN CHEMERINSKY*

When historians look back at the Rehnquist Court, they will without a doubt say that its greatest changes in constitutional law were in the area of federalism. Over the past decade, and particularly over the last five years, the Supreme Court has dramatically limited the scope of Congress' powers and has greatly expanded the protection of state sovereign immunity. Virtually every area of law, criminal and civil, has been touched by these changes. I began teaching constitutional law in 1980. Without question, the most significant differences in constitutional law since then are a result of the Supreme Court's revival of federalism as a constraint on federal power.

In a series of 5-4 decisions, the Court has dramatically changed the law. First, the Court created major new limits on the scope of Congress' powers, particularly Congress' authority to legislate under the Commerce Clause and under Section 5 of the Fourteenth Amendment (see e.g., *United States v. Morrison; United States v. Lopez; City of Boerne v. Flores*). Second, the Court greatly expanded the scope of state sovereign immunity and protection from suit in federal court (see, e.g., *Alden v. Maine; Seminole Tribe v. Florida*). Third, the Court reversed course and held that the Tenth Amendment is a limit on congressional power, specifically, that Congress cannot compel state legislative or regulatory action (see e.g., *Printz v. United States; New York v. United States*). Individually and especially, collectively these three doctrines have dramatically changed the law.

The federalism decisions are the product of a Court with five conservative members deeply committed to protecting state governments from federal encroachment. Virtually all of the recent Supreme Court cases have been 5-4 decisions, with the majority comprised of Justices Rehnquist, O'Connor, Scalia, Kennedy, and Thomas.

---

*Author's Note: I want to thank Anieko Webb for her excellent research assistance. It also should be disclosed that I did legal work for the Gore side during the Florida election litigation. I argued in the Florida trial court in the "butterfly ballot" case for a new election in Palm Beach County. Also, I worked on various briefs in the *Bush v. Gore* litigation, including the Supreme Court brief.

The same five Justices who comprise the majority in these federalism decisions were also the majority in *Bush v. Gore*. Thus, it is interesting and important to look at *Bush* from a federalism perspective. Although an enormous amount has been written about *Bush v. Gore* (see e.g., Hasen, this volume), this is a perspective that has largely been overlooked. From the point of view of federalism, it is very difficult to reconcile the conservative five Justices' commitment to states' rights with their decision in *Bush v. Gore*. This is telling because it helps to show the unprincipled nature of *Bush v. Gore* and that the conservative Justices were influenced by the underlying politics much more than by legal doctrine.

In this chapter, I examine three federalism aspects of the Court's decision in *Bush v. Gore*. First, the Court's stay of the counting of the uncounted votes on December 9, 2000, was inconsistent with basic principles of judicial federalism. Second, the Court's review of the Florida Supreme Court's decision, before it had been implemented and was ripe for review, was an affront to federalism and important principles limiting federal court power. Finally, and most importantly, the Supreme Court's choice on December 12 to end the vote-counting based on Florida law violated the fundamental principle that state courts should have the last say as to matters of state law. The final section of the chapter offers some concluding thoughts about the future implications of *Bush v. Gore*.

These criticisms are particularly important because the five Justices in the majority in *Bush v. Gore* have repeatedly emphasized protecting the prerogatives of state governments and state courts. My central point is that the five Justices in *Bush v. Gore* abandoned their usual principles because of their desire to rule in favor of George W. Bush.

I am not suggesting that they did so for consciously partisan reasons, desiring to make Bush the president because they, like him, are Republicans. Rather, the politics were more subtle. Virtually all of the Republicans I know thought that the Florida Supreme Court was wrong and that no additional recounts should have occurred. But almost all of the Democrats I know believed that the Florida Supreme Court was correct and that the most important principle was to ensure that every vote was accurately counted.

The five Justices in the majority in *Bush v. Gore* were all Republicans. It was not surprising to me that they saw the case the same way that all the Republicans that I know did. As with so much in law and life, the perspective one starts with greatly influences the conclusion. But in this light, the federalism issues underlying *Bush v. Gore* become all the more important. The five Justices in the majority should be criticized for not getting past their politically influenced views and for abandoning their usual commitment to federalism principles.

THE COURT SHOULD NOT HAVE STAYED THE COUNTING ON DECEMBER 9

Perhaps the Court's most egregious action in the entire saga was its order, on Saturday, December 9, staying the recount in Florida. The law is clear and long established that the Supreme Court may halt another court's order only if the person seeking the stay demonstrates that he or she would suffer an "irreparable injury" without one. This is especially important when the Supreme Court is reviewing the decisions of a state court because of the federalism aspects of such a stay. The Supreme Court often, especially in reviewing state court convictions in criminal cases, has expressed the need for great deference to the decisions of state courts (see e.g., *Engle v. Isaac; Stone v. Powell*, proclaiming the need for deference to state courts).

There was no plausible basis for the Supreme Court to have found such an irreparable injury to Bush in allowing the ballots to be counted while the case was pending before it. Justice Antonin Scalia released a short concurring opinion stating that there was "irreparable harm." His reasons, however, are specious.

First, Scalia said that "the counting of votes that are of questionable legality does in my view irreparable harm to [Bush] by casting a cloud on what he claims to be the legitimacy of his election." What, then, according to Scalia, is the harm to Bush? The claim is that if the recount were to put Gore ahead, but the Supreme Court later invalidated the recount, then Bush's victory would lack legitimacy.

But the irony is that Bush's election was robbed of its legitimacy—at least in the eyes of forty-nine million people who voted for Al Gore—because it resulted from a Supreme Court order that kept the votes from being recounted. Much of the public perceives the Supreme Court's 5-4 ruling to halt the recount, split entirely along ideological lines, as an act of partisan politics to give Bush the election. Justice Scalia professed to be concerned about legitimacy, but he ignored how the Court's action would harm the credibility of both the Supreme Court and the Bush presidency.

The Supreme Court gets to decide whether the recounted votes are included in the tally, but it cannot and should not try to control public perceptions. Stopping the recount to enhance the public's view of a Bush victory is simply not an appropriate role for the Supreme Court. No prior Supreme Court decision—or any prior decision from any court—ever found that such a harm is legally cognizable or could be the basis for finding irreparable injury.

Second, Justice Scalia argued that allowing the recount to occur while the case was pending could prevent a proper recount later because "it is generally agreed that each manual recount produces a degradation of the ballots, which renders a subsequent recount inaccurate." This is a factual question decided by Justice Scalia without any evidence whatsoever. There was absolutely nothing in the record to support this assertion. More importantly, this argument ignores the reality that it was then or never for a recount that mattered in this election; Justice Scalia halted the recount so as to protect a mythical recount that never could occur in time to meet the Tuesday, December 12, deadline that the Court emphasized in its subsequent decision.

The simple reality is that Bush would have suffered no irreparable injury if the recount continued pending a Supreme Court decision, while Gore incurred a potentially irreversible harm when the recount was stopped. Under traditional legal principles the Supreme Court's stay order is indefensible. Halting a state court order on this basis should have been very troubling to the majority of the Justices who profess a commitment to principles of federalism and states' rights.

On Friday afternoon, December 8, when the Florida Supreme Court handed down its decision, I told a reporter from the *Los Angeles Times* that the key move to watch for would be whether the Supreme Court issued a stay. If the Court did not stay the counting, there was a real chance that Gore would have been ahead when the Court heard oral arguments on Monday, December 11. The Court would have had a much more difficult time ruling in favor of Bush if it meant disqualifying a count that had Gore ahead. My sense is that the stay was motivated by the Court majority's desire to avoid this and to make it much easier to rule in favor of Bush.

THE COURT OFFENDED FEDERALISM PRINCIPLES BY PREMATURELY REVIEWING THE FLORIDA SUPREME COURT'S DECISION

The ripeness doctrine seeks to separate matters that are premature for review, because the injury is speculative and never may occur, from those cases that are appropriate for federal court action (*Abbott Laboratories v. Gardner*). Ripeness is based on Article III's requirement for cases and controversies (see, e.g., *O'Shea v. Littleton*, dismissing as not ripe a suit contending that the defendants, a magistrate and a judge, discriminated against blacks in setting bail and imposing sentences). Ripeness, like all of the Article III justiciability doctrines,[1] has an important federalism dimension, particularly when the Court is reviewing state government conduct and state court decisions. Above all, the justiciability doctrines, such as ripeness, are meant to prevent unnecessary federal judicial review and thus avoid federal courts needlessly overturning state laws and state court decisions.

The Court's premature, and possibly unnecessary, decision in *Bush v. Gore* was inconsistent with a commitment to federalism. A further irony is that it traditionally is the conservative Justices who are most concerned with ensuring that a case is justiciable.[2] Here, however, the conservative majority in *Bush v. Gore* ignored the justiciability problems in the case.

For several reasons, the issues before the Supreme Court in *Bush v. Gore* were not ripe for review. The central issue was whether the counting of votes would deny equal protection. There would be a constitutional violation only if similar ballots were treated differently in the counting process. But it could not be known if this would occur until the counting occurred and the trial judge in Florida, Judge Lewis, ruled on all of the challenges. Until then, it was purely speculative as to whether there would be a problem with similar ballots being treated differently. Judge Lewis, on Friday night, December 8, announced a procedure whereby he would rule on disputes. It certainly was possible that by the time he was finished doing this, a clear standard for treating all ballots equally would have emerged and been applied.

The Supreme Court, in its *per curiam* opinion, focused on inequalities that already had occurred. The *per curiam* opinion points to differences in the Miami-Dade and Palm Beach counting (*Bush v. Gore* 2000, 533). But the counting that already had been done was not the issue before the Supreme Court.[3] The only issue was whether the counting should continue. The prior experience was not predictive of what was to occur because of a key change: a single judge was overseeing the counting under the Florida Supreme Court's decision. This judge was to hear all of the disputes and potentially could eliminate any inequalities by applying a uniform standard.

Justice Stevens emphasized exactly this point in his dissent. He wrote:

> Admittedly, the use of differing substandards for determining voter intent in different counties employing similar voting systems may raise serious concerns. These concerns are alleviated—if not eliminated—by the fact that a single impartial magistrate will ultimately adjudicate all objections arising from the recount process. (*Bush v. Gore*, 541)

Justice Stevens, however, did not draw a key conclusion from his observation: The challenge to the counting was not ripe for review. Only after the counting was completed could the parties claim that there was inequality and thus a constitutional violation.

Phrased another way, the Supreme Court improperly treated an "as applied" equal protection challenge as if it were a facial challenge. Bush was not arguing that the Florida election law was unconstitutional on its face. Neither in the briefs nor in the oral argument did Bush's lawyers suggest such a facial attack. Rather, Bush's argument was that counting without uniform standards denied equal protection. This is an equal protection violation only if, after the counting and the resolution of disputes by the judge, similar ballots are treated differently. But that cannot possibly be known until the ballots are all counted. Until then, it was purely speculative as to whether there would be a denial of equal protection.

The ripeness doctrine is intended to prevent federal courts from deciding such speculative claims (*Abbott Laboratories v. Gardner*). The Court has applied the ripeness doctrine in the voting context. For example, in *Texas v. United States*, the Supreme Court refused to rule as to whether the preclearance provision of the Voting Rights Act of 1965 applied to the possible appointment of a magistrate to oversee school districts that failed to meet performance standards. The Court noted that no magistrate had yet been appointed and that the appointment of a magistrate was a last resort to be used only if all other means failed. The Court concluded that the case was not ripe because it was too speculative whether a magistrate ever would be appointed. Likewise, it was completely speculative as to the nature and extent of inequalities that would exist in the counting that was occurring under Judge Lewis's oversight.

Bush v. Gore was not ripe for an even more basic reason: George W. Bush might well have ended up ahead after the counting. In that event, there obviously would have been no need for the Supreme Court to decide his appeal. The Supreme Court repeatedly has held that a case is not ripe when it is unknown whether the injury will be suffered. For example, in *Reno v. Catholic Social Services*, the Supreme Court held that a challenge to Immigration and Naturalization Service (INS) regulations had to be dismissed on ripeness grounds because it was too speculative that anyone would be injured by the rules. The Immigration Reform and Control Act of 1986 provided that before illegal aliens residing in the United States could apply for legalization, they had to apply for temporary resident status. Temporary resident status required showing that the person continually resided in the United States since January 1, 1982, and had a continuous physical presence since November 6, 1986. The INS adopted many regulations to implement this law. A class of plaintiffs, Catholic Social Services, challenged some of the INS regulations. The Supreme Court, in an opinion by Justice Souter, held that the case was not ripe for review. The Court said that it was entirely speculative whether any members of the class would be denied legalization because of the regulations. The Court said that the case might be ripe for review if the immigrants took the additional step of applying for legalization.

Bush v. Gore was not ripe for review on December 9, when the stay was issued, nor on December 11, when the case was heard, nor on December 12, when it was decided. The case would have been ripe only after all the counting was done if (1) Gore came out ahead in Florida *and* (2) Bush could present evidence of inequalities in how the ballots were actually counted. Until and unless these eventualities occurred, the case was not ripe and should have been dismissed.

THE SUPREME COURT VIOLATED PRINCIPLES OF FEDERALISM BY ENDING THE COUNTING BASED ON FLORIDA LAW

The Supreme Court's *per curiam* opinion made two arguments. First, counting the uncounted votes without standards violates equal protection (*Bush v. Gore*, 530). Second, *Florida law* prevents the counting from continuing past December 12. This second point is indispensable to the Court's decision to end the counting. Assuming that there were inequalities in the counting that violated the Constitution, there were two ways to remedy this: Count none of the uncounted ballots or count all of the ballots with uniform standards. The latter would involve remanding the case to the Florida Supreme Court for development of standards and for such relief as that court deemed appropriate.

It must be emphasized that the Supreme Court did not hold that federal law prevented the counting from continuing. The only reason for not remanding the case—as Justices Souter and Breyer argued for—was the Court's judgment that Florida law prevented this. In two paragraphs near the end of the per curiam opinion, the Court explains why it stopped the counting:

> The Supreme Court of Florida has said that the legislature intended the State's electors to "participat[e] fully in the federal election process," as provided in 3 U.S.C. §5. . . . That statute, in turn, requires that any controversy or contest that is designed to lead to a conclusive selection of electors be completed by

December 12. That date is upon us, and there is no recount procedure in place under the State Supreme Court's order that comports with minimal constitutional standards. Because it is evident that any recount seeking to meet the December 12 date will be unconstitutional for the reasons we have discussed, we reverse the judgment of the Supreme Court of Florida ordering a recount to proceed.

Seven Justices of the Court agree that there are constitutional problems with the recount ordered by the Florida Supreme Court that demand a remedy. The only disagreement is as to the remedy. Because the Florida Supreme Court has said that the Florida legislature intended to obtain the safe-harbor benefits of 3 U.S.C. §5, Justice Breyer's proposed remedy—remanding to the Florida Supreme Court for its ordering of a constitutionally proper contest until December 18—contemplates action in violation of the Florida election code, and hence could not be part of an "appropriate" remedy authorized by Fla. Stat. §102.168(8) (2000). (*Bush v. Gore*, 533)

This passage is recited at length to show that the sole reason the Court gave for ending the counting was based on its interpretation of Florida law. However, no Florida statute stated or implied that the counting had to be done by December 12. The sole authority for the Supreme Court's conclusion was one statement by the Florida Supreme Court.

That statement, however, was made in a very different context and was made when the Florida Supreme Court was not faced with the issue posed by the Supreme Court's ruling. After the Supreme Court decided on December 12 that the counting without standards violated equal protection, the issue was what remedy was appropriate under Florida law: to continue the counting past December 12 or to end the counting to meet the December 12 deadline. The Supreme Court could not possibly know how the Florida Supreme Court would resolve this issue because it never had occurred before. Prior Florida decisions emphasized the importance of making sure that every vote is accurately counted. The Florida Supreme Court might have relied on this to continue the counting past December 12. Alternatively, the Florida Supreme Court might have ended the counting, treating December 12 as a firm deadline in Florida.

Indeed, after *Bush v. Gore* was decided, the Florida Supreme Court issued a decision dismissing the case. Justice Shaw, in a concurring opinion, declared:

[I]n my opinion, December 12 was not a "drop-dead" date under Florida law. In fact, I question whether any date prior to January 6 is a drop-dead date under the Florida election scheme. December 12 was simply a permissive "safe-harbor" date under the Florida election scheme. It certainly was not a mandatory contest deadline under the plain language of the Florida Election Code. (*Gore v. Harris*)

Perhaps a majority of the Florida Supreme Court would have followed this view, perhaps not. The point is that this was a question of Florida law to be decided by the Florida Supreme Court. Of course, it is established clearly that state supreme courts get the final word as to the interpretation of state law. In

Murdock v. City of Memphis in 1875, the Supreme Court held that it could review only questions of federal law and that the decisions of the state's highest court are final on questions of state law. The Court explained that Section 25 of the Judiciary Act was based on a belief that the Supreme Court must be available to ensure state compliance with the United States Constitution, but there was no indication that Congress intended the Court to oversee state court decisions as to state law matters.

From a federalism perspective, it is inexplicable why the five Justices in the majority—usually the advocates of states' rights on the Court—did not remand the case to the Florida Supreme Court to decide under Florida law whether the counting should continue. The Supreme Court impermissibly usurped the Florida Supreme Court's authority to decide Florida law in this extraordinary case.

Moreover, an analogy can be drawn to the political question doctrine. This justiciability doctrine is based on the premise that some issues are best left to others to resolve. The interpretation of Florida law was for the Florida Supreme Court to resolve, and that determination should have been final in the Supreme Court. In *Baker v. Carr*, the Court spoke of a political question based on "the impossibility of a court's undertaking independent resolution without expressing lack of the respect due coordinate branches of government." Yet the Court's deciding rather than remanding in *Bush v. Gore* did exactly this.

FUTURE IMPLICATIONS OF *BUSH V. GORE*

Before concluding, it is worth considering some of the future implications of the Court's decision in *Bush v. Gore* (see also Hasen, this volume). I want to focus on two that seem most important: what the decision will mean for the Court's legitimacy and what will it mean for future elections.

The Claim that *Bush v. Gore* Will Undermine the Legitimacy of the Supreme Court

Immediately after the decision, one of the most frequent questions I was asked by reporters was whether the ruling would irreparably damage the credibility of the Supreme Court. Certainly, many on December 13, 2000, and the days following expressed this concern. Justice Stevens eloquently expressed this fear in his dissent in *Bush v. Gore*:

> The position of the majority of this Court can only lend credence to the most cynical appraisal of the work of judges throughout the land. Although we may never know with complete certainty the identity of the winner of this year's Presidential election, the identity of the loser is perfectly clear. It is the nation's confidence in the judges as an impartial guardian of the rule of law. (*Bush v. Gore*, 542)

Yet this loss of confidence has not manifested itself. According to Gallup polls, 65 percent expressed confidence in the Court as an institution in September

2000 and 62 percent expressed confidence in June 2001 (see Gallup Organization 2001a). Why has there not been the loss in legitimacy that so many predicted on December 12? There are many possible explanations, none mutually exclusive.

First, *Bush v. Gore* enhanced the Republicans' view of the Court and lessened the Democrats' perception of the Court, so it evened out. Again, the Gallup polls provide some support for this. According to them, approval of the Court among Republicans went from 60 percent in August 2000 to 70 percent after the decision in December, while approval among Democrats shrunk from 70 percent in August to 42 percent in December (see Gallup Organization 2001b).

Second, any harm to the Court's credibility was likely short-lived. The country quickly accepted that George W. Bush was president, no matter how he got there, and moved on. This was true even before September 11, 2001, and certainly, as the nation's focus has shifted, *Bush v. Gore* has faded in significance (see Crigler, Just, and Buhr, this volume).

Third, in such a close election most people were willing to accept any result. The margin of statistical error was larger than the number of votes that decided the election. Most people understand that our system of voting and counting votes is simply not precise enough to definitively resolve such a close election (see also McCaffery, Crigler, and Just, this volume; Krosnick, Miller, and Tichy, this volume, discussing the ambivalence of the electorate).

Fourth, people accept that the Court makes political choices. Those who suggested that the Court's legitimacy would be permanently harmed based this on the assumption that people would be shocked by *Bush v. Gore* and the seemingly partisan split in the Court. But, after decades of high-profile cases, ranging from *Brown v. Board of Education* to *Miranda v. Arizona* to school prayer, people realize that the Court is making value choices in deciding the meaning of the Constitution. The rejection of Robert Bork for the Supreme Court in 1987 was all about recognition of the role of an individual Justice's ideology in Constitutional decision making.

Finally, and most profoundly, the Supreme Court's legitimacy is not fragile. Claims about the Supreme Court having fragile legitimacy have been very important in American constitutional law. Justice Felix Frankfurter based his jurisprudence around it; recall his dissent in *Baker v. Carr*, in which he opposed the Court's involvement in reapportionment because of fear that it would undermine the Court's legitimacy (*Baker v. Carr*, 738). Scholars such as Alexander Bickel and, more recently, Jesse Choper have built theories of judicial review around the premise that the Court must conserve its limited public legitimacy (see Bickel 1962; Choper 1980). But *Bush v. Gore* requires that we rethink what is even meant by the Court's legitimacy. Is it approval ratings in Gallup polls? Is it something deeper and less susceptible to measurement? However defined, *Bush v. Gore* indicates that the Supreme Court's legitimacy is robust, not fragile, and no single decision is likely to make much difference in the public's appraisal of the Court. The credibility of the Court is the product of over two hundred years of American history; it is the result of confidence in the Court's methods and overall decisions. It reflects popular understanding of the desirability of resolving disputed questions in the courts and under the Constitution, even though it means that everyone knows that, at times, they will be on the losing side.

What Are the Implications of the Court's Equal Protection Analysis?

The *per curiam* opinion in *Bush v. Gore* held that counting the uncounted votes without legal standards violated equal protection. In other words, the Supreme Court said that significant variations within a state in a presidential election deny equal protection. But this has profound implications for the conduct of elections in the United States (see Hasen, this volume). By this reasoning, the entire election in Florida denied equal protection and was unconstitutional. There were major differences in Florida among counties in how the ballots were designed, how absentee ballots were handled, how minority voters were treated at the polls, and what types of voting machines were used. By the Court's reasoning all of these variations violated equal protection.

These intrastate differences, of course, were not limited to Florida. In every state except Oklahoma, county officials have significant discretion with regard to aspects of conducting elections. Does this mean that all of these elections are unconstitutional?

The Supreme Court in *Bush v. Gore* tried to duck these implications by declaring: "Our consideration is limited to the present circumstances, for the problem of equal protection in election processes generally presents many complexities" (*Bush v. Gore*, 532). In other words, the Court said that it was deciding the issue only for this case and only for this day.

But that, of course, is not how the legal system operates. Decisions do create precedents, and litigants undoubtedly will base lawsuits on the reasoning of *Bush v. Gore*. Immediately after September 11, 2001, I asked Mark Rosenbaum, the legal director of the Southern California American Civil Liberties Union (ACLU), whether he planned to bring a suit based on *Bush v. Gore*. He said yes, but he was going to ask his assistant to go through the Los Angeles phone book to find people named Bush to be the plaintiffs; he said that he thought the Supreme Court's decision only might have precedential effect with a plaintiff named Bush. The Southern California ACLU did file suit challenging the differences in voting machines used among counties in California, with varying degrees of accuracy (*Common Cause v. Jones*, pending in the United States District Court for the Central District of California). Lawsuits have been filed across the country based on *Bush v. Gore* (Palermo 2000; Hasen, this volume).

The key question is which intrastate variations violate equal protection. The core basis for the Court's decision in *Bush v. Gore* was that voting is a fundamental right under equal protection. This, of course, is not new. Challenges to intrastate differences might have been brought even without *Bush v. Gore*. But *Bush* certainly has brought the issue to everyone's attention: Which variations violate equal protection? This is the crucial question for courts and scholars to consider in the months and years ahead.

CONCLUSION

There is much to criticize in the Supreme Court's decision in *Bush v. Gore*. But the federalism dimensions of the decision seem particularly important because of the conservative majority's professed concern for states' rights and deference to state courts.

The pattern that emerges is a disturbing one. The conservative majority invokes federalism when it wants to strike down federal civil rights laws, such as the Violence Against Women Act and the ability to sue state governments for age or disability discrimination. But the same five Justices ignore federalism considerations when they want to rule in favor of George W. Bush.

Early in the twentieth century, there was a much-repeated quote from a political pundit that the Supreme Court reads the election returns. In *Bush v. Gore*, for the first time, the Supreme Court created the election returns and decided who would be president.

NOTES

1. The justiciability doctrines are important limits on the power of any federal court to hear a case. They include the prohibition on federal courts issuing advisory opinions, the requirement for standing, the need for the case to be ripe, the bar on courts hearing moot cases, and the prohibition of federal courts hearing cases deemed political questions. See Chemerinsky 1999.
2. For example, decisions restricting standing to sue are almost always a product of a conservative majority, with the more liberal Justices in dissent. See, for example, *Lujan v. Defenders of Wildlife*, denying standing to enforce the Endangered Species Act in an opinion by Justice Antonin Scalia; *Allen v. Wright*, denying standing to plaintiffs challenging tax exemptions for private schools engaged in racial discrimination in an opinion by Justice Sandra Day O'Connor.
3. At one point, the *per curiam* opinion argues that the past inequalities were relevant. The Court stated: "That brings the analysis to a further equal protection problem. The votes certified by the court included a partial total from one county, Miami-Dade. The Florida Supreme Court's decision thus gives no assurance that the recounts included in the final certification must be complete" (*Bush v. Gore*, 531–532). But even the Supreme Court's phrasing acknowledges that it was speculative as to whether there would be incompleteness by the time the counting was finished. The existence and extent of this incompleteness could not be known when the Supreme Court decided the case on December 12 precisely because the Court had stayed the counting process.

7

Federal Election Authority
Jurisdiction and Mandates

TREVOR POTTER*

MARIANNE HOLT VIRAY

The United States Constitution provides Congress with broad-based authority to regulate federal elections and to ensure equal protection of citizens' rights in state and local elections. In the past, Congress has used this authority to regulate registration, election qualifications, and procedures, but it had not provided states with financial assistance for implementation. In the aftermath of the 2000 election, the Help America Vote Act of 2002 (HAVA) became law. This long needed improvement offers states funding to improve the electoral process and ensure compliance with federal mandates. The federal government's authority to oversee elections and its ability to offer federal subsidies for election administration are the foundations for building greater, uniform standards of access, accuracy, and accountability in the national electoral system.

OVERVIEW

The United States is unique among worldwide federal systems in authorizing the states rather than the national government to administer elections to national office. The profound variation in election administration among states and even local jurisdictions in the United States results from the Constitutional assignment of responsibility for election administration to the states. In approaching the question of electoral reform, many observers assume that the federal government would be prohibited from any initiative to improve elec-

*Authors' Note: Various general resource materials were utilized for this chapter. Professor Pamela Karlan's memo to the Constitution Project, entitled "Congressional Authority to Regulate Elections and Elections Technology," was useful; Professor Karlan's memorandum is available online at www.constitutionproject.org/eri. See also the General Accounting Office Report on Elections: *The Scope of Congressional Authority in Election Administration* (GAO-01-470, March 13, 2001); Davidson 2001.

tion administration. This is not the case. The U.S. Congress has broad constitutional authority to regulate the times, places, and manner of federal elections (United States Constitution, Article I, Section 4). As a result of this authority, as well as the authority to ensure equal protection of citizens' voting rights in state and local elections,[1] the federal government is already an active participant in establishing election rules on issues ranging from voter registration to enforcement of equal access to voting booths.

Congress has only recently offered funds to state or local governments to assist in election administration. While the primary responsibility to administer elections should remain with the states, where the Congress has placed most of the administrative burden, it is necessary for the federal government to assist states and localities in modernizing and improving the nation's election system in order to fulfill the federal government's dual obligations of administering federal and presidential elections and protecting the right to vote.

This chapter reviews Congress' constitutional and legislative authority to administer federal elections. It then describes the current role of the federal government and concludes with a discussion of what Congress could and should do.

CONSTITUTIONAL AUTHORITY OVER ELECTIONS

The federal government operates according to powers granted by the United States Constitution. There are seven separate sources of constitutional authority— three general, four more specific—that have become the foundation of Congress' regulatory power over state and local administration of federal elections. The three general sources are the Elections Clause in Article I, Section 4; the Spending Clause in Article I, Section 8, Clause 1; and the Enforcement Clause in the Fourteenth Amendment. Four additional specific areas in the Constitution mandate congressional involvement in elections. In fact, Congress and the states have added more amendments to the Constitution on voting rights than on any other individual subject. These amendments prohibit the denial of the right to vote on the basis of race (Fifteenth Amendment), gender (Nineteenth Amendment), failure to pay poll tax (Twenty-fourth Amendment), and age (eighteen or over) (Twenty-sixth Amendment). Each amendment endows Congress with the power to protect voting rights established through proper legislation.[2]

Elections Clause

> The Times, Places and Manner of holding Elections for Senators and Representatives, shall be prescribed in each State by the Legislature thereof; but the Congress may at any time by law make or alter such Regulations, except as to the Places of chusing [*sic*] Senators. (*United States Constitution, Article I, Section 4*)

Article I, Section 4 of the Constitution, the so-called Elections Clause, provides the primary federal authority over elections. This provision states that states may enact rules governing the administration of federal elections, but Congress may "alter" state election procedures or "make" them in advance of states, whereas no state may change an act of Congress in this way. This provision offers states their only Constitutional mandate for election administration, while it is only one of several Constitutional provisions addressing the federal government's responsibility in election administration. The Supreme Court has explained the Election Clause by defining it as

> a default provision; it invests the States with responsibility for the mechanics of congressional elections, but only so far as Congress declines to preempt state legislative choices. Thus it is well settled that the Elections Clause grants Congress the power to override state regulations by establishing uniform rules for federal elections, binding on the States. The regulations made by Congress are paramount to those made by the State legislature; and if they conflict therewith, the latter, so far as the conflict extends, ceases to be operative. (*Foster v. Love*)

The Supreme Court has also identified Congress' exceedingly broad authority under the Elections Clause in a separate case, *Smiley v. Holm*. In this decision, the Court defined what election-related activities were appropriate for Congress to oversee:

> These comprehensive words embrace authority to provide a complete code for congressional elections, not only as to times and places, but in relation to notices, registration, supervision of voting, protection of voters, prevention of fraud and corrupt practices, counting of votes, duties of inspectors and canvassers, and making and publication of election returns; in short, to enact the numerous requirements as to procedure and safeguards which experience shows are necessary in order to enforce the fundamental right involved. (*Smiley v. Holm*)

The lower federal courts and the Supreme Court have consistently widened Congress' power over elections, most recently in 2001 in a balloting case, *Cooke v. Gralike*. The Court has expanded Congress' original election practices to include everything from voter registration to certifying election results post-election and punishing state election administrators for violating state obligations in conjunction with federal elections (*United States v. Gradwell; ex parte Clarke*).

For presidential elections, the express power given to Congress is more limited. Article II, Section 1, Clause 4 of the U.S. Constitution grants to state legislatures the power to direct "the Time of chusing [*sic*] the Electors, and the Day on which they shall give their Votes; which Day shall be the same throughout the United States." Article II, Section 2, Clause 2 also grants states authority over the manner of presidential electors being appointed. Nevertheless, the Supreme Court held in *Buckley v. Valeo* that "Congress has power to regulate Presidential elections and primaries." Congress has established that presidential elections shall take place "on the Tuesday next after the first Monday in November, in every fourth year" (2 U.S.C. 2(c)). Inevitably, the manner of administering congressional elections is also the manner of administering presidential elections.

In sum, the Elections Clause grants to Congress the broad authority to regulate the "times, places, and manner" of holding federal elections, including presidential elections. Furthermore, Court interpretations have consistently expanded the power given to the federal government under the Elections Clause.

The Spending Clause

> The Congress shall have Power To . . . provide for the . . . general Welfare of the United States. *(United States Constitution, Article I, Section 8, Clause 1)*

The "General Welfare Clause," or "Spending Clause," as it is alternately called, gives Congress the power to provide states with federal funds to implement federal acts. Congress may offer these funds on a conditional basis to motivate states to act in a certain way, even if Congress does not have authority to regulate in that area. In *South Dakota v. Dole*, the Court identified three General Welfare Clause requirements for this kind of conditional federal funding. First, the spending must be according to the "general welfare" of the people. Second, Congress must clearly delineate qualification requirements for federal funding. Third, the conditions for funding must relate to the intent of the spending (*South Dakota v. Dole*). In the area of election law, the Court interpreted the General Welfare Clause in *Buckley v. Valeo* to mean that Congress can use its spending power "as a means to reform the electoral process."

In legislating electoral reform, Congress could easily meet the first two conditions for spending as specified in *Dole*. Any congressionally offered requirements for election administration, and the associated funding, would be for the "general welfare" of Americans. The second requirement, of clear and unambiguous regulations so that states know exactly the terms of receipt of federal funds, can be resolved by the clear drafting of the law. The third condition (relevance to the intent of the spending) is more complicated. Congress must decide whether to attempt to attach conditions on already existing funds that conceivably relate to election administration or if there is to be a new system of appropriations to states and localities to upgrade their election equipment to meet greater accuracy standards.

Congress has not exercised its spending power with respect to conducting federal elections beyond limited appropriations for enforcement of certain federal laws and the Federal Election Commission's voting system standards, which will be discussed later. Congress has an obligation to assist financially its own federal agency responsible for election and voting standards, but it also has the responsibility to appropriate funds for state and localities for federal elections administration.

Fourteenth Amendment

[N]or shall any State deprive any person of life, liberty, or property, without due process of law; nor deny to any person within its jurisdiction the equal protection of these laws. . . . The Congress shall have power to enforce, by appropriate legislation, the provisions of this article. *(United States Constitution, Fourteenth Amendment, Section 1 and Section 5)*

The Equal Protection and Due Process clauses in the Fourteenth Amendment are the main provisions protecting the right to vote. The Court has acknowledged that voting is a "fundamental" right and that any limitation or restriction of that right warrants examination (see, e.g., *Harper v. Virginia Board of Elections*).

The Equal Protection Clause of the Fourteenth Amendment grants Congress the power to enforce these rights. This clause has increased electoral significance in the wake of *Bush v. Gore* (see Hasen, this volume). Given the state legislatures' authority to decide the method of selecting presidential electors, the Supreme Court found that "the right to vote as the legislature has prescribed is fundamental; and one source of its fundamental nature lies in the equal weight accorded to each voter" (*Bush v. Gore*). The Court also held that

[t]he right to vote is protected in more than the initial allocation of the franchise. Equal protection applies as well to the *manner* of its exercise. Having once granted the right to vote on equal terms, the State may not, by arbitrary and disparate treatment, value one person's vote over that of another. (530)

The *Bush v. Gore* decision potentially opens the door to future challenges against existing state election procedures on the basis of equal protection (see Hasen, this volume) and demonstrates the potential power of the federal government—both legislative and judicial—in determining election administration. It is difficult to determine how expansively *Bush v. Gore's* equal protection "doctrine" will be applied, if at all, because as the Court noted, "[o]ur consideration is limited to the present circumstances, for the problem of equal protection in election process generally presents many complexities" (532).

THE HISTORY OF FEDERAL INVOLVEMENT IN ELECTIONS

The Constitutional Convention

There was very little debate on the Elections Clause at the Constitutional Convention. However, the federal power to "make or alter election regulations" was "assailed by the opponents of the Constitution, both in and out of the state conventions, with uncommon zeal and virulence" (Story 1833; see Davidson 2001 for further history on the debate over the Times, Places and Manner Clause at the Constitutional Convention, during ratification debates, and in the first Congress). The primary defense of this provision was that Congress needed to be able to regulate elections if the states failed to act in this regard. The clause was also defended on two grounds that are used in today's discussion of election reform: the need "to insure [*sic*] free and fair elections" and the "equal rights of elections" (Elliot 1888), or that all citizens have the right to vote.

Alexander Hamilton and James Madison both supported the Election Clause and wanted states to have primary responsibility for election regulations while Congress retained ultimate authority to make reforms. Hamilton noted that the Convention delegation

> submitted the regulation of elections for the Federal Government in the first instance to the local administrations, which in ordinary cases, and when no improper views prevail, may be both more convenient and more satisfactory; but they have reserved to the national authority a right to interpose, whenever extraordinary circumstances might render that interposition necessary to its safety. (Hamilton, Jay, and Madison 1787, Federalist No. 59)

At the Virginia Constitutional Convention, James Madison argued that

> were they [election regulations] exclusively under the control of the state governments, the general government might easily be dissolved. But if they be regulated properly by the state legislatures, the congressional control will very probably never be exercised. (Elliot 1888)

Congress first acted on the timing of federal elections in 1792 when it established a uniform day for House of Representative elections. In 1914, after the ratification of the Seventeenth Amendment allowed the popular vote rather than state legislators to choose senators, Congress set the elections for the same day as House elections. Together, these provisions mandate all federal and presidential elections to be held on the same day throughout the nation.

The Reconstruction Era and Disenfranchisement

Congress acted extensively on the manner of conducting elections in three separate measures enacted at the time of the ratification of the Fifteenth Amendment in 1870. This amendment held that no one could be denied the right to vote on the basis of color or race. The Enforcement Act of 1870 created criminal consequences for interference with voting rights, and the 1871 Force Act offered federal oversight of elections.

These measures were largely repealed in 1894 during a period of disenfranchisement after two separate Supreme Court decisions in 1875 limited the scope of congressional authority under the Enforcement and Force Acts (see *United States v. Cruikshank*; *United States v. Reese*). The consequences of these decisions, coupled with federal troops being removed from the South as part of the Hayes-Tilden Compromise, resulted in a suppression of minority turnout and increased voter fraud. A series of laws were enacted that chipped away at what was left of the Enforcement and Force Acts, as well as directly assaulting the Fifteenth Amendment. Poll taxes, literacy tests, "crimes of moral turpitude" disqualification, and "good character" vouchers were all designed to exclude minority citizens from voting at the determination of white election officiators. Other infringements took place in the form of racial gerrymandering. It would take many more years for Congress to address the fraud and discrimination that transpired in state and federal elections during the late 1800s.

MODERN VOTING RIGHTS AND FEDERAL REGULATION OF ELECTIONS

Further congressional legislation on the manner of conducting federal elections took place during the twentieth century civil rights era, beginning with the Voting Rights Act (VRA) of 1965. Other major acts included the Voting Accessibility for the Elderly and Handicapped Act (VAEHA) of 1984; the Uniformed and Overseas Citizens Absentee Voting Act (UOCAVA) of 1986; the National Voter Registration Act (NVRA) of 1993; and HAVA.

The Voting Rights Act of 1965

The most sweeping of the modern laws is the Voting Rights Act of 1965 (as amended), which addresses discriminatory election practices. The VRA and subsequent amendments established minority voting rights and protections against discrimination on the basis of race, language, or color (42 U.S.C. § 1973). It abolished the use of literacy tests, "good character" vouchers, and other requirements impeding the right to vote, and it granted language minorities the right to register and vote in their own language. The VRA also enabled voters to challenge discriminatory voting practices.

Under the act, the federal government also required all changes to state voting standards, practices, or procedures to be approved by the Department of Justice (43 U.S.C. sec. 1973c). The act states:

> Whenever [a covered jurisdiction] shall enact or seek to administer any voting qualification or prerequisite to voting, or standard, practice, or procedure with respect to voting different from [before], such [jurisdiction] may institute an action . . . for a declaratory judgment that such qualification, prerequisite standard, practice, or procedure does not have the purpose and will not have the effect of denying or abridging the right to vote on account of race or color, or in contravention of the guarantees [protecting certain language minorities,] and unless and until . . . such judgments no person shall be denied the right to vote for failure to comply with such qualification, prerequisite, standard, practice, or procedure. (42 U.S.C. sec. 1973c (sub sec. 5))

A state must demonstrate that the proposed changes do not limit or deny the right to vote in any way. The Department of Justice's civil rights division reviews all proposed changes and the U.S. Attorney General is given sixty days to object and to deny the proposed change. A state may also make changes in state election regulations by filing suit in a U.S. district court. The local district court has the authority to allow or prevent the state's implementation of the change until the attorney general or the District of Columbia district court reviews the change and makes its determination.

Voting Accessibility for the Elderly and Handicapped Act of 1984

The federal Voting Accessibility for the Elderly and Handicapped Act of 1984 (VAEHA) requires all polling places to be accessible to elderly and handicapped voters for federal elections (42 U.S.C. § 1973ee-1). This act has had less effect than other federal voting rights legislation because it allows states to establish their own guidelines and does not permit damages or attorney fees to those who sue states under the act.

Uniform and Overseas Citizens Absentee Voting Act of 1986

The 1986 Uniform and Overseas Citizens Absentee Voting Act permits "absent uniformed services voters and overseas voters to use absentee registration procedures and to vote by absentee ballot in general, special, primary, and runoff elections for Federal office" (42 U.S.C. § 1973ff-1). According to the General Accounting Office, the act covers nearly 6.1 million citizens, including 3.4 million citizens living abroad and 2.7 million active military personnel and their families (Walker 2001).

UOCAVA requires states to do several things: to ensure ballot access for overseas and military voters, to override their own deadlines to accommodate overseas registrants, and to accept a write-in absentee ballot in federal general elections.[3] Enforcement of UOCAVA is the responsibility of the civil rights division of the Department of Justice. It typically brings enforcement actions against states after being notified by the Federal Voting Assistance Program (FVAP) that state overseas voter absentee ballots were sent so late that a substantial risk exists that overseas voters will miss state ballot deadlines. The civil rights division has brought suit under this law more than twenty times since the act was established in 1986.

The National Voter Registration Act of 1993

The National Voter Registration Act of 1993 codifies the federal government's broad authority over voter registration for federal elections. "Motor voter," as the act was nicknamed, was written to "create procedures to increase the number of eligible citizens who register to vote, to protect the integrity of the voting process and to ensure accurate and current voter registration records" for presidential and congressional elections (Pub. L 1003-31, § 2, 107, Stat. 77).

Motor voter requires states to register individual voters for federal elections at state division of motor vehicles offices at the time of applying for a driver's license; at schools, libraries, unemployment offices and disability services offices; and by mail (Traugott, this volume). NVRA also requires states to maintain accurate voter records and requires removal of ineligible voters because of change in residence, violation of the law, or death. No person's name can be removed from the records for failing to vote.

The final way that motor voter regulates state election registration is through a provisional ballot allowing voters whose records indicate a recent change of address and who affirm in person on the day of the election that they have not changed addresses. Written confirmation of the address occurs after the voter is allowed to cast a ballot, but written confirmation of the address must take place before the vote will be counted.

According to the Federal Election Commission's 2001 biennial report to Congress on the National Voter Registration Act, NVRA was responsible for registering 22.4 million new registrants this election cycle. Thirty-eight percent, or 17.3 million, of these registrants were in conjunction with driver's license applications ("The Impact of The National Voter Registration Act of 1993" 2001).

Help America Vote Act of 2002

The Help America Vote Act (H.R. 3295) passed the U.S. House of Representatives on December 13, 2001. The Senate unanimously passed an amended version of the House's bill on April 19, 2002 and the legislation was sent to a conference committee to reconcile the differences between the two versions. On October 8, 2002 the conference committee resolved the discrepancies between the bills and the approved bill was voted on in the House for final passage on October 10, 2002. The President signed the Help America Vote Act of 2002 into law on November 7, 2002. The act is wide-ranging, seeking to provide the states with large amounts of funding as well as to improve and implement election system standards. In particular, the law:

- Authorizes $650 million to buy punchcard voting machines from the states
- Creates an Election Assistance Commission that will serve as a national clearinghouse for information and review of procedures for federal elections
- Allocates $3.86 billion in election fund payments to the states over four years to help finance a variety of election improvement projects
- Establishes minimum standards for state election systems and directs the Department of Justice to monitor and enforce these standards
- Creates the Help America Vote Foundation and College Program to encourage college students to assist in the administration of state and local elections
- Mandates provisional ballots by 2004 and statewide computerized voter database by 2006
- Reduces postage rates for official election mail

Conclusions on Congressional Legislation to Date

Through its legislative and judicial branches, the federal government today is a more active participant in conducting federal elections than ever before in U.S. history. Existing federal mandates are costly, and the U.S. Attorney General has sued numerous states over implementation of certain federal requirements. In the case of the NVRA, the courts found in favor of the act and re-quired the states to implement it. Thus, given the reality of federal authority in this area and the overarching importance of federal elections to the federal government, the question is not *whether* Congress can extend federal regula-tion of election procedures, but *how* federal, state, and local governments can work together to implement new solutions to the current electoral problems.

REMEDIES AND ROLES FOR THE FEDERAL GOVERNMENT: WHERE TO GO NEXT?

Commentators vigorously debate the question of how best to allocate roles be-tween the federal, state, and local governments in election administration (see, e.g., Chemerinsky, this volume). Most observers agree, however, that the fed-eral government could or should play a role in one or more of four major areas in the electoral process: disseminating information, engaging in research, es-tablishing standards, and providing financial assistance. This section looks at each in turn.

Disseminating Information about Best Practices

Justice Brandeis once wrote, "It is one of the happy incidents of the federal sys-tem that a single courageous state may, if its citizens choose, serve as a labo-ratory; and try novel social and economic experiments without risk to the rest of the country" (*New State Ice Co. v. Liebmann* [Brandeis, J., dissenting]). This statement is particularly fitting in the context of election administration, for not only are the fifty states able to serve as independent testing grounds, but the myriad of counties within each state also serve as individual areas of experi-mentation. Many observers argue that perhaps the strongest role the federal government can serve entails disseminating information regarding state and local jurisdictions' improvements.

Many associations and academic projects believe that the federal govern-ment should collect information on a diverse array of topics ranging from bal-lot format to voting equipment and make this information publicly available. In collecting this information, the federal government can identify those prac-tices and equipment in the states that are the most and least effective. This eval-uation will allow election administrators to take advantage of the ingenuity and experiences of their colleagues. The National Association of Counties urges that Congress create a "central repository of information on voting equip-ment problems and solutions reported by election officials," and the National Commission on Election Reform proposes that the federal government "maintain a national clearinghouse of information on best practices in election administration."[4] One of the challenges facing the new Election Assistance Commission (EAC) created by HAVA will be carrying out these requests.

Technological Research

In addition to facilitating the exchange of information, states also need the federal government's involvement in researching and developing accurate equipment technologies through substantive testing of voting machines. In each election, potentially millions of ballots go unmarked or spoiled (Alvarez, Sinclair, and Wilson, this volume). In 2000, Florida's error rate was 3 percent, while cities such as Chicago and New York had higher rates of spoiled or uncounted ballots. These numbers could diminish greatly if the federal government were to take a greater role in researching and testing direct recording electronic (DRE) and optical scanning equipment as well as in providing states with the necessary funds to replace machinery that does not meet basic accuracy standards.

The Constitution Project, a not-for-profit research and advocacy organization, released a report recommending that

> Congress should provide funds for research and development on voting equipment, with particular emphasis on ease-of-use, enhanced accessibility for people with disabilities or low levels of English literacy, and measures to protect the accuracy and integrity of election results. (The Constitution Project 2001)

A primary goal of the federal government should be to research and develop machinery that will count ballots accurately as well as accommodate individuals with disabilities, allow voting in multiple languages, compensate for illiteracy, provide voters with confirmation that their vote is exactly as they want it, and recount ballots effectively. The federal government is best suited to conduct the research and disseminate the findings in a broad and unbiased fashion. Research costs do not need to be incurred by each individual state or local precinct—all these costs could be absorbed by the federal government, enabling each state to evaluate its current system, its needs, and what technologies it should implement to improve the integrity of the voting process. The role that the new EAC will play in this regard is not yet clear.

Standards

Prior to 1990, the states were left to themselves to select voting machines for all elections. According to the Federal Election Commission (FEC), few states created guidelines for testing or appraising the accuracy of voting machines. In 1975 the National Bureau of Standards issued a report concluding that the basic election-related problem was "the lack of appropriate technical skills at the State and local level for developing or implementing written standards, against which voting system hardware and software could be evaluated" ("The Impact of the National Voter Registration Act of 1993" 2001).

Responding to the report, Congress asked the FEC to analyze the possibility of creating equipment and performance standards. The three-year effort resulted in the *Voting System Standards: A Report on the Feasibility of Developing Voluntary Standards for Voting Equipment*. These voluntary standards addressed punchcard DRE voting systems' performance. According to the FEC, to date, thirty-seven states have reported that they have already adopted, or intend to adopt, the FEC's voting systems standards.

Congress created voluntary standards ten years ago to help states exercise the responsibility to approve all voting machines. State-level organizations complain that these voluntary standards are too narrowly defined and are unhelpful in the changing world of voting technology. State and local election administrators and those within the FEC agree that these voluntary national standards need to be updated and need to reflect independent testing conducted on equipment and data collection. The National Association of State Election Directors (NASED) and the National Association of Counties (NACO) argue for national standards that include operational or managerial as well as technical standards. Poll workers and election administrators should be better trained on the rights of voters, state law, and how to use and verify the accuracy of equipment. Better training for state precinct workers—as well as mailing sample ballots to registered voters and voter pamphlets describing the voting process and voter's rights—could also be implemented to increase the standards of election administration. NASED is currently working with the FEC's Office of Election Administration (OEA) to update the voluntary standards and widen their purview. HAVA now creates such minimum standards.

Federal Funding

The federal government needs not only to spend money at the federal level to conduct research, develop technology and standards, and disseminate the findings broadly among the states, but also to assist the states in the direct costs of administering state and federal elections—something that up until HAVA, it failed to do. In public statements by election administrators and national commissions, a demand has been identified for: (1) a grant program designed to assist state and local governments to acquire new voter systems and registration lists and (2) a permanent federal program to facilitate sharing the cost of elections with state and local governments. HAVA only provides for the first of these programs.

One-Time Federal Investment in Elections

There is a strong argument to be made for the federal government to cover a one-time upgrade cost for hardware, software, and other related supplies to improve voter registration systems and voting equipment, as HAVA accomplishes. Registration lists should be electronic in either a single database or linked databases (Motor Vehicle records, Post Office records, state and federal prison lists, and other sources) that are accessible for immediate voter registration confirmation at polling places.

Currently, voter registration systems are kept to define eligible participants and to ensure that voters vote where they are registered to vote. These registration lists tend to be quite decentralized, with each county or state maintaining a database separate from other county databases, taxation lists, and license registration lists. Assisting states to unify all registration lists statewide would produce cleaner registration records. This process of integration would be initially costly, but would simplify maintenance of such lists, authentication, and protect against improper "purging" of voter records.

According to the U.S. Census' most recent population survey, 7 percent of all registered voters who did not vote in the election said they failed to vote because of registration difficulties (Caltech/MIT Voting Project 2001b). One academic study released this year by the California Institute of Technology and the Massachusetts Institute of Technology estimates that three million votes were lost because of registration problems. These registration problems were compounded by the fact that many polling places did not allow voters to submit provisional ballots while authorities attempted to verify their voter registration information. As a result, the Caltech/MIT study recommends

> improved database management, installing technological links to registration databases from polling places, and use of provisional ballots. . . . Aggressive use of provisional ballots alone might substantially reduce the number of votes lost due to registration problems. (Caltech/MIT Voting Technology Project 2001b)

The 2000 election showed that many localities are using voting equipment that is decades old (see Alvarez, Sinclair, and Wilson, this volume). While these older voting technologies are functional, some of them have numerous problems that newer technologies solve. In particular, older equipment may not provide voters with the ability to alter a vote cast in error; or, if votes are correctly cast, they may fail to be counted. The cost of purchasing new equipment, however, can be great. Therefore, many have argued that the federal government should help finance the cost of overhauling election equipment nationwide in order to ensure that every locality can afford reliable voting technology. The federal government should also subsidize voting machine administration so that poll workers can be trained and educated on the voting systems and voters' rights. According to the U.S. Census, twice as many people failed to vote in 2000 compared to 1996 because of polling place problems such as long lines, insufficient hours, and difficulty finding locations or other operational complications (Caltech/MIT Voting Technology Project 2001b). Federal funding could be made available for poll worker education and training and an increased number of workers for the next election cycle.

Permanent Supplemental Funding in Election Administration

There is also a strong argument for the federal government permanently to increase its funding for election administration. Developing standards, engaging in research, and disseminating information all require federal financing. Currently, Congress funds the OEA to handle many of these activities; however, many observers argue that funding for the OEA is inadequate. For example, in 1999, the House Appropriations Committee passed over the OEA for additional funds. On June 17, 2001, despite the OEA receiving additional attention following the 2000 election and expanding its work to include "acquisition of new voting systems, administering elections, training election workers, ballot design, and public education," the House Appropriations Committee denied the OEA's request for a 2002 budgetary increase of $4.8 million. These actions suggest that the federal government has yet to assume the financial responsibility necessary for a long-term role in the administration of elections.

Additionally, there is widespread support for a permanent and ongoing federal investment in the administration of elections at the local level. Advocates argue that the federal government should distribute additional funds to local jurisdictions to defray the costs of election administration. The National Association of Counties and the National Association of County Recorders, Election Officials and Clerks stated in their report on election standards and reform that "[f]unding for administration should be distributed to local election jurisdictions based upon measures of election activity and financial need" ("Report of the NACO/NACRC Commission on Election Standards and Reform" 2001).

One proposal in particular that has generated a good deal of support is the establishment of an Elections Class postage rate. This proposal would establish a class of mail that would provide first class service at 50 percent of cost. This would enable local jurisdictions to pay a great deal less for the current election-related mailings distributed via first class mail during election cycles. While this form of federal financing is not a direct grant of funds to states, it does have enormous potential to defray the costs of administering elections at the local level. This provision was included in HAVA.

Regardless of the method of federal financing, politics governs the distribution of federal funds. Some states, counties, and cities want additional funds but don't want the potential mandate attached. Some jurisdictions may decide that the federal money available is not worth the headache of compliance with national mandatory standards and could then opt just to abide by the current acts and voluntary national standards set by the OEA. Or, if the money is given to the states, a conflict over priorities between election officials and state legislatures could ensue. Regardless of how the money is distributed, there is undoubtedly a role for the federal government in assisting in the financing of election administration.

CONCLUSION

The federal government has the authority and constitutional mandate to do much to assist state and local jurisdictions manage elections. It has already implemented wide-reaching legislation such as the VRA and the motor voter act that require states to administer elections in particular ways. The federal government can address problems of election administration by researching and developing reliable technology for voting registration and election machinery, disseminating election-related information, setting mandatory and voluntary standards, and offering financial subsidies in exchange for meeting mandatory requirements and for the purchasing of necessary equipment to ensure accurate elections. Existing federal election mandates are costly. The ongoing congressional debate about whether there should be a "federal mandate" for state election reform is not a constitutional and legal question—that issue has been settled—but a policy one: What is the best way to ensure the optimum functioning of our election system? HAVA is Congress' initial response to this issue. It seems likely that more will need to be done following the 2004 elections.

NOTES

1. "All persons born or naturalized in the United States, and subject to the jurisdiction thereof, are citizens of the United States and of the state wherein they reside. No state shall make or enforce any law which shall abridge the privileges or immunities of citizens of the United States; nor shall any state deprive any person of life, liberty, or property, without due process of law; nor deny to any person within its jurisdiction the equal protection of the laws." United States Constitution, Fourteenth Amendment, Section 1.

2. *Fifteenth Amendment (race)*: "The rights of citizens of the United States to vote shall not be denied or abridged by the United States or by any state on account of race, color, or previous condition of servitude."

   Nineteenth Amendment (gender): "The right of citizens of the United States to vote shall not be denied or abridged by the United States or by any state on account of sex."

   Twenty-fourth Amendment (poll tax): "The right of citizens of the United States to vote in any primary or other election for President or Vice President, for electors for President or Vice President, or for Senator or Representative in Congress, shall not be denied or abridged by the United States or any state by reason of failure to pay any poll tax or other tax."

   Twenty-sixth Amendment (age): "The right of citizens of the United States, who are 18 years of age or older, to vote, shall not be denied or abridged by the United States or any state on account of age."

3. The act designated the Department of Defense as the federal agency responsible for regulating all related federal activities. In turn, the Secretary of Defense, the Presidential designee tasked with fulfilling the statutory provisions, created the Federal Voting Assistance Program (FVAP) to administer the act, compile and distribute state absentee ballot registration and voting guideline information, write a report to Congress and the president on the effectiveness of the act, and design a write-in absentee ballot for overseas voters.

4. "Report of the NACO/NACRC Commission on Election Standards and Reform" 2001; The National Commission on Election Reform 2001. Additional reports from the Constitution Project, the National Association of State Election Directors, Caltech/MIT Voting Technology Project, and the Election Center all support a publicly accessible federal clearinghouse of election information.

8

Congressional Compromise on Election Reform

A Look Backward and Forward

JEB BARNES

INTRODUCTION

The 2000 presidential election produced a flurry of activity on Capitol Hill (see generally Lipton 2000; Squitieri 2000; Vita and Dewar 2000; see also Calmes 2001b; Steel and Posner 2001). In the Senate, well before the Supreme Court decided the presidential race (see Hasen, this volume; Chemerinsky, this volume), then chairman of the Rules and Administration Committee Senator Mitch McConnell (R-KY) announced his intention to hold hearings on poll closing times, ballot design, voting equipment, absentee voting, and "the timeliness and accuracy of vote-counting." Senator Barbara Boxer (D-CA) asked the General Accounting Office to explore ways to minimize fraud and other irregularities under state election laws. Senator Arlen Specter (R-PA) proposed a commission to study the best available voting technologies. Senator John Warner (R-VA) promised reform of voting procedures for military personnel. Senator-elect Hillary Rodham Clinton (D-NY) called for the abolition of the Electoral College. Senator John McCain (R-AZ) pressed for consideration of campaign finance reform. And Senator Charles Schumer (D-NY) promised a bill that would provide $10 million to the Federal Election Commission (FEC) to study Internet voting, computerized voting machines, and expanded polling hours as well as make grants to states for modernizing their voting infrastructures.

Members of the House of Representatives similarly promised to leave no stone unturned in seeking reform. Shortly after the election, Minority Leader Richard Gephardt (D-MO) advocated Electoral College reform and suggested that federal elections be held on Saturdays. Representative W. J. "Billy" Tauzin (R-LA), chairing a House Commerce subcommittee, announced plans to call television executives and pollsters to explain mistaken and premature election night projections. Members of the Black Congressional Caucus urged immediate improvement of voting equipment in poor and minority communities. And

Representatives Peter DeFazio (D-OR) and James Leach (R-IA) proposed a twelve-person commission to look into the historical rationale of the Electoral College as well as voter registration rules, mail-in and absentee voting, voting technologies, polling locations and closing times, ballot design, and multiday voting.

Despite this spate of post-election activity on both sides of the aisle, the political prospects of federal election reform were up and down. In the immediate aftermath of the election, many feared that Congress would act precipitously, passing reforms without adequate deliberation. After months of foot dragging and partisan jockeying, the prevailing fear became that Congress would do nothing, especially as budget negotiations, midterm elections, and the tragic events of September 11, 2001, threatened to push election reform off the agenda (Broder 2001; Seelyee 2001).

In the end, both fears proved unfounded. Congress neither acted in haste nor failed to act. Instead, the House and Senate have acted incrementally, passing targeted measures that aim to improve voting equipment and procedures, but not enacting more sweeping reforms such as abolishing the Electoral College. Of course, one might counter that banning "soft money" in federal elections—or unregulated campaign contributions to political parties—does represent major reform. But insiders disagree, including FEC Chairman David Mason (see also Estrich, this volume). They argue that, even if the ban on soft money withstands court challenges and congressional attempts to create new loopholes for contributors in the tax code, it will be ignored or easily circumvented (Anderson 2002b). In fact, the national parties have reportedly begun to establish so-called shadow parties, which promise to serve as new conduits for soft money (Rasky 2002).

From a purely political perspective, the modest results are not surprising. After all, Congress' fragmented policymaking process features multiple "veto points" that make it easier to play defense in Washington—to block or water down legislation—than to play offense and pass significant reforms. This may be particularly true for election reform proposals because sitting members of Congress are often reluctant to change a system that overwhelmingly returns them to office.

As the dust settles on the political reaction to the 2000 presidential election, the time is ripe to look back on Congress' likely policy accomplishments—such as they are—and look forward to the next round of election reform. In that spirit, this chapter evaluates three approaches to election reform from the perspective of "participatory" and "minimalist" (McCaffery, Crigler, and Just, this volume)—or what I prefer to call "Madisonian"—democracy: (1) voting methods reform, which aims to improve the accuracy and reliability of recording votes; (2) Electoral College reform, which seeks to abolish—or substantially modify—the Electoral College in order to give votes for president equal, or at least more equal, weight; and (3) choice method reform, which seeks to enhance information about voters' preferences in close elections by allowing citizens to vote for more than one candidate.[1]

Looking backward, I argue that the passage of targeted voting methods reform and the rejection of Electoral College reform represent a clear victory for

Madisonian democracy, which favors enhancing the accuracy and reliability of voting procedures without tampering with the American system of checks and balances. Looking forward, I argue that choice method reform, although often ignored, offers an intriguing policy option because it builds on participatory and Madisionian democracy's shared commitment to improving the accuracy of the vote, while promising to avoid some of the daunting political obstacles facing Electoral College reform. Throughout I stress issues that have arguably been overlooked in the current debate, which may prove useful when the electoral process returns to center stage.

PARTICIPATORY VERSUS MADISONIAN DEMOCRACY: AN OVERVIEW

Before turning to specifics, a brief overview of participatory and Madisonian democracy is needed (see McCaffery, Crigler, and Just, this volume). The outline of participatory democracy is simple. It holds that the quality of democracy rests on the breadth and depth of citizen participation in elections. Or, as Daniel Ortiz suggests in a later chapter, participatory democracy should feature wide, if not universal, suffrage, equality among voters, and some degree of voter thoughtfulness (Ortiz, this volume). From this perspective, the 2000 presidential election was an unqualified disaster, culminating in the Supreme Court's crowning of a president who lost the popular election by over five hundred thousand votes.

Advocates of Madisonian democracy would counter that American democracy was not founded on the principles of broad suffrage, voting equality, and voter deliberation. To the contrary, the Framers believed unchecked popular participation represented a primary *threat* to republican government. More precisely, the Framers feared the "mischief of faction": the natural tendency of individual citizens to form groups—either majority or minority groups—that pursue narrow self-interests, which are inimical to others or the aggregate interests of the community (Madison 1788). Given this definition of the problem, the challenge was creating a system of governance that would tame the threat of minority and majority factions without extinguishing the spirit of popular sovereignty or unduly restricting individual liberty.

With respect to tyranny of the minority, the solution was straightforward. The Framers provided regular elections, which offer citizens ample opportunities to remove corrupt or biased representatives from office. Accordingly, the ideal of majority rule as well as open and fair elections are integral to Madisonian democracy. They are not, however, the only—or even the most important—attributes. Why? The Framers' primary fear was tyranny of the majority, and elections cannot overcome this threat, because a majority faction, by definition, cannot be voted out of office.

To address the problem of majority tyranny, the Framers designed a system of government that resists domination by any single group. Specifically, they employed a twofold strategy. First, they fragmented lawmaking authority among separate but overlapping legislative, executive, and judicial branches of government. As a result, even if a faction managed to capture one branch of government, it could not unilaterally impose its preferences on others. Instead, the faction would have to persuade the other branches to endorse its preferences. Second, to reduce the likelihood that a single faction might gain simultaneous control of all branches of government, each branch is accountable to different political constituencies. Thus members of the House of Representatives answer directly to voters in congressional districts; senators initially were accountable to state representatives (and now are accountable to voters in statewide elections); the president is selected by the Electoral College, whose members represent all the states; and federal judges are insulated from the electoral process as political appointees with lifetime tenure and salary protection. As a further safeguard against a tyrannical majority sweeping into office on a wave of popular sentiment, the Constitution staggers the terms of the Senate, House, and presidency and provides that the Senate would be a continuing body, in that only one-third of its members run for reelection at a time.

According to the ideal of Madisonian democracy, this elaborate dispersal of power not only serves the negative function of thwarting majority tyranny but also plays a positive role in creating dynamic tension among the branches of government. This tension, in turn, promises to enrich democracy by promoting interaction among diversely representative lawmakers and mutual accommodation among a wide range of groups, which must build broad and stable coalitions in order to run the gauntlet of the American system of separate institutions sharing power (see generally Dahl 1956; Peretti 1999, 209–217; Sunstein 1993b; see also Madison 1788, Federalist Nos. 10 and 51). Thus, the ultimate touchstone of Madisonian democracy is not the breadth and depth of voter participation; it is the preservation of a complex system of checks and balances, which resists capture by tyrannical factions and fosters bargaining among diverse lawmakers and groups.

From this perspective, the 2000 presidential election raised legitimate concerns about the mechanics of federal elections, but it did not raise serious concerns about the quality of American democracy. To the contrary, it demonstrated the flexibility of a system of government whose stability—and legitimacy—does not rest on the potentially contradictory goals of universal and thoughtful voter participation (see Ortiz, this volume), but rather on overlapping and diversely representative policymaking forums, each of which has a voice in resolving political conflict.

Two points emerge from this thumbnail sketch. First, despite their many differences, participatory and Madisonian democracy require open and accurate electoral processes, albeit for different reasons. Participatory democracy requires open and accurate elections because wide suffrage, equality of votes, and voter deliberation are meaningless if ballots are unclear and voter preferences are inaccurately recorded. Madisonian democracy requires open and accurate elections because a majority of citizens must have reliable means to oust tyrannical minority factions.

Second, although both sides value majority rule and voter equality, they prioritize these values differently. Specifically, advocates of participatory democracy place the values of majority rule and voting equality first and view nonmajoritarian aspects of American government with suspicion. Advocates of Madisonian democracy, in contrast, believe that the threat of majority tyranny outweighs the threat of minority tyranny. As a result, they will always oppose election reforms that threaten to reduce structural tension between the branches of government, even if such reform undeniably promotes majority rule and the equality of votes. To make these points concrete, consider voting methods reform and Electoral College reform.

VOTING METHODS REFORM: PARTICIPATORY AND MADISONIAN DEMOCRACY'S COMMON GROUND

Background

Regardless of where one falls on the outcome of the 2000 presidential election, the election undoubtedly raised red flags about the states' reliance on a hodge-podge of ballot designs and voting technology, some of which were confusing and unreliable. A case in point is the infamous "butterfly ballot" in Palm Beach County, which listed candidates alternatively on two sides of a page to accommodate larger type. Democrats argued that this ballot design caused a significant number of votes intended for Vice President Al Gore to be miscast for Patrick Buchanan, the archconservative Reform Party candidate. And they may be right (Brady 2002). Buchanan, who reportedly did not campaign in Palm Beach, received over thirty-four hundred Palm Beach votes, more than (1) three times his total in any other Florida county, including the most staunchly conservative, and (2) more than six times enough to swing the election in favor of the Democratic ticket.[2] Even Buchanan conceded that many of his Palm Beach votes were probably not intended for him and could have provided enough votes for a Democratic win (Bruni and Yardley 2000).

Punchcard balloting offers another example. About one-third of American voters use punchcard technology (Alvarez, Sinclair, and Wilson, this volume). Introduced in the 1960s, punchcards are notoriously finicky, producing post-election scenes worthy of the Keystone Cops. In a small Georgia town, for example, humidity warped voters' punchcards, causing counting machines to reject thousands of ballots. To remedy the problem, election officials reached for their blowdryers and blasted the misshapen ballots. Fran Watson, the election superintendent, explained: "As weird as it sounds, it's standard procedure" (Bruni and Yardley 2000). Fortunately, it seems to work, representing a victory for both big hair and democracy in the South. In Florida, however, problems with punchcards were not so easily fixed, resulting in the troubling spectacle of Florida election officials trying to divine voters' intent from hanging and dimpled chads.

Immediately following the election, voting methods reform seemed like a political slam-dunk. One public opinion poll found 88 percent of Americans favored a national ballot; 86 percent supported national standards for counting and recounting votes; 87 percent backed requiring reliance on a single type of voting machine; and nearly two-thirds supported outlawing punchcard ballots (Morin and Deane 2000; Crigler, Just, and Buhr, this volume). Elite media opinion, as reflected in newspapers such as the *New York Times*, *Wall Street Journal*, and *Los Angeles Times*, also supported swift congressional action to improve the nation's voting technology ("The Ballot Reform Imperative" 2000; Harwood 2000, culminating in a special series on election reform; "Vote Counting: Fix It" 2000; see also Ornstein 2001). Moreover, Democrats, especially members of the Black Caucus, seemed determined to pressure newly elected President Bush to deliver on promises to change American election procedures (Allen 2001; Calmes 2001a).

Things inside the Beltway, however, are rarely so simple, even though public support for voting methods reform has remained reasonably stable (Crigler, Just, and Buhr, this volume). Indeed, congressional reaction to voting methods reform proposals provides an object lesson on the political obstacles and opportunities facing popular election reforms. The main political obstacles are twofold.

First, because neither side wants to be seen as the enemy of popular reforms, each side will fight bitterly to set the terms of the debate, even if such conflict robs reform of political momentum. For example, in late January 2001, House Speaker Dennis Hastert (R-IL) announced the creation of a bipartisan panel to study reform alternatives. House Democrats almost immediately rejected the Republican proposal because it required a one-vote GOP majority on the panel. The spokesperson for Minority Leader Richard Gephardt, Laura Nichols, explained: "This can't be truly bipartisan unless you have an even split on the committee." John Feehery, the spokesperson for Speaker Hastert, rejoined: "We [the GOP] have a majority of the House; we will have a majority on this committee" (Eilperin 2001). Within two weeks, the initiative died, and Democrats created a Special Committee on Election Reform, chaired by Representative Maxine Waters (D-CA). It should be added that the choice of Representative Waters was hardly an olive branch to House Republicans or the Bush administration; she was one of a handful of Democrats who walked out in protest during the official reading of the Electoral College votes in Congress.

Second, popular reforms create strong incentives for ideological extremes of the parties—especially the minority party—to push politically unviable proposals, which allow them to claim credit for taking the lead on reform, while blaming others for failing to take action. Consistent with this expectation, when the Democrats were in the minority of both the House and Senate, the most substantively ambitious measures tended to be the most liberal, as measured by the Americans for Democratic Action (ADA) scores of their sponsors. More specifically, as of April 18, 2001, several broad searches on the Library of Congress' Thomas database revealed eight voting methods reform bills that called for direct substantive changes. Democrats sponsored each bill. Four received a substantial number of cosponsors: H.R. 1170 John Conyers's (D-MI) bill (eighty-two cosponsors); H.R. 775, Steny Hoyer's (D-MD) bill (sixty-six cosponsors); and H.R. 1151 and 1482, newly elected James Langevin's (D-RI) bills (twelve and seven cosponsors, respectively). The median 1998 ADA scores for the sponsors of these bills—95, 97.5, 97.5, and 100 out of a possible 100, respectively—suggest they are far to the left of even the most moderate Republicans.

The political news for popular reforms, however, is not all bad. Although such reforms create strong incentives for partisan gamesmanship, they also attract the attention of political entrepreneurs who seek to champion high-profile issues that lay the foundation for future runs at higher office. These entrepreneurs tend to push politically viable reforms, which either gain momentum on their own or trigger others to act. In early May 2001, for instance, Senator John McCain (R-AZ) who seems determined to build on his impressive showing in the 2000 GOP presidential primary, publicly indicated his intention to push a voting methods reform bill out of the Senate Commerce Committee. The Committee quickly held hearings (Mitchell 2001). Faced with the prospect of Senator McCain's garnering credit for campaign finance reform *and* election reform, Democratic and Republican senators, such as Senators Charles Schumer (D-NY) and Robert Torricelli (D-NJ) as well as Republican Senators Mitch McConnell (R-KY) and Sam Brownback (R-KS), joined forces and proposed a series of compromise measures aimed at gaining broad bipartisan support (Seelyee 2001c).

After months of posturing and maneuvering, members of Congress collectively blinked. Instead of risking a public backlash for taking no action, the House and Senate each passed bipartisan reform packages. On the anniversary of the Supreme Court's decision that decided the election, the House—in a 362-63 vote—passed a bill that would provide $2.65 billion over three years to states to upgrade voting equipment, improve voter registration lists, train and recruit election day volunteers, and enhance access to voting places for the disabled. In addition, it would provide a one-time grant of $400 million to states for replacing punchcard ballots. In April 2002, the Senate—in a 99-1 vote—passed a similar bill, which would provide about $3.5 billion to states for improving voting technology and voter registration lists as well as require new voting procedures, such as allowing voters to cast provisional ballots if their names did not appear on the rolls on election day.

Not surprisingly, hammering out the final details in Conference Committee produced another round of partisan squabbling. Nevertheless, Congress managed to pass a compromise measure titled the Help America Vote Act of 2002, which President George Bush signed into law on October 29, 2002. The Act provides $3.86 billion for election system upgrades, including $650 million for replacing antiquated punchcard and lever voting machines. It also creates a new Election Administration Commission and calls for a host of changes to voting procedures, such as imposing some voter identification requirements, mandating provisional voting by 2004 and statewide voter databases by 2006, and requiring better access to the polls for the disabled and voters with limited English proficiency. (Public Law No. 107-252; Walsh 2002; "Election Reform Since November 2001: What's Changed, What Hasn't, and Why" 2002).

The View from Participatory and Madisonian Democracy

From the perspective of both participatory and Madisonian democracy, the final passage of voting methods reform is cause for some celebration. Under the logic of participatory democracy, the quality of democracy turns on the quality of elections. Accordingly, clear ballots and reliable voting technology is a necessary condition for a healthy democracy. Advocates of Madisonian democracy would agree that American voting technology needs to be upgraded, but for different reasons. Under the logic of Madisonian democracy, citizens must have the *opportunity* to vote in regular elections as a means to remove tyrannical minority factions. Thus, if citizens take the initiative to vote, their ballots should be reasonably clear and their votes should be accurately recorded. Equally important, voting methods reform does nothing to threaten the complex system of checks and balances that reins in the threat of tyranny of the majority.

ELECTORAL COLLEGE REFORM: PARTICIPATORY AND MADISONIAN DEMOCRACY AT LOGGERHEADS

Background

In addition to revealing outdated voting technology, the 2000 presidential election provided Americans with a primer on the quirks of the Electoral College. To elaborate briefly, Americans do not directly elect their president; they choose "electors" who later assemble to select the president. The Constitution leaves states considerable discretion in determining how electors are selected, and most states (as of the 2000 election) choose electors by popular vote in winner-take-all elections. Under this system, by narrowly winning enough states, a candidate can win the election while losing the overall popular vote. As a result, a relatively small number of votes in one state can outweigh thousands of votes cast in all states, which plainly violates the ideals of majority rule and one person, one vote (see Gelman, Katz, and King, this volume). That, of course, is what happened in the 2000 presidential election. According to the final official tally, slightly more than five hundred votes cast for Governor George Bush in Florida trumped over five-hundred thousand votes cast for Vice President Al Gore nationally (see Jost and Giroux 2000, for an accessible overview of the Electoral College controversy).

Predictably, the 2000 presidential election renewed calls to abolish—or substantially modify—the Electoral College. To this end, several pending resolutions proposed (1) replacing the Electoral College with a national, popular election or (2) substantially modifying the Electoral College by allocating states' electoral vote proportionally according to popular vote or victories in congressional districts (see e.g., H.J. Res. 3, 5, 25, calling for the abolition of the Electoral College; H.J. Res. 17, calling for the allocation of Electoral College votes by proportion of statewide popular vote; H.J. Res. 1, 18, 37, calling for the allocation of Electoral College votes by winner of popular vote in congressional districts).

Equally predictably, Electoral College reform faced formidable opposition in Congress and quickly died. Most notably, Senate Majority Leader Tom Daschle (D-SD) indicated his opposition to any reform that hurt small states, such as his home state of South Dakota. In addition, Senator Orrin Hatch

(R-UT), the ranking minority member on the Judiciary Committee, which would have jurisdiction over any Constitutional amendment to the Electoral College, has stated: "I'll die before I'll let that constitutional amendment pass" (Wolf and Harrie 2000).

Senator Hatch seems safe for the foreseeable future. Prior to the current session, an estimated 1,028 federal proposals to reform the Electoral College have been introduced in Congress. Almost all have failed. (Of course, Congress did pass—and the states ratified—the Twelfth Amendment, which amended the Electoral College in 1804 to avoid having a president and vice president from different parties.)[3] Indeed, it is instructive that the most sweeping reforms of presidential elections in recent memory—the post-1968 Democratic convention reforms of presidential primaries—were not implemented through Congress at all. Instead, they resulted from changes in the Democratic Party that courts made binding on state parties (see Polsby 1983 for more on these reforms and their consequences).

The View from Participatory and Madisonian Democracy

Advocates of participatory and Madisonian democracy would sharply differ over the recent failure to enact Electoral College reform. From the perspective of participatory democracy, the Electoral College is an anachronism that violates the core principle of one person, one vote and threatens to produce countermajoritarian results in close elections. As a result, it should have been abolished, and its survival following the 2000 presidential election is a real—although not wholly unexpected—disappointment (but see Gelman, Katz, and King, this volume, suggesting that such beliefs may be overstated).

Advocates of Madisonian democracy would disagree, arguing that the Electoral College was never intended as a majoritarian institution and has evolved into an integral part of the American system of checks and balances (see generally Polsby and Wildavsky 2000). From this perspective, the Electoral College remains worthwhile and should not be substantially reformed. The argument is somewhat complex, and, perhaps for that reason, often receives short shrift in the public debate. To summarize, advocates of Madisonian democracy oppose Electoral College reform because the Electoral College promises to ensure that the president and Congress have different political constituencies. As a result, it arguably contributes to preserving structural tension among the elected branches of government, which is central to the Framers' strategy for curbing tyranny of the majority and forcing mutual accommodation among diverse interests. To illustrate this argument, it is useful to compare the strategic incentives under the current system versus a popular presidential election (with a 40 percent runoff provision), the most politically viable federal Electoral College reform in recent history.

The Current System

As noted earlier, the current Electoral College features two main rules: (1) Under the Constitution, votes are apportioned to each state according to their total number of House and Senate seats; and (2) under state law, most states award electors on a winner-take-all basis. Clearly, the least populous states benefit from the apportionment rules because votes in small states carry greater weight. For example, the ratio of citizens to electoral votes in Wyoming is about 206,500 to 1; in Texas, that ratio is about 626,400 to 1. Based on these ratios, presidential votes in Wyoming have more than three times the weight of votes in Texas.

What is often missed, however, is that winner-take-all rules greatly benefit the most populous states (Polsby and Wildavsky 2000; Gelman, Katz, and King, this volume). Consider California. Winning California by one vote in the 2004 election will garner fifty-five electoral votes, which is more than the total amount for winning fifteen small races.[4] This fact alone encourages presidential candidates—whether Democratic or Republican—to appeal to voters in large, urban states. It should be added these states often have well-organized minorities, meaning that candidates should avoid alienating such interests (Polsby and Wildavsky 2000), which arguably accounts for President Bush's emphasis on "compassionate conservatism" during the 2000 campaign.

Another factor encourages presidential hopefuls to concentrate on large, urban states under the current system: Many smaller states are frequently "safe" for presidential candidates from the leading political parties. For example, in recent presidential elections, Massachusetts and Connecticut have strongly favored Democrats in presidential elections, whereas Utah and Alabama have reliably voted Republican. Obviously, it makes little sense for presidential candidates to run up popular vote margins in these states under the Electoral College; a simple majority captures all the state's Electoral College votes and a majority is nearly certain. By contrast, competitive, more populous states, such as Florida, Ohio, and Michigan, become key battlegrounds under the current system because a narrow victory in these states delivers a payload of Electoral College votes.

To make matters more concrete, consider the key strategic states for the Democrats and Republicans in the last presidential election, as measured by the states' total number of Electoral College votes. As seen in Table 8.1, the top six Electoral College states for Vice President Al Gore and Senator Joseph

TABLE 8.1 Comparison of Each Political Party's Top Six States in the 2000 Election, by Electoral Votes

Key Democratic States during the 2000 Election under the Electoral College	Key Republican States during the 2000 Election under the Electoral College
California (54)	Texas (32)
New York (33)	Florida (25)
Pennsylvania (23)	Ohio (21)
Illinois (22)	North Carolina (14)
Michigan (18)	Georgia (13)
New Jersey (15)	Virginia (13)

Lieberman were large to medium-sized states in the West, Northeast, and Midwest region: California (54 votes); New York (33 votes); Pennsylvania (23 votes); Illinois (22 votes); Michigan (18 votes); and New Jersey (15). For Governor George W. Bush and Dick Cheney, the key Electoral College states in 2000 were large to medium-sized states in the South and one Midwest state: Texas (32 votes); Florida (25 votes); Ohio (21 votes); North Carolina (14 votes); Georgia (13 votes); and Virginia (13 votes).

Direct Elections

Putting aside, for the moment, the effects of a runoff provision, how would a direct popular vote change the incentives of presidential candidates in building winning coalitions? In general, candidates would be expected to target states that produce the largest popular vote margin (as opposed to the largest electoral vote payoff) (Polsby and Wildavsky 2000). As a result, little incentive would exist to target highly competitive states, such as Florida, Michigan, and Ohio, because such states tend to split the popular vote. Vice President Al Gore would have had strong incentives to spend additional time turning out the vote in California, New York, and the larger New England states, such as Massachusetts, whereas President Bush would have had reason to focus on his home state of Texas and on the relatively large number of small and medium-sized Western and Southern Republican states.

To illustrate this point, compare the strategic importance of various states for each party in a popular vote, as indicated by the states' total popular vote margin in the 2000 presidential election. As seen in Table 8.2, "safe" states for Democratic and Republican nominees would benefit under a direct popular vote system as expected; however, the effect would be more dramatic on the Republican side. Specifically, for the Democratic ticket in 2000, these data suggest that three of the top four states would remain the same under either system: California, New York, and Illinois. New Jersey would move up a notch to fifth place, while Massachusetts and Maryland would move up into the top six, replacing Pennsylvania (which drops from third to ninth place) and Michigan (which drops from fifth to eighth place). In sum, these data suggest the

TABLE 8.2 Comparison of Each Political Party's Top Six States in the 2000 Election, by Popular Vote Margin

Key Democratic States during the 2000 Election Based on Popular Vote Margin (in 1,000s) (Electoral College Rank)	Key Republican States during the 2000 Election Based on Popular Vote Margin (in 1,000s) (Electoral College Rank)
New York (1,704) (2)	Texas (1,366) (1)
California (1,294) (1)	North Carolina (373) (4)
Massachusetts (738) (7)	Indiana (738) (6)
Illinois (570) (4)	Utah (312) (20)
New Jersey (505) (6)	Georgia (304) (5)
Maryland (333) (11)	Oklahoma (270) (16)

target states for Democratic presidential candidates would remain a mix of populous Western, Midwestern, and Northeastern states with added emphasis on medium-sized, Democratic bastions, such as Massachusetts and Maryland.

On the Republican side, these data suggest that President Bush's home state of Texas would retain its top strategic spot under a direct popular vote. However, the other strategically important, populous states for the Republicans under the Electoral College—Florida and Ohio—would drop precipitously. Florida would fall from second to last place; Ohio would drop from third to fifteenth place. By contrast, North Carolina—a medium-sized, Southern state— moves from fourth to second place. The real beneficiaries from abolishing the Electoral College, however, would be several small and medium-sized Republican states. For instance, Utah's strategic rank rises from twentieth under the Electoral College to fourth under a popular vote system, and Oklahoma moves from sixteenth to sixth place. In sum, these data imply that medium-sized one-party states would dominate GOP presidential coalitions.

Admittedly, popular vote totals under the current system are imperfect proxies for the counterfactual results under popular presidential election. If the 2000 presidential election were decided by popular vote, candidates presumably would campaign differently, resulting in different vote totals in each state. Nevertheless, these totals are indicative of where large popular vote margins are likely to emerge and hence which states would be attractive *strategic* targets for presidential candidates under a popular vote system. Moreover, even if one wholly rejects these numbers as illustrative of popular vote totals, the general point remains: Moving from the current system to direct presidential elections would change the strategic incentives of presidential candidates and encourage them to maximize their voting margins in "safe" states.

The bottom line? As a political matter, where one sits on abolishing the Electoral College depends on where one stands on states like Utah and Massachusetts gaining importance in their respective parties' presidential coalitions. From the perspective of Madisonian democracy, however, the increased importance of such states in the presidential coalition would be troubling, because small, one-party states have traditionally been overrepresented in Congress because of the apportionment rules as well as the norm of seniority promotions (which has weakened recently but remains important in awarding committee chairs). As a result, abolishing the Electoral College risks a step toward aligning the political bases of the executive and legislative branches. Such alignment, in turn, would reduce the political tension among the branches of government, which is crucial to maintaining the ideal of diversely representative policymaking forums that force coalition-building among varied interests.

What about Runoff Provisions?

To prevent the possibility of a candidate gaining the Oval Office with only a small percentage of the popular vote, proposals for direct presidential elections usually require a runoff if no candidate receives more than 40 percent of the total vote. Such a rule obviously gives well-organized groups an incentive to contest the first election (Polsby and Wildavsky 2000). Why? As in continental

European systems, forcing a runoff would enable groups to gain concessions from the leading parties in exchange for forming a majority. If successful, such strategies would undermine the simplicity and majoritarian appeal of a popular vote system. More important from the Madisonian perspective, such factionalism undermines a hidden benefit of the Electoral College: Namely, state-by-state, winner-take-all races reward coalition-building among factions and punish splinter groups, such as the Green Party, who fail to join forces with the leading parties.

Other Electoral College Reform Strategies at a Glance

Much more could be—and has been—said about the relative merits of the Electoral College and other commonly proposed modifications: Allocating states' Electoral College votes proportionally by statewide popular vote or by winners of congressional districts (Polsby and Wildavsky 2000; Gelman, Katz, and King, this volume). Suffice to say that allocating electoral votes proportionally by statewide popular vote raises many of the same issues as moving to a direct popular vote system; however, its anticipated effect on larger states is more dramatic because they are already underrepresented under the Constitution's allocation rules. Allocating electoral votes by winners in each states' congressional districts, which is gaining favor in some states, seems the worst of all worlds: It retains winner-take-all rules (and thus fails to eliminate the possibility of countermajoritarian election results), it provides no guarantees against deadlock (e.g., George Wallace would have done even better under this system), and it exaggerates the importance of one-party states in presidential coalitions.

VOTING CHOICE REFORM: AN INTRIGUING FUTURE OPTION

Background

In addition to revealing unreliable voting technology and quirks of the Electoral College, the 2000 presidential election highlighted a third limitation in the presidential election process: We only count voters' first choices. As a result, election results in close races may leave many important questions about voters' preferences unanswered.

Consider again the Florida vote in the presidential election. According to the official count, Bush received 2,912,790 first place votes (or 49 percent of the total vote); Gore received 2,912,253 votes (or 49 percent of the total vote); and Green Party candidate Ralph Nader received 97,488 votes (or about 2 percent of the total vote). The rest of the field accounted for about 40,500 votes, representing about 0.007 percent of the total vote.

From the perspective of majority rule, these results raise a number of questions. For example, did a majority of Florida voters prefer Al Gore to George Bush? Or did a razor thin plurality of Floridians favor Bush? The answer is unclear based on first place votes, even if the numbers are 100 percent accurate,

TABLE 8.3   The Vote-Splitting Scenario

Voter	Green Party Voters (2%)	Democratic Party Voters (49%)	Republican Party Voters (49%)
Acceptable candidates (by rank)	Nader, Gore	Gore	Bush
Unacceptable candidates	Bush	Nader, Bush	Gore, Nader

because the official tally is consistent with a range of normatively distinct voter preferences. One possibility is that Ralph Nader split the Democratic vote, as shown in Table 8.3. In this case, Al Gore would be the only candidate acceptable to a majority (51 percent) of voters. As a result, from the perspective of majority rule, Al Gore should have won.

Another scenario is that votes for Ralph Nader represented a protest *against* the established parties, as shown in Table 8.4. Unlike the vote-splitting scenario, *none* of the candidates is acceptable to a majority in the protest vote scenario. Thus, Gore would have no special majoritarian claim to the Florida election, and then Bush, as the winner of a slim plurality of votes in the official tally, should have won. Moreover, knowing that no candidate received a clear majority of votes in Florida may have rendered the Supreme Court's role as the final arbiter of the election more broadly acceptable.

These scenarios, of course, do not exhaust the possibilities, but that is the point. In close elections, counting first place votes more does not distinguish among very different structures of voter preferences. We will never know if a clear majority of Floridians found Gore acceptable (and Bush unacceptable), or whether no majority found a single candidate acceptable. In principle, choice method reform that establishes a system of approval voting, which allows voters to vote for all acceptable candidates, would more accurately reflect voter preferences, but better technology in a "first choice only" system cannot (see Brams and Fisherman 1978 for more on approval voting).

A View from Participatory and Madisonian Democracy

Regardless of its merits, choice method reform was almost entirely ignored in the aftermath of the 2000 presidential election. That is not too surprising as a political matter. Choice method reform would represent a dramatic change in the way Americans vote, and, as such, it would face steep political challenges

TABLE 8.4   The Protest Vote Scenario

Voter	Green Party Voters (2%)	Democratic Voters (49%)	Republican Voters (49%)
Acceptable candidates (by rank)	Nader	Gore	Bush
Unacceptable candidates	Bush, Gore	Bush, Nader	Gore, Nader

in a fragmented policy process that favors incremental reform. At the same time, choice method reform represents an intriguing possibility for future consideration. Why? It promises to build on participatory and Madisonian democracy's shared commitment to improving the accuracy of elections in close races without affecting the Electoral College, which is almost sure to remain protected by a coalition of states including small states and the hotly contested battleground states, such as Florida, Michigan, and Ohio.

More specifically, from the perspective of participatory democracy, choice method reform could increase the voice of voters in the process, allowing them to convey more information through their votes. In addition, although it clearly does not eliminate the paradox of participatory democracy—which holds that the goals of expanding the vote and improving voter deliberation are at odds (see Ortiz, this volume)—choice method reform may lessen this tension in an age of significant third-party presidential candidates because it may be easier for voters to identify acceptable candidates as opposed to choosing a single candidate.

Advocates of Madisonian democracy should also approve choice method reform. Such reforms would provide more information about majority preferences in elections, which is central to curbing minority tyranny. At the same time, unlike Electoral College reform, choice method reform does nothing to affect the underlying system of checks and balances, which provides the main bulwark against majority tyranny. Of course, the fact that choice method reform may build on common ground between participatory and Madisonian democracy does not guarantee passage—or even consideration—on Capitol Hill, but it may provide a basis for coalition-building among groups with diverse viewpoints, which is one ingredient for potential success in Washington.

CONCLUSION

Looking back, the 2000 presidential election did not produce bold congressional action, as many had hoped. Instead, promises of vigorous action predictably gave way to partisan politics and the passage of compromise measures. From the perspective of participatory democracy, Congress' muted response to the 2000 presidential election represents a squandered opportunity to enhance dramatically the equality of the federal election process and hence the quality of American democracy. From the perspective of Madisonian democracy, by contrast, Congress' focus on improving the nuts and bolts of the states' voting infrastructures was an appropriate and measured reaction to the drama of the 2000 presidential election. If passed and properly implemented, targeted voting method reforms should eventually enhance the accuracy of counting votes without threatening our system of checks and balances, the cornerstone of American democracy.

Looking forward, perhaps the greatest legacy of the 2000 presidential election will have been meaningful debate over the goals and nature of American democracy. This debate has revealed two competing views of democracy that are not dusty academic concepts; they have real policy implications that may be instructive to future reform efforts. Specifically, taking participatory and Madisonian democracy seriously has suggested that future reform efforts should entertain proposals, such as choice method reform, which build on a shared commitment to improving the accuracy of election results in close races without changing the Electoral College. In so doing, reformers may be better prepared to overcome the inevitable political resistance to changing an incumbent-friendly system and to enhance American democracy the next time extraordinary events force us to take a hard look in the mirror.

NOTES

1. Of course, these are not the only reform strategies considered following the 2000 presidential election. Approaches other than voting methods reform, Electoral College reform, and choice method reform include the following: voter participation reform (which seeks to improve access to the voter); campaign coverage reform (which aims to eliminate premature and/or mistaken election night forecasts); campaign finance reform (which primarily seeks to ban so-called soft money contributions, i.e., unregulated contributions to political parties); and several miscellaneous measures, such as Senator Lieberman (D-CT) and Representative Eleanor Norton's (D-D.C.) efforts to provide full voting rights for citizens of the District of Columbia. Given this volume's focus on federal election processes—as opposed to funding campaigns, voter participation, or campaign media coverage—I focus on voting methods reform, Electoral College reform, and choice method reform. It is hoped that what is lost in breadth will be somewhat offset by analyzing a few strategies in some depth.
2. The next closest county total for Buchanan was about 1,000, in Pinellas County, Florida. See "Buchanan Votes in Florida, County by County" 2001; see also Brady 2002, 7, concluding that his models suggest "with a very high degree of scientific certainty that essentially none (at most perhaps a handful) of the Bush supporters mistakenly supported Buchanan while at least 2000 Gore supporters mistakenly supported Buchanan."
3. There has been greater success in changing the Electoral College at the state level. In the nineteenth century, the states responded to pressure to democratize the presidential election process and adopted the current system in which electors are selected by popular vote within the states (and almost always on a winner-take-all basis). In the aftermath of the 2000 presidential election, some states are already moving to adopt the Maine and Nebraska model, which allocates electoral votes district-by-district and awards the popular vote winner in the states an additional two votes.
4. E.g., Alaska (3), Delaware (3), District of Columbia (3), Montana (3), North Dakota (3), South Dakota (3), Vermont (3), Wyoming (3), Hawaii (4), Idaho (4), Maine (4), Nebraska (4), New Hampshire (4), Nevada (5), and New Mexico (5).

9

Do Institutions Matter?

The Consequences of Electoral Reform for Political Participation

PIPPA NORRIS

Worldwide parliamentary elections in the 1990s revealed stark contrasts in the percentage of citizens who cast their vote. Turnout in established democracies ranged from over 80 percent in Iceland, Greece, Italy, Belgium, and Israel to fewer than one-half the eligible voters in the United States. Indeed, turnout in the United States continues to fall well below the level common in nearly all other affluent postindustrial societies. Policymakers seeking to improve turnout in the United States have often been attracted to institutional reforms, ranging from initiatives such as "motor voter" registration laws to liberalization of postal voting (see Traugott, this volume).

The core question addressed by this chapter is whether institutional reforms can overcome barriers to electoral turnout in the United States, and in particular whether there is evidence from other countries that institutional changes, legal rules, and voting facilities have a systematic impact on voting participation.[1]

Political institutions refer to variables such as party competition, type of electoral system, and level of the contest; *legal rules* determine who is eligible to cast a ballot; and *voting facilities* include such technological factors as proxy or postal ballots, or the ease with which those eligible can in fact register and vote. This chapter analyzes the impact of all these arrangements on turnout. The first part outlines a motivational theory of voting, which assumes that citizens are motivated by the rational tradeoff between the cost of voting, electoral choices, and decisiveness of the vote, and then summarizes the results of previous literature of voting. Subsequent parts examine the impact of institutions, rules, and facilities on turnout, measured by the ratios of vote/voting age population (VAP) in 405 national (parliamentary and presidential) elections held during the 1990s worldwide.[2] The results demonstrate that political institutions do matter. In particular, voting participation is likely to be maximized in elections using proportional representation, with small electoral districts, regular but relatively infrequent national contests, and competitive party systems, and in chief executive contests. Legal rules also play a role. In contrast, voting facilities are relatively unimportant for turnout. The conclusion summarizes the main findings and considers their implications for the process and prospects of electoral reform in the United States.

FACTORS IN THE VOTE DECISION

Why would institutions be expected to affect turnout? The motivational theory of voting developed in this chapter suggests that the structural context shapes voters' incentives to participate by influencing electoral costs, electoral choices, and decisiveness of the vote.

Electoral Costs

Electoral costs concern the time, energies, and informational demands required to register and cast a ballot. The difficulties of voting can be reduced by making arrangements for voters with special needs. Mail, proxy, and absentee ballots; mobile polling facilities for voters who cannot travel; and elections held on holidays or weekends are some ways in which voting can be made more accessible. Registration procedures can be an important hurdle to voting. In many countries, registration is the government's responsibility, conducted via a door-to-door canvas or annual census, so that most eligible citizens are automatically enrolled to vote. In others, such as the United States, France, and Brazil, citizens have to apply to register to vote, often well ahead of the election, and complicated, time-consuming, or restrictive practices can depress participation levels (Katz 1997). In general, the greater the cost of voting, the lower electoral participation.

Electoral Choices

Electoral choices are determined by the options available on the ballot, notably the range of parties and candidates and the policy choices listed for referenda issues. Elections can be classified as competitive, semicompetitive, and controlled contests (see Rose 2000b). The ability of organized opposition parties to contest elections is limited under many authoritarian regimes, where parliamentary assemblies function primarily to legitimize the government. In semicompetitive elections there is a genuine contest for power between major parties but certain opposition groups are legally banned. In contrast, competitive democratic elections let voters choose among two or more parties. In Israel, for example, the May 1999 elections to the 120-member Knesset returned seventeen parties, and no single party won more than 14 percent of the popular vote. As a rule, the greater the range of choices available on the ballot, the more various segments of the public will find a party, candidate, or referendum option that reflects their viewpoint, and therefore the stronger will be their incentive to vote.

Electoral Decisiveness

Yet there may well be a trade-off between electoral choices and electoral *decisiveness*. A voter may perceive a political benefit from casting a vote that is likely to determine the composition of government and its public policy agenda or the outcome of referenda issues. Decisiveness (see Gelman, Katz, and King, this volume, describing voting impact) is enhanced when elections are anticipated to be close. Voters are likely to feel far greater incentive to get to the polls in close elections than in those where the outcome appears to be a foregone conclusion. For example, British election studies of the postwar era have found that the closer the difference in the national share of the vote between the major parties, the greater the level of electoral participation (see Heath and Taylor 1999).

The incentives motivating electors to cast a ballot represent a product of electoral costs (in registering and voting), electoral *choices* (how many parties are listed on the ballot), electoral *decisiveness* (to what extent votes cast for each party determine the outcome for parliament and government), and perceptions of competitiveness of the election. If voters face restricted options, so that they cannot choose a party that reflects their views, they are less likely to participate. And if casting a ballot expresses support for a party, candidate, or cause, but makes little difference to the composition of government, the marginal value of the vote is reduced, along with incentives for voting.

Although political institutions are often regarded as largely stable phenomena and therefore unable to account for fluctuations in levels of turnout, the way that institutions operate may change significantly over time. Institutional reforms that may affect turnout include expanding the franchise to women and younger voters; abandoning restrictive practices such as poll taxes, property qualifications, and literacy requirements; changing the laws concerning compulsory voting; increasing the frequency of elections; the use of referendums; and changing patterns of party competition, for example, the rise of the Greens and the collapse of some Communist parties in Europe. Case studies within particular countries can provide important insights into the impact of these developments. Major Constitutional reforms during the 1990s provide "before" and "after" experiments monitoring the impact of institutional changes on levels of electoral turnout (Karp and Banducci 1999).

What remains unclear from previous studies is the relative importance that citizens give to electoral costs, electoral choices, and electoral decisiveness in weighing the decision to participate. It may be, for example, that elections can be very costly (for example, if there are several complex referenda issues on the ballot that create high information hurdles), but citizens may nevertheless participate if they expect their votes to be decisive (such as in close contests or those that are important to voters' interests). Moreover, the link between the broader institutional context and how voters perceive and weigh the costs, choices, and decisiveness of elections is poorly understood. Individuals' motivation can also be influenced by many other factors, such as mobilization efforts by particular groups; political attitudes, including a sense of political efficacy; trust in government; civic duty and interest in current affairs; and voters' education and income (Norris 2002). Nevertheless, the institutional context can be expected to play an important role in structuring voters' choices, and we can test the evidence for these claims.

INSTITUTIONAL MODELS EXPLAINING TURNOUT

To examine the impact of political institutions on turnout, we here report a series of predictive multivariate models that use ordinary least squares regression analysis. The dependent variable in each model is turnout, measured by the ratio of turnout to voting age population (vote/VAP) in 405 national, parliamentary, and presidential elections held during the 1990s in all the countries worldwide where there are consistent indicators.

Model A in Table 9.1 examines the impact of modernization without any institutional factors to explain vote as a proportion of voting age population. Model A includes levels of "human development" (using the United Nations Development Program (UNDP) human development index combining longevity, education, literacy, and per capita gross domestic product) and levels of "democratization" (gauged by the Freedom House Gastil Index of political rights and civil liberties). These two factors alone explain 18 percent of the variance in turnout.

Model B then adds two sets of factors: the main political institutions and the legal rules commonly thought to influence voter participation (for reasons discussed in detail later). The institutional factors include type of electoral system, size of electoral districts, frequency of national elections, whether the contest was presidential or parliamentary, and the type of party system. Model B also tests for the impact of legal rules determining the eligibility to vote, including the use of compulsory voting, the age at which citizens are eligible to vote, the length of time that women have been enfranchised, and the use of any literacy requirements. After including these structural factors, the overall level of variance explained by the model (shown by the R^2 statistics) rises from 18 percent to 29 percent. This suggests that the factors included in Model B improve the goodness-of-fit, although considerable variance remains to be explained. Let us consider these results in terms of each of the structural factors that can be expected to influence turnout.

Electoral Systems

The seminal work of Maurice Duverger (1954) and Douglas Rae (1971) classified the main types of electoral systems and sought to analyze their consequences (also Lijphart 1994). Systems vary according to a number of key dimensions, including district size, ballot structures, effective thresholds, malapportionment, assembly size, and the use of open or closed lists. The most important variations concern electoral formulas that determine how votes are counted to allocate seats. There are four main types: *majoritarian* formulas, plurality formulas;

TABLE 9.1 Explaining Turnout in National Elections, All Countries in the 1990s

	Model A Socioeconomic Development				Model B Development plus Institutions			
	b	s.e.	St. Beta	Sig.	b	s.e.	St. Beta	Sig.
Constant	45.67	(5.82)		***	76.77	(12.64)		***
Development								
Human development	0.03	(.01)	.31	***	0.02	(.01)	.19	**
Level of democratization	0.95	(.33)	.16	**	0.84	(.33)	.14	**
Political Institutions								
Electoral system					2.65	(1.02)	.13	**
Mean population per Member of Parliament					−.001	(.00)	−.09	*
Frequency of national elections					−3.47	(.56)	−.34	***
Predominant party system (1 = yes)					−3.98	(2.47)	−.08	
Fragmented party system (1 = yes)					−6.23	(3.76)	−.08	
Presidential (1) or Legislative (0) contests					4.54	(1.77)	.11	**
Legal Rules								
Age of voting eligibility					−.99	(.62)	−.07	
Length of women's enfranchisement					.19	(.052)	.19	***
Use of compulsory voting					1.96	(2.11)	.04	
Literacy requirements					−20.69	(6.17)	−.15	***
Number of elections	405				405			
Adjusted R²	.182	(16.7)			.294	(15.5)		

Notes: *Vote/VAP* is measured as the number of valid votes as a proportion of the voting age population in 405 parliamentary and presidential national elections held in 139 nations during the 1990s. The figures represent unstandardized regression coefficients (b), standard errors (s.e.), standardized beta coefficients (St. Beta), and significance (Sig.), with mean vote/VAP as the dependent variable. *p < .05; **p < .01; ***p < .001.

Human development: Human Development Index 1998 combining longevity, literacy, education and income. United Nations Development Program.

Level of democratization: Freedom House Index in the year of the election. Combined reversed fourteen-point scale of political rights and civic liberties. Freedom House. www.freedomhouse.org.

Electoral system: Coded as majoritarian/plurality (1), semiproportional (2), and proportional representation (3).

Party system: Predominant party systems are defined as those in which the party in first place gets 60 percent of the vote or more. Fragmented party system are those in which the party in first place gets 30 percent of the vote or less.

Compulsory voting: The following twenty-three nations were classified as currently using compulsory voting: Australia, Belgium, Costa Rica, Cyprus, Greece, Italy, Luxembourg, Argentina, Bolivia, Chile, Dominican Republic, Ecuador, Liechtenstein, Panama Canal Zone, Thailand, Uruguay, Brazil, Guatemala, Honduras, Peru, Venezuela, Singapore, and Egypt.

Source: Calculated from International Institute for Democracy and Electoral Assistance (IDEA) database *Voter Turnout since 1945*. www.idea.int.

semiproportional systems, and *proportional representation* (PR) (see Reynolds and Reilly 1997 for details of these electoral systems and definitions).

Previous studies have found that the type of electoral formula affects participation, with proportional representation systems generating higher voter participation than majoritarian or plurality elections (Blais and Dobrzynsky 1998; Jackman 1987; Jackman and Miller 1995; Ladner and Milner 1999; Powell 1986). This pattern seems supported by the evidence in established democracies, although the exact reasons for this relationship remain unclear (see Blais and Dobrzynska 1998). Motivational explanations focus on the differential incentives facing citizens under alternative electoral arrangements. Under majoritarian systems, such as first-past-the-post used for the House of Representatives in the United States Congress, Westminster, and states employing the unit rule for votes in the Electoral College, supporters of minor and fringe parties like the Greens—whose geographic support is dispersed widely but thinly across the country—may feel that casting their votes will make no difference to who wins in their constituency, still less to the overall composition of government and the policy agenda. The "wasted votes" argument is strongest in "safe seats," those where the incumbent party is unlikely to be defeated. In contrast, PR elections with low vote thresholds and large district magnitudes, such as the nationwide party list system used in the Netherlands, increase the opportunities for minor parties with dispersed support to enter parliament even with a relatively modest share of the vote, and therefore increase the incentives to participate. This proposition can be tested by classifying national elections around the world into three categories: PR, semi-PR, and plurality/majoritarian electoral systems (Reynolds and Reilly 1997). Table 9.1 shows that, even after controlling for levels of development, the basic type of electoral system is a significant indicator of turnout, with PR systems generating about 10 percent higher levels of voting participation than plurality/majoritarian systems.

Electoral Districts

District size, and in particular the population of the average electoral district, can be especially important, since this may determine the linkages between voters and their representatives. A relationship between the size of a country and the stability of democracy has long been suspected, although the reasons for this association remain unclear (see Dahl 1998). It is possible that the smaller the number of electors per member of government, the greater the potential for elected representatives to maintain communications with local constituents, and therefore the higher the incentive to turnout based on any "personal" vote (see Cain, Ferejohn, and Fiorina 1987, for a discussion about this in the context of Britain and the United States). Voters may not be able to shape the outcome for government, but in smaller single-member or multimember districts they may have greater information, familiarity, and contact with their elected representative or representatives, and therefore they may be more interested in affecting who gets elected (see e.g., Katz 1999 for a discussion of role orientations of MEPs and MPs in different electoral systems). Representatives of small homogeneous districts may also find it easier to support constituent interests while representatives of large diverse districts must balance many interests (see Madison 1788, Federalist No. 10).

The simplest way to measure the effect of district size on turnout is to divide the number of seats in the lower house of the legislature into the total population in each country. The results in Table 9.1 confirm that the size of electoral districts measured in this way was a significant negative predictor of turnout: Smaller districts were generally associated with higher voter participation.

Frequency of Contests

The frequency of elections has also been thought to be important for participation because it increases the costs facing electors and may produce voting fatigue. Franklin, van der Eijk, and Oppenshuis (1996) have demonstrated that the closer national elections were in time before direct elections to the European parliament, the lower the turnout in the European elections. The cases of Switzerland and the United States are commonly cited as exemplifying nations with frequent elections for office at multiple levels, as well as widespread use of referenda and initiatives; both are characterized by exceptionally low voter participation among Western democracies (Franklin 2001; Lijphart 2000). California, for example, has primary and general elections for local, county, and state government, including for judicial, mayoral, and gubernatorial offices; congressional midterm elections every two years for the House and Senate; presidential elections every four years; as well as multiple referenda issues on the ballot—all producing what Anthony King has called the "never-ending election campaign" (King 1997). If the frequency of elections generates voter fatigue, then the increase in primary contests in the United States after 1968, the introduction of direct elections to the European parliament in 1979, and contests for regional bodies following devolution and decentralization in countries like Spain, France, and the United Kingdom could help to explain their declines in turnout in recent decades. A simple measure of electoral frequency can be calculated by the number of national-level parliamentary and presidential elections held during the decade of the 1990s, ranging from only one contest in a few semidemocracies up to seven or more elections in the United States, Ecuador, and Taiwan. Although not definitive, the results in Table 9.1 confirm that the frequency of national elections was highly and negatively significant: the more often national elections are held, the greater voter fatigue. This result could provide important clues to some of the sharpest outliers in turnout, such as Switzerland and the United States, both some of the richest and most developed countries on earth, with highly educated populations and a substantial middle class, yet characterized by relatively low (and falling) levels of voter participation.

Party Systems and Electoral Competition

The type of party system and the levels of electoral competition are likely to be closely related to the basic type of electoral system, although the fit is not perfect. Ever since Duverger (1954) it has been well known that the plurality method of elections favors two-party systems by systematically overrepresenting the largest party when translating votes into seats. Lijphart's (1999) comparison of thirty-six established democracies demonstrates that as disproportionality rises, the effective number of parliamentary parties falls. Yet there are a number of important exceptions to this rule, with plural societies such as Papua New Guinea and India characterized by multiple parties in majoritarian electoral systems, as well as Malta and Austria with two-party and two-and-a-half party systems despite PR elections.

In addition to party system arrangements, the very closeness of the vote in a particular election may increase citizens' incentives to participate and parties' incentives to mobilize supporters to get them to the polls. Patterns of electoral competition can therefore be expected to influence voter turnout, but there is little agreement in the literature about the exact nature of this relationship, or how best to gauge competition. Some suggest that the greater the range of alternative parties listed on the ballot, from the nationalist far right to the post-Communist left, the more people are stimulated to vote (Colomer 1991). This claim assumes that wider electoral choices across the ideological spectrum mean that all social groups are more likely to find a party to represent their views, preferences, and interests. Yet the counterargument is also heard from those who suggest that the higher the level of party fragmentation, the higher the probability of coalition government, the less the share of votes cast determines the formation of government, and therefore the lower the inducement for electors to turn out (Blais and Carty 1990). As Jackman (1987) has argued, voters in multiparty systems that produce coalitions do not directly choose the government that will govern them; instead they vote for the parties that select the government that determines the policy agenda. Under multiparty coalitions voters appear to have a more decisive choice among policies, whereas in fact they have a less decisive one (Jackman 1987).

The most important proposition based on the motivational theory already discussed is that under conditions of free and fair elections, all other things being equal, we would expect to find a *curvilinear* relationship between the *effective number of electoral parties* and *levels of voting turnout*. More parties standing for office simultaneously increases electoral choice, but it also decreases electoral decisiveness (what Gelman, Katz, and King, this volume, refer to as voter impact). The share of the national vote for the strongest party in first place provides a simple and effective summary indicator of electoral competitiveness. In highly fragmented party systems, the strongest parliamentary party in each election commonly wins less than a third of the popular vote. In contrast, predominant one-party systems characteristically have the winning party with vote shares of 60 percent or more.

Table 9.1 confirms that both predominant one-party systems and fragmented multiparty systems are characterized by lower than average levels of turnout, although in the multivariate models the difference was only significant at the relatively weak .10 level. Turnout rises steadily with a more evenly balanced vote share, before dropping again in cases where the winning party received 30 percent or less of the vote, indicating a highly fragmented multi-party system and coalition government.

In contrast, participation is likely to be higher in elections with more competitive party systems. Two-party systems vying for power in unitary parliamentary government usually produce a decisive electoral outcome and regular rotation of government and opposition parties in power. Where two fairly evenly divided major parties compete for marginal seats, the "winners' bonus" or "manufactured majority" characteristic of majoritarian and plurality electoral systems means that a modest tremor in the popular vote can trigger a dramatic shift in parliamentary seats. In such systems, as in a finely balanced mechanism, even a small swing in electoral support may change the party that forms the government. Two-party systems usually offer voters clear and simple choices between two alternative sets of public policies, and this pattern of competition also forces parties to maintain their core base and to compete for the "swing" or median voter in the center ground.

Moderate multiparty systems, typified by Germany or Norway, are characterized by more than two and less than five or six parliamentary parties. This pattern of competition provides voters with a range of electoral choices. However, these systems also simultaneously decrease the decisiveness of the electoral result and the salience of casting a ballot because the outcome is more likely to produce coalition governments that rest on negotiations among parties rather than on the share of the vote and allocation of seats.

Presidential versus Parliamentary Executives

Another constitutional factor commonly believed to influence the motivational incentives to turnout concerns the power of the office and, in particular, whether there is a parliamentary or presidential system of government. *First-order elections* are the most important national contests, including legislative elections in countries with parliamentary systems of government and presidential contests in countries with strong presidencies. *Second-order* elections are all others, including state, provincial, or local contests; referenda and initiatives; and direct elections to the European parliament among the fifteen-member European Union (EU) states (Reif and Schmitt 1980). In a parliamentary system, the head of government—such as the prime minister, premier, or chancellor—is selected by the legislature and can be dismissed by a legislative vote of no confidence. In a presidential system the head of government is popularly elected for a fixed term and is not dependent on the legislature for tenure in office (see Lijphart 1992 for a fuller discussion of the nature of presidential systems). In countries with presidential systems of government where elections for the president and legislature are held on separate occasions, such as the midterm elections in the United States, more people are likely to participate in executive contests. Where presidential and legislative elections are held on the same date, there is likely to be no substantial difference in levels of turnout in both types of contest. The result of the analysis presented in Table 9.1 confirms that, overall, presidential elections produced significantly greater turnout than legislative contests.

THE IMPACT OF LEGAL RULES

Direct arrangements more closely related to legal eligibility include restrictions of the franchise based on age, gender, and literacy tests, along with the use of compulsory voting laws.

Eligibility for the Franchise

The minimum age at which people qualify to vote is important, since in most Western European countries for which we have survey data the young are consistently less likely to vote than older groups, and similar patterns are well established in the United States (Miller and Shanks 1996; Topf 1995; Traugott, this volume).

Ceteris paribus, we would find that the lower the ages at which citizens are eligible to vote, the lower the turnout. Blais and Dobrzynska (1998) confirmed that turnout is reduced by almost two points when the voting age is lowered by one year. Latin American states were the first to lower the age of the franchise from twenty-one to eighteen, beginning in the nineteenth century; it was only in the 1970s that the United States and Western European countries followed suit (Grotz 2000). This remains an important issue given that some countries are discussing lowering the age of suffrage. Yet the results of the analysis in Table 9.1 show that today the age of voting eligibility was not significantly related to turnout, probably because most countries have now standardized to within a relatively similar age bracket.

Restrictions on the franchise vary from one country to another, such as the disenfranchisement of felons, bankrupts, resident aliens, and groups like the mentally incapacitated (Blais, Massicotte, and Yoshinaka 2001; see also Katz 1997). Waves of immigration or increases in the prison population can have an important dampening effect on vote/VAP. In the United States the claim of steadily declining turnout since 1972 has been challenged as an artifact of an increase in the size of the voting age population by those ineligible to vote (see McDonald and Popkin 2000). One of the most important restrictions concerns the use of literacy requirements to qualify to vote, abolished in the United States in 1965, which served mainly to disenfranchise less educated and ethnic minority groups (for details see Katz 1997, Tables 13.1 and 13.2). Where these requirements were enforced, they would have depressed the number of eligible voters, and the abolition of these requirements should have served to boost vote/VAP. Table 9.1 confirms that turnout is significantly lower among the few countries that still employ this practice.

The enfranchisement of women has had a dramatic impact on electoral participation. Only four countries enfranchised women before the start of World War I. Women attained suffrage by the end of World War II in 83 nations, and in 171 nations in total by 1970. Women today continue to be barred from voting in Qatar, Saudi Arabia, Oman, and the United Arab Emirates (see Bartolini 2000; Rule 2000 for details). The first election after women's enfranchisement has usually seen a sudden drop in levels of vote/VAP, as women suddenly become eligible to vote, followed by a slow recovery in rates of turnout. In the

United States and Britain women were first enfranchised in the early 1920s, and the first election afterward saw an immediate sharp drop in overall turnout. Subsequent decades saw a slow and steady increase in levels of female turnout until the early 1980s, when women came to participate at similar, or even slightly higher, levels than men (Traugott, this volume). Similar patterns have been found elsewhere (Norris 2002). The residual effect of this pattern is found more widely; countries that enfranchised women prior to 1945 had average turnout (vote/VAP) of 69 percent in the 1990s, compared with 61 percent for countries that granted women the vote in the postwar era. In the multivariate model in Table 9.1 the difference proves to be strong and significant; countries that enfranchised women earlier tend to have higher turnout today than those that reformed in more recent decades. The enfranchisement of women brings groups into the electorate who have never acquired the habit of voting from an early age. Due to the process of generational turnover, as younger women gradually replace older women, this disparity gradually fades over time.

Compulsory Voting

Compulsory or mandatory voting laws would seem to have an obvious impact on turnout, although the strength of the effect depends upon how strictly such regulations and any associated sanctions are implemented and enforced (Hirczy 1994, 2000; Lijphart 1997). In practice, legal rules for voting may be de jure or de facto. The most common legal basis is statutory law, although the obligation to vote may also be rooted in constitutional provisions.[3]

Implementation ranges from minimal de facto enforcement to the imposition of various sanctions. Fines are most common, although other punishments include the denial of official documents such as passports, identity cards, driver's licenses, or government benefits and even occasionally the threat of imprisonment for a criminal offense. The effectiveness of any legal penalties depends on the efficiency of the prior registration process and, where the initiative falls on the elector, whether fines or other penalties are associated with failure to register. Where implementation is loosely enforced, the impact of any mandatory regulations has to operate largely through the impact of the law on social norms, similar to the effect of no-parking restrictions on city streets.

Mandatory voting regulations may be genuine attempts to increase public involvement in the political process, or they may be employed by less democratic regimes to compel the public to vote, hoping to legitimize one-party contests. Even in democratic states the use of legal regulations may have unintended consequences for participation, since they may reduce the incentive for parties to organize and mobilize their heartland supporters to get them to the polls (McAllister 1986).

Previous studies have found that compulsory voting is associated with higher turnout, but these have been limited mainly to established democracies, most of which are in Western Europe. Where these laws exist in established democracies, the registered electorate, the group most obviously subject to any sanctions, is far more likely to cast a ballot. Yet in all other types of political systems the result is very different, with vote/VAP actually slightly lower among newer democracies and semidemocracies with mandatory laws and far lower in Egypt and Singapore, the only two nondemocratic states with mandatory regulations and somewhat competitive elections. Table 9.1's comparison of the use of compulsory voting in all countries (not just older democracies) shows that this has no significant impact on voting turnout.

What explains this finding? First, the law may be enforced more strictly, and the registration processes may be more efficient in the older democracies, so that voters face stronger negative incentives to participate. Second, the impact of mandatory laws may depend primarily on broader social norms about obeying the law and those in authority, which may prove stronger in established democratic states in Western Europe than in many Latin American cultures. Third, it is possible that newer democracies characterized by low electoral turnout are more likely to introduce laws in the attempt to mobilize the public, but that without strict implementation these laws prove to be ineffective correctives. Fourth, the penalties facing voters vary in terms of the level of any fine (from three Swiss francs up to three thousand schillings in Austria), the possibility of imprisonment for failure to pay the fine, potential disenfranchisement (in Belgium and Singapore), and other sanctions (such as the difficulties Greek nonvoters face in getting a new driver's license or passport) (see Gratschew 2002). We cannot establish the relative importance of each of these reasons, but they may help to account for some of the striking differences in the impact of compulsory voting laws in different types of political systems, and they suggest the need for caution in generalizing from how these laws work in established democracies to other nations.

THE IMPACT OF VOTING FACILITIES

Turnout may also be affected by the administration of registration procedures and facilities for voting that alter the costs for certain groups. Absentee, advance, overseas, and postal ballots; proxy votes; mobile polling facilities for special populations such as the institutionalized elderly, infirm, or disabled; and polling scheduled for weekend or holidays rather than workdays increase the administrative burden of electoral regimes while lowering the costs for individual voters (Blais and Dobryzynska 1998; Crewe 1981; Franklin et al. 1996; Jackman 1987; Jackman and Miller 1995; Lijphart 1997; Powell 1986; Traugott, this volume).

Registration Processes

The facilities for registration and casting a ballot are commonly expected to affect turnout. Evidence that the registration process matters is most persuasive when comparing variation in regulations from state to state within the United States. Rosenstone and Wolfinger (1980) examined the difference in turnout between those states with the easiest registration requirements, for example, those that allow election day registration at polling places, and those with the strictest requirements. Their estimates suggest that if all American states had same-day registration, this would provide a one-time boost of turnout by about 5–9 percent (Fenster 1994; Wolfinger, Glass, and Squire 1990). Since their study in the 1970s, many states have experimented with easing the requirements through initiatives such as "motor voter" registration (where citizens can register to vote while getting their driver's licenses), although with limited effects on American voter participation (Knack 1995; Martinez and Hill 1999; see Traugott, this volume). Some states have also experimented with postal voting. The 1993 National Voter Registration Act requires all states to make voter registration available in Motor Vehicle bureaus and by mail, and it also forbids removing citizens from the rolls simply for not voting. Nevertheless, as Florida vividly illustrated in the 2000 presidential contest, the efficiency of the registration and voting procedure at state levels can leave much to be desired. Studies suggest that easing voter registration processes has slightly improved American voter turnout, with a one-time bump when new processes are introduced, but that the impact is not uniform across the whole electorate. It has had the most impact increasing participation among middle-class citizens (Brians and Grofman 1999; Karp and Banducci 2000; Knack and White 2000).

The comparative evidence is less well established. Studies have long assumed that voluntary registration procedures, in which citizens need to apply to be eligible to vote, are an important reason why American turnout lags well behind many comparable democracies (Wolfinger et al. 1990). In countries with application processes, prospective voters must usually identify themselves before an election, sometimes many weeks in advance, by registering with a government agency. In other countries the state takes the initiative in registering eligible citizens through an annual census or similar mechanism. But what is the impact of this process? Katz (1997) compared the electoral regulations in thirty-one nations and found that nineteen states used an automatic registration process, while twelve registered citizens by application. The analysis of electoral participation based on this classification of countries suggests that the registration hurdles may be less important than is often assumed, since average vote/VAP proved to be identical in both systems.[4] Contrary to the conventional wisdom, the use of automatic or voluntary registration procedures seems unrelated to levels of turnout within the universe of established democracies.

Polling Facilities

In terms of other voting facilities, most countries hold their elections on a single day, usually on the weekend, making it easier for employed people to vote. In some places, however, elections are spread over more than one day. India, for example, has more than six hundred million voters and some eight hundred thousand polling stations, so balloting takes place on a staggered basis during a month across the whole country. Different countries treat absentee, overseas, postal, and advance ballots; proxy voting; and polling station distribution differently.[5] Franklin (2002) compared average turnout in parliamentary elections in twenty-nine countries from 1960 to 1995 and found that compulsory voting, Sunday voting, and postal voting facilities all proved important predictors, along with the proportionality of the electoral system, but that the number of days that polls were open did not. A broader comparison of twenty-five older democracies where information about voting facilities is available found that only voting on a rest day provided a significant boost to turnout in established democracies; in contrast, the use of proxy voting (where the act of casting a ballot was delegated legally to someone else, such as a spouse, parent, or friend) and the number of days that the polling stations were open were negatively associated with voter turnout, perhaps because countries concerned about low turnout are the ones that try to increase the opportunities to get to the polls. Other special voting facilities all proved to be unrelated to turnout. Overall, a comparison of older democracies found that voting facilities explained far less variance in electoral participation than the role of institutions and legal rules.

Nevertheless, despite this pattern, other evidence from recent experimental pilot schemes suggests that lowering the barriers to participation may have a more positive effect than the cross-national comparison indicates. Pilot programs trying Internet remote e-voting include the Arizona Democratic primary election (Gibson 2002; Solop 2001) and local elections in Geneva (Auer and Trechsel 2001). One of the most innovative experiments was conducted by the British government when they introduced easier voting facilities in selected pilot wards during the May 2002 local elections. The pilots used a variety of methods, including casting a vote by post; by mobile phone text messaging; by the Internet at remote home/office sites, local libraries, and information kiosks; and by digital television, as well as extending the opening hours for polling stations and using early voting. The results remain under review by the Electoral Commission, but preliminary comparisons appear to show a dramatic increase in turnout in wards using all-postal ballots, almost doubling levels of participation in some places.[6] The evidence remains under review, as the changes could be the result of a "Hawthorn" effect, if voters and parties change their behavior in the light of the experiments, and some security concerns remain in certain wards. The difference between the cross-national evidence and the British results could also be due to the particular way in which postal voting is implemented, for example, the ease or difficulty of registering and voting by mail, and in particular whether postal votes are automatically issued to all electors or whether they are only available for certain restricted categories, such as the disabled or those living overseas. Nevertheless, innovative pilot schemes exemplified by those in Britain appear to be a promising way to evaluate the public's response to alternative voting facilities in the context of real elections, and more should be attempted to evaluate alternative proposals.

CONCLUSIONS

The primary incentives facing citizens in national elections may be understood as a product of the electoral *costs* of registering and voting, the party *choices* available to electors, and the *impact* of the vote on government composition. The costs include the time and effort required to register and to vote, any legal sanctions imposed for failure to turnout, and the frequency with which electors are expected to vote. Among affluent societies we expect turnout to be higher in political systems with lower voting costs, such as those with automatic processes for maintaining the electoral register and electoral arrangements that maximize party competition.

The main findings in this chapter can be summarized as follows:

- In multivariate models predicting turnout in national elections around the world during the 1990s, after controlling for levels of human and political development, *political institutions and legal rules were strongly and significantly associated with voter participation.*

- In the worldwide comparison, among the *political institutions* that matter, voting participation is likely to be maximized in elections that employ any of the following: proportional representation, small electoral districts, regular but relatively infrequent national contests, competitive party systems, and elections for the chief executive.

- In terms of the *legal rules*, the worldwide comparison showed that voter participation was lower in countries that had enfranchised women more recently and that employed literacy requirements, although the age of voting eligibility and the use of compulsory voting made no significant difference to turnout.

- When the comparison is limited to established democracies, the evidence shows that *the combination of political institutions and legal rules influence turnout more strongly than specific voting facilities*, such as registration processes, proxy voting, or advance voting, which all proved insignificant.

- In national elections held *in established democracies, the use of compulsory voting regulations was an important indicator of higher turnout, whereas this was not found in the broader comparison of elections worldwide.* Although it cannot be proven here, the reasons for this difference probably concern the efficiency of the implementation process of the registration system, sanctions for nonvoting, and cultural traditions concerning obeying the law.

The implications for the United States are that many of its basic institutional arrangements act to depress electoral participation. Voting participation is usually lower in countries using majoritarian first-past-the-post electoral systems, in districts with large electorates like the Senate and House, and in nations where there are frequent contests producing voter fatigue, all of which characterize the American political system. This suggests that some of its most important reforms—such as the introduction of party primaries—have had the opposite effect on turnout to that intended. In established democracies, the use of compulsory voting is an effective tool for boosting participation (see Hasen, this volume). The two-party system in America also limits voters' ability to express their preferences at the ballot box (see Barnes, this volume). Yet among all the reforms that are currently under debate, none of the basic institutional arrangements shown to make a difference are under serious consideration. Instead, most attention has focused on reforms to specific voting facilities that are unlikely to prove an effective remedy (see Traugott, this volume). The problem is *not* that postwar turnout has declined significantly in the United States, as many popular accounts falsely claim, but rather that postwar American turnout has *always* been lower than nearly all comparable postindustrial societies. This systemic pattern is unlikely to alter as a result of tinkering with modest reforms. At the same time, whether persistently low turnout should even be a cause for concern in America remains a matter worthy of serious debate.

NOTES

1. It should be noted that this chapter is drawn from a larger comparative project; see Norris 2002.
2. When comparable models in Table 9.1 were run with vote as a proportion of the registered electorate (vote/reg) as the dependent variable, no substantial differences were found to the results, suggesting that this is not simply a matter of the selected measure used for analysis.
3. I am most grateful for help received in identifying the countries that use compulsory voting from Gillian Evans, Lisa Hill, Marian Sawer, Ian McAllister, and Wolfgang Hirczy.
4. The mean vote/VAP in the 1990s was the same (72 percent) in the countries classified by Katz as using automatic and those using application registration procedures, and the mean vote/reg in the 1990s was slightly higher (78.1 percent) in countries with application procedures than in those with automatic processes (75.1 percent).
5. The best discussion of the administrative arrangements for registration and balloting found around the world can be found at www.ACE.org, developed by International IDEA and IFES. For further details, see Maley 2000. See also Blais and Louis Massicotte 2000.
6. For details see http://www.press.dtlr.gov.uk and http://www.electoralcommission.gov.uk/.

Part III

Should the Problems Be Fixed?

10

Cleavage and Consensus
The Public and Electoral Reform

ANN N. CRIGLER

MARION R. JUST

TAMI BUHR

ELECTION 2000 AND SUPPORT FOR ELECTION REFORM

While the minimalist and participatory debate about electoral reform has divided political elites, it is not clear that the public reflects these cleavages. Both sides in the debate appeal to basic values held by Americans. Minimalists, for example, argue that swift and clear election outcomes are essential for stable democracy. Participatory advocates maintain that the electorate should coincide as closely as possible with the citizenry to make democracy effective. But the arguments about the specific procedures and processes necessary to achieve these democratic goals can be technical or even obscure. It would be no surprise, therefore, if the public were not engaged by the discussion of electoral reform. The 2000 presidential election, however, changed the political landscape. As many observers agreed, the aftermath of the election gave Americans a vivid civics lesson (see, for example, Schwarz, 2000; Toedtman, 2000; Walker, 2000).

This chapter analyzes public opinion about the electoral process in light of the 2000 presidential campaign. We consider the minimalist and participatory values underlying the reform measures that do and do not garner public support as well as the hardy persistence of public support for election reform long after the 2000 campaign was decided (see McCaffery, Crigler, and Just, this volume; Barnes, this volume). We expect election minimalists to emphasize protection from electoral fraud and equal counting of votes and participatory advocates to emphasize not only equality of votes cast but also ensuring and expanding access to the vote. Given the ideologies of the Republican and Democratic parties, we hypothesize a greater affinity for minimalist attitudes toward voting among Republicans and participatory views among Democrats. The minimalist position coincides with the Republican emphasis on political stability over expressive politics. The participatory view coincides with Democrats' traditional base of support, claiming more egalitarian goals, including support for expanding the franchise to African Americans and language minorities. The partisan divide is also reflected, although imperfectly, in the conflict between federal and state responsibility with respect to electoral reform. Who should be responsible for restoring Americans' faith in their electoral processes?

The short and bumpy road from election day, November 7, 2000, to Al Gore's concession on December 13 illustrates the problem of coordinating federal and state, authority in presidential elections. Federal, state, and local election officials oversee different aspects of the election to the presidency. The relationship between the state standards and federal intervention highlights some of the constitutional and jurisdictional issues about elections that remain contested among government elites as well as members of the public. For example, eighteen months after the 2000 election, the Justice Department announced it would file suit against three Florida counties for alleged voting rights violations stemming from that race. The goal of the suit was to ensure that federal electoral laws are followed, and its implementation may require placing federal monitors at polling places (Lichtblau, 2002). The 2000 election also focused public attention on the disparities among states in voter registration, voter assistance, maintenance of election rolls, polling hours, recording votes, absentee ballots, as well as the counting and recounting of ballots (Traugott, this volume).

Until now, only a few electoral issues captured the public's attention—the Electoral College, election night media projections, and changes in voter registration procedures (such as "motor voter"). The more mundane, technical issues of balloting—such as ballot formats and types of voting machines—had not made it onto the public radar screen since the first decades of the twentieth century (see Alvarez, Sinclair, and Wilson, this volume; Norris, this volume), when voting machines were being adopted in cities all over the country (Zukerman 1927).

After the 2000 election, all of these issues were on the table—from the Electoral College to voting machines. Many Americans thought about what went wrong in 2000 and how elections should be carried out in the future. Weekly national surveys conducted from November 1999 to January 2001 showed that interest in the presidential campaign was 50 percent greater in the week after the election than at any time during the 2000 campaign (Vanishing Voter).[1] Many Americans registered surprise that numerous votes cast in the 2000 election did not count at all or counted for the wrong candidate (Fox News/Opinion Dynamics Poll November 29–30, 2000).[2] For some citizens, surprise turned to astonishment when they discovered that not counting votes was routine in U.S. elections. Opinion surveys conducted in the aftermath of 2000 revealed public concern about the fairness and democratic effectiveness of the country's electoral system. Public opinion coalesced on different sides of the federal/state divide over election jurisdiction. Public opinion surveys showed that citizens' opinions about how elections should be conducted were consistently related to minimalist or participatory orientations and partisanship.

Our analysis of public opinion is based on surveys during and following the 2000 election.[3] Surveys during the campaign highlight the public's response to many issues of electoral reform raised by the election process. Later surveys show just how much public support for electoral reform remained after President Bush was inaugurated. Did the public lose interest in reform once the outcome was settled, or is desire for electoral reform a stable set of opinions? Our focus is on public opinion about specific reforms and compares citizens' support for minimalist and participatory approaches to change. We find that egalitarian reforms are the most widely supported by the public. Notably, both minimalist and participatory advocates regard vote equality as an essential ingredient of the democratic process. In the deciding case of the 2000 election, *Bush v. Gore*, the Supreme Court insisted that the "right to vote is protected in more than the initial allocation of the franchise. Equal protection applies as well to the *manner* of its exercise." Furthermore, egalitarianism has long been the touchstone of American democracy. As de Tocqueville commented, "democratic peoples [such as the Americans] show a more ardent and more lasting love for equality than for freedom" (de Tocqueville, Mansfield and Winthrop, 2000).

SUPPORT FOR REFORM MEASURES

The vast majority of Americans believe that some kind of electoral reform should be undertaken. Several months after the 2000 presidential election had been decided, a national sample of Americans was asked, "How important to you personally is election reform in this country?" (ISA/Caltech Survey 2001). Fully 77 percent of adult respondents considered electoral reform important or very important. Although electoral reform is somewhat higher on the agenda of Democrats (86 percent) than Republicans, 74 percent of Republicans and 75 percent of independents agreed that election reform was important (or very important).

Specific aspects of electoral reform, however, are not immune to partisan division. In particular, if either party expects a specific electoral reform to change the partisan balance of the electorate, the reforms become mired in controversy. A reform that is perceived to expand the electorate or to increase turnout is likely to be opposed by the Republicans. For example, the Republican Party historically opposed motor voter legislation that made registration easier and was, therefore, expected to enlarge the pool of voters (see Traugott, this volume). Similarly, in the 2001 ISA/Caltech survey, Republicans are about 15 percent less likely to support a twenty-four-hour election day or its establishment as a holiday from work. They likely see these reforms as making it easier for people to vote, and thus as favoring Democrats more than Republicans. Republican opposition is based on the increased costs of administering extended hours as well as on the demography of nonvoters, who are generally poorer and less educated and more likely to vote Democratic than Republican. The authors of a recent study, however, argue that "one of the ironies of the intensely held partisan assumption about turnout is that there is so little empirical evidence to support it" (Calvert and Gilchrist 1993, 696; see Traugott, this volume). Support for voting reform takes place in a context of perceptions about partisan advantage as well as ideological attachment to minimalist or participatory orientations toward democracy.

Electoral College

The minimalist/participatory and partisan tensions are epitomized by Americans' divided opinion about the Electoral College. Support for direct election of the president may reflect a simple participatory view that there should be no barriers between the public expression of support and the election of the president. Minimalists argue that the Electoral College system has worked for more than two hundred years and preserves an essential tension between majoritarianism and diversity (see Barnes, this volume).

Supporters of direct election have pointed out that campaigns would be played out more evenly across states if the Electoral College were eliminated. In 2000, as in other post-television presidential elections, candidates targeted only a few "battleground" states in which a significant number of Electoral College votes were at stake and in which voter preferences were closely divided along partisan lines. Neither Bush nor Gore broadcast a single political advertisement in nearly half of the largest seventy-five media markets because they were located in noncontested states. *New York Times* reporter Peter Marks described the country as "divided into electronic haves and have-nots [those who did not see TV ads]" (Marks 2000). More than half the country was not exposed to candidates and their messages. The candidates were no more willing to waste their time than their money. Combined, the Bush and Gore campaigns made 220 separate visits to different states during the final four weeks of the 2000 campaign, of which 69 percent were visits to thirteen battleground states.[4] Residents of "have-not" states received a different campaign. As Gerald Schmitt, the mayor of Dodge City, Kansas, put it, "You wouldn't hardly know that there's a presidential campaign on. Nobody asks us what we think. We sit here and observe what's happening, but there's nothing we can do"(quoted in Marks 2000).

Results from the Vanishing Voter surveys confirm that residents of battleground states did indeed experience a more personal campaign than did residents of other states. Compared to citizens in other states, more respondents in battleground states reported receiving a phone call (47 percent to 31 percent), mail (57 percent to 46 percent), or a visit to their home (9 percent to 7 percent) on behalf of a candidate during the final few weeks of the campaign. Many more respondents in battleground states than in other states could recall a candidate visiting their state during the final two to three weeks of the campaign (84 percent to 51 percent).

The special attention paid to the residents of battleground states boosted citizen involvement with the campaign in those states. During the final month of the campaign, the Vanishing Voter surveys found that respondents in battleground states compared to those in other states were more likely to have thought about the campaign (58 percent to 54 percent), talked about it (49 percent to 43 percent), and recalled seeing, hearing, or reading a campaign news story (46 percent to 43 percent).[5]

The increased interest and participation of citizens in hotly contested states suggest that promoting direct election of the president might stimulate interest and turnout throughout the country. If the Electoral College did not strategically draw candidates to particular states, they might distribute their campaign efforts more evenly or at least differently (Barnes, this volume). Public opinion seems to favor direct election of the president. For at least the past thirty-five years, Gallup polls have shown that a majority of Americans support a Constitutional amendment to replace the Electoral College with direct popular election[6] (see Figure 10.1).

The ISA/Caltech survey of March 2001 shows a lower level of support for eliminating the Electoral College than was prevalent in the preceding years. On a five-point scale, only a slight majority, 54 percent, of respondents approved of eliminating the Electoral College to "allow for direct election of the president," 40 percent disapproved, and 6 percent had no opinion. The March figures even show a slight drop in support for eliminating the Electoral College compared to the Gallup results for December 2000. Looking at the pattern over time, there is a modest trend since 1968 of *declining* support for eliminating the Electoral College. More and more people "disapprove" of eliminating the Electoral College (see Figure 10.1).

One explanation for the current equivocation about the fate of the Electoral College may be the result of increasing partisan polarization of minimalist and participatory views. Republicans believe they hold a partisan advantage in the

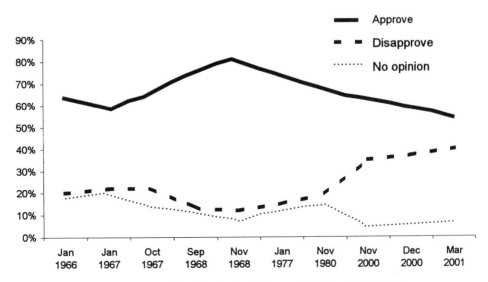

Figure 10.1 Public support for eliminating Electoral College, 1966–2001

current distribution of Electoral College votes, understandably since Gore won the popular vote in 2000 and Bush won the election (but see Gelman, Katz, and King, this volume). In contrast, Democrats perceive greater support for their own partisan interests among more marginal participants in elections who might be drawn into a direct popular election of the president. The ISA/ Caltech Survey shows that Republicans and Democrats have very different opinions about the Electoral College. The majority of Democrats (59 percent) approved of eliminating the Electoral College, while a majority of Republicans (54 percent) disapproved. Notably, independent voters sided with the Democrats. Fifty-two percent of independent voters supported eliminating the Electoral College in favor of direct election of the president.

Is majority opinion that favors eliminating the Electoral College going to have any political consequences? In the past, public support for eliminating the Electoral College has not been translated into a change in policy (see Barnes, this volume).[7] The minimalist view of democracy has weighed in on the side of the Electoral College, seeing it as a stabilizing, if imperfect, translation of popular votes. In the wake of the 2000 presidential election, the newly elected Democratic Senator from New York, Hillary Clinton, expressed a participatory view of the Electoral College: "I believe strongly that in a democracy we should respect the will of the people, and to me that means it's time to do away with the Electoral College and move to the popular election of our Presidents" (quoted in Lewine and Gest 2000). Charles Fried, former Solicitor General, supported the retention of the Electoral College in an op ed piece in the *New York Times* only a few days after Clinton's remarks. He wrote: "The Electoral College is one of the political safeguards of federalism: those structural features of our constitutional system—like the allocation of two senators to each state, whatever its size—that of their own force and without court intervention assure that the states count as distinct political entities, not merely administrative units of one central government" (Fried 2000). These remarks reflect the ideological nature of the debate over eliminating the Electoral College, which makes a Constitutional change unlikely.

If the question is reform rather than elimination of the Electoral College, partisan support is reversed. An overwhelming majority of Republicans support *reform* of the Electoral College. It seems that in the case of the Electoral College, even minimalists want some kind of change to make the vote more proportional, but they are reluctant to scrap the Electoral College altogether. Republican Party leaders should not assume that the Republican rank-and-file prefer a continuation of the present Electoral College system. Furthermore, both parties' leaders may be underestimating independent voters' support for either change. Independents register approval of both elimination and reform of the Electoral College. Most Americans of all political stripes would prefer that the results of the Electoral College be more in line with the popular vote. That said, other electoral reforms that have reached the agenda since the 2000 presidential election are even more popular with the public than reform of the Electoral College.

Media Projections

For some time the public has been concerned about the impact of media projections of the results before balloting is complete on election night (see Frankovic, this volume). In 1980, Jimmy Carter conceded the presidential election just after the networks projected a Reagan victory, but *before* polls had closed on the West Coast. There were complaints that Carter's early concession diminished turnout and may have affected contests lower down on the California ballot. In 1985, Congress held hearings to investigate and consider legislation for regulating the media's projection of election results before all polls had closed in the contiguous forty-eight states. In response, the major television networks' news directors voluntarily agreed to delay projecting winners in any state until most of the polls in that state closed (Grossman 2000). The emergence of the Internet as a news source has challenged these voluntary restrictions on information. In 2000, some Internet sites, such as the Drudge Report, explicitly stated that they would publish projections as soon as they had the information regardless of what the networks did (Powers 2000). In addition, all of the networks projected a Gore win in Florida a few minutes before 7 P.M., when most, but not all, of the polls had closed in that state. It was still several minutes before counties in the Florida panhandle closed their doors (see Frankovic, this volume).

A large majority of the public believes that media projections of election results have a significant effect on election outcomes. A CNN/Gallup/USA Today poll conducted on November 26–27, 2000, found that 62 percent of respondents thought the networks' election night coverage had a "great deal" or a "moderate amount of influence on the results of the Florida election." Only 35 percent thought there was little or no effect from election night miscalls.

The public not only believes that the media are powerful but also thinks that their impact is detrimental. In their November 11–12, 2000, survey CNN/Gallup reported that 55 percent of respondents disapproved of "the way the news media handled the situation surrounding the results" of the just completed presidential election. Public disapproval of election night coverage exceeded even the rate of disapproval of either of the presidential candidates by opposing partisans. The miscalls on election night evoked an emotional response among members of the public. Of those respondents who disapproved of media handling of election night, 65 percent said it made them feel angry.

Four months after the 2000 election dust had settled, a large majority, 78 percent, of the respondents to the ISA/Caltech March poll still agreed that the media should be "prohibited from reporting election results until every American has voted." The same percentage also agreed that the media should be prohibited from "reporting exit poll projections until all of the polls have closed." Clearly, media intimations of the results before citizens have voted strike a negative chord with the public. A full year after the election, 55 percent of those polled by Scripps Howard/Ohio University in an October/November 2001 survey approved banning television projections of election outcomes. As much as the media may proclaim "the public's right to know," citizens would rather not have their own votes scooped by media projections. Although the public may or may not be correct in its assumptions about media impact, the widely shared belief in the power of the media and disapproval of their performance suggests that this is one area of reform that could receive bipartisan support.

Uniform Poll Closing

Media projections would be less problematic if the whole country were situated in a single time zone or if all polls closed at the same time. In recent years, the news media have supported uniform poll closing throughout the country as a way to eliminate the problem of calling elections before some citizens have voted (Frankovic, this volume). After the 2000 election, the public overwhelmingly supported a policy of uniform national poll closing. CBS News polls on November 19 and December 9–10, 2000, respectively, showed 71 percent and 73 percent of adults favored "setting a uniform poll closing time on election night so that all polling places across the country close at the same time" (23 percent opposed in both polls). Shortly after the election, an ABC News Washington Post poll conducted December 14–15, 2000, showed 64 percent of likely voters favoring "a federal law setting a single poll closing time across the entire country" (34 percent opposed and only 4 percent had no opinion). Interestingly, a CBS News poll showed that Bush supporters were somewhat more likely than Gore supporters to favor uniform poll closing (77 percent compared to 71 percent).[8]

Efforts to impose uniform poll closing will affect some states more than others. Under the current rules, citizens in western states feel that their votes are devalued when the national election outcome is apparently decided further east. Under uniform poll closing, however, citizens in the western part of the country would likely have less time to vote than citizens farther east. Minimalist and participatory views converge in support of uniform poll closing, but for different reasons. Minimalists may take comfort in standardizing the rules, while participatory advocates prefer uniform poll closing because all voters in the contiguous United States would have a chance to cast a ballot before media projections seemed to make their votes irrelevant. This is especially important for local and statewide races during presidential election years. The ISA/Caltech survey showed that in March 2001, an overwhelming majority of respondents from both parties (72 percent) still supported uniform poll closing.

There is no doubt that the news media support uniform poll closing because it would make their job easier. If all of the polls in the country closed at the same time, then all of the networks would feel comfortable putting off their projections until that moment. Without the pressure to scoop the opposition, networks will be less tempted to make projections with marginal data. It seems that the public's support for uniform poll closing intuits these incentives. Uniform poll closing, by eliminating questionable media projections, appeals to citizens across party lines. Both Republicans and Democrats thought that the media miscalls on election night damaged their side. Furthermore, the egalitarian principle of uniform poll closing appeals to both minimalists and participatory advocates.

Other aspects of election day reform do not garner the same level of support that uniform poll closing does. Efforts to extend polling hours are clearly participatory proposals that would make it easier for some people to vote. Reforms to extend polling hours can be accomplished by allowing votes to be cast before election day or by keeping polls open later on election night. Poll hours can be extended prior to election day by allowing voting by mail (see Traugott, this volume). Public opinion, however, is evenly divided on mail voting. The Scripps Howard/Ohio University survey found that 47 percent of respondents approved of allowing voting by mail, while 49 percent disapproved.[9]

An alternative to early balloting is to extend polling hours (see Traugott, this volume). Twenty-six states, accounting for 51 percent of the voting age population, close their polls at or before 7:30 P.M. local time. A comparison of voter turnout figures from the 2000 election shows that states that closed their polls before 8 P.M. had lower turnout rates than states that closed their polls at 8 P.M. or later (50 percent to 53 percent). It could be argued that states with later closing times might be more progressive states populated by people who are more predisposed to vote regardless of closing times. A multivariate analysis isolated the impact of later poll closing times on turnout. Controlling for all other relevant factors such as education, income, race, and age, the analysis shows that closing time matters. More people went to the polls in November 2000 in states where polls closed at 8 P.M. than in states where polls closed before 8 P.M.

The public supports later poll closing times. In a Vanishing Voter survey conducted in January 2001, respondents were asked when they thought the polls should close and were given a choice of four times ranging from 7 P.M. to 10 P.M. Only 21 percent thought the polls should close at 7 P.M. The rest felt that the polls should close later, with 10 P.M. being the most popular time (34 percent). Younger adults, minorities, the less educated, and the less wealthy, groups that traditionally turn out at lower rates, are particularly supportive of a later closing time. By supporting increased polling hours the public supports the participatory side of the debate. The minimalist argument against extending polling hours focuses on the increased costs of staffing the polls. If the question is, "Is increased turnout worth the increased costs?" then minimalist and participatory advocates disagree.

ELECTION DAY REFORMS

In the wake of the 2000 presidential election were several calls to bring American election procedures in line with those of other democracies. Many European nations vote on Sundays. That invasion of the Sabbath would probably not pass muster in the United States, but the bipartisan National Commission of Presidential Election Reform came out strongly in support of making elec-

tion day a holiday. Public support for these proposals is mixed. Forty-six percent of respondents to the ISA/Caltech March 2001 survey favored making
election day a holiday, and 43 percent supported extending voting hours to a
full twenty-four-hour period. More than six months later, in November 2001,
the Scripps Howard/Ohio University poll found that 62 percent of their sample approved making election day a national holiday. It appears that these more
novel approaches to election day are supported by about half the public. Democrats and independents particularly support these participatory reforms to
broaden electoral participation.

   Given the coincidence of partisan and minimalist/participatory views, it
is not surprising that election day changes are supported differentially by Republicans and Democrats. On the whole, a majority of Democrats supports expanding election day hours and establishing an election holiday, while a
majority of Republicans does not. The differences range from 10 percent to 15
percent. It may be that a sophisticated sense of Republican advantage is the
cause of partisan differences, or it may be that Republicans already vote in large
numbers and, as good minimalists, do not see any need for change, especially
when the costs are taken into account. The independent voters, however, side
with the participatory advocates.

Election Day Voter Registration

Election day voter registration (EDR) takes the process of increasing access a
step further than election day holidays and longer polling hours. EDR increases
the pool of potential voters by allowing any eligible citizen to register to vote
on election day. Currently, six states allow their residents to register to vote at
the polls on election day.[10] Twenty-three states require registration a month in
advance of the election. The remaining twenty states close their registration
rolls between one and three weeks before the election. A number of studies
provide evidence that permitting election day registration increases voter
turnout (Fenster 1994; Knack 2001; Mitchell and Wlezien 1989; Rhine 1995;
Rosenstone and Wolfinger 1978). These studies estimate that if the whole country adopted same-day voter registration, turnout would increase by between 5
percent and 9 percent. Such an increase would bring the United States several
notches up from the bottom of the list of national election turnout (Norris, this
volume; see also Traugott, this volume).

   EDR reduces the burden on citizens. The Vanishing Voter surveys found an
additional benefit to EDR—it is easy to remember. During the October 2000 surveys, respondents who were not registered to vote were asked if they planned
on registering before the election and if they knew their state's registration deadline. Most people do not know their states' deadline, but as Figure 10.2 shows,
respondents who lived in states with EDR were more likely than those in non-
EDR states to know their registration deadline, even after taking into account
the respondents' age, sex, education, race, party attachment, and campaign interest. In fact, in states with EDR, no one has to remember to register.[11]

   States that set their registration closing dates well in advance of the election also limit the extent to which the campaign can mobilize voters. The Van-

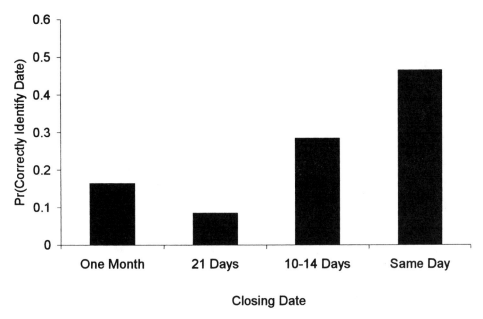

Figure 10.2 Impact of registration closing date on knowledge of date

ishing Voter's Voter Involvement Index shows that voter interest in the 2000 presidential election peaked just before election day.[12] Many of the nonregistered who become interested in the election during its final month were not able to vote because they missed their state's registration deadline. Interestingly, in the case of battleground states, only four of the thirteen have EDR.

Because parties appeal to different groups of voters, EDR is preferred by Democrats more than Republicans. Republicans are likely to oppose same-day registration because of its potential to transform nonvoters into non-Republican voters. Minimalists fear that EDR will bring ill-informed, less interested citizens to the polls and claim that these are not the people who should be deciding elections (see Ortiz, this volume). However, past research provides little evidence that EDR actually will affect the partisan or demographic composition of the electorate. Calvert and Gilchrist's analysis of same-day election registration in Minnesota showed that "rather than goading the disadvantaged to the polls, [EDR] appears to simply provide a further convenience for those already inclined to vote by virtue of their social class position" (1993, 699). Wattenberg and Brians (1999) found that allowing citizens to register on election day increases turnout among the middle class but not among the least educated and poor. In a study of states that adopted EDR in the early 1990s, Knack and White (2000) found that EDR brought more young people and recent movers to the polls but did not affect the income and educational profile of the electorate (see also Traugott, this volume). The fact that EDR increases turnout without making the electorate more representative of the underlying population may eventually result in bipartisan support. Democrats may take comfort in increasing turnout, while Republicans may be satisfied that the partisan balance is not changed.

Uniform Ballot Standards

Support for uniformity of voting equipment and ballots, however, is clearly a consensual view. Uniformity strikes an egalitarian chord and is reflected in broad public support for various standardizations of election procedures (such as machines and ballots). Following the 2000 election, two-thirds of those surveyed agreed that "the federal government should pass laws that would establish the same ballot and voting procedures in all states for all presidential elections." And less than one-third thought that "decisions on ballots and voting procedures should be left to state and local officials, as is currently the case" (CNN/Gallup/USA Today survey, November 11–12, 2000). Although majorities of citizens in both parties favored uniform standards, support for change among Gore voters was substantially greater than among Bush voters: almost 80 percent compared to 54 percent for Bush voters. Since it became clear in the 2000 election that less accurate voting equipment was concentrated in minority and lower income districts, it is not so surprising that minority and low-income respondents favor a uniform system that would have the effect of upgrading their polling equipment. What is important in the survey results, however, is that the appeal of making all voters equal crosses partisan and ideological lines.

An ABC News/Washington Post poll (December 14–15, 2000) asked respondents how much they supported changes in voting that would introduce greater uniformity to the process. See Figure 10.3, which compares the December 2000 ABC results with the ISA/Caltech March 2001 survey.

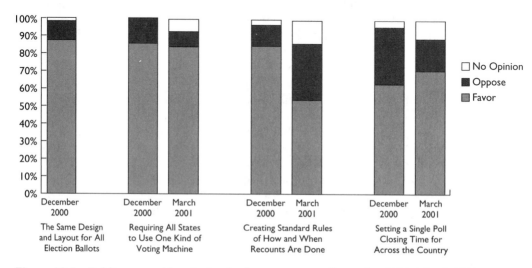

Figure 10.3 Public support for electoral reform measures, December 2000–March 2001

Support for uniform standards in elections declined slightly between December and March, yet 45 percent of respondents still agreed that "the federal government rather than the states [should] . . . set rules for counting ballots." Fifty-nine percent of Democrats and 58 percent of independents favored a federal rule for counting ballots. Notably, Republicans (48 percent) supported a federal rule almost as strongly as Democrats did. A year after the election, a CNN/Gallup/USA Today poll indicated even greater support—68 percent—for the federal government to require all states to meet certain standards for their voting systems.

The idea of uniform voting machines, as opposed to the more abstract "uniform rules for counting ballots," had consistent popular support in the months after the 2000 election. In the ISA/Caltech March 2001 survey, substantial majorities in both parties as well as independents wanted to see voters use the same (and presumably reliable) voting equipment. Eighty-six percent of Democrats, 84 percent of independents, and fully 75 percent of Republicans supported the "use of the same voting machines across the country." No doubt the Palm Beach County butterfly ballot and the uncounted hanging chads, so well covered by the media, have galvanized public support for reform of voting equipment.

The idea of uniform vote-counting rules and uniform voting equipment seems to have the same appeal to equality that is apparent in the support for uniform poll closing. Certainly after the 2000 ballot-counting debacle, people of all political persuasions thought that standards for counting votes should be implemented. If there is going be any change in the way that Americans vote, the most popular reform will be to improve the most tangible aspect of voting by providing uniform, reliable equipment (Alvarez, Sinclair, and Wilson, this volume).

From what we can judge so far, policymakers at the state and federal level are reluctant to implement uniform ballot standards. First of all, any standardization will be costly. The Secretaries of State and the Directors of Elections hoped that after the 2000 election, Congress would provide funds to upgrade election processes or facilities. But Congress has been slow to act as parties have struggled to balance minimalists' protections against vote fraud and participatory advocates' civil rights concerns (Potter and Viray, this volume). One year after the December 12, 2000, Supreme Court decision in *Bush v. Gore*, the House passed an election reform bill (H.R. 3295) that provided grants to states to upgrade punchcard voting machines and to set standards for counting ballots within each state. The House bill would also establish a commission to help states implement improved voluntary standards. On April 11, 2002, the Senate overwhelmingly passed a compromise election reform bill (S. 565) that allocated $3.5 billion to help states improve their voting systems. Whereas the House version focused primarily on improving voting standards and technologies, the Senate version additionally called for funds to make polling places accessible and to help disabled people vote. The Senate bill also required voters who register by mail to provide identification or another validating document (a utility bill, a pay stub) the first time they vote. Clearly, resolving these tensions between minimalist, accuracy-related goals of mini-mizing fraud and participatory goals of increasing turnout was central to the success of the conference committee's efforts and the ultimate fate of any elec-toral reform (see also Barnes, this volume).

WHAT IS TO BE DONE?

The impression that something went wrong with the electoral process in the 2000 presidential election has led to widespread and lasting public support for electoral reform in the United States. An analysis of public opinion, how-ever, suggests that support for reform continues to show the effects of the minimalist/participatory debate. The minimalist side of the debate would limit reform to fixing only things that went demonstrably wrong in the 2000 elec-tion, such as voting machines, uniform poll closings, and media projections. Minimalists favor reforming but not eliminating the Electoral College to better reflect the popular vote. The participatory side of the debate is represented by support for popular election of the president and improved access to the polls: making Election Day a holiday and keeping polls open longer. Uniformity in voting machines and poll closing and federal rules for counting ballots, along with banning media projections and reports of exit polls, transcend the minimalist/participatory divide. Figure 10.4 shows that these most widely sup-ported reforms receive the endorsement of Republicans, Democrats, and inde-pendents alike.

The consensus around electoral reform focuses on making votes equal. The public overwhelmingly supports reforms that would ensure reliable and stan-dard voting machines, enact uniform poll closing, and prohibit media projec-tions until polls close throughout the country. Of these proposals, the only one

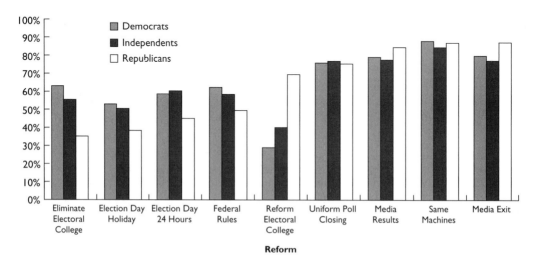

Figure 10.4 Public support for electoral reforms by partisanship, 2001 survey

that has been successful so far in gaining congressional consideration is the improvement in voting equipment to set minimal voting standards. Following the 2000 election, representatives of the television networks were called to testify before Congress, but no legislation relating to uniform poll closing or media projections has made it through the gauntlet of congressional committees, despite overwhelming public support for these measures (see Frankovic, this volume). It is possible that the networks have been sufficiently traumatized by the events of 2000 that they will voluntarily move in the direction desired by the vast majority of the public. Whether the networks act or not, it is important to keep working on these consensual reforms. Even if research suggests that reforms have little impact on electoral outcomes, they can help to increase the legitimacy of the electoral process. When elites act to support these popular reforms, they will help to restore Americans' faith in elections.

NOTES

1. The Vanishing Voter Project is a study of the Joan Shorenstein Center on the Press, Politics, and Public Policy at Harvard University's Kennedy School of Government, funded by the Pew Charitable Trusts, that sought to understand the factors that affected public involvement in the 2000 presidential campaign. From November 1999 through January 2001, the Project asked questions on a weekly national omnibus telephone survey conducted by International Communications Research (ICR). Each survey was in the field for five consecutive days and asked questions of approximately one thousand people age eighteen and older. Almost one hundred thousand surveys were completed over sixty weeks. Margin of error ±3.0 percent. The results reported in this chapter were drawn from nine surveys, each conducted over five days during October and November 2000.
2. Fox News/Opinion Dynamics Poll; nine hundred registered voters surveyed, margin of error ±3 percent.
3. Vanishing Voter Survey details in note 1. Under the auspices of the USC-Caltech Center for the Study of Law and Politics, a fifteen-minute telephone and Web-based survey was conducted of Americans' political attitudes and opinions about election reform. Surveys were in the field from March 26 to April 29, 2001. This chapter reports results from the telephone survey that was conducted by the Interview Service of America (ISA) for the California Institute of Technology (CalTech). The sample was a national RDD sample of 1,500 adults with a margin of error of ±2.5 percent. Response rate was 45.05 percent calculated as [(total sample − ineligible cases − nonsample cases)/total sample]. ABC News poll November 14–19, 2000, conducted by ICR-International Research: RDD sample 1,015 adults, margin of error ±3 percent. ABC News/Washington Post poll December 14–15, 2000: RDD sample 807 likely voters, margin of error ±3.5 percent. CBS News polls—November 19, 2000: sample 822 adults; December 9–10, 2000: sample 1,014 adults; December 14–16, 2000: RDD sample 1,048 adults; total margin of error for all polls ±3 percent. Scripps Howard/Ohio University survey October 21–November 1, 2001: surveyed 1,127 adults; margin of error ±3.5 percent. CNN/Gallup/USA Today surveys–November 12, 2000: RDD sample 1014 adults, margin of error ±3 percent; November 26–27, 2000: RDD sample 881 adults, margin of error ±4 percent; November 2–4, 2001: RDD sample 1,012 adults, margin of error ±3 percent.

4. Based on the Cook Political Report, thirteen states were identified as battleground states: Florida, Iowa, Maine, Michigan, Minnesota, New Hampshire, New Mexico, Ohio, Oregon, Pennsylvania, Tennessee, West Virginia, and Wisconsin.

5. For $n = 1,000$ in these surveys, margin of error is ±3.0 percent. The increased interest at the end of the campaign contrasts with the early period of the campaign, when residents of battleground states were somewhat less involved with the election than the rest of the country. A multivariate analysis was conducted controlling for a number of demographic characteristics that are associated with political involvement to ensure that the battleground states were not more involved simply because they are populated by people who are more interested in politics in general. Results are similar. Residents of battleground states were significantly more involved with the fall campaign than residents of other states. There were no differences between battleground and nonbattleground states' residents during other periods of the campaign.

6. An early Gallup poll during the election of 1944 already found a majority of Americans supporting a change in the Electoral College. In response to the question, "It has been suggested that the electoral vote system be discontinued and presidents of the U.S. be elected by total popular vote alone. Do you favor or oppose this proposal?" 65 percent favored, 23 percent opposed, and 13 percent had no opinion. Data from 1966 forward from http://www.gallup.com/poll/releases/pr001116.asp. Other polling organizations, including CBS News/New York Times and ABC polls, using different question wording have found similar results. See http://nationaljournal.com.members/polltrack/2000/races/whitehouse/wh2000recount.htm.

7. In September 1997, the House Judiciary Committee debated eliminating the Electoral College in favor of direct election of the president (H.J. Res. 28 and H.J. Res. 43). The Committee heard testimony from law school professors and the League of Women Voters.

8. The margin of error for Gore voters was ±5 percent, ±6 percent for Bush voters.

9. This Scripps Howard/Ohio University poll was conducted from October 21 to November 1, 2001; surveyed 1,127 adults; margin of error ±3.5 percent.

10. Idaho, Maine, Minnesota, New Hampshire, Wisconsin, and Wyoming have EDR. North Dakota does not require its residents to register to vote, which has the same effect as EDR.

11. The more obscure the deadline, the more difficult it is to remember. Residents of states with a deadline three weeks in advance of the election had only an 8 percent chance of knowing their deadline compared to a 49 percent chance for residents of states that permit registration on election day. A one-month deadline is twice as likely to be recalled than a three-week deadline, but no deadline matches EDR for its simplicity. Voters only have to know that they can show up at the polls on election day and can vote.

12. For the complete Voter Involvement Index, see http://www.vanishingvoter.org/graphs/vi-currents.html.

11

Why Electoral Reform Has Failed

If You Build It, Will They Come?

MICHAEL W. TRAUGOTT

Electoral reform in the United States over the past fifty years has been an upstream battle to design and implement structural and legal changes to facilitate voting set against a decline in attitudes about civic engagement, government responsiveness, and personal efficacy. Especially since 1960, a high point in voter turnout in the postwar era, changes in the socioeconomic characteristics of the electorate should have pointed to increased voter participation. So should have the reenfranchisement of African American and Hispanic voters and the mobilization of women. Changes in election administration procedures such as "motor voter" registration, increased access to absentee ballots, and innovations like "early voting" and voting-by-mail (VBM) should have had the same effect. Yet, despite all these changes, the decline in participation has been relatively steady and proportionately deep. The drop from 64 percent turnout in 1960 to around 50 percent turnout in the last two presidential elections represents a 22 percent decline in participation across that period.[1]

The problem for reformers has been the general failure of changes in election procedures to produce the kinds of changes in American voting behavior and in the electorate for which they were designed. In general, there have been two goals for the changes: *increasing levels of participation and altering the composition of the resulting electorate.*[2] Neither has been obtained.

More particularly, there has been almost no discussion of how much of the recent 14 percentage point decline in turnout is a reasonable goal to recapture, or how much higher turnout should go. There also has been little discussion of how much more representative the resulting electorate should be. Most of the empirical analysis of the reforms tried to date suggests that the improvements they can produce are modest. Worse, analysis of the impact of the reforms has highlighted a puzzle: Even when there have been incremental increases in the number of participants, the characteristics of the new voters most closely resemble those of the existing core of participants. They generally do not reflect increased representation of those who previously had declined to participate. This raises troubling issues for democratic theorists in the participatory vein (McCaffery, Crigler, and Just, this volume), as well as for the technocratic reformers.

This chapter explores the puzzle. After first considering various theories of why citizens do or do not vote, it turns to the factors thought to affect turnout and analyzes the state of present knowledge about the efficacy of these diverse reform efforts. Before concluding, the chapter looks in depth at Oregon as a particular case study. The dominant theme throughout is questioning whether or not anything at all can be done to advance participatory democracy at the voting booth.

UNDERSTANDING WHY CITIZENS DON'T VOTE

To some extent, different conceptions of the electorate come from researchers using different units of analysis that reflect aggregate statistics for geographical units or individual-level data on who votes. Research perspectives differ further depending on whether the analysis is conducted cross-sectionally, that is, within a single election, or dynamically, that is, across elections. Within a single election, researchers can focus on a variety of attributes of individual voters to classify or categorize them in different ways.

Virtually every proposed reform to the registration and voting system in the United States has two stated goals: to increase the *number* of people who vote and to make the electorate *more democratic* by making the voting population more accurately reflect the characteristics of the population as a whole. In addition to raising participation rates, for example, most reforms are intended to make the U.S. voting population include more people of color, more people with high school diplomas or less schooling, and more people who do not already feel involved in the political system. Based on current voting patterns and an understanding of who participates and why, the belief has been that reducing administrative barriers to registration and voting will produce a larger, more representative electorate.

Some reforms have had a significant effect on the political participation of specific groups in the population. For example, the Voting Rights Act of 1965 enabled significant numbers of minorities to enjoy the same participation rights that majority citizens do. The Twenty-sixth Amendment to the Constitution reduced the voting age from twenty-one to eighteen years of age, in principle enfranchising millions of young citizens for the 1972 election. The "women's movement" that flowered in the 1970s was the kind of mobilizing force that boosted women's voting rates higher than men's and in fact made women the majority of the electorate. But these actions did not forestall the overall secular decline in turnout. The recent period of turnout decline not only has proportionally decreased the number of participants but has also, along most dimensions, made the electorate less representative relative to the population as a whole.

Comparative studies indicate that turnout rates in the United States are among the lowest of any currently functioning democracy, approximated only by those in Switzerland (see Norris, this volume). These comparisons have been made across different time periods with slightly different calculations of turnout, but they produce remarkably similar conclusions. Avey (1989) found that average turnout in the United States ranks twenty-third among twenty-four liberal democracies in national elections since 1945. By this calculation, turnout in the United States averaged 58.5 percent. Franklin (1999) presented a compilation of data for average turnout in "free elections to the Lower House" for twenty-five countries between 1960 and 1965 and found the United States and Switzerland tied for last, with 54 percent each.

RECONCEIVING THE ELECTORATE AND THE ELECTORAL PROCESS

Progress in developing an improved understanding of the American voter and the impact of election administration procedures on voting has required a changing view of the electorate and the act of voting. In addition, better understanding depends on the development of improved data resources for the study of these issues, increasingly involving the combination of contextual information with individual-level data. Research has been marked by the application of improved statistical techniques that permit analysis of dynamic elements of the process and the determination of direct and indirect effects of the main predictors.

One central element in almost every study of turnout is Campbell's "surge and decline" model (Campbell 1966). Campbell's research found a regular ebb and flow of voters between presidential and midterm elections and focused on factors such as the short-term stimulation of campaigns and underlying political interest as the main factors in determining who votes. In particular, Campbell described a set of "core voters" who are highly interested and who are "joined in a high-stimulus election by additional 'peripheral voters' whose level of political interest is lower but whose motivation to vote has been sufficiently increased by the stimulation of the election situation to carry them to the polls" (43). While originally describing the regular pattern of variation in turnout levels between presidential and midterm elections, over time Campbell's work has been interpreted to produce an image of an electorate that consists of a series of layers or strata. Each is characterized by different levels of interest, or in some cases different levels of individual resources.

Elements of subsequent research have indirectly raised questions about the appropriateness of this imagery. The first refinement is that voting is now understood to be a two-step process (Kelley, Ayres, and Bowen 1967); only those who are registered already or who are stimulated enough to register can be drawn into the voting population. Second, longitudinal studies of voting, especially those that involve individuals' voting histories from administrative records, suggest an alternative perspective. According to this view, there are really three groups of citizens among the registered: those who vote all the time, those who never vote, and those who wander in and out of the electorate as personal circumstances and political contexts change. A more appropriate image than that of strata might be one of a permeable membrane between fully active voters and somewhat or occasionally active voters—those who could be drawn through the membrane under some circumstances—with a virtually impermeable membrane between both of these groups of voters and habitual nonvoters.

In his original analysis, Campbell illustrated the degree to which net changes in turnout seriously understated the degree of flux in the electorate. While there was a tendency for a core set of voters to participate in every election, the level of churning in the electorate was substantial (for a related analysis, see Burnham 1987). In two different pairs of successive elections, Campbell found that more than one-half of the citizens voted in both, one-fifth in neither, and another fifth in one but not the other.

Campbell's analysis makes clear that there are two ways, not one, through which the electorate can grow. The voting pool grows when voters join the electorate, but it expands even more when existing voters fail to drop out of it. Sigelman et al. (1985) extended this analysis using validated registration and voting data from Kentucky for the period from 1978 to 1982. In these four years, when there were ten possible elections in which citizens could participate, about three in ten citizens (28.7 percent) were not registered. Of those who were, 13 percent voted in no elections; half (50 percent) were classified as "marginal voters"(voted in one to four elections), while "hard-core voters" (those who voted in five or more elections) comprised the remaining 36.5 percent of those registered.

Sigelman and Jewell (1986) conducted a more direct test of such a model. Extending the analysis to a Kentucky voter database consisting of a 10 percent sample of 1,840,000 registrants, Sigelman and Jewell looked at individual voting histories to see whether there was any cumulative pattern of voting behavior. The lack of such a pattern suggested that although voting in presidential and congressional elections may be scalable—that is, those who vote in congressional elections would be likely to vote in presidential elections but not vice versa—other factors determine whether or not an individual votes in a particular election, including levels of interest and contextual factors related to specific elections and variations in personal circumstances that coincide with particular election dates.

More recent data from Oregon (Berinsky, Burns, and Traugott 2001) demonstrated this same structure of voting patterns. Using validated vote histories of a sample of survey respondents to compare their participation in pairs of elections, a high level of individual volatility became apparent. For example, aggregate turnout in the general election in November 1994 was 68.4 percent, whereas it "declined" to 66.3 percent in a special general election for a U.S. Senate seat in January 1996, a difference of 2.1 percentage point. But the individual-level data indicate that 63 percent voted in both elections, 11 percent voted in neither, 11 percent did not vote in November but did in January, and 14 percent voted in November but not in January. In sum, that means that a quarter of the electorate was inconsistent, voting in one election but not the other.

When the number of elections under study increased, the proportion of individuals demonstrating persistent behavior decreased further, as in the

Sigelman and Jewell analysis. Across a series of five Oregon elections from 1994 to 1996, 25 percent of the registered voters voted in all of the elections and 10 percent voted in none. Thus, 65 percent moved in and out of the electorate across this sequence, a much greater proportion than the 25–30 percent who were "in-and-out voters" between any pair of elections—a proportion roughly comparable to the "middle stratum" observed in Kentucky.

These examples from Kentucky and Oregon suggest that individual-level shifts in voting behavior are the result of different processes that can increase aggregate turnout. If the electorate is conceived of as consisting of four strata—citizens who are not registered, are registered but never vote, are registered and vote in some elections but not others, and are registered and always vote—then there are two distinct processes at work. Thinking about each process separately can help set appropriate goals for electoral reformers. One is a process of *mobilization*. This could work in two areas: first, encouraging the unregistered to register or otherwise make themselves eligible to vote, and second, getting registered people who are not habitual voters to the polls for a specific election. There is also a process of *retention*, whereby registrants who are inclined to vote by past behavior can have their participation in any particular election facilitated by lowering the obstacles to casting a ballot.

FACTORS IN THE VOTING DECISION AND THE EFFECTIVENESS OF REFORM ATTEMPTS

The literature on voting (or nonvoting) and turnout consists of five different sets of explanations for the decisions to vote (or not):

- Legal and administrative restrictions on registration and voting
- Socioeconomic characteristics of citizens and the resources they do or do not provide to voters
- Social psychological precursors of political involvement and a sense of personal effectiveness
- The impact of economic conditions
- Political mobilization

Understanding the impact of any particular reform ideally requires taking all of these factors into account, but most studies have focused on only one or two of these possible explanations, primarily because of the different and divergent data needed for each set of explanations.

The attitudinal basis for voting was first incorporated in a systematic and thorough way in the "Michigan model" developed by Campbell et al. (1960). The "funnel of causality" that preceded turnout and vote choice decisions was a combination of long-term predispositions such as identification with a political party, a sense of personal effectiveness, and support for the political system, along with short-term factors associated with a specific campaign, including assessments of the candidates and an ability to distinguish both the differences in their positions and the consequences of one's winning rather than the other.

One of the strongest countertrends to eased registration and voting requirements has been a decline in the levels of key attitudinal predictors of voting. Using the full set of American National Election Study (NES) datasets between 1952
and 1980, Abramson and Aldrich (1982) identified two strong time series: declining partisanship and beliefs about government responsiveness (external efficacy). Using individual-level data alone, they estimated that between two-thirds
and 70 percent of the decline in turnout can be explained by these two factors.
A second study of the attitudinal basis for the turnout decline between 1960 and
1980 concluded that the best explanation was a decline in caring which party
wins the presidential elections. In contrast, Miller and Shanks (1996) believe that
the major factor in turnout decline was the generational replacement of the
pre–New Deal with a post–New Deal cohort, with their different experience and
attitudes about government and political involvement.

Assessing the Impact of Mobilization

One of the key determinants of turnout is how much and what kind of effort
the major parties and their candidates make to get out the vote (GOTV) on election day. The earliest studies of GOTV efforts go back to the advent of social
science research on turnout (Gosnell 1927; Merriam and Gosnell 1924). The results were reproduced with subsequent experimental designs (Blydenburgh
1971). Since then, the concept of mobilization has taken on different meanings
and, as a result, has been operationalized differently. In the earliest work, a distinction was made between direct mobilization in the form of contact from parties and candidates, as opposed to the stimulation of campaign events. In more
recent work, a distinction has been drawn between direct efforts, in which the
candidate, party, or some other organization makes the contact, and indirect
mobilization, where intermediaries such as family, friends, or coworkers provide a stimulus to vote.

In these studies, analysts have turned to individual-level data from surveys, typically from NES, and supplemented that information with contextual
data about how vital and active campaigns were in their locales (Caldeira, Patterson, and Markko 1985; Patterson and Caldeira 1983). Taking into account
voter characteristics and attitudes, the economic climate, and legal restrictions
on participation, these researchers showed that political mobilization could increase turnout by an additional 4–7 percent.

Jackson (1996) looked at the impact of campaigns separately on citizens'
likelihood of registering and likelihood of voting, using validated registration
and voting information from the 1984, 1986, 1988, and 1990 NES studies. He
found that personal demographic characteristics, reflecting resources relevant
to dealing with administrative requirements, were the most important predictors of registration. In the voting model, campaign factors representing the stimulus of the specific electoral environment were the most important factors.

Rosenstone and Hansen (1993) looked at the impact of campaign contact
by candidates, parties, and other interested individuals and groups using a
pooled sample of eighteen NES surveys from 1952 to 1988, as well as the

panel studies of 1972–1974–1976. They concluded that the "level of political participation in the United States waxes and wanes in response to political mobilization" (227).

Understanding the Impact of Registration

The analysis of the impact of registration requirements on turnout began with aggregate level data. Kelley et al. (1967) highlighted the fact that voting is a two-step process that must begin with registration before voting in an election can be contemplated. Employing a framework suggested by Downs (1957), their analysis of variations in registration and turnout in 104 cities showed that turnout was higher in cities where it was more convenient to register. A similar analysis at the state level showed that turnout rates were higher in the 1960 presidential election in cities where it was easier to register.

While the impact of registration requirements on turnout seemed small, there was a continued focus on their impact because changes in registration rates were feasible. Teixeira (1992) used a combination of Current Population Survey and NES data through 1988 to assess the impact of eased registration requirements and estimated that the adoption of same-day registration, evening and Saturday hours, and the elimination of purging (removal of citizens from the roles based on nonvoting) could increase turnout by 7.8 percentage points. In another approach, Highton (1997) compared turnout in North Dakota, a state with "easy registration" that could be accomplished on election day, and "easy registration" states that included Maine, Minnesota, and Wisconsin. Highton found a difference of about the same magnitude as Teixeira (10 percent), but multivariate analysis showed that a substantial portion of this could still be attributed to higher education levels among residents of these states, compared to the rest of the country.[3]

Fenster (1994) took a different look at the impact of election day registration on turnout by comparing aggregate-level data from three states that adopted it—Maine, Minnesota, and Wisconsin—in relation to the others. Fenster used a quasi-experimental approach in an analysis of data from 1960 to 1972 to see whether actual turnout levels and the relative rankings of these states changed. He concluded that the turnout increase was approximately 5 percentage points and that this was a one-time increase that did not accumulate.

Motor Voter and the National Voter Registration Act

As evidence began to accumulate about the consistent if modest relationship between eased registration requirements and turnout based on variations in state practices, pressure built for a change in registration requirements at the national level. While this eventually resulted in the passage of the National Voter Registration Act (NVRA) of 1993, there were states that had already adopted the innovation and provided a laboratory for assessing the likely impact of such a law. The main provision of "motor voter" was that citizens could register to vote on occasions when they had other routine contacts with governmental institutions, including occasions when they renewed their driver's licenses with the Department of Motor Vehicles.

Knack (1995) conducted one of the first studies to estimate *in advance* the likely effects of the motor voter provisions in the NVRA on registration and turnout rates.[4] He found that "active" motor voter programs (similar to the NVRA requirement) were significantly related to higher registration and turnout rates, with a 10 percent cumulative effect on registration and 4 percent increase in turnout up to the fifth election. An unexpected finding was that the impact would be disproportionately felt in midterm compared to presidential elections. Knack also cautioned that these results might be biased because these estimates were based on states that embraced these changes and not on states that were forced to do so by national legislation.

Another study that analyzed in advance the likely impact of motor voter reached a similar conclusion by a somewhat different route (Highton and Wolfinger 1998). These researchers reclassified states according to the correspondence between their motor voter procedures and those embodied in the NVRA.[5] They concluded that the NVRA would have its greatest impact through its motor voter provision, while the effects of mail registration and the elimination of the purging of voter rolls would be slight. They also estimated that the greatest effects of the NVRA would come among the youngest and most mobile citizens, but the law would not have an impact on the racial composition of the electorate.[6]

Since the NVRA was passed in 1993, its first effects should have been felt in the 1996 election. The first official report that the Federal Election Commission prepared for Congress on the impact of the act focused on the increase in registration rolls (Federal Election Commission 1997), as more than fourteen million registration applications or transactions were processed in its first two years, although Wolfinger and Hollman (2000) have revised this figure downward in terms of new registrants. However, 1996 was the first election since 1972—when the voting age was lowered to eighteen—in which the percentage of citizens registered increased but voter turnout declined. Between 1992 and 1996, voter turnout in the presidential election fell again, from a rate of 51.1 percent to 49.1 percent, while the number of Americans actually voting fell by more than 5 percentage points. This obviously created a dilemma for the act's proponents.

Knack (1999) published an analysis of the impact of the NVRA on turnout in 1996 and 1998. This was a complicated task since in the first presidential election after adoption of NVRA, turnout dropped nationally to 49.1 percent, the largest four-year decline since 1920 and the lowest point since 1924. It also declined in every single state. In addition, there was also a record low turnout in the 1998 midterm election. Knack constructed an argument that the *declines* in presidential turnout were lower in the newly reformed states than in the five "no-reform" states, although even this difference (3.6 percentage points on average) was lower than all of the previous estimates of the impact of motor voter. Using regressions on state-level data, Knack also found no differences in the composition of the electorate between the no-reform states and those where

NVRA provisions were adopted; the slight differences he found in the party vote in these states favored Republican over Democratic candidates. Knack argued that the passage of time, permitting successive waves of citizens to receive an opportunity to register along with the renewal of their driver's licenses, would be the true test of the effectiveness of the NVRA.

A second analysis of the impact of the NVRA on turnout in 1996, employing a slightly different classification of the states, reached essentially the same conclusion (Martinez and Hill 1999). Their estimate of the relative declines from 1992 was 7.1 percent among the states that had prior adoption of motor voter, compared to 5.7 percent among those who changed only in order to comply with the new law. In a multivariate analysis, the NVRA was found to increase turnout by .3 percent. A separate analysis revealed that, contrary to expectations, there was no lessening of educational inequality in the electorate in the newly adopting states, and the racial effects favored nonblacks.

Hanmer (2000) analyzed the 1996 CPS data in order to assess the effect of motor voter set against election day registration. He found that motor voter did add many citizens to the rolls of registered voters, but a relatively smaller proportion of those newly registered by motor voter cast votes than those residing in election day registration states. Election day registration, whether in its mature form or as a recently adopted innovation, was more likely to increase turnout than motor voter did in the presidential election, although the greatest increases in turnout occurred where both programs were in place.

Easing Access to the Ballot

A second set of proposals for increasing turnout involves increasing access to the ballot for those who are already registered. One strategy is to make absentee ballots more easily available. In early versions of "mail voting," citizens could apply for a ballot to be delivered routinely to their residence; they could then cast the ballot in advance and return it. Prior to this, registrants often had to provide an explanation for why they could not vote in person, a requirement that has now been abandoned in many jurisdictions. Oliver (1996) found that turnout increased with the availability of absentee ballots, but primarily as a function of party mobilization efforts to see that their supporters received ballots. Using data from the 1992 CPS, he estimated that turnout increased by 2 percentage points where absentee ballots were easily available compared to other locations, and the resulting electorate was slightly more Republican—or less representative of the population as a whole—in demographic terms.

"Early voting" is another technique adopted in several states; it allows registered voters to cast their ballots in person before election day at familiar and dispersed sites such as shopping malls and grocery stores. A study of the use of early voting in Tennessee in 1994, based upon aggregate data, shows a slight increase in turnout (5 percentage points) over the average of the nine previous midterm elections (Richardson and Neeley 1996). This increase was relatively larger in the primary compared to the general election. Stein and a colleague (Stein 1998; Stein and Garcia-Monet 1997) studied the impact of early voting in Texas, using both aggregate and individual-level data. Analyzing aggregate data from the 1992 election, Stein and Garcia-Monet concluded that early voting increased turnout as a significant number of registered voters (24.6 percent) cast their votes early. For every 1 percent increase in the level of early voting, overall turnout increased by .07 percent. The turnout increased more in places where registration efforts took place and the parties and candidates engaged in mobilization campaigns to stimulate turnout.

Because the Clinton–Gore campaign was more likely to mobilize voters, it benefited from the increased turnout, but the researchers did not interpret the outcome to mean that there is an inherent Democratic advantage in early voting. In a subsequent analysis of exit poll data from individual voters in the 1994 midterm election, Stein compared early voters to those who cast their ballots on election day and found no partisan advantage associated with this voting method in either the senatorial or gubernatorial election. Although there was no difference in overall partisanship between the two methods, there was a tendency for strong partisans and those more interested in politics to vote earlier, as well as for older voters and those with lower incomes.

Voting by mail (VBM) is one of the latest strategies designed to increase turnout. This procedure can be distinguished from absentee voting, where only some registrants receive a ballot, in that every registered voter receives a ballot that they can mail back or drop off. The ballots are processed and checked for validity as they come in, but they are not counted until a fixed time on election day. This is distinctly different from the absentee ballot because those votes are not usually counted until all of the "in-person" votes have been tabulated. For administrative and regulatory reasons, the hybrid form of balloting that combines easy access to absentee ballots with polling place voting has sometimes produced very long counts that can take days.

VBM elections began as a local option in a number of municipal and special district elections across the United States in 1977, and thousands of elections were held with this method up to 1988 (Hamilton 1988). Two claims were made for the advantages of VBM elections: They would increase turnout and would lower the costs of election administration.[7] Magleby (1987) studied a series of VBM elections in seven cities, all of which involved referenda, and concluded that turnout did go up when VBM was adopted, on average by 19 percentage points. Education was the best predictor of turnout in these elections, and age and race were significant in some but not all cities. He concluded that there were "few significant demographic differences when comparing elections within cities" (89). He also cautioned that the available time series might not have been long enough to determine whether or not the effect was durable because "it is difficult to predict whether the mail ballot response rate will remain high after the 'newness' wears off" (88).

OREGON: A CASE STUDY OF VOTING REFORM

In 1981, Oregon began to experiment with VBM for local elections, and in 1987 the legislature made it legal as an option for local or special elections. An analysis of 48 statewide elections, controlling for type of election and electoral competitiveness, suggested that VBM increased turnout in Oregon by 10 percent, or 5–7 percentage points in the typical election (Southwell and Burchett 2000). The authors concluded "the state of Oregon adopted a unique method of conducting its elections, which is likely to boost the voter turnout above the state's already relatively high level" (77).

Subsequently, proposals were made to adopt VBM for all elections, but they were defeated at first in the legislature and then with a gubernatorial veto because of a fear that Democrats would benefit and Republicans suffer as turnout increased. An innovative and aggressive Secretary of State, Phil Keisling, began to take advantage of the provision in the Oregon law that allowed the use of VBM in special elections. In December 1995, after Bob Packwood was forced to resign his U.S. Senate seat, Oregon held the first statewide partisan primaries using VBM; in January 1996, Oregon held a special general election to select Packwood's replacement. These two VBM elections are the most heavily studied (Berinsky et al. 2001; Magleby 1996; Southwell 1997; Southwell and Burchett 2000; Traugott 1997; Traugott and Mason 1996).

Using both aggregate and individual-level data, Berinsky et al. (2001) estimated that VBM increased turnout in Oregon's 1996 special general election by between 4 and 6 percentage points, controlling for the characteristics of the elections in the former case and on relevant attitudes, demographic characteristics, and personal voting histories in the latter. Of equal significance, they assessed the impact of an electoral innovation in the context of individual voters' usual behavior. By paying attention to the dynamics of electoral behavior, they acknowledged the reality of people flowing in and out of the electorate rather than simply looking at increases and decreases in aggregate turnout levels.[8]

This review of past studies on the impact of innovations in election administration suggests a number of generalizations. Based on the conditions under which the studies were conducted, the effects on turnout were small, virtually none producing greater than single-digit increases in turnout. They also show that there were even smaller or nonexistent effects on changing the composition of the electorate. Most of this work has been cross-sectional, with little study of effects over time. Furthermore, most of the studies focus on only one innovation at a time, so there has been little attention to the impact of combined effects. This suggests a need for more research that discriminates between impacts on registration as opposed to impacts on voting. Many of these issues have been addressed in recent research on the implementation of VBM in Oregon.

What Can We Learn from Oregon?

The December 1995 special primary and the January 1996 special general elections to elect a U.S. senator from Oregon are the most intensively studied administrative reforms because of the range and quantity of data resources assembled. Both of the general election candidates were well funded and well matched financially. In his winning effort, Ron Wyden reported expenditures of $4.2 million to the Federal Election Commission. Gordon Smith, the loser in January, ended up running two campaigns in 1996, counting his successful effort in the fall general election; he reported expenditures of $9.3 million. Tom Bruggere, the losing Democratic nominee in the fall, spent an additional $3.3 million. So the Oregon electorate, comprising less than two million registered voters, was exposed to more than $17 million of campaigning in about a twelve-month period. By comparison, Bob Packwood spent a total of $6.1 million for his reelection campaign in 1992; his opponent, Les Au Coin, spent $2.6 million, for a total of less than $9 million.

For the general election, county officials mailed ballots to every registered voter in Oregon between January 10 and 12, 1996. Voters could mail in their ballots, providing their own postage, or they could drop them off at a number of locations. The Secretary of State reported that 86 percent of the returned ballots came by mail and 14 percent were dropped off at a site or the local election office.

How did the flow of the vote affect the partisan division? Magleby (1996) analyzed the partisan division of the vote in the January election by the time of balloting, and he did not find any differences by time period, nor did he find differential patterns of turnout suggesting that one or the other party was more successful in mobilizing its supporters at different points in the campaign. When survey data were analyzed by strength of party identification, however, there was a relationship between strength of partisanship and time of vote. Strong identifiers cast their votes earlier in the period (within the first week), while weak identifiers were more likely to vote near the end. Those who classified themselves as independents also voted earlier.

There were significant mobilization efforts in Oregon for these elections. Both candidates and groups organized efforts to contact citizens to get them to vote. For example, 47 percent of the respondents indicated that a political party contacted them about the campaign. These contacts were relatively evenly divided between the parties. A total of 26 percent of the respondents reported being contacted by the Republicans, 21 percent by the Democrats, and 39 percent by both the major parties. Some respondents could not remember who contacted them or refused to answer. In the entire sample, people who were contacted in this fashion were more likely to vote than those who were not (80 percent compared to 56 percent). Only 8 percent of the survey respondents reported that someone other than the political parties contacted them. In this case, there was little impact on turnout from such contacts. These groups included labor unions, groups concerned with moral or religious issues, and employers.

The Impact of Voting-by-Mail at the Individual Level

The post-election survey measured demographic data, political attitudes, and self-reported voting behavior. Self-reports about registration status and voting behavior were subsequently validated in administrative records in the county clerks' offices. The first way to assess the impact of VBM was an analysis of voting behavior in pairs of elections. For the primaries, voting patterns in two May elections were compared, between 1995 (a VBM election) and 1994 (a polling place election). These elections were used because all registered voters could participate. For the general election, voting in the January 1996 U.S. Senate election was compared to voting in the November 1994 election, which employed voting at polling places.[9]

For each pair of elections, turnout for individuals was generally higher in the VBM election compared to the polling place election, especially so for citizens with briefer periods of residence. For example, the longer a person reported living at their current address, the more likely he or she was to vote. This is predicted by past research suggesting that residential stability is related to registration status and is also linked to a greater sense of community and a stake in it. Turnout in the general election was consistently higher than in the primary and increased as residency did. This is likely because these individuals did not have to devote much energy to finding out where to vote, for example, because a ballot was delivered to their home.

Since the late 1980s, women have been voting at a higher rate than men have. They have become a majority of the electorate, reflecting their majority status in the population as a whole. VBM should reduce the differential in turnout by gender by making it easier to vote. The data presented in Figure 11.1 suggest that this is the case in Oregon. In each pair of elections, turnout was higher among women than among men, and turnout was higher in the VBM election in each pair than in the polling place election. Again, the "improvement" in turnout was greatest in the primary election for men compared to women under the condition of VBM compared to at a polling place.

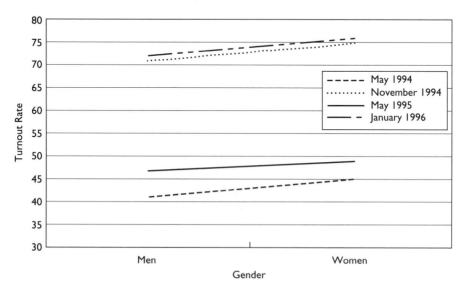

Figure 11.1 Comparison of primary and general election turnout by gender

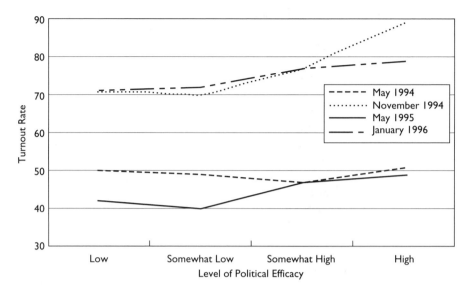

Figure 11.2   Comparison of primary and general election turnout by levels of political efficacy

As a final check on the impact of balloting method, turnout by levels of political efficacy was assessed. Efficacy measures a person's sense of his or her ability to have an impact on the political system. Individuals with higher levels of political efficacy are more likely to participate in politics. The data presented in Figure 11.2 show that this was the case in Oregon in both the primary and general elections, although the overall relationship is weaker than that typically observed in national surveys. Turnout tended to be higher in the VBM elections in each pair, and the differential (or improvement with VBM) was greatest for low efficacy individuals in the primary election pairing.

The relationships between individual-level characteristics and voting by mail and at polling places conformed to expectations from past research about the increase in turnout when voting is made more convenient. However, these increments were small, typically ranging from 2 to 10 percentage points, although they appeared in the expected direction and among appropriate subgroups. The magnitude of the shift was so slight that it did not result in any significant change in the compositional characteristics of the electorate.

The next step was to pursue a multivariate analysis that had several unique attributes (Berinsky et al. 2001). First, the analytical approach assessed VBM in terms of two different potential effects: mobilizing new voters to participate and retaining past voters who might not have voted in a particular election. The model contained vote histories and measures that represented the standard attitudinal and demographic explanations for voting at the individual level, as well as contextual data on the type of election and whether or not VBM was used.

This analysis highlighted several interesting aspects of the impact of VBM. First of all, the overall impact of VBM on turnout was an increase of 6 percentage points. Second, the statistical technique allowed a separate estimation of the retention versus the mobilization effect of the innovation. Using information from individual vote histories, the analysis showed that the increase in turnout among registered voters was a result of greater success in retaining previous voters in a VBM election than in mobilizing new voters. The retention effects were most pronounced for younger, less well educated and less interested voters. VBM actually accentuated existing stratification in the electorate rather than ameliorating it. The significant exception is that VBM did not favor either party over the other; it ensured that partisans of both stripes kept voting. Another way to think of these effects is that VBM stabilized the electorate by slightly increasing turnout over the long run through the retention of participants in previous elections.

Another important question is whether or not the effects of VBM will be durable. Illustrating how difficult these analytical issues can be, the preliminary indication in the aggregate data is that turnout in Oregon is headed back down. Turnout in the 1998 general election, held with easy registration conditions whereby a citizen could register as a permanent absentee voter enabling a ballot to be mailed to one's home, was 34.9 percent compared to 38.2 percent in 1994 (under the old system) or 66.2 percent in the 1996 special general election held under VBM. Turnout in the May 1997 special primary, held by mail, was 42.1 percent compared to 43.7 percent in the May 1995 primary, also held by mail. Turnout in the 2000 presidential election, one of the closest and most competitive on record, was up, but not to the level of the 1996 special general election. While the time series is too short to draw definitive conclusions, there is a suggestion that a substantial portion of the original burst in turnout might be attributable to novelty and to the high levels of media coverage associated with implementation, as Magleby suggested. At the least, the suggestion is that experience with VBM does not accumulate across successive elections. This is clearly an area where research must be continued.

CONCLUSIONS

This chapter has analyzed a number of electoral reforms in order to assess the magnitude and direction of their effects on registration and voting. These include motor voter provisions for registration, election day registration, increased availability of absentee ballots, early voting, and voting by mail. Using a variety of data sources and analytical techniques, we conclude that the effects of these reforms have been modest both in terms of increasing the size of the participating electorate and in altering its demographic and attitudinal characteristics.

When the focus is registration, it appears that motor voter provisions and election day registration can add reasonably large numbers of people to the rolls. But there is little to suggest in the analysis of the 1996 or the 2000 presidential election that these new registrants have the same propensity to vote as those who were inclined to register on their own in previous years. That is to say, turnout goes up but not at the same rate as it has in the past when new people were added to the lists. Suggestions that we must wait until a full cycle of license renewals takes place before assessing the law's impact may or may not be well grounded, based on these early returns. The fact that turnout did not go up in a presidential election suggests it will be difficult to produce expanded voting in off-year elections.

Analyses of alternative voting methods suggest similar modest results for turnout. These reforms seem to exert a small influence on the levels of participation, certainly not more than increases in the high single digits. It must be asked whether recent innovations will have any cumulative effects over a series of elections, or how durable some of these shifts might be, once the novelty of the changes and the associated high media coverage of their adoption wear off. In compositional terms, where most of the work has been among voters as opposed to registrants, these procedural changes do not seem to produce a less stratified electorate than we have now, or one that better reflects the underlying demographic or attitudinal characteristics of the population.

A commitment to participatory democracy means that we are obliged to do what we can to spur participation and change the character of the electorate, within reasonable cost. But one thing that is needed now is a conversation that distinguishes normative goals from reasonable expectations for change or improvement based on our current state of empirical knowledge. How much of an increase in turnout should we expect from any particular reform? What is "enough" change? Is there a reasonable amount of change? And does it make any difference when some reforms are combined with others?

Central to the discussion is an appropriate conceptualization of the dynamics of voting that underlies aggregate shifts in turnout in order to design subsequent reform proposals. One way is to distinguish three distinct segments of the population and the processes needed to activate them. Employing the concepts of mobilization and retention as discussed earlier, three groups can be characterized: inactive, unregistered citizens; registered people who almost never vote; and habitual voters who sometimes drop out.

Getting new voters on the rolls through motor voter and election day registration is essentially a mobilization effort directed at nonregistrants; there is no equivalent retention effort for them. The registered but occasional voters can be mobilized by providing easier access to ballots, by mail as either absentee or VBM ballots. These techniques also play a role in retaining existing voters in the electorate at any particular election. While there is no need to mobilize habitual voters, improving ballot access will help them to participate when events like travel, illness, or complications of family life might otherwise keep them away from a polling place. These categorizations are briefly summarized in Table 11.1.

It would also be useful to have a conversation about reasonable expectations for effect sizes. Normatively, this could include a conversation about goals for increased turnout, set against a research-based notion of how much of an increase it is reasonable to expect. Given that past research suggests that even

TABLE 11.1 Schematic Representation of the Expected Impact of Some Electoral Reforms

Target Population	Mobilization	Retention
Getting unregistered citizens registered	Registration drives	
	Motor voter	
	Election day registration	
Getting registered, infrequent voters to vote more often	Eased absentee ballots	Eased purging requirements
	Voting by mail	
Keeping habitual voters voting		Eased absentee ballots
		Voting by mail

double-digit increases in turnout are not likely, and after acknowledging the lack of compulsory voting in the United States (Franklin 1999; Lijphart 1997), is it fair to continue to compare turnout here to European democracies (see Norris, this volume)? Based on the results of the first set of discussions, comparative studies should be directed at understanding the differences in the same three groups in the populations of other democracies. Does higher turnout there reflect the same attitudinal and demographic characteristics but in different relative proportions? Or is there a different pattern of interactions between administrative procedures and these personal characteristics?

The evidence that reforms have little impact on composition of the electorate is likely to be a more difficult problem to address, normatively and in terms of the prospects of proposing new reform proposals. Many reforms make it easier for occasional voters (people who look more like voters than nonvoters) to cast another ballot rather than to mobilize previous nonparticipants into the electorate. The newest registrants today may have several attributes (age, cohort, and attitudinal characteristics) that make it unreasonable to expect them to vote at the same levels that past segments of newly registered citizens did.

NOTES

1. There is some dispute in the literature about whether there really is a decline in turnout in the United States since 1960 and, if so, how unique and troublesome such a trend is. McDonald and Popkin (2000) suggest that the denominator of most calculations—the *voting-age population* measured by the Bureau of the Census—is seriously flawed. They argue for the use of a more refined measure called the *voting-eligible population*. Nardulli and collaborators (Nardulli, Dlager, et al. 1996) have written about turnout in the United States in historical perspective, providing important insights and a context for interpreting current trends. Using county-level data from 1828 to 1992, they argue, first, that the decline that began in 1960 is not without precedent in U.S. history and was surpassed by a decline almost twice as large between 1896 and 1924. Second, they argue that using 1960 as the base point for assessing current trends is misleading because turnout in that election was the highest since 1900.

2. This chapter does not deal with the question of whether or not reforms change the patterns of voting among those who do show up at the polls, especially roll-off or split-ticket voting. For examples of this research, see Nichols and Strizek 1995; Rusk 1970; Walker 1966.

3. Fenster (1994) took a different look at the impact of election day registration on turnout by comparing aggregate-level data from three states that adopted it (Maine, Minnesota, and Wisconsin) in relation to the others. Fenster used a quasi-experimental approach in an analysis of data from 1960 to 1972 to see whether actual turnout levels and the relative rankings of these states changed in relation to other states. He concluded that the turnout increase was approximately 5 percentage points and that this was a one-time increase that did not accumulate.

4. He employed state-level data on registration and voting from 1976 to 1992 in a pooled time-series cross-section model looking at the effects of prior adoption.

5. Using CPS data at the individual level for 1992, they treated Colorado as a "pure" case study. Then they simulated the national impact of the changes election day registration might have produced in 1992, suggesting it would have been 8.7 percentage points.

6. Franklin and Grier (1997) analyzed state-level turnout data for the 1988 and 1992 presidential elections, comparing nine states and the District of Columbia, where motor voter provisions were in effect, to the remaining forty-one. They did not find significant differences in registration rates between the two groups of states in 1988, but they were present in 1992. They found that motor voter increased registration by 2.3 percentage points and turnout by 2.1 percentage points. And they found no significant partisan bias in motor voter states after controlling for the normal vote.

   Another analysis used a pooled cross-section of state-level data from 1970 to 1992 to assess the likely impact of registration reforms embodied in the NVRA on voter turnout in both presidential and midterm congressional elections (Rhine 1995). Using the variation in state-level adoption of reforms as a natural experiment, Rhine found that election day registration produced a 3-percentage point increase in turnout. The adoption of a motor voter provision added only a small but significant amount to turnout, about 1 more percentage point. And the adoption of mail registration had no significant effect on turnout at all.

7. This chapter does not address election officials' assessments of innovations like VBM, but there is some literature that demonstrates their strong support of the procedure based upon interests in reducing costs (Hamilton 1988; Traugott 1997). These studies do not imply that the transition to such a new procedure is a guaranteed way to reduce costs. In Oregon, heavy computerization of election administration offices reduced the burden of validating signatures. Other jurisdictions might have to make heavy initial investments in appropriate technology before they could begin to benefit from reduced costs for holding a particular election.

8. The use of individual vote histories enabled them to investigate two distinct forms of impact of the innovation. They did not find any partisan consequence of VBM in this election, but they did develop a method for extrapolating from the Oregon data to other jurisdictions where equivalent information is available.

9. Because there are other factors besides balloting method that can affect turnout, two different pairs of elections were used—one in a set of statewide primaries, usually relatively low turnout elections, and the other in a pair of general elections. The 1994 general and January 1996 special general election was also an appropriate comparison because it was also an "off-year" statewide general election in which the office of president of the United States was not at stake.

12

After the Storm

The Uses, Normative Implications, and Unintended Consequences of Voting Reform Research in Post–Bush v. Gore Equal Protection Challenges

RICHARD L. HASEN

INTRODUCTION: BACK TO THE FUTURE

Imagine the following scenario: The presidential election of 2024 is expected to be the closest election since the infamous campaign of 2000. Democratic candidate Karenna Gore is locked in a tight battle with Republican candidate Jenna Bush, especially in the key state of California. The election could be decided by just a few thousand votes in the state. California law requires that candidates be listed on the ballot using a "randomized" alphabet created by the California Secretary of State. This randomization was put in place in response to social science research showing that the person listed first on the ballot tends to gain some additional votes based solely on the ballot placement (see Krosnick, Miller, and Tichy, this volume; *Gould v. Grubb*). The randomized alphabet created by the Secretary of State for the November 2024 election will place Bush's name before Gore's name.

Gore goes to court challenging California's means for determining ballot order. She argues that her equal protection rights under the Fourteenth Amendment to the United States Constitution and the equal protection rights of California voters who support her will be violated by a system for ballot selection that fails to *rotate* the order of candidates throughout the state. Rotation, used in some states, varies the order of candidates on ballots through the printing of multiple ballots. The practice appears to neutralize the ballot order effect (Steen and Koppell 2001). A social scientist is prepared to testify for Gore that the first presidential candidate listed on the ballot throughout the state gets about a 3 percent advantage in votes. Given the closeness of the election, the social scientist would testify, ballot order may well dictate who the next president will be. The California Secretary of State issues a press release stating that California does not use rotation because no state law demands it,[1] rotated ballots increase printing costs to the state, and ballots that differ from published sample ballots may confuse voters.

How should such a case be decided? Is there a constitutional right to ballot rotation? Or does the state get to decide how best to allocate resources and make other choices regarding its own election practices, such as what steps are necessary to avoid voter confusion? Perhaps the only United States Supreme Court precedent on point in 2024 will be the 2000 opinion of *Bush v. Gore*, which, as will be discussed later, was quite opaque about the standards for challenging nuts-and-bolts election procedures as violating equal protection. How the hypothetical case of Karenna Gore and Jenna Bush gets handled may depend very much on how intervening cases have interpreted *Bush v. Gore* and what social science has been able to teach us about the problems and pitfalls with holding elections.

Although social scientists have focused on nuts-and-bolts voting reform issues for some time, research in this area gained unprecedented attention and importance in the wake of the controversies surrounding the 2000 presidential election (see Alvarez, Sinclair, and Wilson, this volume). Questions regarding the means for casting and counting votes, the form of the ballot, and increasing voter registration and turnout became the topic of everyday conversation (if not obsession) in the extremely close and bitter recount battle between Al Gore and George W. Bush over Florida's twenty-five electoral votes.

The focus on voting reform continued following the 2000 election, as the issues arose (and continue to arise) in at least three separate contexts: state legislative and congressional consideration of voting reform bills; research and recommendations by private and public commissions and groups considering reforms; and a spate of lawsuits challenging election procedures, most notably the use of punchcard balloting systems (challenged in lawsuits in California, Florida, Georgia, and Illinois).

The contributions to this volume by Michael Alvarez, Betsy Sinclair, and Catherine Wilson; Jon Krosnick, Joanne Miller, and Michael Tichy; and Michael Traugott demonstrate, each in its own way, that despite a large number of studies previously conducted on voting methods and mechanisms, much more research is necessary to get a handle on empirical questions surrounding voting reform. Such questions include the following: What technological method for counting votes produces the lowest rate of error, and how does this interact with race and other demographic variables (Alvarez, Sinclair, and Wilson, this volume)? How do methods for facilitating voter registration affect turnout, and do such methods improve or skew the representativeness of the electorate (Traugott, this volume)? How does ballot form and voting procedure influence voter choice (Krosnick, Miller, and Tichy, this volume)? These contributions take important first steps in filling in gaps about how voting reforms have and are likely to affect the workings of the American democratic process. But they also leave many questions still pending.

This chapter explores the legal and normative implications of social scientific voting reform research. It begins by discussing the state of election law leading up to the United States Supreme Court's December 12, 2000, opinion in *Bush v. Gore*, which ended the recount in Florida, and then comments on what that case did for the law. Even though *Bush v. Gore* ultimately may have *no* precedential value, it is also possible that it has created a window of opportunity for a host of legal challenges aimed at voting reforms. Social science research may well be decisive in resolving such challenges.

The next section considers the possible future and normative implications of the social science research that *Bush v. Gore* may have let into the election law mainstream. Social scientists studying voting have focused much of their attention on boosting turnout, but the focus raises the normative question whether high turnout is desirable (Traugott, this volume; Ortiz, this volume). If a high turnout itself is desirable, some means for increasing turnout raise their own normative questions. Carrots, such as payments for turnout, or sticks, such as compulsory voting laws, may be objectionable, even if the goal of increasing turnout is considered a good. This section also explores some unintended consequences of proposed voting reforms. For example, social scientists are now debating and testing various means for voting in nontraditional ways, such as in cyberspace. Although such means may increase turnout, they also may facilitate voter bribery and fraud.

The final section concludes with a call for the Supreme Court to move slowly in formulating rules in response to election reform litigation. It may seem counterintuitive, but the Court may do best—or at least do the least damage—by adopting initially murky equal protection standards. Such "judicially unmanageable" standards will allow lower courts to experiment with various controls over the electoral process and the Supreme Court to learn from the varied experimentation before committing to more rigid rules governing the electoral process.

THE PAST AND PRESENT OF ELECTION LAW

Legal Standards in Election Law Cases before *Bush v. Gore*

Before *Bush v. Gore*, the basic legal terrain regarding election disputes was complex but not very much in dispute. What follows is a brief and somewhat simplified thumbnail sketch.

Some of the law in this area was (and remains) statutory (Potter and Viray, this volume). The Federal Election Campaign Act (FECA, 2 U.S.C. § 431 et seq.) provides rules regarding contribution limitations and disclosure provisions for campaign finance regulation. The Voting Rights Act (VRA, 42 U.S.C. § 1971 et seq.) contains a number of key provisions regulating voting rights. Section 5, for example, requires that certain (mostly Southern) jurisdictions obtain "preclearance" from the Justice Department or a federal court before making changes in voting practices or procedures. The statute provides that preclearance be granted when the law has neither a discriminatory purpose nor effect on protected minority groups. Section 2 allows minority plaintiffs to sue in any jurisdiction challenging a voting procedure that prevents the plaintiffs from participating in the political process and electing representatives of their choice (Lowenstein and Hasen 2001, chapter 6).

On the constitutional level, the Supreme Court has applied a variety of standards for evaluating election law claims. Laws establishing limits on campaign expenditures, for example, are subject to strict scrutiny (*Buckley v. Valeo*),[2] but laws establishing campaign contribution limits are subject to a less strict standard (*Nixon v. Shrink Missouri Government PAC*; see also Estrich, this volume). These different levels of scrutiny apply even though the Court has said that both contribution and expenditure limits burden the freedom of speech and association guaranteed by the First Amendment of the United States Constitution. Laws preventing citizen and resident adults from voting in most elections are subject to strict judicial scrutiny because they may violate the Fourteenth Amendment's Equal Protection Clause (Lowenstein and Hasen 2001, chapter 4).

Before *Bush v. Gore*, Constitutional challenges to a jurisdiction's garden-variety election laws—for example, laws regulating the order in which candidate names appear on the ballot—were not subject to a single standard of scrutiny. Instead the Supreme Court explicitly eschewed a "litmus-paper" test for evaluating the constitutionality of election laws challenged on a variety of grounds in favor of a balancing test:

> When deciding whether a state election law violates the First and Fourteenth Amendment associational rights, we weigh the "character and magnitude" of the burden the State's rule imposes on those rights against the interests the State contends make the burden necessary. Regulations imposing severe burdens on plaintiffs' rights must be narrowly tailored and advance a compelling interest. Lesser burdens, however, trigger less exacting review, and a State's "important regulatory interests" will usually be enough to justify "reasonable, nondiscriminatory restrictions." No bright line test separates permissible election-related regulation from unconstitutional infringements on First Amendment freedoms. (*Timmons v. Twin Cities Area New Party*)

Under this balancing test, the Supreme Court has proven to be most willing to uphold numerous state election laws against constitutional challenge, such as a ban on write-in voting (*Burdick v. Takushi*) and a ban on "fusion" candidacies, whereby a minor party nominates a candidate also nominated by a major party (*Timmons v. Twin Cities Area New Party*).

Lower courts have followed the Supreme Court's lead. To take an example out of the issues raised by the initial hypothetical lawsuit of *Karenna Gore v. Jenna Bush* over ballot order, the Alaska Supreme Court in 1998 (before *Bush v. Gore*) considered a challenge to an amendment to the Alaska constitution that ended the practice of rotating the order of candidates' names on the ballots and replaced it with a random determination of order (*Sonneman v. State of Alaska*). Applying the balancing test, the court determined that the burden on the candidates was minor and that the state had an important regulatory interest in saving approximately $64,000 per election cycle in the printing of ballots and in reducing voter confusion: Election officials testified that rotational ballots confused voters because the actual ballots might differ from the sample ballots distributed.

This sliding scale approach to "garden-variety" disputes stands in sharp contrast to those Constitutional cases involving voting rights to which the Court has applied (what is now called) strict scrutiny. Two leading cases—both from the 1960s—are *Reynolds v. Sims* and *Harper v. Virginia Board of Elections*. *Reynolds* held that it violates the Equal Protection Clause of the Fourteenth Amendment to elect members of a state legislative body from unequally populated districts. According to *Reynolds*, "[d]iluting the weight of votes because of place of residence impairs basic constitutional rights under the Fourteenth Amendment just as much as invidious discriminations based upon factors such as race, or economic status." In *Harper*, the Court relied upon *Reynolds* in striking down a poll tax on equal protection grounds: "[W]ealth or fee paying has . . . no relation to voting qualifications; the right to vote is too precious, too fundamental to be so burdened or conditioned."

As the next subsection argues, *Bush v. Gore* may have blurred the line between the flexible, balancing, standard applied in garden-variety election disputes, on the one hand, and the strict scrutiny standard applied to laws that the Supreme Court viewed as impinging on the fundamental right to vote, on the other.

Bush v. Gore Changed Everything (or Nothing)[3]

One large open question following the United States Supreme Court's decision in *Bush v. Gore* is the extent to which the case has precedential value in other election law cases. Perhaps the case was, as Posner (2001) and others might argue, simply a pragmatic way out of a practical puzzle—a convenient coin flip dressed up in a jurisprudential ruse to break a statistical tie. But if we take *Bush v. Gore* more seriously, and if the case has such precedential value, it may have the perhaps unintended effect of replacing the "balancing test" for garden-variety election disputes with the strict scrutiny standard. The result would be that courts will strike down many more election practices as violating the equal protection rights of the complaining party.

The road to *Bush v. Gore* began with what would have been a garden-variety election dispute had the stakes not been so high. Following the certification of Florida's presidential election vote in favor of Republican George W. Bush, Democrat Al Gore contested the result of the election (Lowenstein and Hasen 2001, chapter 2, for a chronology of events before the contest). Gore asserted that a recount of "undervotes" from certain Florida counties would show enough legally valid votes cast in his favor but not counted by the vote-tabulating machines to make up the extremely small difference in votes between himself and Bush. Undervotes are votes that vote-tabulating machines recorded as containing no votes in the presidential contest (Alvarez, Sinclair, and Wilson, this volume). The trial court held that Gore failed to meet the statutory standard for a contest, and Gore appealed to the Florida Supreme Court.

The Florida Supreme Court, in a 4-3 vote, reversed the trial court. The court held that the trial court applied the wrong legal standards in judging the merits of Gore's claim (*Gore v. Harris*). Rather than remand the case for the trial court to apply the correct legal standard to the facts, however, the court ordered that certain recounts conducted after the deadline set by the Florida

Supreme Court in an earlier case should be included in the totals and that a recount of undervotes go forward. And rather than allow Gore to pick the counties for the recounts, the Florida court held that all Florida counties—and not just the counties singled out by Gore—had to conduct manual recounts of the undervotes. The court failed to respond to Chief Justice Wells's observation in dissent that it was unfair to count only undervotes and not "overvotes," that is, votes that the machine recorded as containing more than one valid vote for president (see Alvarez, Sinclair, and Wilson, this volume).

The court further held that in examining the undervotes to determine if the ballots indeed contained a valid vote for a presidential candidate, the counters should judge the ballots using a "clear intent of the voter" standard, as indicated in Florida statutes (Fla. Stat. Ann. § 101.5614(5)). The court failed to be more specific, perhaps out of fear that a more specific standard would violate the United States Supreme Court's understanding of Article II of the United States Constitution (Hasen 2002b). Article II requires that the state *legislature* set the manner for choosing presidential electors, and the Supreme Court had indicated in its first look at the Bush–Gore controversy that the Florida Supreme Court might violate Article II by coming up with new rules—not enacted by the Florida legislature—for resolving Gore's election challenges (*Bush v. Palm Beach County Canvassing Board*). In any case, the Florida court ordered that the trial judge manage the statewide recount, which needed to be completed in short order.

The Florida court remanded the case to the original trial judge, who recused himself. Another trial judge ordered the manual recounts to begin of the Miami-Dade ballots (which had been shipped to Tallahassee for the election contest) and in counties across Florida. Meanwhile, Bush filed a petition for a writ of certiorari and a stay in the U.S. Supreme Court. As the recounts began on Saturday December 9, the Supreme Court, by a 5–4 vote, stayed the Florida Supreme Court's order, thereby suspending the recount, and agreed to hear a second case from the Florida controversy just days after it issued its first opinion.

Late in the evening of Tuesday, December 12, the Supreme Court issued its opinion on the merits. Five justices (Chief Justice Rehnquist and Justices Kennedy, O'Connor, Scalia, and Thomas) joined in a *per curiam* opinion reversing the Florida Court on equal protection grounds (*Bush v. Gore*). The Chief Justice, joined by Justices Scalia and Thomas, issued a concurring opinion presenting as alternative grounds for reversal that the Florida Supreme Court's order violated Article II of the Constitution. Four justices dissented (Justices Breyer, Ginsburg, Souter, and Stevens), although Justice Souter and, to a lesser extent, Justice Breyer expressed support for the equal protection rationale (although not the remedy) (see also Chemerinsky, this volume, whose account of *Bush v. Gore* focuses on its federalism aspects. The concern in this chapter is with the equal protection rationale).

The Court held that the recount mechanism adopted by the Florida Supreme Court did "not satisfy the minimum requirement for non-arbitrary treatment of voters necessary to secure the fundamental right" to vote under the Equal Protection Clause for four related reasons:

1. Although the Florida court had instructed that those individuals conducting the manual recounts judge ballots by discerning the "intent of the voter," it failed to formulate uniform rules to determine such intent, such as whether to count as a valid vote a ballot whose chad is hanging by two corners (*Bush v. Gore*, 530).

2. The recounts already undertaken included a manual recount of all votes in selected counties, including both undervotes and overvotes, but the new recounts ordered by the Florida court included only undervotes (*Bush v. Gore*, 531).

3. The Florida Supreme Court had ordered that the current vote totals include results of a partial recount from Miami-Dade County. From this fact the Supreme Court concluded that "[t]he Florida Supreme Court's decision thus gives no assurance that the recounts included in a final certification must be complete" (*Bush v. Gore*, 532).

4. The Florida Supreme Court did not specify who would count the ballots, forcing county boards to include team members without experience in recounting ballots. Nor were observers permitted to object during the recount (*Bush v. Gore*, 532).

The Supreme Court then declined to remand the case to the Florida Supreme Court to order procedures satisfying these concerns, as Justices Souter and Breyer urged. The Court held that the Florida Supreme Court had recognized the Florida legislature's intention to participate fully in the federal electoral process. Under a federal statute, 3 U.S.C. section 5 (designated a "safe harbor" provision by the Court), states that designate their electors by a certain date—in this election by December 12—cannot have their choice challenged in Congress when Congress later counts the electoral votes.

> That date [of December 12] is upon us, and there is no recount procedure in place under the State Supreme Court's order that comports with minimal constitutional standards. Because it is evident that any recount seeking to meet the December 12 date will be unconstitutional for the reasons we have discussed, we reverse the judgment of the Supreme Court of Florida. (*Bush v. Gore*, 533)

Much focus on the case has been placed elsewhere, such as on the question whether the Court's remedy was appropriate to prevent a crisis (compare Posner 2001 with Hasen 2002b). The focus here is perhaps more parochial to the election law context: How did this case go from being a garden-variety election dispute to which a balancing test should have applied to a case where the Court applied strict scrutiny?

In setting forth the equal protection standard to be applied in the case, the Court stated that "the right to vote as the legislature prescribed is fundamental; and one source of its fundamental nature lies in the equal weight accorded to each voter and the equal dignity owed to each voter." The Court continued:

> The right to vote is protected in more than the initial allocation of the franchise. Equal protection applies as well to the manner of its exercise. Having

once granted the right to vote on equal terms, the State may not, by later arbitrary and disparate treatment, value one person's vote over that of another.
Harper v. Virginia Board of Elections. . . . It must be remembered that "the right
of suffrage can be denied by a debasement or dilution of the weight of a citizen's vote just as effectively as by wholly prohibiting the free exercise of the
franchise (*Reynolds v. Sims*) . . ." (*Bush v. Gore*, 530)

In setting forth the substantive standard to apply in *Bush v. Gore*, the
Supreme Court anchored itself in the language and cases of fundamental rights,
speaking in high and mighty terms about "valuing one person's vote over that
of another." The opinion does not read like a *Timmons*-style review of a garden-
variety election dispute, where the "burdens" on the candidates are compared
to the state's "important regulatory interests" in elections. Instead, we have
the "litmus test" of strict scrutiny—which usually means that the state loses the
challenge.

As a matter of case analogies, *Reynolds* and *Harper* were far off the mark
from the recount questions in *Bush v. Gore*. As noted earlier, *Reynolds* involved
malapportioned districts and *Harper* involved poll taxes, both systematic problems with the allocation of voting power. *Bush v. Gore* involved no such claim,
yet the Court still spoke the language of fundamental rights. The result is all
the more curious because the Court could have struck down the law under the
more forgiving balancing test by stating that no "important regulatory interests" were served by the failure to have a uniform standard for the recounting
of punch card ballots. Given the Court's view of the recount procedures, it conceivably could have reversed the Florida Supreme Court through the application of a "rational basis" standard of review.

Perhaps the sweeping language and reliance on *Reynolds* and *Harper* demonstrate no more than the sloppy work of a court under tremendous time pressure and political pressure. However, some observers see these features of
the opinion as a signal of more activist oversight by the judiciary of garden-
variety election disputes (Issacharoff 2000).

There are, however, at least three good reasons for doubting that the
Supreme Court majority intended anyone to take their equal protection holding seriously. First, language in the *per curiam* opinion limits it to the facts of
the case, or, at most, to cases where jurisdiction-wide recounts are ordered. The
Court wrote that "[o]ur consideration is limited to the present circumstances,
for the problem of equal protection in election processes generally presents
many complexities" (*Bush v. Gore*, 532). The Court further noted that "[t]he
question before the Court is not whether local entities, in the exercise of their
expertise, may develop different systems for implementing elections" (*Bush v.
Gore*, 532).

Second, the Court's own analysis was superficial. It failed to explain or jus-
tify its large extension of precedent (how are sloppy recounts like malapportioned districts or poll taxes?), and, most importantly given the fact that a
"fundamental right" was involved, the Court appeared to speak the language
of strict scrutiny but actually applied something much less than strict scrutiny.

If fundamental rights were at stake, it is unclear why Florida's desire to take advantage of the federal "safe harbor" for its electors trumped the rights of all Florida voters to have their votes counted. If the evidence showed that Florida election officials had deliberately failed to count the votes of Miami residents and then certified the results without the Miami returns, who believes that the Court would have allowed the safe harbor to trump the right to have those votes counted?

Finally, the kind of equal protection claim favored by the conservative justices in the *Bush v. Gore* majority is a strong departure from the usual equal protection jurisprudence they favor. Before the case, no Rehnquist Court opinion had ever relied upon *Reynolds* or *Harper* to expand oversight of the electoral process or to expand the franchise. Instead, the leading voting case of the Rehnquist Court applying equal protection analysis is *Shaw v. Reno*, a case in which the Court limited the extent to which race may be taken into account in redistricting to benefit minority-preferred candidates for elective office.

A POSSIBLE FUTURE FOR ELECTION LAW

Legal Standards in Election Law Cases after *Bush v. Gore*

Time will tell whether the Court follows an ambitious new equal protection jurisprudence. But even assuming the Court ultimately backs away (or takes away) from any precedential value for the case (meaning that Karenna Gore may be out of luck in 2024), there will be a window of opportunity, perhaps lasting as long as a decade or more, in which lower courts may have to construe the meaning of *Bush v. Gore* to evaluate challenges to a host of voting practices, including the use of punchcard ballots, procedures for recounting votes, and ballot position challenges. As long as a plaintiff can plausibly argue that a particular voting procedure effectively "values one person's vote over that of another," there appears to be a plausible claim for an equal protection violation under *Bush v. Gore* (see e.g., Alvarez, Sinclair, and Wilson, this volume).

If this analysis is correct, it appears that plaintiffs in cases like *Sonneman* (the Alaska case holding there is no constitutional right to rotation of candidate names on the ballot) will have an easier time convincing courts to strike down particular election laws. Arguably, *Bush v. Gore* mandates the use of strict scrutiny rather than the more flexible balancing test in evaluating these kinds of claims, which will now be recast as equal protection claims. Under strict scrutiny, it does not appear that an interest in saving $64,000 will trump a Constitutional right to equality. Nor should a mere assertion that voters might be confused by various ballot forms, at least in the absence of empirical evidence of confusion, suffice to answer the plaintiff's objection to Alaska's end to candidate rotation on the ballot.

During the post–*Bush v. Gore* window of opportunity, we can expect plaintiffs to file a number of lawsuits challenging voting procedures with a greater chance of winning such challenges. Initial lawsuits filed in California, Florida, Georgia, and Illinois challenged a host of practices, including the use of punchcard ballots. Many legislatures and election officials have acted to preempt or moot such lawsuits. Florida, for example, has outlawed punchcard ballots and required the use of optical scan machines or electronic voting devices. Congressional allocation of money for state and local electoral reform may lead additional jurisdictions to change their voting systems (see Potter and Viray, this volume).

Still, we likely will begin to see appellate decisions discussing the precedential value of *Bush v. Gore* in election cases by the middle of this decade. Initial election reform has been aimed at the *mechanics* by which votes are counted. Little reform so far has been carried out on the state level to change state laws governing other election procedures, such as ballot order or even the means for conducting recounts. These laws are ripe for challenge through litigation.

The Role of Social Science Research in Election Law Cases after *Bush v. Gore*

Social science research will be crucial in this new round of litigation surrounding voting procedures. Social science has sometimes played a role under the balancing test. In a recent but pre–*Bush v. Gore* challenge by the Conservative party to New Jersey's ballot order laws placing the Democratic and Republican party candidates first and second on state ballots, a New Jersey court rejected the challenge in part because of the lack of empirical evidence that a ballot order effect existed: "If the plaintiffs and defendants believed in the legitimacy of the Easter Bunny, this court would not be required to find as a fact . . . that such a creature truly exists" (*New Jersey Conservative Party v. Farmer*).

Not all courts applying the balancing test before *Bush v. Gore* cared all that much about empirical evidence. Indeed, the Supreme Court in a 1986 case upheld Washington state's laws regulating third-party access to the general election ballot on grounds that it prevented voter confusion. The Court explicitly declared that proof of confusion would not be necessary, or even desirable: "To require states to prove actual voter confusion, ballot overcrowding, or the presence of frivolous candidacies as a predicate to the imposition of reasonable ballot access restrictions would invariably lead to endless court battles over sufficiency of the 'evidence' marshaled by a state to prove the predicate" (*Munro v. Socialist Workers Party*).

In the post–*Bush v. Gore* era, however, empirical evidence may play a much more central role. In considering lawsuits now pending regarding the constitutionality of punchcard ballots, courts will have to evaluate whether such ballots indeed present a greater risk of error than other systems. Before the 2000 election controversy, courts and litigants would have been hard-pressed to find such research. In light of the controversy, some of our brightest academic minds have turned their attention to these questions (Caltech/MIT Voting Project 2001b; Alvarez, Sinclair, and Wilson, this volume). Both states and litigants will rely increasingly on social scientists to demonstrate whether voting reform methods pursued during litigation indeed are likely to have the effect alleged by plaintiffs. As Michael Traugott's chapter in this volume demonstrates, however, we have a long way to go before we will have social science data in this area about which we can be very confident. Indeed, the chapters by Alvarez, Sinclair, and Wilson and by Krosnick, Miller, and Tichy raise almost as many social scientific questions as they provide answers.

In addition to new *Bush v. Gore* claims, social science will remain relevant in other election disputes. For example, in considering whether Internet voting procedures should be granted preclearance under Section 5 of the VRA, it will be crucial to evaluate empirical evidence of a digital divide (Alvarez and Nagler 2001). The digital divide might indicate that Internet voting has a "discriminatory effect," making it ineligible for preclearance in covered jurisdictions under Section 5. Indeed, social science has and will continue to play a major role in all Voting Rights Act litigation (Pildes 2002). Moreover, empirical studies of the effects of campaign finance laws have and will remain relevant to challenges in this area as well. The future for social scientists as expert witnesses in election law litigation is bright indeed.

One important caveat: Most voting reform challenges, as in the introductory hypothetical case, will be aimed at *prospective* change. Post-election challenges, where there has been an opportunity before the election to challenge voting procedures, are very difficult to win—as they well should be. If a candidate knows or should know of a problem with a voting procedure, we should not give the candidate an "option" to sit on information about the problem and sue after the election only if the candidate loses.

My caveat, however, does not mean post-election challenges will *never* succeed. One unprecedented recent example of a successful post-election challenge occurred in an election contest involving the small southern California city of Compton. The trial court held that the Compton city clerk violated state law by placing one candidate's name before the other candidate's name in violation of the "randomized" alphabet order that state law mandated be used for the election. The court credited the testimony of Professor Krosnick that it is extremely likely that the ballot order affected the outcome of the election. Surprisingly, the judge did not simply order a new election; she ordered the losing candidate declared the winner and immediately sworn into office. The California appellate courts reversed the trial judge and reinstated the original winner.

Social science created chaos in a small, poor southern Californian city. Here we see the first unintended consequence of social science research: The Compton trial court decision elevated social science above the democratic process by treating these statistics as if they represented actual votes (Hasen 2002a).[4] The case suggests caution for the future.

Normative Implications and Unintended Consequences

Within the *Bush v. Gore* admonition not to "value one person's vote over that of another" is a normative value of political equality, a key element in the participatory view of democracy (see McCaffery, Crigler, and Just, this volume; Barnes, this volume). Supporters of the one person, one vote standard articulated by the Supreme Court in *Reynolds v. Sims* also spoke in the name of political equality. The Supreme Court, unlike a good social scientist, doesn't have to define its terms, and it may well be that the conception of political equality at work in these two cases (not to mention the myriad of other political equality cases decided since the 1960s) are different from—and perhaps even inconsistent with—one another (see McCaffery, Crigler, and Just, this volume).

The voting reform research agenda itself has some normative implications, albeit typically somewhat implicit ones. The focus on turnout questions—whether in regard to registration methods or voting methods like vote-by-mail (Traugott, this volume; Berinsky, Burns, and Traugott 2001)—presupposes a concern with both the absolute number of voters who vote and with whether those who do turn out to vote are representative of the population of eligible voters.

But why do we care so much about turnout? The often-implicit assumption of these studies is that high turnout is important to democratic legitimacy. Moreover, the concern with any skew in the representativeness of turnout suggests a normative view that if the effects of voting methods are not randomly distributed in the population, and voting itself is not representative of the wider population, then electoral outcomes will be biased toward those groups of voters whose turnout is higher.

If the concern about turnout is indeed that a "representative" (however defined) group of voters turn out and vote in elections, we can conceive of any number of ways to boost turnout that are likely to be more effective than the methods such as the NVRA (motor voter law) discussed in Michael Traugott's or Trevor Potter and Marianne Viray's chapters. One possibility is a compulsory voting law, which appears to boost turnout in democracies on average by 10–15 percentage points and has very low enforcement costs (Hasen 1996; Lijphart 1997; Norris, this volume). Another possibility is to pay people to turn out to vote (although not, of course, to vote for a particular candidate or ballot measure) (Hasen 2000).

Compulsory voting is an unlikely reform in the United States, but placing it on the table calls attention to the question of why we care about turnout. One's views on compulsory voting may turn on whether voting is conceived of as a test where we want the most competent or qualified people voting or, instead, a means of allocating political power among political equals (or, indeed, on whether voting matters much at all, as in the minimalist view) (see McCaffery, Crigler, and Just, this volume). Those who care about voter competence are less likely to favor methods like compulsory voting than those who seek political equality. The evidence on ballot order effect, for example, merely amplifies the case that voting sometimes is a thoughtless act. Those who are concerned about voter competence may see low turnout as a blessing and not a curse (Ortiz, this volume).

Calls to pay people to turn out to vote raise difficult social science measurement and normative problems. Would such payments change the nature of the vote, leading more voters (even those who don't take the payment) to vote in their self-interest? Social scientists would have a hard time defining voters' self-interest and then determining whether a vote that aligned with a voter's self-interest in fact was *determined* by self-interest. Answers to these questions may be hard to come by, but even more difficult is evaluating what to do with the answers if we do get them. If, for example, payments for turnout lead to more self-interested voting, is that an argument *for* or *against* such payments?

Besides the normative implications, we need to keep our eye on the unintended consequences of various voting reforms that are currently being explored. It may be that social science research showing a bias in various voting methods, combined with a vigorous reading of *Bush v. Gore* in the lower courts, will combine to stifle experimentation with different voting methods at the state and local levels. For example, Riverside County, California, conducted an experiment with touch screen voting during the 2000 election (see Alvarez, Sinclair, and Wilson, this volume). The American Civil Liberties Union, in its lawsuit challenging California's use of punchcard voting, pointed to the results of the Riverside County experiment to argue that the punchcard system was inadequate (*Common Cause v. Jones*). California will have to think twice about experimentation if it will provide ammunition for plaintiffs who will sue the state over voting methods. The Arizona Democratic Party faced a lawsuit for choosing to experiment with Internet voting in its party primary (Larson 2001).

Finally, a number of voting methods aimed at boosting turnout by making it more convenient to vote—on-demand absentee voting, Internet voting, vote-by-mail—raise the specter of vote buying. Here we have an historical precedent that social scientists have studied. By the end of the nineteenth century, states began adopting the secret, or Australian, ballot (Heckelman 1995). Before this time, each party printed up ballots with the party's candidates listed and gave those ballots to party members to cast. No doubt part of the impetus for passing laws establishing the secret ballot was to provide voters with the ability to vote their conscience. An unforeseen consequence of the move to the secret ballot, however, was a decline in turnout of about 6 percent (Heckelman 1995). Heckelman's hypothesis for the decline posits that the move to the secret ballot eliminated the possibility of effective bribery by making verification of vote-buying contracts more difficult.

If this hypothesis is correct, bribery of voters may recur as voting moves outside the voting booth and into the home. One recent vote fraud prosecution involved two competing candidates in a race for Dodge County, Georgia, county commissioner who bid against each other for absentee ballots inside the county courthouse. The candidates' staff marked the absentee ballots, thereby eliminating the verification problem raised by the secret ballot. "At trial, a Dodge County magistrate described the rowdy courthouse atmosphere during the absentee voting period as 'a successful flea market.' One of the vote buyers in [one candidate's] camp also testified that the open bidding for votes was '[l]ike an auction.'" (*U.S. v. McCranie*).

Certainly social scientists that study methods for increasing voter turnout and the ease of voting do not intend to facilitate bribery. In the area of election law, perhaps more than any other area, however, we need to be vigilant in considering how political operatives may attempt to gain political advantage from proposed voting reforms (see Estrich, this volume). It is a lesson we should not lose sight of as legislatures and courts consider ways of reforming our system of conducting elections.

CONCLUSION: HIKING SLOWLY IN THE POLITICAL THICKET

Justice Frankfurter, who opposed Supreme Court intervention in most election law cases, warned of the dangers of the Court entering the "political thicket." In *Baker v. Carr*, a Court majority rejected Frankfurter's claim and agreed to hear malapportionment claims. Just two years later, in *Reynolds*, the Court struck down the apportionment plans of virtually every state in the union. The Court has hardly turned back to look at what it has done and now regularly intervenes in election law disputes.

As this chapter has shown, there is a good chance that in the wake of *Bush v. Gore* courts are going to be called on to resolve a greater number and variety of election disputes than ever before and that social scientists are going to provide reams of new data that bear on how the courts should resolve the disputes. In this atmosphere, it is quite possible that the courts will get some things wrong, and actually make the electoral system worse. The social science could be wrong, unintended consequences may occur, or normative positions may change. One way of mitigating this danger, at least on the Supreme Court level, is for the Court to articulate initially opaque or "mushy" standards in novel equal protection cases (Hasen 2002b). This strategy of adopting "judicially unmanageable" standards allows the Court to observe how lower courts respond to the murky signal sent by the Court and ultimately to choose the best form of electoral reform in the particular case.

Consider, for example, one unintended consequence of the Supreme Court's decision in *Avery v. Midland County* to apply the one person, one vote rule to local legislative bodies. The rule has frustrated workable regional government plans that require "federal"-like compromises among entities of different sizes (Cain 1999). Had the Court in *Avery* (or even *Reynolds*) begun with a murkier standard for judging malapportionment claims rather than with the rigid mathematical rule of one person, one vote, it might have been able to protect basic equality claims but still have left room for such regional compromises.

The murkiness point brings us back to *Bush v. Gore*. Indeed, the best (and probably unintended) feature of the otherwise poor *per curiam* opinion is its opacity on the scope of equal protection claims it is meant to cover. The case's holding is novel and unprecedented, which should call for some initial murkiness. Before the Court ventures even further into the political thicket to constitutionalize garden-variety election disputes, it can, like a good social scientist, collect data. The data will come in the form of lower court opinions, many of which will rely upon the important work of social scientists studying voting reform. Armed with competing notions of political equality and the workability of various rules culled from these lower court cases, the Court can decide to move more confidently (or to stay put) through this new corner of the political thicket.

NOTES

1. Contrary to the hypothetical, California does require ballot rotation. See Cal. Elec. Code § 13111(b) (West 2002).
2. Under the strict scrutiny standard, the government must show that the law is narrowly tailored to promote a compelling government interest. Under lesser standards, the government need show less to defend a law. Under the easiest standard, "rational basis" scrutiny, the government must come forward with a "legitimate" interest and show that the means chosen are reasonably related to promoting that interest.
3. I explore the legal implications of the case in much greater detail elsewhere (Hasen 2002a,b). The analysis in the next few paragraphs appears in slightly different form in these articles.
4. As a matter of full disclosure, I advised the city of Compton on the election dispute.

13

A Tale of Two Worlds

SUSAN ESTRICH

A BRAVE NEW WORLD?

"Corporate democracy" has always struck me as an oxymoron in a world where board members are appointed insiders but denominated as independent outsiders, a world that has been harder for women and minorities to crack than even the world of partisan politics. Electoral politics is by no means the last plantation. The longest lasting impact of the Enron scandal on politics may be not as an agent of campaign finance reform—although it has surely been that— but, rather, as a window into corporate America and as an engine for reform of the democracy of business (Khanna 2002; Shaw 2002).

There is a magnificent theory of how "publicly held companies" in America are run and regulated for the benefit of their shareholders, a theory holding that corporate executives work for their boards and that independent directors are in no way dependent on management for their selection or retention. On that theory, Ken Lay, as the CEO of Enron, worked for its employees, whose pensions were locked in (Miller 2002). This naïve and happy theory is similar, of course, to the theory that holds that money has nothing to do with influence in politics, that corporations give millions of dollars to politicians with no hope or expectation that the cash will impact the policies as to which they have billions of dollars at stake.

I have spent much of my adult life as a student of electoral politics— doing it and teaching it. I thought I had seen it all. I thought I understood the tradeoffs between freedom and regulation, how to write laws and how to stretch them to their limits and perhaps beyond, and why people like me will find ways around any law written by people like me, which is not necessarily a reason not to try to write good laws in the first place. I considered myself a pol of the highest order.

And then I found myself in the brave new world of corporate politics: a world where Big Brother regulates every word you say—where, for all intents and purposes, there is no First Amendment and democracy is the exception, not the rule, subject to strict limits. A world where the lawyers are kings and the strategists work for them, not the other way around. I found myself in this world of big business, a world that seems far too important to trust to the messy mechanics relied on, say, to pick a president of the United States of America.

I came away from this latest adventure with two beliefs: (1) that the world of electoral politics could use more of the fair play that is required when elections are held in corporate America, but also, (2) that corporate America could certainly use more democracy and reform—for which it can afford to pay—and that the participants in this world would have no constitutional cause to complain. Think of the difference it might make.

Perhaps then, the world of big business should be a laboratory for thinking about the world of more traditional electoral politics.

WELCOME TO THE CORPORATE WORLD

A corporation whose chairman was under fire retained me for a brief period to assist in "communications strategy;" in this case, the action was coming in the form of a dissident slate of directors. The chairman was of the view that his problem was in large part "the lawyers." He did not view me as a lawyer, but as someone who would stand up to them. I say this to make clear the capacity in which I was functioning: I was *part* of the client, not one of its lawyers.

I wrote a press release. It was the subject of a conference call. On the line, among others, was one of America's best and most respected private investigators, himself a lawyer, who worked with our company. In the press release I quoted from *Forbes* magazine—a direct and accurate quote from a reputable source. For anyone who has worked in political campaigns, to quote from a mainstream publication is itself impressive; pols like me quote out of context from anything printed on paper and consider that to form the basis of a "comparative" ad. To quote *Forbes* magazine for the proposition that our opponent was "controversial"—based on his association in an earlier proxy fight with famed financier Marc Rich (famed, if nothing else, for his highly controversial pardon by President Clinton [O'Rourke 2001]), seemed like nothing less than gold from the perspective of a political operative like me. On the conference call, someone asked whether we still thought our opponent was "controversial," giving me the opportunity to ask our investigator what he'd come up with. He went on about secret investors, offshore accounts, and investments in companies that made mobile gas chambers. The eyes of a political hack like me were dancing! I said something like, "You're telling me this guy invests in companies that made mobile gas chambers for World War II?" *In my political head, I was thinking about how we could do an ad using the image of the mobile gas chambers, maybe even with Anne Frank.* Being lawyerlike—albeit not acting in my official capacity as a lawyer—I just stood by the quote from *Forbes*.

Not everyone on the call was so sure my plan was proper. "Do you really think you can say that?" someone asked. *I was a veteran of four presidential campaigns; did I think I could say this? I had an investigator on the phone that had legal documents about investments in companies that started out in the mobile gas chamber business.* "It's nothing compared to the ads we're *going* to run," I said. "We'll have the directors he's running—they'll look like puppets—and there'll be strings, and we'll have this guy up here pulling them." I was having a wonderful time. I thought to myself, *This corporate world is great.*

Forty-eight hours later we had to retract from this press release the sentence that quoted *Forbes* magazine.

I didn't get it. I called up the senior partner on our team, a top lawyer at a top New York firm, someone I respected enormously. I explained my problem to him: I had run political campaigns for the highest office in the world where I had seen people—members of the United States Senate, party chairpersons—flat out lie. They would say, "So and so's wife burned a flag," or "Somebody was mentally depressed." And what happens? The next day you would lose points in the polls, and the truth never caught up (Kenney 1988). This wasn't even kid's stuff, and we were tripping over ourselves with retractions. The lawyer said, "This is different. This is the corporate world." *Excuse me. I was just trying to elect a president.* I said, "This was an accurate quote."

What is absolutely stunning to me, as I now inhabit it, is the extent to which regulation is a fully accepted aspect of voting contests in corporate America. "Fight letters" are carefully constructed lawyer's letters, even at their toughest; disclosure requirements dictate content and prohibit any form of targeted messaging at all; you're not allowed to quote a newspaper article in the context of a proxy fight without contacting the author of the article to make certain that it is still accurate (Sidel 2001). You're not allowed to attack the character of your opponent. *Imagine not attacking the character of your political opponent!* In another meeting, I asked for a copy of the report on the private lives of the three middle-aged men we were running against. And everyone at the table looked at me and said "What?" as if I had landed from Mars. And in some sense, I had: I'd landed from the First Amendment, as it is understood in the political world, that is. In labor elections, if the labor union says anything that is in any sense considered misleading or false, or it says it in too many triplicates or it hands it to too many people, they take away the election. The reason labor lives with these rules is because business had the power to push them through Congress. And in the corporate world, as I learned, based on hundreds of rulings by the Securities and Exchange Commission (SEC), if I ever dreamed of doing an ad with the guy with the strings—*and it really was a good idea*— we'd get killed.

The chairman of my client corporation chafed under the lawyers' rules, but no one went to court to challenge the SEC's authority. After all, one of the securities lawyers pointed out, we had every reason to be happy with rules that prohibited character attacks. Our own chairman was "colorful," as we fondly put it.

THE GULF BETWEEN THE CORPORATE
AND POLITICAL WORLDS

Why is it that in corporate America, regulation of speech and conduct is widely accepted, whereas in politics any effort to limit the amount of money you spend or what you can say with it is viewed as utterly inconsistent with the First Amendment (see e.g., *Buckley v. Valeo; Republican Party of Minnesota v. White*)?

The obvious answer, which is that the First Amendment is a prohibition of government action, not private action—and so the government cannot regulate private citizens' political speech (*West Virginia State Board of Education v. Barnette*)—underscores the central importance of freedom of political speech, but it doesn't automatically give government the right to regulate the content of corporate speech. A recent corporate battle, the Hewlett-Packard fight between Chairman Carleton Fiorina and dissident board member Walter Hewlett, was viewed as one of corporate America's fiercest, certainly since the heyday of hostile takeovers (Swisher 2002), but it paled in comparison to the average congressional race in tenor (Roeper 2002). The participants in proxy contests, even if they do not live in utter fear of the SEC, certainly approach the agency and its rules with a level of deference and respect that I have never, in twenty years in politics, heard expressed by anyone toward electoral politics' regulatory body, the Federal Election Commission (FEC).

Iowa, 1988

Of course, I've had much more experience in the political world. In 1988 I ran the Michael Dukakis presidential campaign. I was in the odd position of being the only former election law professor ever to sign an actual FEC report. I will never forget sitting there—the campaign was about to lose badly in the Iowa caucus (Shapiro 1988), where we needed to spend more money. I had played every game I could think of, but we were still going to get *killed* in Iowa. We had the money, we needed to spend it; the spending "caps"—limits on how much you could spend in each state, based on that state's population, not its political significance—were in the way.[1] Once again, and not coincidentally, I was *part* of the client, not acting as its lawyer. We political operatives said, to our very smart lawyers, "We need to spend more money in Iowa. We're hitting the cap and it seems to us that Congressman Dick Gephardt is spending more than us because we're tracking his expenditures and comparing our expenditures to his. Somehow he is spending more money." I said to the lead lawyer, "How can he be doing this? More important, how can *we* do it?"

He said, "We'll think of something."

He came back a week later with a plan. There was a precedent. Not a really great precedent, but a possible precedent from the John Glenn campaign for fundraising ads (*Glenn v. Federal Election Commission*). As fundraising expenses were exempt from the cap, any expense allocated to a fundraising ad wouldn't count against a state limit. We could run these ads that said why you should be for our guy and not for the other guy. Then, we'd flash a statement on the screen that said, "Mike Dukakis does not accept PAC money (*which, by the way, was a really good political issue*); to contribute call 1-800-USA-MIKE." I said, "We're going to raise money that way?" The lawyer said, "No, we're going to have a fund-raising ad that way." Twenty-nine seconds out of thirty was devoted to the case of why you should vote for us; the card flashed at the end. I said, "Are you serious?" He said, "Yes."

Now I realized that I was being too clever by half—I was the client, not the lawyer. I said, "Fundraising ads. So we're going to deduct a percentage of this ad and apply it to our fundraising, and not to our Iowa cap?" He said, "Yes, that's the precedent from the Glenn campaign." I said, "What percent? I need a lot of these ads." He said, "Wouldn't you say that these ads are at least 50 percent fundraising?" *Now I can tell you with a straight face that there was no way— we raised almost no money in Iowa, certainly none in that last week. Those ads were being paid for by money raised in New York and California; my motivation in airing them was 100 percent political, and if anything, the use of the tag* "Mike Dukakis uses no PAC money" *was entirely for political purposes, too.* I asked, "How much am I going to be raising in downtown Des Moines with these ads?" One of our strategists looked at me and said, "If we come in fourth, we could be dead."

I said, "Dead."

He said, "If we come in third, we could be president, right?"

I said, "Right. Fifty percent." And I signed the FEC form and we did it.

The joke of this story is that I think Gephardt went for sixty percent.

Further Reflections on the Political World

A year and a half later the FEC was reviewing our filings from the Dukakis campaign. We were by this time ancient history—it didn't matter.

I knew it might come to this at the original time. As I sat in the meeting in Iowa, before the vote, I thought, *I could be attorney general or I could go to prison. Give me the form. If I am attorney general, I won't go to prison; and if I'm not attorney general, I won't care and they won't bother to send me to prison.* What I learned in that moment (and came to understand increasingly well as the campaign went along) is that the incentives when you're in the midst of a political campaign are to violate, twist, push, shove, and put off the application of every rule on the twin theory that either you're going to be running the world or you're going to be on vacation in the Bahamas and let them come after you and find you if they want to. This makes the regulation of a political environment one of the most difficult challenges that exist. Politicians will find a way around almost any regulation; someone will push at the edges, and they're apt to be the winners.

I remember sitting with Michael Dukakis later in 1988 and explaining "soft money" (Dukakis 1998; Wertheimer and Manes 1994). And he said to me about halfway through, "You got better grades than me at Harvard Law School." *Which was true, and which he always held against me.* I said, "Yes, I did and that is why I can say to you with great certainty that there are no limits here; we are in the brave new world." *And I remember when he looked at me; this was after a year of these one thousand dollar caps, Iowa, and 50 percent, and my explaining that we were not going to go to prison but that we were running ads in Iowa that we were calling fundraising ads that weren't really going to raise any funds. Then, the day after, we got the nomination. I sat down with him, and I said, "Now the world is about to change. Upstairs, all those people that work for me, they still work for me but they answer the phone in a different way. They now answer, 'Democratic Victory Fund.' Same number, same desks, same people; new way of answering the phone. What is the significance of this new way? They still work for me, mind you. It's not like they're allowed to spend Victory Fund money without our approval. But, they are no longer on our staff." (In the state of California in 1988, I had one person who officially worked for me.)*

So I said to Michael Dukakis, "Listen, we're going to raise more money. Now we're not at a thousand."

Dukakis said, "Well, how much can they give?"

I said, "They can give whatever they want."

He said, "What are you talking about?"

I said, "Well, you know, any amount."

He said, "What can we do with it?"

I said, "Virtually anything. The only thing we're not going to do with it is put the ads on the bottom that say 'Vote for Dukakis.'"

He said, "Are you telling me that there is, after all this regulation—after all of these endless meetings about landing a plane in Boston so you can count it as a Massachusetts expenditure not a New Hampshire expenditure, and writing back to each person that gave us a thousand dollars, saying, 'Wouldn't you like to have five hundred of it credited to your wife so we can get a double match?'—after nine months of doing this, you're telling me that you're now going to go out and raise unlimited funds?"

I said, "That's what I'm telling you."

He said, "I'm not comfortable with that; I'm going to put a limit on it."

I said, "How much of a limit?"

We went back and forth. Finally, he laid down the law and said no one is allowed to give more than $100,000—and I settled for $100,000. *In retrospect, this seems so naïve.*

"And I'm supposed to go to these events and raise $100,000 from people?" he asked.

I said, "Well, do you think they're going to give *me* $100,000? They're not going to give $100,000 without meeting you." I used to keep in the center drawer of my desk at all times a list of everyone who had given us $100,000. I insisted that everyone know who was on that list. And what did these contributors call about? Anything they wanted. There was one who wanted to be ambassador to St. James. Another wanted Moscow. I always promised to pass it on. Make it happen. I promise you that when you take $100,000 from someone, two things follow: One, everyone knows it; you know it, everyone in the campaign knows it. Two, they want something in return.

There I was with a very decent candidate and we got blown out of the water, financially speaking, because we were taking $100,000 and the opposition was taking $250,000.

And every day I was on the phone with my best friend from the 1988 campaign, the person who stood by me, got the numbers from me every morning, and got my list at the end of the day. He was the governor of Arkansas, and he said to me, "Why are you limiting it to a hundred?" I said, "You know, Michael doesn't want to take more than one hundred from anybody." And all Bill Clinton could say to me was, "What's the difference between taking a hundred and taking two-fifty?"

SAME OLD, SAME OLD

The distinction between the two worlds of corporate and political America does not begin or end in the arcania of constitutional law. In fact, on closer examination, there is no real distinction at all—there is just one loud, resounding similarity. Money wins in corporate America. The boys with the bucks don't want their dirty laundry aired in public, and it isn't. The law backs them up. In politics, these same old boys still get the usual bang for their bucks. They want to call the shots. They can and they do. And the law backs them up.

It's the oldest story in books—OK, *one* of the oldest stories—and women know it all too well.

Money and Power, Women and Men

When Catalyst, the research and advocacy group that, among its other actions, counts the number of women who serve on corporate boards, first started doing its surveys, the world soon discovered that all one had to do was to ask and the number of women serving on boards would increase ("Women Still Rare on Boards of Directors" 1998). Disclosure was enough to prod corporate America to act. Of course at that time there was no where to go but up: from 2 percent women to 10 percent (Apgar 1997). Not much has happened since this initial "surge." In board membership, in top executive suites, and in state legislatures, there has been very little movement of late. Board membership is flat; the number of women serving in state legislatures has actually decreased. The percentage of women who are law firm partners has gone down, even as the percentage of women in law schools has increased (Fleischer 2000; Smolkin 2001a; Wells 2001; "Women Still Rare on Boards of Directors" 1998).

Why? Because the rules haven't changed. There is little accommodation for mothers; no sense of a need to be inclusive, and no effort made to be. Discrimination persists at the top. Even the most ambitious women report that the old boys' network continues to flourish at the highest reaches. After a certain point, all but the most ambitious women give up, or hit the concrete wall. It's the same old boys, doing their same old tricks.

The irony, of course, is that women have enormous wealth and power in this country, more than enough to change the rules economically and politically—if they used their money and their power and if institutions were structured to allow them to use it. I have long argued that it would make a difference if half the Congress, half the state legislatures, half the governors in America were women

(Estrich 2000). By the same token, I would argue that it could make a real difference to the women in a company if a majority of its board's members were women, particularly if they were women who were committed to changing the rules for women.

Back to the Board Room

In the corporate proxy fight I worked on, one of our candidates was a woman, a distinguished former prime minister of Canada. She was the first woman on the company's board, added at my suggestion. She was running against a slate of three men.

Voters in corporate proxy battles fall into two groups. "Retail" voters are men and women who own stock. "Institutional" voters include banks, money managers, pension funds. Every morning, just as in any campaign, we would go over the list of targets, mainly institutional voters. What was striking to me, a newcomer, a pol, was how many of these targets were familiar to me— liberal employee pension funds and teachers' funds (*which is to say, predominantly women*). One of the largest was CALPERS, the giant California Public Employee Pension Fund (Benson 2002). During the fight, then afterward, I spoke to the one woman on its board, California state controller Kathleen Connell. CALPERS was voting for the dissident slate. Kathleen is my friend; the woman on our slate was a mutual friend of ours. When Kathleen asked the staff why they were voting to replace the only woman on the board, the all-male senior staff told her that gender was simply not an issue that CALPERS considered in voting.

Here is a pension fund whose membership is 60 percent female that doesn't consider gender in its voting decisions? Why not? California's public employee unions are among the most progressive in the country. Diversity is a firm commitment of public employee unions, teachers' unions, universities, and labor unions across the country.[2] Why shouldn't their money be *voted* that way in elections? It could be.

TIAA-CREF, the pension fund that counts university faculty among its members, has pressed hard for governance resolutions demanding that independent directors be truly independent (Thornton and Henry 2002). TIAA-CREF defines this to mean that they not be paid by the corporations, which many corporations are now considering stopping (Romans, Velshi, and Marchini 2002). But, with or without side payments, the reality is that independent thinking is not always or often a sought-after trait among those looking to fill seats on most corporate boards. The Enron debacle certainly is not a product of independent thinking by independent board members (McNamee, Byrnes, and Lavelle 2002). Women need to reach a critical mass on corporate boards, well above the 10 percent "quota" (Catalyst 2002; Donovan 2001) before their presence will have a real impact. But, when it does, is there any doubt that having boards half of whose members are women will matter? Those who have never been admitted to the club are less likely to be enforcers of its rules and customs. Diversity and independence are goals that could and should go hand in hand.

Bringing It All Back Home

In the corporate world, truly independent candidates need to be able to run against the candidates selected by management. And, to do that, they need money. One of the very pleasant aspects of working on the corporate side—like working for a rich, self-financed candidate—is that you just open up the checkbook. Most people, unless they are fighting for control of a company, or backed by an institutional investor, simply can't afford to take on a management-backed candidate in a proxy contest. Management will outspend them and management will win. The advantages of incumbency, beginning with money, not to mention setting the rules of the game, are enormous.

Wherever it might occur, real democracy demands a level playing field, or at least a floor. If this is true in political America, why not also in corporate America? As for funding, the answer is obvious. We have in place, or propose, public funding of elections (Briffault 2000). Why not corporate funding of both sides in board elections? We need to think how better to spread the money in the corporate world, and how better to keep it out—or at least limit its deleterious effects—in the political world.

Perhaps naively, I continue to believe that the participatory project for democracy (McCaffery, Crigler, and Just, this volume) is possible. But it needs to take head on the role of money, money everywhere. We need to finance the outsiders in the corporate world and limit the financial clout of the insiders in the political world.

Is there any possibility of making these dreams come true? Perhaps the last, best hope of meaningful democracy was closer to home than we might have thought when women first started asking for the most basic right, namely their right to vote. If women can learn to use their increasing money and their increasing power as men have, then maybe, one day—irony of ironies—we can get to a promised land where money is no longer the enemy of freedom. Women, perhaps, can use their money as freedom's ally.

LAST THOUGHTS

Imagine what Trevor could have done with a real agency. Imagine Trevor with an agency like the SEC. Imagine giving him just a bit of their power. . . .

Trevor Potter is the former chairman of the FEC, a contributor to this volume (see Potter and Viray, this volume), and a serious student of the political system. He spent years doing the best that could be done. But the FEC is not an agency that commands the respect of those it regulates. It isn't supposed to; it isn't allowed to. Unlike every other agency that Congress creates, the mandate of the FEC puts it head to head with the life support system of those who have created it. Even reformers in Congress understand that incumbency protects them, and the FEC generally doesn't (Lochner and Cain 1999; Wertheimer and Manes 1994). So they shortchange it in every way possible at the outset (Wertheimer and Manes 1994).

And then people like me kick mud in everyone's faces, pushing the law to the limits, determined to win.

Which provides us the set of questions, not the answers. We in the political world are subject to the rule of law, just not easily so. That is one of our great challenges in the days and decades ahead: How can we make democracy in general—and its central act, voting, in particular—meaningful and participatory in a world of old boys flush with ever-new money? I don't know the answer for sure. But I know that it will have something to do with following the money and the power.

NOTES

1. 2 U.S.C.A. § 441(b) (1)(A).
2. Women make up 36.3 percent of college and university teachers and 70.9 percent of teachers other than college and university ones (U.S. Census Bureau 2001).

14

The Paradox of Mass Democracy

DANIEL R. ORTIZ

What does democracy mean? Although everyone agrees it entails governance by "the people" rather than by some select group or by one individual, agreement begins to disappear after that. How widely must suffrage extend? Which offices must it cover? How actively must people participate? What kinds of voting procedures must be in place? As the 2000 presidential election showed, debate about democratic processes can be just as vigorous as debate about proper democratic outcomes.

THREE CONDITIONS OF DEMOCRACY

Most of us agree, however, that any truly democratic system must at a minimum meet three necessary conditions: (1) relatively wide, if not universal, suffrage; (2) a great degree of equality among those allowed to vote; and, perhaps most controversially; (3) some degree of thoughtfulness among voters. Thoughtfulness does not require voters to deliberate deeply with others or to transcend their private interests in pursuit of some conception of the public good. Thoughtful voters can be good, old-fashioned interest group pluralists. But if they are pursuing their narrow private interests, they must do so thoughtfully. As John Mueller, a proponent of minimalist democracy, has put it: "people do not need to be good or noble, but merely to calculate their own best interests, and, if so moved, to express them" (Mueller 1992, 991; see also McCaffery, Crigler, and Just, this volume). In other words, thoughtful voters must choose on the basis of a candidate's positions, character, experience, political party affiliation, or ability to achieve some end, not randomly or on some basis unrelated to how well the candidate will advance certain values. Both the assembly of Athens and the New England town meeting, exemplars of democracy, satisfied these three necessary conditions. In both, a broader swath of the populace voted than in most other systems at the time; individuals who voted did so on at least formally equal terms; and those individuals decided how to vote after participating in a public debate that educated them about different choices.

This has always been, of course, an idealized picture. Suffrage has never been truly universal. In both Athens and New England, many could not vote. Both systems excluded women, for example, approximately half of the populace. And until the middle of the twentieth century, many American states barred from voting those who did not pay a special tax or who failed to attain a certain degree of literacy. Both requirements effectively disenfranchised many poor and uneducated citizens and often were intended, in fact, to suppress the vote of African Americans. Second, equality among those voting has seldom been exact. Before the United States Supreme Court enforced the principle of one person, one vote, many states drew districts to overrepresent rural interests. Even later, racial majorities drew single-member districts and employed multimember districts in order to depress minority representation. Third, people have long cast their votes on less than thoughtful grounds. Even shortly after the Revolution, a time when we like to think Americans engaged in politics more deeply than at present, many cast their votes for those candidates who promised to give them the most beer or whiskey. More recently, many complain that mass political advertising leads American voters to chose candidates on civically irrelevant grounds, such as candidate affect or the sheer number of advertisements (Ortiz 1998, 902–903).

Still, as Alexander Keyssar reminds us, although unsteady, our course has been one of progress (Keyssar 2000). Even if we reject the self-congratulatory myths of American democratic triumphalism, we have moved far forward since the founding. We have gradually abolished property and income qualifications, literacy tests, poll taxes, and many other bars to participation, and we have extended the suffrage to women, African Americans, and those between eighteen and twenty-one (see McCaffery, Crigler, and Just, this volume; Potter and Viray, this volume). Our uneven path should, however, lead us to acknowledge how much remains to be accomplished and cause us to rededicate ourselves to democracy's fulfillment. As Keyssar puts it, "[d]emocracy . . . must remain a project, a goal, something to be endlessly nurtured and reinforced, an ideal that cannot be fully realized but always can be pursued" (Keyssar 2000, 323).

CONFLICTING DEMOCRATIC IMPERATIVES

This project, however, is impossible—at least as we presently conceive it. Democracy's three necessary conditions increasingly and embarrassingly conflict. For perfectly understandable reasons, the more we broaden and equalize political participation, the more difficult we make thoughtful individual political choice. In other words, there is some tradeoff between the quantity and quality of individual political engagement. Only in exceptional moments can politics be both broad and deep. This is the paradox of mass democracy. We cannot promote some necessary conditions without undercutting others. Thus, although Keyssar is right that we have made progress on democratic equality and participation, he neglects the cost that such progress has exacted on the thoughtfulness of individual decision making. Some steps forward come with some steps back.

Two separate factors explain why this painful tradeoff is unavoidable. First, the more people who vote, the less any one individual's vote matters (Downs 1957, 260–276; Popkin 1991, 10–43; Gelman, Katz, and King, this volume). If one is a dictator, one's "vote" makes all the difference. Dictators thus have a great incentive to inform themselves about all major matters they decide. At the other extreme, however, someone whose individual vote is very unlikely to make a difference has little reason to spend time, money, and energy learning about issues. What use would such investments serve? Such people might invest, of course, because they find politics provides fulfillment or entertainment. To them, politics is an idiosyncratic consumption good—something like a hobby. Some others might invest because they see voting as a civic duty and believe unthoughtful voting would be irresponsible. They too invest because politics provides fulfillment—this time of a social norm they have internalized. But for most voters mass participation creates disincentives to thoughtful voting. Their own individual vote stands so little chance of making a difference that investing in information and worrying through a decision is irrational. The puzzle is not that so few people actively seek political information, but that anyone does at all.

Each expansion of the franchise, moreover, makes this problem worse. As we grant new groups the right to vote, we do not grant them exactly the same vote that those before them enjoyed. With each addition to the franchise, the value of each vote declines somewhat—both for those newly enfranchised and for those already enfranchised. When the Nineteenth Amendment dramatically expanded the franchise by granting women the right to vote, for example, the value of each vote was much less than before. Although every man and every woman's vote counted equally, each individual vote made even less difference than it did previously and each voter had correspondingly less reason to engage politics deeply. It is not surprising, then, that as the right to vote has expanded the rates of actual voting have often declined (Norris, this volume; Traugott, this volume). When one's vote makes less difference, there is less reason to bother to cast it or, if one does, less reason to think about the issues.

The second factor exacerbating the tradeoff between broad participation and thoughtfulness revolves around the important cultural function served by admission to the franchise. Just as enfranchisement grants political power, it also signals that the newly enfranchised group is worthy of respect. Allowing a group to vote lifts a major civic disability and signifies that the group has gained significant social status. Status, however, like voting, is a relative good: Its value depends on who else has it and how many others have it. The more the right to vote expands, the less social privilege it confers on all those who enjoy it and the less reason they have to exercise it to express their difference from and superiority to others. Those newly enfranchised, of course, may vote often at first in order to reaffirm their elevation in civic status. But as they gradually become more confident of their position and others come to accept it, they too will have less reason to vote. In short, the less socially selective the club, the less status it confers on its members. As Groucho Marx once quipped, "I don't want to belong to any club that will accept me as a member" (Marx 1959,

321). Lest anyone doubt the continuing importance of this cultural dimension to the franchise, it currently underlies much of the demand from citizens with disabilities that they be allowed to vote on the same terms as every other citizen rather than at home by absentee ballot. It also underlies much of the plea by felons who have served their time that they should be allowed to vote. Voting is as much a means to reaffirm one's civic and social status as it is a means to make collective choices. As one writer has put it, "[d]isenfranchisement is a symbol. . . . It is a symbol of rejection, not reconciliation; a symbol of difference, rather than commonality; a symbol of domination instead of equality" ("The Disenfranchisement of Ex-Felons" 1989, 1317).

Voting's expressive function may exacerbate the problem of low thoughtfulness and information. Since voters can reaffirm their civic status by merely casting a ballot, they may be tempted to gain these expressive benefits on the cheap. That is, they may vote and so formally express their membership in the polity without investing in any information or even bothering to think about any information that may come to them for free. Indeed, Jon A. Krosnick, Joanne M. Miller, and Michael P. Tichy have discovered one piece of evidence that such unthinking voting regularly occurs (Miller and Krosnick 1998; see Krosnick, Miller, and Tichy, this volume). They show that some voters choose candidates not on grounds of how effectively they would advance certain values, but simply on where the candidates' names appear on the ballot. Even in high-profile races, they point out, many voters are powerfully drawn to the first candidate listed for any office. One wonders why these voters vote. Since ballot position conveys no direct information about substance (and any information it might indirectly convey about political party is more easily and directly obtained from the indication of party affiliation on most ballots), these voters must be voting largely for other reasons—perhaps to reaffirm their civic status or to satisfy a perceived civic obligation to vote. In either case, their participation in the civic ritual gains them benefits at little cost. Such unthoughtful participation, however, undermines one of the very conditions of democracy. It represents participation without thoughtful engagement.

Some argue that voters do not need to actively invest in information to vote thoughtfully since much political information comes for free (Popkin 1991). Political parties, candidates, outside groups, and individuals all provide information to voters. A voter's own personal experience, moreover, may provide highly relevant information. Many aspects of tax policy, for example, are painfully felt by voters every April 15 and economic policy can make itself felt through inflation rates, job security, and general well-being. But such information alone may not take the voter very far. A voter may, for example, feel that current tax and economic policy is clearly misguided, but still not know which of the various candidates would work best to redirect it. And although it is true that thoughtful individual decision making may not require great investments in information, it is also true that the availability of some free information does not ensure thoughtful decision making.

Pointing to the tension between broad participation and meaningful engagement is certainly not to say that we should roll back the franchise or discourage political participation through other, less formal means. Such a course not only would run against the current of American history, but would also violate important norms of civic inclusion we have worked very hard to vindicate. In a series of amendments to the Constitution and in legislation ranging from the Voting Rights Act of 1965 to the more recent National Voter Registration Act, Americans have fought to ease participation for individuals and various groups (see Traugott, this volume; Potter and Viray, this volume). While some of these laws have accomplished less than hoped and a few may have had some unexpected, perverse results, they all reflect a single and noble ambition: expanding voting participation to broader and broader groups. They all aim to make government "by the people" more than a misleading slogan by including more people in the process of self-governance. That is an ambition we renounce at our peril.

At the same time, however, we may worry whether increasing participation does at some point bring negative returns. Several commentators have suggested, for example, paying people to vote either in currency or in some substitute, like coupons or lottery chances (Hasen, this volume). Pamela Karlan, for example, has argued that such payments would bring many benefits:

> If nominal payments can have significant effects at the margin in bringing nonvoters to the polls . . . then perhaps the government ought to pay eligible citizens to vote. At the very least, such payments would remove the financial barriers now faced by indigent voters who require transportation to the polls. Moreover, paying voters directly could circumvent the implicit coercion and group stereotyping associated with candidate-paid haulers and get-out-the-vote efforts. If the two central ways in which citizens participate in the process of self-government are voting and jury service, then it is unclear why compensating voters would be any more controversial than the accepted practice of compensating jurors. . . .
>
> Voters might, for instance, be given vouchers exchangeable for public transportation or admission to public events. Or voters might be allowed to assign their vouchers to nonprofit organizations. In such a regime, if a church's congregation wanted to set up a free breakfast program, its members could vote and then donate their vouchers to the church. Such a system would both provide a tangible demonstration of the importance of voting and allow individual voters the choice of how to aggregate themselves instead of ceding that power to middlemen vote-packagers. Perhaps most importantly, turnout would be enhanced, with a concomitant increase in political competition in general and in competition for the votes of traditionally ignored groups in particular. On any model of the political process, pluralist or republican, this would represent an improvement, for the gain would be not just quantitative but qualitative as well. (Karlan 1994, 1472–1474)

As Karlan notes, moreover, some countries, like Australia, currently fine people who are able to vote and do not. Although she would use a carrot and Australia uses a stick, both have the same aim: to get people who do not care enough to overcome the costs of voting to actually vote. Karlan would subsidize, Australia would penalize. But both aim for the same effect.

But would either a subsidy or penalty improve politics? It surely would, as Karlan argues, increase participation. Those who now almost, but not quite, make it to the polls would vote. And if those voters fell into social groups that turn out at low rates, then equality would increase as well—although perhaps not by as much as reformers would hope (see Traugott, this volume). The first two of the three conditions of mass democracy would be better met. But what about the third? Would subsidies or penalties increase thoughtfulness among voters?

Karlan thinks so, as her last few words show. In a footnote that fleshes out her intuition, she makes two arguments. First, "[a]lthough uninterested voters may make bad choices, it is entirely possible that voters who know they will be voting will in fact become better informed, either out of a sense of obligation or because candidates, knowing these people are going to the polls, will invest in informing and persuading them" (Karlan 1994, 1474 n.60). This is entirely correct. Some will make bad (meaning uninformed) choices and some may become better informed. But which way will the balance run? I am less sanguine than Karlan that informed choices will outnumber uninformed choices, especially when all, not just the top, decisions on the ballot are considered. The "sense of obligation," moreover, can run in the opposite direction than she believes. If the obligation extends to voting but not to informed voting—and, after all, the little seals of civic approval we bestow on people as they step out of the booth on election day say "I voted," not "I voted thoughtfully"—then we are creating an incentive to vote but little, if any, incentive to be thoughtful. Also, candidates already "invest in informing and persuading" these voters. The problem is that the voters do not have an adequate incentive to listen. This is, in other words, largely a demand, not a supply, problem and subsidies and penalties directed at merely showing up will do little to fix it. Overall, then, we may well see less informed choices.

Second and more interestingly, Karlan seems to challenge the whole notion that we can judge the "quality" of voting—a somewhat odd position for someone who claims that the "gain" under her proposal "would be not just quantitative but qualitative as well." The difficulty she sees is "epistemological." As she puts it, "in a democracy where the franchise is at least formally open to virtually all adult citizens, how is an observer to decide which voting preferences are "bad" (Karlan 1994, 1474 n.60)? In other words, if we allow all adults to vote and many of them are bad (meaning uninformed) voters, how can we object to more of them? This answer won't quite do, however. There is a clear difference between tolerating a certain degree of uninformed voting and encouraging it. It is one thing for a political system to decide that the benefits of increased participation and equality may outweigh a certain decline in thoughtfulness; it is another to say that tolerating some amount of uninformed voting means we should tolerate any amount at all.

Karlan may actually mean something different by this comment. If one believes that mass democracy entails not just equality among voters but also among different ways of making political decisions, then thoughtful decision making cannot be essential. In this view, mass democracy is agnostic about how individuals should make political decisions. It cares only *that* people make them, not *how* they make them. Whether I choose a candidate because of that candidate's views, because of that candidate's looks, or because of a coin-toss does not matter. Democracy cares only that I make a choice under whatever criteria I want. Only this view, one could argue, fully respects decisional autonomy among voters, an important component of equality among voters themselves. This is truly minimalist democracy.

But is mass democracy so minimalist? Does it make *no* judgments about how people make political decisions? People may argue over how much information voters may properly base their votes on, but does anyone believe that they can properly choose on the basis of no information at all? Unless one entertains such an empty vision of democracy, there is no "epistemological" difficulty here. And very few of us do entertain such a vision. Most of us, for example, would describe a system where individuals could freely vote but where each chose candidates by flipping coins or by the order of letters in candidates' last names not as democratic, but as random and alphabetical, respectively. Even proponents of minimalist democracy accept that some degree of thoughtfulness is absolutely necessary. People's "common sense and arithmetic . . . [their] canny, if perhaps not terribly sophisticated, ability to assess reality and their own interests and to relate things in a fairly logical and sensible way" are what ultimately make minimal democracy possible and even attractive (Mueller 1992, 992). In Mueller's view, in fact, democracy can dispense with both elections and equality—but not minimal thoughtfulness—and still remain in some deep sense democratic (Mueller 1992, 984–90). In other words, mass democracy is not truly agnostic about how people make decisions. If it were, Karlan would be right. There would be no conflict between participation and equality, on the one hand, and "quality," on the other, because "quality" would simply not matter. But this only solves the paradox by making mass democracy something less than democratic. Thoughtless voting fails to ensure that government is responsive to the people—the central aim of democracy.

CLASSIC STRUCTURAL SOLUTIONS

Recognizing the imperative of broadening participation, several commentators have sought to finesse the troubling implications of the paradox of mass democracy. Some, including many advocates of deliberative democracy, argue that we should change our political culture to engage voters more deeply (Gutmann and Thompson 1996; Sunstein 1993a, 244–245). Of this I am deeply skeptical, since remaking culture ultimately first requires remaking voters themselves. Others have suggested minimizing the paradox's troubling implications through the structures of government. The Framers, for example, famously tried to overcome the paradox through two structural mechanisms: bicameralism and the Electoral College. Within Congress, of course, the House of Representatives expressed the democratic conditions of participation and equality. Its members were to be elected every two years by direct popular vote. Although the franchise excluded many social groups, most notably women, African Americans, and those without property, it did, relatively speaking, allow broad and equal participation. In the Framers' eyes, however, this virtue entailed a vice. The closeness of the House to the people meant that it, like they, would sometimes act unthinkingly. For this reason, among others, the Framers created a structural counterweight: the Senate. As *Federalist No. 63* puts it:

> [The Senate] may be sometimes necessary as a defense to the people against their own temporary errors and delusions. As the cool and deliberate sense of the community ought, in all governments, and actually will, in all free governments, ultimately prevail over the views of its rulers; so there are particular moments in public affairs when the people, stimulated by some irregular passion, or some illicit advantage, or misled by the artful misrepresentations of interested men, may call for measures which they themselves will afterwards be the most ready to lament and condemn. In these critical moments, how salutary will be the interference of some temperate and respectable body of citizens, in order to check the misguided career, and to suspend the blow meditated by the people against themselves, until reason, justice, and truth can regain their authority over the public mind. (Hamilton, Jay, and Madison 1787, 403–04)

To achieve this purpose, the Senate had to be constituted differently than the House. It had to be more distant from the people and not subject to their regular, direct control. The Framers thus gave senators a term of six, not two, years and allowed state legislatures, not the voters themselves, to choose them. Through these two structural means the Framers provided distance from the people and ensured a longer and steadier view in the legislative process. One chamber of the legislature could be counted on not to pander to the people when the masses themselves were not thinking things through thoughtfully.

Although we now may think of the Senate as a somewhat undemocratic feature of American government, one justified largely on historical political grounds by the need to gain the assent of small states to the Constitution, it was originally thought to serve an important democratic function. Although it violated the first two conditions of democracy (wider participation and relatively equal voting power), which were well served by the House of Representatives, it promoted the third (thoughtfulness in decision making), which in the Framers' eyes was just as important. Part of the Framers' solution to the paradox of mass democracy, then, was to have Congress straddle it. One house promoted two conditions at the expense of the third; the other promoted the third at the expense of the other two. Together they balanced competing democratic concerns. In this view, the elite Senate not only made the more seemingly democratic House tolerable but also provided the Congress overall with a perspective necessary to make the whole institution truly democratic. It was a solution that *Federalist No. 63* itself described as "paradoxical" (Hamilton et al. 1787, 402).

The Senate, of course, no longer plays this democratic role. As participation and equality grew in importance, the Senate's distance from the people began to appear unwholesome. The Senate came to be perceived as an elite, not democratic, feature of governance. In 1913 the states passed the Seventeenth

Amendment, which provides for the direct election of senators. At this point the Senate lost much of its democratic distinctiveness and effectively switched from serving democratic values complementary to those served by the House to serving the very same values. With the rise in importance of participation and equality, the Framers' paradoxical solution to the paradox of mass democracy could no longer be sustained.

The other major structural feature meant to ease the paradox's implications was the Electoral College. Here a different solution was called for. The need for a unified executive made the congressional bicameral solution infeasible. There was no way to counterbalance a directly elected executive with a thoughtfully elected one. The Framers had to find a different way of addressing the conflict among the different democratic values at stake, and their resolution reflects their weighing of the three democratic conditions. Participation and equality largely gave way to thoughtfulness.

The Framers did not provide for the direct election of the president. Instead they created what now appears to be one of the more Byzantine features of the American political landscape: the Electoral College. It provides for the election of the president by a group of people selected by the legislature of each state. It resembles the original selection mechanism of the Senate. In both cases, the state legislatures, not the citizens themselves, make the operative choices. But in the case of the president, of course, the selection is even one more step removed. The state legislatures themselves do not choose the president but rather the group of people who then will make that choice. It is a curious but carefully designed scheme. As *Federalist No. 68* explains it:

> [Although i]t was desirable that the sense of the people should operate in the choice of the person to whom so important a trust was to be confided[,] . . . [i]t was equally desirable, that the immediate election should be made by men most capable of analyzing the qualities adapted to the station, and acting under circumstances favorable to deliberation, and to a judicious combination of all the reasons and inducements which were proper to govern their choice. A small number of persons, selected by their fellow-citizens from the general mass, will be most likely to possess the information and discernment requisite to so complicated an investigation.

> It was also peculiarly desirable to afford as little opportunity as possible to tumult and disorder. . . . The choice of *several*, to form an intermediate body of electors, will be much less apt to convulse the community with any extraordinary or violent movements, than the choice of *one* who was himself to be the final object of the public wishes. (Hamilton et al. 1787, 435)

The Framers allowed each state's legislature to choose members of the Electoral College however it wished. A state legislature could allow their direct election, appoint electors itself, or choose them on some other basis. But by providing generally for two degrees of separation from the people, the Framers ensured that even in cases where a state provided for the electors' direct election there would still be some distance. To their eyes, this distance would ensure some degree of thoughtfulness in decision making.

Like the Senate, however, the Electoral College no longer fulfills its original democratic purpose. First, as all states have moved from legislative appointment of electors to appointment through popular election, the distance between the president and the voters has decreased. We have gone from two degrees to one degree of formal separation. Whether the decision rule in a particular state is winner-take-all or some form of rough proportional representation, the voters now choose the electors themselves. Second and more important, the rise of political parties, a circumstance unforeseen by the Framers, makes even this one degree of separation illusory. No longer do we encourage electors to deliberate. We expect them to mechanically reflect the preferences of the electorate (or its larger part) and, except in extreme circumstances, would think it wrong for electors to vote for any candidate other than the one to whom they are slated (*Ray v. Blair*).

The Electoral College today—to the extent it well serves any interests at all—serves interests opposite to those it was originally designed to serve (see Barnes, this volume; Gelman, Katz, and King, this volume). By effectuating the popular vote in a somewhat crude fashion, it furthers participation and equality, not thoughtfulness in decision making. Along with the Senate, it now serves the values it was originally intended to oppose and underscores, rather than helps resolve, the paradox of mass democracy.

DOWNSIZING THE ELECTORATE

Perhaps we can avoid the paradox of mass democracy by giving voters greater incentives to become engaged. Much of James Fishkin's work on the presidential primary system, for example, explores this strategy (Fishkin 1991, 1995). He starts from a recognition of the paradox. As he notes, "[t]he move towards mass democracy—a move realized by increasing participation and political equality—has had a cost in deliberation" (Fishkin 1995, 173). Moreover, Fishkin finds, all proposals for reforming the early stages of the presidential primary system fall neatly on one side of the paradox or the other. The first type of proposal, which would broaden the early primaries beyond Iowa and New Hampshire, two admittedly unrepresentative states, aims to make the primary selection process more representative of the country as a whole. The second type of proposal, which would move to some form of convention where a smaller group would choose the party's nominee, aims to make the process more thoughtful. As Fishkin describes them, these proposals present a choice "between politically equal but relatively incompetent masses and politically unequal but relatively more competent elites" (Fishkin 1991, 9). In other words, the first type of proposal vindicates participation and equality at the expense of thoughtfulness while the second type vindicates thoughtfulness at the expense of participation and equality. Although the reformers make the tradeoff differently, they all see it as unavoidable.

Fishkin seeks a way to vindicate participation, equality, and thoughtfulness all at the same time. His proposal, "deliberative polling," would randomly assemble a relatively small group of voters from across the country, educate them as they need and desire, let them argue and deliberate, and then publicize their choices. By assembling a small, representative sample of the electorate, Fishkin hopes to break through the democratic paradox. His central insight is that if we can create a micro-electorate with the same characteristics and values as the whole we can allow democracy to proceed unencumbered by the disincentives to thoughtfulness that large numbers create. Since all participants in the sample will feel that their votes actually matter in a way they did not before, we can count on them to care and think through their choices. By radically but representatively downsizing the electorate, in other words, we can create the conditions of small-scale, face-to-face electoral participation on which real democracy depends.

The problem with Fishkin's proposal is that it either has no bite or cheats on equal participation. If it is advisory only, as Fishkin envisions it, it is likely to be ignored by unthoughtful voters, who will help choose the winners. If it is given some official weight, on the other hand, those in the sample participate more fully than do others and their opinions matter more. This is necessarily so. If everyone participated equally, the large numbers of participants would rob any individual vote of its value and the whole project would collapse.

Fishkin tries to minimize this conflict between deliberative polling and equal participation in two ways. First, although relatively few voters actually participate in the deliberative polling, those who do, he insists, participate on behalf of others. Because they are chosen fairly they represent us all, and because they participate more deeply the rest of us actually participate more significantly than we would if we voted directly. Under this type of "virtual participation," everyone's views are represented in the right balance—just by others, not themselves. Second, Fishkin is careful to leave some room after deliberative polling for everyone else to participate. In the presidential selection context, for example, the sample of voters would not choose the president, but merely help narrow the field. Everyone, then, would have some voice even if some have a greater voice than others.

I doubt, however, that citizens will view virtual participation any more favorably than their forebears viewed virtual representation. What does it matter that someone else had your educated interests at heart if you had no voice? Interests that lose in the deliberative polling are likely to wonder whether the sample was truly representative. And if the deliberative polling process actually led some of a group's representatives to vote after deliberation against the group's unreflective position, the group might be more apt to challenge their representatives' legitimacy than to accept their representatives' judgments as their own. To the extent that deliberative polling works to change people's initial positions, in other words, it may make virtual participation harder to accept. The plea that a particular group would vote in a particular way if it only knew better will be greeted with great suspicion. Citizens are also likely to believe that deliberative polling violates deep norms of democratic equality. As long as the results of deliberative polling are given any concrete effect—whether those results choose the president or just narrow the field of presidential candidates—the process creates two classes of citizens and those sampled simply have greater power than those who are not.

RAISING BARRIERS IN THE NAME OF DEMOCRACY?

Is there no way out? Two strategies present themselves—one often used outside of politics but that poses troubling issues in voting and one less tried but that appears more promising.

One might first try to allow all to participate equally as a formal matter while informally discouraging unthoughtful participation. My hometown, for example, currently holds city elections on a different date from state and federal elections and is considering moving them to the same day in November. On the one side, people argue that holding separate elections wastes money and that consolidating them would dramatically boost voting in city races where turnout is now very low. On the other side, people argue that holding the elections on different days decreases the likelihood of unthoughtful voting in local elections. They contend that if local elections were moved to November many people who informed themselves only about the high-profile federal and state elections would still vote in the local races and inappropriately influence the outcome. As the candidate name order studies suggest (see Krosnick, Miller, and Tichy, this volume), voters cannot be counted on to stop voting when their information runs out. Instead they might vote randomly, vote according to where the candidate's name appears on the list, or vote according to whatever cues—racial, gender, class, or personality—they feel the names themselves supply.

Holding the elections on different dates lessens this danger because many voters who do not care enough to inform themselves about local candidates will not care enough to go to the polls for that election. Although allowed to participate, they would self-select out of these particular elections because the cost of participating in them—a separate trip to the polls—would exceed the small additional benefits they would receive from voting in the second set of races (see Norris, this volume, for a similar motivation account of voting). Separating higher- and lower-profile elections screens out less interested and engaged voters from the local races where they are likely to be disproportionately unthoughtful. This is a standard economic strategy akin to charging congestion fees on a busy road. By effectively raising the cost of voting in local elections it screens out people who do not highly value participation, just as congestion fees screen out those who receive less value from driving their car on a particular road at a busy time.

Separating elections, however, poses some troubling issues. For one thing, placing an informal toll on participation will depress participation rates overall. If the price of voting goes up, demand will go down. Although the average voter who participates may be more thoughtful, fewer will participate at all. In this view, separating elections resembles not just congestion fees but poll taxes and might make us uncomfortable for the same reasons they do. For another thing, separating elections may change the type of person who participates. By effectively raising the cost of voting, it ensures that mostly those who care will show up and they will disproportionately consist of party activists and others whose views may be unrepresentative. In primaries, for example, a party's more passionate—and partisan—members are most likely to vote (Gerber and Morton 1998, 309–310). Separating elections might thus make voting more thoughtful but at the same time less representative. Is it better to have a more thoughtful but skewed electorate? The costs of this strategy may be unacceptably high.

NEO-MADISONIAN SOLUTIONS

A more promising approach to unthoughtful voting notes that although the paradox of mass democracy implies that tradeoffs between broad participation and thoughtful *individual* political decision making are inevitable, it does not necessarily imply any conflict between broad participation and thoughtful *overall* political decision making. In other words, although we cannot escape the paradox individually we may be able to do so collectively. The challenge is to design social procedures that neutralize the effects of unthoughtful individual decision making that accompany broadened participation. Although this might sound a tall order, several existing electoral practices arguably achieve it in particular contexts.

Many have long suspected that the position of a candidate's name on a ballot makes a difference to her success, and research confirms this (Krosnick, Miller, and Tichy, this volume). As already described, those candidates whose names appear first for an office typically receive a "name order" bonus. They gain some votes purely by virtue of appearing first. Some voters must, in other words, choose at least some of their candidates by ballot position. To them, ballot structure, not policy, character, experience, or political party, drives their choice and in close cases can change the overall outcome of the election. Montana and Ohio address this problem in a very practical way (Montana Code Annotated § 13-12-205; Ohio Revised Code § 3505.03-.04; see generally Krosnick, Miller, and Tichy, this volume). Rather than trying to convince voters to make more thoughtful choices or trying to discourage participation by those likely to cast such unthoughtful ballots, these states structure the ballot itself in such a way as to neutralize any net name order voting effect. By rotating the order of names on the ballot so that each candidate appears equally often in each position, they ensure that votes made on the basis of name order flow equally to all candidates and so have no overall effect on the election. Name order rotation causes name order votes to cancel each other out and so allows only the remaining, more thoughtful votes to decide the result.

At first glance, this regulatory strategy appears shallow. It does, after all, address only the symptoms of the pathology and leaves the underlying pathology itself untouched. It neither improves the way individual voters make their decisions nor restricts participation to more civically competent voters. Yet this shallowness is its strength. Attempts to refashion voters themselves are apt to be coercive and offensive, not to mention ineffective. Barring some from voting would violate two of the three necessary conditions of democracy: broad participation and equality. Addressing only the symptoms of unthoughtful voting, however, avoids these difficulties. By restructuring the ballot to neutralize the overall effect of uninformed voting, everyone can still participate equally—no matter how they make decisions—but choices made on the basis of where a candidate's name appears will not likely affect any collective outcome. An unthoughtful voter cannot complain, moreover, that his choice was not counted or respected. It was—even though it was canceled out by other votes chosen on the same basis. This shallow strategy of addressing symptoms rather than pathologies allows us to promote participation, equality, and overall, if not individual, thoughtfulness in decision making. Although it does not overcome the paradox of mass democracy, it allows us to avoid its bad collective effects. Like Madison's solution to the problem of faction, it provides a structural means of collectively overcoming individuals' civic disabilities.

Campaign finance reform often works similarly. At bottom much campaign finance regulation rests on the fear that some voters choose candidates unthoughtfully—in particular, that they respond to campaign advertising as pure stimulus. Under this view, the problem with unequal resources lies in the way it permits campaigns to sway some voters by the sheer amount and gloss of advertising (see Estrich, this volume). If voters were always thoughtful and carefully weighed what they saw and heard, there would be no reason to worry about advertising inequalities at all. In fact, advertising, even if unequal, would likely improve voters' individual decision making. It would either provide voters with information that they found useful and thus enable them to make better choices, or it would provide no such information and the thoughtful voter would simply discard it. In neither case would it ever lead thoughtful voters to make worse decisions. If voters do not carefully weigh advertising, however, the situation looks very different. In particular, if citizens respond positively to sheer advertising stimulus—favoring those candidates who advertise more often and more slickly—unequal advertising may degrade the thoughtfulness of their individual choices. In this view, choosing a candidate because she advertised more heavily is like choosing her because her name appears first on the ballot. Neither represents a respectable basis for democratic choice.

Restricting money in politics might address this danger in two ways. First, limits can redirect available money from more expensive media, like television, to less expensive media, like print and mass mailings. If print and mass mailings convey more hard information or are less likely to provoke a pure stimulus-type response, this redirection of spending would improve the quality of individual decision making. In this view, campaign finance limits work to change the character of appeals campaigns make. They shift advertising toward media that allow thoughtful voters to make more informed choices and at the same time deny unthoughtful voters the stimulus to which they respond. Proposals to regulate the format of political advertising on television by requiring that commercials consist only of shots of the candidates themselves speaking aim in this same direction (Fairness in Political Advertising Act 1984).

By avoiding voiceovers and forcing the commercial to focus visually on the candidate, these proposals hope to encourage listeners to focus on substantive differences. Similar to campaign finance limits, these proposals seek not to remake unthoughtful voters or bar them from voting but to deny them the types of appeals most likely to stimulate unthoughtful choices.

The media exception, one of the more controversial aspects of current campaign finance regulation, has the same ambition. Under federal law, corporations and unions cannot contribute money directly to federal candidates or make expenditures for them. Federal law, however, exempts "any news story, commentary, or editorial distributed through the facilities of any broadcasting station, newspaper, magazine, or other periodical publication, unless such facilities are owned or controlled by any political party, political committee, or candidate" (2 USC § 431(9)(B)(i)). A media company can spend money to endorse a candidate in its pages or programming while other companies cannot. As many have pointed out, this puts media companies in a privileged position. They alone can spend money to advertise the fact that they think particular candidates should win or lose.

To many, this distinction is indefensible. Media companies, like other businesses, have their own interests and will be tempted to pursue them, sometimes have bad judgment, and can be highly partisan. Any justification for the exception, then, cannot lie in the nature of the business media companies pursue, media companies' superior wisdom, or their neutrality. The exception must rest rather on the nature of the communication itself. To some, a "news story, commentary, or editorial" likely imparts a different kind of message than does a standard political advertisement. It is more likely to engage voters' thoughtful capacities and less likely even to catch the attention of less thoughtful voters. Editorial endorsements, for example, make notoriously uncaptivating copy. If they persuade at all, it is because of their arguments, not their gloss.

Second, by seeking to limit the funds available to each side, campaign finance limits can try to prevent one side from vastly outspending the other. Even if some voters then choose on the basis of sheer advertising stimulus, both sides can make roughly the same number of such appeals, if they wish. This constraint produces an effect like that produced by rotating candidates' names on a ballot. Since both sides can produce roughly the same amount of stimulus, these voters' ballots largely cancel each other out. Equalizing budgets, in other words, allows all voters to participate equally as voters but neutralizes the overall effect of choices made on the basis of advertising stimulus. Like name order rotation, it seeks to address symptoms rather than the underlying democratic pathology itself. But that is again its strength.

FINAL THOUGHTS

The paradox of mass democracy condemns us to increasingly unthoughtful individual decision making as we make government by "the people" more and more a truth. We simply cannot deepen and broaden individual participation at the same time. The only remedy to unthoughtful individual decision making—narrowing participation—carries costs too high to contemplate. We can, however, seek to mitigate, if not neutralize, the effects of such individual decision making on our collective choices. The paradox of mass democracy has no collective corollary. Our challenge, then, should be to design new democratic structures appropriate for a mass electorate. We should learn from our experiments with name order rotation that we can sometimes collectively overcome the paradox's bad individual effects. But as the contentious history of campaign finance reform suggests, innovation here is likely to be difficult not least because it challenges many attractive notions we like to hold about the voter in traditional democracy.

Postscript

15

Keeping Hope Alive

EDWARD J. McCAFFERY

MARION R. JUST

ANN N. CRIGLER

BACK TO THE BEGINNING

We began the project of rethinking the vote both many pages ago, and in the wake of the 2000 presidential election. We noted then, and in our introductory chapter, that much of the heated rhetoric that surrounded Bush versus Gore, the election, and *Bush v. Gore*, the case, could be traced to two competing conceptions of what democracy was all about, with correspondingly divergent views of the role of the vote.

To "minimalists" such as Richard Posner, a broad popular vote is little more than a crude and pragmatic check on elected officials, helping to prevent the worse alternative of despotism and to facilitate peace, prosperity, and stability. Such a minimal role for the vote fits with these theorists' minimal view of the realities and possibilities for individuals as fully participating political citizens (Mueller 1992; Plato 1957; Riker 1982). Less is fine.

To "participatory" democrats like Lani Guinier and Cass Sunstein, in contrast, the vote is the central constitutive act of democracy, which is after all a form of government "of the people, by the people, and for the people." Democracy is democracy because the people have the power. The vote is the literal instantiation of that power. Participatory theorists place great faith in the realities and possibilities of individual citizen participation in governance. More is always desired.

In the pages since our first words—and in the time since the 2000 election—the minimalists seem to have had the better of things. Nothing truly dramatic in the way of actual electoral reform has occurred since November 7, 2000, as the chapters by Barnes, and Potter and Viray, have pointed out. This might even be a good thing, as the chapters by Hasen, Ortiz, and others suggest.

Further favoring the minimalist side of things is the fact that, while nothing is precisely what some good minimalists might have hoped for in the

prospects for American electoral reform, the path toward reasonably acceptable *minimal* reform, at least, seems clear. The technology of voting and of vote-
counting should be improved, as the chapter by Alvarez, Sinclair, and Wilson
so clearly demonstrates; based on their solid evidence and analysis, one would
hope that punchcard ballots will soon become a thing of the past. Ballot ordering and design are subjects that deserve far more attention than they have
historically received, as Krosnick, Miller, and Tichy convincingly show. The
media should, at the margin, get its act together by taking more time to report
results, using better statistical models, and being more cautious about how they
describe vote projections, as Frankovic points out. Popular ideas like twenty-
four-hour voting, same-day registration, and making election day a holiday
warrant further study, as the chapter by Crigler, Just, and Buhr underscores.
And there is a strong case, for all but the most ardent minimalist, for strengthening the Federal Election Commission and making voting and electoral standards more uniform across the country, as Potter and Viray argue. So much
can be achieved without stirring revolutionary fervor or disrupting the calm
characteristic of the minimalist pose: better voting without anything "carniva-
lesque," as Posner (2001) would have it. But what of the participatory project?
As we have seen, nothing of any great consequence has been done. More troubling still, the very means for furthering the ideal of more and better participation are far from clear. What, if anything, can and should be done to advance
the dream of making "all the votes count, and count equally"?

The small steps even considered so far can hardly sate the participatory
democrat's urge to answer "the clarion call for major democratic reform"
(Guinier 2000). What has actually been accomplished is even less satisfying.
Yet, since we first invoked Guinier's plea, the intervening pages have been
filled with skeptical warnings to the participatory crowd. If any or even all of
the agenda just sketched out were acted on—if we had better and clearer ballots, no punchcards, clearer and more uniform vote-counting rules, and so on—
there is good reason to believe that nothing very significant would change.
Perhaps in the next rare case of a statistical tie things would come out differently, but that is hardly certain: It is not clear that Bush versus Gore came out
"wrong," in point of fact. The lesson that even dramatic legal and institutional
changes are unlikely to have major impacts on voter registration and turnout
emerges quite clearly in the U.S. context from Traugott's chapter and, worldwide, from Norris's. Indeed, Traugott suggests that easier registration and voting protocols might make the electorate *less* representative of the whole than
it already is, dealing a blow to the ambitions of a good many participatory theorists. Ortiz more darkly suggests that there is a nearly unavoidable tradeoff
between quantity and quality in voting, that more participation might inevitably lead to less informed participation. Hasen cautions that chaos can result from an over-quick embrace of the equal protection door opened by the
Supreme Court in *Bush v. Gore*—the one potentially *beneficial* aspect of the opinion, to participatory believers such as Chemerinsky, Guinier, and Hasen himself. Gelman, Katz, and King demonstrate that even seemingly radical solutions
such as eliminating the Electoral College are unlikely to make any major difference and, again, may make things worse by the light of many participatory

theorists: Repealing the Electoral College may only disempower the average voter. Truly radical solutions, such as Barnes's invocation of rank order preference voting, or Ortiz's suggestion of small deliberative communities of voters, seem little more than pipe dreams.

In the light of all this darkness, is it even worth keeping hope alive for the participatory vision of democracy? Or should we just do the minimal things, and get on with other more important political matters?

WHAT IS TO BE DONE?

In terms of voting and electoral reform, two answers to the familiar question of what is to be done emerge from the discussions in these pages.

First, there is a good deal to be said for the impact of technocratic changes. Alvarez, Sinclair, and Wilson show, for example, that eliminating punchcard ballots may reduce racial and ethnic bias in voting. This should be done. Other chapters raise other strong arguments for simple changes that might matter, such as Krosnick, Miller, and Tichy's suggestion of ballot order rotation. Even most minimalists ought to endorse such reform in the name of technocratic accuracy. But we should all be realistic about the transformative possibilities of such minimalist changes. After all, to connect the dots, minimalists can endorse such changes precisely *because* they are so minimal. It is hard to object to small changes that will make small differences. But participatory theorists cannot be blamed for asking if that is all that should be done in the wake of the seeming crisis of Bush versus Gore.

Second, then, is the participatory answer. This does not emerge as simply or as directly from what we have learned. But on reflection a strong case can be made for some participatory response nonetheless: As we have seen, the small and (relatively) uncontroversial technocratic changes most likely to happen will not satisfy any clarion call for major democratic reform. Believers in participatory democracy should therefore keep doing what they have always done: Ignore the minimalists and continue to work to get more people more engaged in the democratic project. After all, Downs's voter's paradox did not spring into being in 1957 when Downs set it to print. It is a brute mathematical fact of the matter. People should not vote expecting to change outcomes, certainly not in national elections in a democracy the size of the United States. Citizens would be better off playing the lottery and using their winnings (if any) to influence the political process, in the manner that Estrich, unhappily, describes, if they want to have real power. That is just the way it is.

Yet dire statements of the arationality of the act of voting have not stopped various "political entrepreneurs" (Popkin 1979)[1] from getting out there and stirring up, imploring, even "rocking" the vote. Voter registration efforts, for example, have been major features of the civil rights movement in the 1960s, the women's liberation movement under Gloria Steinem and other feminist leaders in the 1970s (Stern 1997; Steinem 1994), and the black empowerment movement under Jesse Jackson and other leaders in the 1990s (Timmerman 2002; Frady 1996; House 1988). There is reason to believe that Latinos today, who vote in relatively lower numbers than other demographic groups, stand poised to benefit from similar mobilization efforts (Arvizu and Garcia 1996; Cassel 2002; Shaw, de la Garza, and Lee 2000).

Unfortunately, there is reason to be skeptical here, too. It is not all that certain, by any of several observable measures, that these relatively late-stage voter turnout efforts have mattered all that much.[2] Of course, there can be no doubt that the Nineteenth Amendment, giving women the legal right to vote, and the Twenty-fourth Amendment, abolishing poll taxes and thus making the black vote initially granted by the Fifteenth Amendment more of a reality, changed things, over time. The Civil Rights Act of 1965 ensured ballot access for ethnic and linguistic minorities around the country. Such landmark constitutional and legislative changes, chronicled by Potter and Viray, resulted in the increased participation of previously marginalized groups and have had significant impact on America's policy agendas.

Yet in the very success of these large-scale enfranchisements lies something of a rub. Now that most large demographic groups have been enfranchised— and now that women and minorities are voting in large numbers—it gets harder and harder to see what additional efforts will matter at the margins, in terms of electoral outcomes. The electorate appears to have stabilized at about one-half of the eligible citizenry. Traugott's and Norris's chapters show how hard it will be to ratchet these numbers up, and Traugott's and Ortiz's chapters suggest that things may not improve if we do. Gelman, Katz, and King show how brutally small each individual's voting power is, in fact, with or without the intermediary of the Electoral College.

In sum: Downs's paradox lives.

ROOM FOR HOPE?

Does all this mean that democracy in the United States and other large Western nations has simply gotten so big and unwieldy that individuals have little real power and that they might as well stay home and not vote—and academics might as well stop writing about how to get them to vote?

Not necessarily.

Maybe we have been looking in the wrong place for the meaning of voting all along, or at least of late. The minimalists are, by and large, consequentialists, narrow empiricists who care about specific, observable outcomes. By their lights, it is hard to argue that any single vote matters. Downs's voting paradox is relentless; an individual has more of a chance of dying on the way to the polls than affecting the outcome in a major election. Bush versus Gore did not disprove Downs; if anything, as we argued in the introductory chapter, it made the paradox more apparent. For even if there ever were a literal tie—and Bush versus Gore got as close to that reality as any presidential election in our more than two hundred year history has—it would be some judge, some elected official, some bureaucrat, and not any individual voter, who decided the outcome.

But maybe the consequentialist lights are the wrong ones under which to analyze the vote. Maybe participation is a good *in and of itself*, not because it does or might in some remote counterfactual case affect actual political outcomes. Perhaps the right to participation that voting entails makes people feel better about themselves, their role in their country, and their country itself. Certainly, people seem to hunger for participation, as Crigler, Just, and Buhr point out. And when this ardent desire for participation is flaunted—by practices that impede access to the ballot booth, by crude and imperfect voting or vote-counting processes, by public statements of the arbitrariness of it all—maybe a harm is done to the people's senses of dignity and self-respect. And maybe these harms matter.

This possibility leaves us with some questions: Are the people who want "all the votes to count, and to count equally" naïve? Are they the same statistically inept people who play the lottery for the wrong reasons?[3] Or are they simply looking for something else, other than the raw power to determine electoral outcomes? And are they right to want that?

Let's return to a statement from Posner, the leading minimalist interpreter of Bush versus Gore, which we quoted in our introductory chapter:

> American democracy is structured, formal, practical, realistic, and both supportive of and supported by commercial values. It is not starry-eyed, carnivalesque, or insurrectionary. *It is not pure or participatory democracy*, and it does not consider political chaos a price worth paying to actualize the popular will. Its spirit is closer to that of Burke than to that of Rousseau. The populism of a Jefferson or a Jackson remains a part of our democratic ideology, but a smaller part than in the days of yore. (Posner 2001 emphasis added)

Maybe Posner is only half-right here. He is right that American democracy has indeed been remarkably stable and supportive of commercial values and prosperity. But maybe—just maybe—it has been stable *because* it has been participatory. Maybe we have avoided "political chaos" as well and as long as we have because of, not despite, our long if uneven trend toward being a more full and participatory democracy. When people are hopeful and feel engaged and participatory in a society they are less, not more, likely to be "insurrectionary." After all, the greatest periods of unrest in our nation's history have come when people or groups have felt disempowered, disrespected, disenfranchised.

Social psychologists know this phenomenon, as do a good many laypeople with common sense and empathetic hearts. People like to be listened to, treated with equal concern and respect. Patients, for example, who feel that their doctors and other caregivers pay them heed often have better clinical outcomes. Neighborhoods are often safer when residents feel that the police listen to them. Students learn more when teachers treat them with respect. And so on.

Maybe voters want, need, deserve the same kind of attention, to feel that they are being treated with equal concern and respect. Consider, for example, that since 1964, the National Election Study (NES) has been asking a question: "How much do you feel that having elections makes the government pay attention to what the people think?" Larry Bartels recently studied the responses to this question and concluded:

> Whether the extraordinary aftermath of the 2000 presidential election will erode American's faith in their electoral process remains to be seen. But the evidence of the past four decades, properly interpreted, seems to suggest that that faith has been remarkably durable. (Bartels 2002, 76)

If the minimalists were to "win" the battle post–Bush versus Gore by keeping actual electoral changes to a minimum, but at the cost of shattering Americans' faith in the central role of the vote as an occasion to be heard, they might just find their victory to be a Pyrrhic one in the end.

LAST WORDS

This is where we have come in our rethinking of the vote. The minimalists are right, for important reasons. We should indeed hesitate to do too much too quickly; we should celebrate and not condemn the calm stability of American democracy. Still, the small steps to be taken are clear, and there is little reason not to take them.

But the participatory theorists are right, too, albeit for different reasons, different even from what they often aver. Greater, purer, wider participation may not generate any better choices among candidates. More participation may not bring a revolution today, tomorrow, or ever. But it may make us all feel better about ourselves and our society, feel that we are being listened to, feel that we are being treated with respect. And these things matter. In the end, America and other Western democracies have discovered the perhaps paradoxical truth that greater popular participation is not an enemy of peace and prosperity, but rather a continuing precondition for their attainment. There is no reason to cease trying to expand the participatory project, born but hardly finished in our founding revolution.

Perhaps this is what Lincoln had in mind in dedicating his life to the ongoing quest to make real a government "of the people, by the people, and for the people." Lincoln knew with his heart that there is something transcendent in political participation and equality; he saw with his eyes that there is something fatal in disenfranchisement. Lincoln, a practical politician, knew from abundant experience that citizen voters could do harm. But he also believed in the possibilities that the "better angels of our nature" might yet one day speak out (Lincoln 1861). In the end, a faith in letting these voices be heard may matter more to the democratic process than Downs's coolly mathematical calculus. We can thank the participatory theorists for keeping such hope alive.

NOTES

1. Samuel Popkin defines a political entrepreneur as "someone willing to invest his own time and resources to coordinate the inputs of others in order to produce collective action or collective goods" (Popkin 1979, 259). The term well fits those individuals dedicated to getting out the vote.
2. For example, U.S. Census Bureau statistics show that the black vote as a percentage of black citizen population peaked in 1984 at 72 percent; it was 70 percent in 1992 and 67.5 percent in 2000. Women's participation peaked in 1968 at 72.8 percent; the number fell to 69.3 percent in 1992 and 65.6 percent in 2000 (U.S. Census Bureau 2002; see also Conway 2000).
3. Compare McCaffery 1994, arguing that lottery play does not reveal rampant ignorance.

Bibliography

Abramson, P. R., and J. H. Aldrich. 1982. "The Decline of Electoral Participation in the United States." *American Political Science Review* 76(3): 502–521.

Ackerman, Bruce. 2001. "Anatomy of a Constitutional Coup." *London Review of Books*, 8 February.

Aldrich, J. H. 1993. "Rational Choice and Turnout." *American Journal of Political Science* 37: 246–278.

Allen, Mike. 2001. "In First Meeting, Bush and Black Caucus Discuss Voting." *Washington Post*, 1 February.

Alvarez, R. Michael, and Jonathan Nagler. 2001. "The Likely Consequences of Internet Voting for Political Representation." *Loyola Law Review* 34(3): 1115–1154.

Alvarez, R. Michael, Tara Butterfield, and Catherine Wilson. 2001. "Counting Ballots." Unpublished manuscript, California Institute of Technology.

Anderson, Nick. 2001. "House OKs an Overhaul of Elections." *Los Angeles Times*, 13 December.

———. 2002a. "Defying Congress, Bush Slashes Anti-Terror Bill." *Los Angeles Times*, 14 August.

———. 2002b. "Soft-Money Rules a Hard Row to Hoe." *Los Angeles Times*, 7 April.

Ansolabehere, Stephen. 2001. "Voting Machines, Race, and Equal Protection." *Election Law Journal* 1: 61–70.

Apgar, Sally. 1997. "Stepping Up: Women Finding Place in Boardroom." *Star-Tribune Newspaper of the Twin Cities Minneapolis–St. Paul*, 28 July.

Arvizu, John R., and F. Chris Garcia. 1996. "Latino Voting Participation: Explaining and Differentiating Latino Voting Turnout." *Hispanic Journal of Behavioral Sciences* 18(2): 104–128.

Auer, Andreas, and Alexander H. Trechsel. 2001. "Voter Part Internet?" Le projet e-voting dans le canton de Geneve dans une perspective socio-politique et juridique. Online. www.helbing.ch.

Avey, M. J. 1989. *The Demobilization of American Voters: A Comprehensive Theory of Voter Turnout*. New York: Greenwood Press.

Bagley, C. R. 1966. "Does Candidates' Position on the Ballot Paper Influence Voters' Choice?—A Study of the 1959 and 1964 British General Elections." *Parliamentary Affairs* 74: 162–174.

Bain, Henry M., and Donald S. Hecock. 1957. *Ballot Position and Voter's Choice*. Detroit: Wayne State University.

Bakker, Eric A., and Arend Lijphart. 1980. "A Crucial Test of Alphabetic Voting: The Election at the University of Leiden, 1973–1978." *British Journal of Political Science* 10: 521–525.

"The Ballot Reform Imperative" [Editorial]. 2000. *New York Times*, 17 December.

Banzhaf, J. R. 1965. "Weighted Voting Doesn't Work: A Mathematical Analysis." *Rutgers Law Review* 19: 317–343.

———. 1968. "One Man, 3,312 Votes: A Mathematical Analysis of the Electoral College." *Villanova Law Review* 13: 304–332.

Bartels, Larry M. 2002. "Question Order and Declining Faith in Elections." *Public Opinion Quarterly* 66(1): 67–79.

Bartolini, Stefano. 2000. "Franchise Expansion." In *International Encyclopedia of Elections*, ed. R. Rose. Washington, DC: CQ Press.

Beck, N. 1975. "A Note on the Probability of a Tied Election." *Public Choice* 23: 75–79.

Benson, Mitchel. 2002. "Questioning the Books: CALPERS Vows to Help Prevent Audit Schemes." *Wall Street Journal*, 22 February.

Berelson, Bernard, Paul Lazarsfeld, and William McPhee. 1954. *Voting: A Study of Opinion Formation in a Presidential Campaign*. Chicago: University of Chicago Press.

Berg, Irwin A., and Geralk M. Rapaport. 1954. "Response Bias in an Unstructured Questionnaire." *Journal of Psychology* 38: 475–481.

Berinsky, A., N. Burns, and M. Traugott. 2001. "Who Votes by Mail? A Dynamic Model of the Individual-Level Consequences of Vote-by-Mail Systems." *Public Opinion Quarterly* 65: 178.

Bickel, Alexander. 1962. *The Least Dangerous Branch*. Indianapolis: Bobbs-Merrill.

Blais, Andre, and R. K. Carty. 1990. "Does Proportional Representation Foster Voter Turnout?" *European Journal of Political Research* 18(2): 167–181.

Blais, Andre, and A. Dobrzynska. 1998. "Turnout in Electoral Democracies." *European Journal of Political Research* 33(2): 239–261.

Blais, Andre, and Louis Massicotte. 2000. "Day of Election." In *The International Encyclopedia of Elections*, ed. R. Rose. Washington, DC: CQ Press.

———. 2001. "Electoral Participation." In *Comparing Democracies 2: Elections and Voting in Global Perspective*, ed. L. LeDuc, R. Niemi, and P. Norris. London: Sage.

Blais, Andre, Louis Massicotte, and A. Yoshinaka. 2001. "Deciding Who Has the Right to Vote: A Comparative Analysis of Election Laws." *Electoral Studies* 20(1): 41–62.

Blydenburgh, J. C. 1971. "A Controlled Experiment to Measure the Effects of Personal Contact Campaigning." *Midwest Journal of Political Science* 15(2): 365–381.

Brady, Henry E. 2002. *Report on Voting and Ballot Form in Palm Beach County*, Survey Research Center, University of California, Berkeley. Online. http://srcweb.berkeley.edu.

Brams, Steven J., and M. D. Davis. 1974. "The 3/2's Rule in Presidential Campaigning." *American Political Science Review* 68: 113–134.

———. 1975. "Comment on 'Campaign Resource Allocation under the Electoral College,' by C. S. Colantoni, T. J. Levesque, and P. C. Ordeshook." *American Political Science Review* 69: 155–156.

Brams, Steven J., and Peter S. Fisherman. 1978. "Approval Voting." *American Political Science Review* 72(3): 831–847.

Brians, Craig Leonard, and Bernard Grofman. 1999. "When Registration Barriers Fall, Who Votes? An Empirical Test of a Rational Choice Model." *Public Choice* 21: 161–176.

Briffault, Richard. 2000. "Law and Political Parties: The Political Parties and Campaign Finance Reform." *Columbia Law Review* 100: 620–664.

Broder, David. 2001. "Election Reform, a Hit Last Year, Goes Amiss." *Washington Post*, 21 April.

Brook, D. and G. J. G. Upton. 1974. "Biases in Local Government Elections Due to Position on the Ballot Paper." *Applied Statistics* 23(3): 414–419.

Brooks, Robert C. 1921. "Voters' Vagaries." *National Municipal Review* 10: 161–165.

Bruni, Frank, and Jim Yardley. 2000. "The 2000 Election: The Texan Governor; Bush Aides, Casting Gore Camp as Sore Losers; Plot Next Steps." *New York Times*, 10 November.

"Buchanan Votes in Florida, County by County." 2001. *Washington Post*, 9 November.

Bullock, Charles S., and Richard E. Dunn. 1996. "Election Roll-Off: A Test of Three Explanations." *Urban Affairs Review* 32(1): 71–86.

Burke, Edmund. [1790] 1969. *Reflections on the Revolution in France*. Reprint, Baltimore, MD: Penguin.

Burnham, Walter D. 1965. "The Changing Shape of the American Political Universe." *American Political Science Review* 59(1): 7–28.

———. 1982. *The Current Crisis in American Politics*. Oxford: Oxford University Press.

———. 1987. *The Turnout Problem Elections American Style*. Washington DC: The Brookings Institute.

"Bush Still Had Votes to Win in a Recount, Study Finds" [Editorial]. 2001. *Los Angeles Times*, 12 November.

Byrne, Donn. 1971. *The Attraction Paradigm*. New York: Academic Press.

Byrne, Gary C., and J. Kristian Pueschel. 1974. "But Who Should I Vote for County Coroner?" *Journal of Politics* 36(3): 778–784.

Cain, Bruce E. 1999. "Election Law as a Field: A Political Scientist's Perspective." *Loyola Law Review* 32: 1105–1120.

Cain, Bruce, John Ferejohn, and Morris Fiorina. 1987. *The Personal Vote*. Cambridge, MA: Harvard University Press.

Caldeira, G. A., S. C. Patterson, and G. A. Markko. 1985. "The Mobilization of Voters in Congressional Elections." *Journal of Politics* 47(2): 490–509.

California Department of Finance, Economic Research. 2001. *California County Profiles*. Sacramento, CA: Author. California Election Code 13111(b). West, 2002.

Calmes, Jackie. 2001a. "Congress Presses to Put Election Reform Atop Bush's List of Legislative Concerns." *Wall Street Journal*, 26 January.

———. 2001b. "Election-Reform Proposals Pop Up All Over the Country." *Wall Street Journal*, 5 February.

Caltech/MIT Voting Technology Project. 2001a. *Residual Votes Attributable to Technology: An Assessment of the Reliability of Existing Voting Equipment*. Unpublished manuscript, California Institute of Technology.

———. 2001b. *Voting: What Is, What Could Be*. Pasadena: California Institute of Technology. July.

Calvert, Jerry W., and Jack Gilchrist. 1993. "Suppose They Held an Election and Almost Everybody Came!" *P.S.*, December: 695–699.

Campbell, Angus. 1966. "Surge and Decline: A Study of Electoral Change." In *Elections and the Political Order*, ed. A. Campbell, P. E. Converse, W. E. Miller, and D. E. Stokes. New York: Wiley.

Campbell, Angus, et al. 1960. *The American Voter*. New York: Wiley.

Campbell, James E. 1992. "Forecasting the Presidential Vote in the States." *American Journal of Political Science* 36(2): 386–407.

Cassel, Carol A. 2002. "Hispanic Turnout: Estimates from Validated Voting Data." *Political Research Quarterly* 55(2): 391–408.

Catalyst. 2002. *Women Board Directors of the Fortune 1000*. Online. http://www.catalystwomen.org/research/censuses.htm.

CBS, Inc. 1964. *Bandwagon: A Review of the Literature*. New York: Columbia Broadcasting System, Office of Social Research.

Chamberlain, G., and M. Rothchild. 1981. " A Note on the Probability of Casting a Decisive Vote." *Journal of Economic Theory* 25: 152–162.

Chemerinsky, Erwin. 1999. *Federal Jurisdiction*. Gaithersburg, MD: Aspen Law and Business.

Choper, Jesse. 1980. *Judicial Review and the National Political Process*. Chicago: University of Chicago Press.

Clausen, A. R. 1966. *Political Predictions and Projections: How Are They Conducted? How Do They Influence the Outcomes of Elections?* Washington, DC: Center for Information on America.

Clubb, Jerome M., and Michael W. Traugott. 1972. "National Patterns of Referenda Voting: The 1968 Election." In *People and Politics in Urban Society*, ed. H. Hahn. Beverly Hills, CA: Sage.

Colomer, J. M. 1991. "Benefits and Costs of Voting." *Electoral Studies* 10(4): 313–325.

Coney, Kenneth A. 1977. "Order-Bias: The Special Case of Letter Preference." *Public Opinion Quarterly* 41(3): 385–388.

The Constitution Project. 2001. "Building Consensus for Election Reform." *The Constitution Project's Forum on Election Reform*, August. Online. www.constitutionproject. org/eri/index.htm.

Conway, M. Margaret. 2000. "Gender and Political Participation." In *Gender and American Politics*, ed. S. Tolleson-Rinehart and J. J. Josephson. Armonk, NY: M. E. Sharpe.

Coombs, Fred S., John G. Peters, and Gerald S. Strom. 1974. "Bandwagon, Ballot Position, and Party Effects: An Experiment in Voting Choice." *Experimental Study of Politics* 3: 31–57.

Cox, G. W., and J. N. Katz. 1999. "The Reapportionment Revolution and Bias in U.S. Congressional Elections." *American Journal of Political Science* 43: 812–840.

———. 2002. *Elbridge Gerry's Salamander: The Electoral Consequences of the Reapportionment Revolution*. New York: Cambridge University Press.

Crewe, Ivor. 1981. "Electoral Participation." In *Democracy at the Polls*, ed. A. Ranney and D. Butler. Washington, DC: AEI Press.

Cronbach, Lee J. 1950. "Further Evidence on Response Sets and Test Design." *Educational and Psychological Measurement* 10: 3–31.

Dahl, Robert A. 1956. *A Preface to Democratic Theory*. Chicago: The University of Chicago Press.

———. 1989. *Democracy and Its Critics*. New Haven, CT: Yale University Press.

———. 1998. *On Democracy*. New Haven, CT: Yale University Press.

———. 2001. *How Democratic is the American Constitution?* New Haven, CT: Yale University Press.

Darcy, Robert. 1986. "Position Effects with Party Column Ballots." *Western Political Quarterly* 39: 648–662.

Darcy, Robert, and Ian McAllister. 1990. "Ballot Position Effects." *Electoral Studies* 9: 5–17.

Darcy, Robert, and Anne Schneider. 1989. "Confusing Ballots, Roll-Off and the Black Vote." *Western Political Quarterly* 42: 347–364.

Davidson, Michael. 2001. "Notes on the History of Article I, Section 4, Clause 1." The Constitution Project, 3 April. Online. www.constitutionproject.org/eri.

Davies, Phillip J. 1992. *Elections USA*. New York: Manchester University Press.

Dean, Michael L. 1980. "Presentation Order Effects in Product Taste Tests." *Journal of Psychology* 105: 107–110.

Delli Carpini, Michael X., and Scott Keeter. 1996. *What Americans Know about Politics and Why It Matters*. New Haven, CT: Yale University Press.

de Tocqueville, Alexis. [1850] 1990. *Democracy in America*. Reprint, Chicago: Encyclopaedia Britannica.

de Tocqueville, Alexis. [1850] 2000. *Democracy in America*. Ed. and trans. Harvey Mansfield and Delba Winthrop. Chicago: University of Chicago Press.

Dinkin, Robert J. 1982. *Voting in Revolutionary America: A Study of Elections in the Original Thirteen States*. Westport, CT: Greenwood Press.

"The Disenfranchisement of Ex-Felons." 1989. *Harvard Law Review* 102: 1300–1317.

Donovan, Aaron. 2001. "No Gains for Women on Corporate Boards." *New York Times*, 24 June.

Downs, Anthony. 1957. *An Economic Theory of Democracy*. New York: Harper & Row.

Dukakis, Michael. 1998. "The Problem Is Not the Phone Calls, It's the Special Interest Money." *Journal of Legislation* 24(2): 201–205.

Duverger, Maurice. 1954. *Political Parties: Their Organization & Activity in the Modern State*. London: Metheun.

Edelman, Murray. 1977. *Symbolic Politics*. Urbana: University of Illinois Press.

Eilperin, Juliet. 2001. "House in Dispute over Election Reform Panel." *Washington Post*, 15 February.

Eilperin, Juliet, and Mike Allen. 2001. "Election Reform Gets Push from Bush, Congress: House Leaders to Create Special Panel." *Washington Post*, 25 January.

Election Reform Information Project, 2000. "Election Reform Since November 2001: What's Changed, What Hasn't, and Why." Washington, DC: electionline.org.

Election Reform Information Project. 2002. "Election Reform Since November 2001: What's Changed, What Hasn't, and Why." Washington, DC: electionline.org.

Elliot, Jonathan. [1888] 1937. *Debates in the Several State Conventions on the Adoption of the Federal Constitution*. Reprint, Charlottesville, VA: Michie Co.

Estrich, Susan. 2000. *Sex and Power*. New York: Berkeley Publishing Group.

Federal Election Commission. 1997. *Report to the Congress on the Impact of the National Voter Registration Act of 1993 on the Administration of Federal Elections*. Washington, DC: U.S. Government Printing Office.

Felsenthal, D. S., and M. Machover. 1998. *The Measurement of Voting Power*. Northampton, MA: Edward Elgar.

Fenster, Mark J. 1994. "The Impact of Allowing Day of Registration Voting on Turnout in U.S. Elections from 1960 to 1992." *American Politics Quarterly* 22(1): 74–87.

Ferejohn, John A., and M. P. Fiorina. 1974. "The Paradox of Not Voting: A Decision Theoretic Analysis." *American Political Science Review* 68(2): 525–536.

Fessenden, Ford, and John M. Broder. 2001. "Examining the Vote: The Overview; Study of Disputed Florida Ballots Finds Justices Did Not Cast the Deciding Vote." *New York Times*, 12 November.

Fishkin, James S. 1991. *Democracy and Deliberation*. New Haven, CT: Yale University Press.

———. 1995. *The Voice of the People*. New Haven, CT: Yale University Press.

Fleischer, Matt. 2000. "Women in NLJ 250 Hit a Glass Plateau: Mergers, Lure of Other Work Keep Numbers at Law Firms Flat." *The National Law Journal* 23(16).

Frady, Marshall. 1996. *Jesse: The Life and Pilgrimage of Jesse Jackson*. New York: Random House.

Franklin, D. P., and E. E. Grier. 1997. "Effects of Motor Vehicles Legislation: Voter Turnout, Registration, and Partisan Advantage in the 1992 Presidential Election." *American Politics Quarterly* 25(1): 104–117.

Franklin, Mark N. 1999. "Election Engineering and Cross-National Differences: What Role for Compulsory Voting?" *British Journal of Political Science* 29(1): 205–216.

———. 2001. "Electoral Participation." In *Comparing Democracies 2: Elections and Voting in Global Perspective*, ed. L. LeDuc, R. Niemi, and P. Norris. London: Sage.

Franklin, Mark N., Cess van der Eijk, and Erik Oppenhuis. 1996. "The Institutional Context: Turnout." In *Choosing Europe? The European Electorate and National Politics in the Fact of Union*, ed. M. Franklin and C. van der Eijk. Ann Arbor: University of Michigan Press.

Frankovic, Kathleen A. 1998. "Polling and the News." In *The Politics of News; The News of Politics*, ed. D. Graber, D. McQuail, and P. Norris. Washington, DC: CQ Press.

Frankovic, Kathleen A., and Monika L. McDermott. 2001. "Public Opinion and the 2000 Election: The Ambivalent Electorate." In *The Election of 2000: Reports and Interpretations*, ed. G. M. Pomper. New York: Chatham House Publishers.

Fraser, Jeanette Lynn. 1985. "The Effects of Voting Systems on Voter Participation: Punchcard Voting Systems in Ohio." Ph.D. diss., Ohio State University.

Fried, Charles. 2000. "How to Make the President Talk to the Local Pol." *New York Times*, 11 November.

Gallup Organization. 2001a. "Hispanics, Whites Rate Bush Positively, While Blacks Are Much More Negative." Princeton, NJ: Gallup News Service.

———. 2001b. "Opinion of U.S. Supreme Court Has Become More Politicized." Princeton, NJ: Gallup News Service.

Gelman, A., and J. N. Katz. 2001. "How Much Does a Vote Count? Voting Power, Coalitions, and the Electoral College." Caltech Social Science Working Paper No. 1121.

Gelman, A., and G. King. 1994. "A Unified Model for Evaluating Electoral Systems and Redistricting Plans." *American Journal of Political Science* 38: 514–554.

Gelman, A., J. N. Katz, and J. Bafumi. 2002. "Why Standard Voting Power Indexes Don't Work." Caltech Social Science Working Paper No. 1133.

Gelman, A., G. King, and W. J. Boscardin. 1998. "Estimating the Probability of Events That Have Never Occurred: When Is Your Vote Decisive?" *Journal of the American Statistical Association* 93: 1–9.

General Accounting Office Report on Elections. 2001. *The Scope of Congressional Authority in Elections Administration*. Online. www.gao.gov.

Gerber, Elisabeth R., and Rebecca B. Morton. 1998. "Primary Election Systems and Representation." *Journal of Law, Economics & Organization* 14: 304–324.

Gibson, Rachel. 2002. "Elections Online: Assessing Internet Voting in Light of the Arizona Democratic Primary." *Political Science Quarterly* 116(4): 561–583.

Gillman, Howard. 2001. *The Votes That Counted*. Chicago: University of Chicago Press.

Gold, David. 1952. "A Note on the 'Rationality' of Anthropologists in Voting for Officers." *American Sociological Review* 17(1): 99–101.

Goldstein, Tom, David McCormick, and Maya Windholtz. 2001. "NBC News Summary of Election Night Review." 4 January.

Gosnell, Harold Foote. 1927. *Getting Out the Vote: An Experiment in the Stimulation of Voting*. Chicago: University of Chicago Press.

Graber, Doris. 1991. "The Mass Media and Election Campaigns in the United States of America." In *Media, Elections and Democracy*, ed. F. Fletcher. Toronto: Dundurn Press.

Gratschew, Maria. 2002. "Compulsory Voting." In *Voter Participation Since 1945*. Stockholm, Sweden: International IDEA.

Greene, William H. 2000. *Econometric Analysis, 4th ed.* Upper Saddle River, NJ: Prentice Hall.

Grossman, Lawrence K. 2000. "Exit Polls, Academy Awards, and Presidential Elections." *Columbia Journalism Review* 39(1): 70–72.

Grotz, Florian. 2000. "Age of Voting." In *The International Encyclopedia of Elections*, ed. R. Rose. Washington, DC: CQ Press.

Guinier, Lani. 2000. "A New Voting Rights Movement." *New York Times*, 18 December.

Gutmann, Amy, and Dennis Thompson. 1996. *Democracy and Disagreement*. Cambridge, MA: Belknap Press.

Hamilton, Alexander, John Jay, and James Madison. [1787] 2001. *The Federalist*. Reprint, New York: Random House.

Hamilton, R. H. 1988. "American All-Mail Balloting: A Decade's Experience." *Public Administration Review* 45(5): 860–866.

Hanmer, M. J. 2000. "Alternative Estimates of the Effects of Election Day Registration and Motor Voter Laws." Washington, DC: American Political Science Association.

Harris, Joseph P. 1934. *Election Administration in the United States*. Washington, DC: The Brookings Institute.

Harwood, John. 2000. "Broken Ballot—America's Dysfunctional Voting System—Electoral Choices—Fixing the System." *Wall Street Journal*, 22 December.

Hasen, Richard L. 1996. "Voting without Law?" *University of Pennsylvania Law Review* 144: 2135–2180.

———. 2000. "Vote Buying." *California Law Review* 88: 1323–1372.

———. 2001. "*Bush v. Gore* and the Future of Equal Protection Law in Elections." *Florida State University Law Review* 29(2): 377–406.

———. 2002a. "Compton Decision: Too Clever by Half." *Los Angeles Times*, 12 February.

———. 2002b. "The Benefits of 'Judicially Unmanageable' Standards in Election Cases under the Equal Protection Clause." *North Carolina Law Review* 80(4): 1649–1503.

Heath, Anthony, and Bridget Taylor. 1999. "New Source of Abstention?" In *Critical Elections: British Parties and Voters in Long-Term Perspective*, ed. G. Evans and P. Norris. London: Sage.

Heckelman, Jac C. 1995. "The Effect of the Secret Ballot on Turnout Rates." *Public Choice* 82: 107.

Herron, Michael C., and Jasjeet S. Sekhon. 2001. "Overvoting and Representation: An Examination of Overvoted Presidential Ballots in Broward and Miami-Dade Counties." Unpublished manuscript, Harvard University.

Highton, B. 1997. "Easy Registration and Voter Turnout." *Journal of Politics* 59(2): 565–575.

Highton B., and R. E. Wolfinger. 1998. "Estimating the Effects of the National Voter Registration Act of 1993." *Political Behavior* 20(2): 79–104.

Hirczy, Wolfgang. 1994. "The Impact of Mandatory Voting Laws on Turnout: A Quasi Experimental Approach." *Electoral Studies* 13(1): 64–76.

———. 2000. "Compulsory Voting." In *The International Encyclopedia of Elections*, ed. R. Rose. Washington, DC: CQ Press.

House, Ernest R. 1988. *Jesse Jackson & the Politics of Charisma: the Rise and Fall of the PUSH/Excel Program*. Boulder, CO: Westview Press.

Hughes, Colin A. 1970. "Alphabetic Advantage in the House of Representatives." *Australian Quarterly* 4(2): 24–29.

"The Impact of the National Voter Registration Act of 1993 on the Administration of Elections for Federal Office 1999–2000, A Report to the 107th Congress." 2001. Issued by the Federal Election Commission's Office of Election Administration, June 21. Online. www.fec.gov/elections.html.

Issacharoff, Samuel. 2000. "The Court's Legacy for Voting Rights." *New York Times*, 14 December.

Jackman, Robert W. 1987. "Political Institutions and Voter Turnout in the Industrialized Democracies." *American Political Science Review* 81(2): 405–424.

Jackman, Robert W., and Ross A. Miller. 1995. "Voter Turnout in Industrial Democracies during the 1980s." *Comparative Political Studies* 27: 467–492.

Jackson, R. A. 1996. "A Reassessment of Voter Mobilization." *Political Research Quarterly* 49(2): 331–349.

Jacobson, Gary C. 1987. *The Politics of Congressional Elections*. Boston: Little, Brown, and Co.

Jenkins, Roy. 2001. *Churchill: A Biography*. New York: Farrar, Straus, and Giroux.

Johnson, Mitzi S. 1986. "The Initial Letter Effect: Ego Attachment or Mere Exposure?" Ph.D. diss., Ohio State University.

Jost, Kenneth, and Gregory Giroux. 2000. "Electoral College: The Issues." *CQ Researcher* 10(42): 980.

Judd, Charles M., and David A. Kenny. 1981. *Estimating the Effects of Social Interventions*. New York: Cambridge University Press.

Kamin, Leon J. 1958. "Ethnic and Party Affiliations of Candidates as Determinants of Voting." *Canadian Journal of Psychology* 12: 205–212.

Karlan, Pamela S. 1994. "Not by Money but by Virtue Won? Vote Trafficking and the Voting Rights System." *Virginia Law Review* 80: 205–212.

———. 2001. "The Newest Equal Protection: Regressive Doctrine on a Changeable Court." In *The Vote: Bush, Gore & the Supreme Court*, ed. C. Sunstein and R. Epstein. Chicago: University of Chicago Press.

Karp, Jeff A., and Susan Banducci. 1999. "The Impact of Proportional Representation on Turnout: Evidence from New Zealand." *Australian Journal of Political Science* 34(3): 363–377.

———. 2000. "Going Postal: How All-Mail Elections Influence Turnout." *Political Behavior* 22(3): 223–239.

Katz, Richard S. 1997. *Democracy and Elections*. New York: Oxford University Press.

———. 1999. "Role Orientations in Parliament." In *The European Parliament, the National Parliaments, and European Integration*, ed. R. Katz and B. Wessels. New York: Oxford University Press.

Kelley, Jonathan, and Ian McAllister. 1984. "Ballot Paper Cues and the Vote in Australia and Britain: Alphabetic Voting, Sex, and Title." *Public Opinion Quarterly* 48(2): 452–466.

Kelley, S. J., R. E. Ayres, and W. G. Bowen. 1967. "Registration and Voting: Putting First Things First." *American Political Science Review* 61(2): 359–379.

Kenney, Charles. 1988. *Dukakis: An American Odyssey*. Boston: Houghton Mifflin Co.

Kendall, Maurice G., and Alan Stuart. 1950. "The Law of Cubic Proportion in Election Results." *British Journal of Sociology* 1: 183–197.

Key, Vladimir O. 1957. Foreword. In Henry M. Bain and Donald S. Hecock, *Ballot Position and Voter's Choice*. Detroit, MI: Wayne State University Press.

Key, Vladimir O. 1966. *The Responsible Electorate*. Cambridge, MA: Harvard University Press.

Keyssar, Alexander. 2000. *The Right to Vote: The Contested History of Democracy in the United States*. New York: Basic Books.

Khanna, Roma. 2002. "Enron Debacle Revives Campaign Finance Reform." *Houston Chronicle*, 25 January.

King, Anthony. 1997. *Running Scared*. New York: Martin Kessler Books.

Klayman, J., and Y. Ha. 1987. "Confirmation, Disconfirmation, and Information in Hypothesis-Testing." *Psychological Review* 94: 211–228.

Knack, Stephen. 1995. "Does 'Motor Voter' Work? Evidence from State-Level Data." *The Journal of Politics* 57(3): 796–811.

———. 1999. "Drivers Wanted: Motor Voter and the Election of 1996." *PS, Political Science and Politics* 32(2): 237–243.

———. 2001. "Election-Day Registration: The Second Wave." *American Politics Research* 29(1): 65–78.

Knack, Stephen, and Martha Kropf. 2001a. "Invalidated Ballots in the 1996 Presidential Election: A County-Level Analysis." Unpublished manuscript, University of Missouri at Kansas City.

———. 2001b. "Roll Off at the Top of the Ballot: Intentional Undervoting in American Presidential Elections." Unpublished manuscript, University of Missouri at Kansas City.

Knack, Stephen, and James White. 2000. "Election-Day Registration and Turnout Inequality." *Political Behavior* 22(1): 29–44.

Konner, Joan, James Risser, and Ben Wattenberg. 2001. *Television's Performance on Election Night 2000: A Report for CNN. Fox News Network Report on Election Night— November 7–8, 2000*, 29 January.

Koriat, A., S. Lichtenstein, and B. Fischhoff. 1980. "Reasons for Confidence." *Journal of Experimental Psychology: Human Learning, Memory and Cognition* 6: 107–118.

Kranish, Michael. 1999. "Who's Ahead? N.H., National Polls Diverge in Key Primary State, Exposure Focuses the Fight." *Boston Globe*, 24 November.

Krosnick, Jon A. 1991. "Response Strategies for Coping with the Cognitive Demands of Attitude Measures in Surveys." *Applied Cognitive Psychology* 5: 213–236.

Krosnick, Jon A., and Leandre R. Fabrigar. Forthcoming. *Designing Good Questionnaires: Insights from Cognitive and Social Psychology*. New York: Oxford University Press.

Ladner, A., and H. Milner. 1999. "Do Voters Turn Out More under Proportional Than Majoritarian Systems? The Evidence from Swiss Communal Elections." *Electoral Studies* 18(2): 235–250.

Lang, Kurt, and Gladys Engel Lang. 1968. *Voting and Non-Voting: Implications of Broadcasting Returns before Polls Are Closed*. Waltham, MA: Blaisdell Publishing Company.

Larson, Kristen. 2001. "Cast Your Ballot.Com: Fulfill Your Civic Duty over the Internet." *William Mitchell Law Review* 27: 1797–1823.

Leonard, Bill. 1964. Internal CBS News memorandum, 14 October.

Lewine, Edward, and Emily Gest. 2000. "Hill Weighs in on Voting Fray." *N.Y. Daily News*, 11 November.

Lichtblau, Eric. 2002. "U.S. to Sue over 2000 Florida Vote; Election: The Justice Department Targets Three Counties for Alleged Voting Rights Violations." *Los Angeles Times*, 22 May.

Lijphart, Arend. 1992. *Parliamentary versus Presidential Government*. Oxford: Oxford University Press.

———. 1994. *Electoral Systems and Party Systems*. Oxford: Oxford University Press.

———. 1997. "Unequal Participation: Democracy's Unresolved Dilemma." *American Political Science Review* 91(1): 1–14.

———. 1999. *Patterns of Democracy*. New Haven, CT: Yale University Press.

———. 2000. "Turnout." In *The International Encyclopedia of Elections*, ed. R. Rose. Washington, DC: CQ Press.

Lijphart, Arend, and Rafael L. Pintor. 1988. "Alphabetic Bias in Partisan Elections: Patterns of Voting for the Spanish Senate, 1982 and 1986." *Electoral Studies* 7: 225–231.

Lincoln, Abraham. 1989. *Speeches and Writings, 1859–1865: Speeches, Letters, Miscellaneous Writings. Presidential Messages and Proclamations*. New York: Viking Press.

Lipton, Eric. 2000. "Problems Stir Calls to End '19th Century' Voting Process." *New York Times*, 13 November.

Littlewood, Thomas B. 1998. *Calling Elections: The History of Horserace Journalism*. Notre Dame, IN: University of Notre Dame Press.

Lochner, Todd, and Bruce E. Cain. 1999. "Equity and Efficacy in the Enforcement of Campaign Finance Laws." *Texas Law Review* 77: 1891–1942.

Locke, John. [1698] 1952. *The Second Treatise of Government*. Reprint, New York: Liberal Arts Press.

Lodge, Milton, Kathleen McGraw, and Patrick Stroh. 1989. "An Impression-Driven Model of Candidate Evaluation." *American Political Science Review* 83(2): 399–419.

Lowenstein, Daniel H., and Richard L. Hasen. 2001. *Election Law: Cases and Materials*. Duharm, NC: Carolina Academic Press.

Mackerras, Malcolm. 1968. "The Donkey Vote." *Australian Quarterly* 40: 89–93.

Madison, James. [1788] 1987. *The Federalist Papers*. Reprint, New York: Penguin Classics.

Magleby, D. B. 1987. "Participation in Mail Ballot Elections." *Western Political Quarterly* 40(1): 71–91.

———. 1996. "When People Vote in Vote-by-Mail Elections." Conference on Evaluating Vote-by-Mail Elections. Millbrae, California.

Maley, Michael. 2000. "Absentee Voting." In *The International Encyclopedia of Elections*, ed. R. Rose. Washington, DC: CQ Press.

Mann, I., and L. S. Shapley. 1960. "The a Priori Voting Strength of the Electoral College." RAND memo, reprinted in *Game Theory and Related Approaches to Social Behavior*, ed. M. Shubik. New York: Wiley.

Mann, Thomas E., and Raymond E. Wolfinger. 1980. "Candidates and Parties in Congressional Elections." *American Political Science Review* 74(3): 617–632.

Margolis, H. 1977. "Probability of a Tie Elections." *Public Choice* 31: 134–137.

———. 1983. "The Banzhaf Fallacy." *American Journal of Political Science* 27(2): 321–326.

Marks, Peter. 2000. "The Forgotten State: Dearth of Ads Makes Race in Kansas a Snooze." *New York Times*, 27 October.

Martelle, Scott. 2000. "Nader Pins Democrats' Woes on Gore." *Los Angeles Times*, 9 November.

Martinez, M. D., and D. Hill. 1999. "Did Motor Voter Work?" *American Politics Quarterly*, 27(3): 296–315.

Marx, Groucho. 1959. *Groucho and Me*. New York: Random House.

Mason, Linda, Kathleen Frankovic, and Kathleen Hall Jamieson. 2001. *CBS Coverage of Election Night 2000: Investigation, Analysis, Recommendations*. CBS News.

Masterman, C. J. 1964. "The Effect of the 'Donkey Vote' on the House of Representatives." *Australian Journal of Politics and History* 10: 221–225.

Mather, George B. 1964. *Effects of the Use of Voting Machines on Total Votes Cast: Iowa—1920–1960*. Iowa City: University of Iowa, Institute of Public Affairs.

Mathews, C. O. 1927. "The Effect of Position of Printed Response Words upon Children's Answers to Questions in Two-Response Types of Tests." *Journal of Educational Psychology* 18: 445–457.

McAllister, Ian. 1986. "Compulsory Voting, Turnout and Party Advantage in Australia." *Politics* 21(1): 89–93.

McCaffery, Edward J. 1994. "Why People Play Lotteries and Why It Matters." *Wisconsin Law Review* 1994(1): 72–122.

McDonald, Michael P., and Samuel L. Popkin. 2000. "The Myth of the Vanishing Voter." Paper presented at the American Political Science Convention, Washington, DC.

McNamee, Mike, Nanette Byrnes, and Louis Lavelle. 2002. "Turn Up the Heat on Board Cronyism." *Business Week*, 22 April.

Mendelsohn, Harold. 1966. "Western Voting and Broadcasts of Results on Presidential Election Day." *Public Opinion Quarterly* 30(2): 212–225.

Merriam, Charles Edward, and H. F. Gosnell. 1924. *Non-Voting: Causes and Methods of Control*. Chicago: University of Chicago Press.

Merrill, S. 1978. "Citizen Voting Power under the Electoral College: A Stochastic Model Based on State Voting Patterns." *SIAM Journal of Applied Mathematics* 34: 376–390.

Miller, George. 2002. "Enron Pension and Benefit Issues." Congressional Testimony by Federal Document Clearing House.

Miller, Joanne M., and Jon A. Krosnick. 1998. "The Impact of Candidate Name Order on Election Outcomes." *Public Opinion Quarterly* 62(3): 291–330.

Miller, Warren E. 1967. "Analysis of the Effect of Election Night Predictions on Voting Behavior." Submitted to Subcommittee on Communications, Senate Commerce Committee (July).

Miller, Warren E., and J. Merrill Shanks. 1996. *The New American Voter*. Cambridge, MA: Harvard University Press.

Mitchell, Alison. 2001. "Blacks and Hispanics in House Balk on Campaign Finance Bill." *New York Times*, 9 May.

Mitchell, Edward P. 1924. *Memoirs of an Editor: Fifty Years of American Journalism*. New York: Charles Scribner's and Sons.

Mitchell, Glenn E., and Christopher Wlezian. 1989. "The Impact of Legal Constraints on Voter Registration, Turnout, and the Composition of the American Electorate." *Political Behavior* 17(2): 179–202.

Montgomery, Michael J. 1985. "Voting Systems and Disenfranchisment." *Election Politics* 2: 16–19.

Morin, Richard, and Claudia Deane. 2000. "Public Backs Uniform Voting Rules; Poll Finds Wide Support for Guidelines on Ballots, Closing Times, Recounts." *Washington Post*, 18 December.

Mueller, John E. 1969. "Voting on the Propositions: Ballot Patterns and Historical Trends in California." *American Political Science Review* 63(4): 1197–1212.

———. 1970. "Choosing Among 133 Candidates." *Public Opinion Quarterly* 34(3): 395–402.

———. 1992. "Democracy and Ralph's Pretty Good Grocery: Elections, Equality, and the Minimal Human Being." *American Journal of Political Science* 36(4): 983–1003.

Nanda, Kristian. 1975. "An Experiment in Voting Choice: Who Gets the 'Blind' Vote?" *Experimental Study of Politics* 4: 20–35.

Nardulli, Peter F., Jon K. Dalager, and Donald E. Greco. 1996. "Voter Turnout in U.S. Presidential Elections: An Historical View and Some Speculation." *PS, Political Science and Politics* 29: 480–490.

National Association of Secretaries of State. Election Reform Resolution. 2001. Online. http://nass.stateofthevote.org/pub/pubs_electionres.html, 6 February.

National Commission on Federal Election Reform. 2001. "To Assure Pride and Confidence in the Electoral Process." Charlottseville, VA: Miller Center of Public Affairs.

Nichols, Stephen M., and Gregory A. Strizek. 1995. "Electronic Voting Machines and Ballot Roll-Off." *American Politics Quarterly* 23(3): 300–318.

Norris, Pippa. 2002. *Democratic Phoenix: Political Activism Worldwide*. New York: Cambridge University Press.

Nuttin, Jozef M. 1985. "Narcissism beyond Gestalt and Awareness: The Name Letter Effect." *European Journal of Social Psychology* 15: 353–361.

Oliver, J. E. 1996. "The Effects of Eligibility Restrictions and Party Activity on Absentee Voting and Overall Turnout." *American Journal of Political Science* 40(2): 498–513.

Ornstein, Norman. 2001. "Election Reform Requires Swift, National Effort—and Money." *USA Today*, 8 February.

O'Rourke, Lawrence M. 2001. "Clinton Advisors Opposed Pardon Aides Argued against Deal for Marc Rich and Thought It Wouldn't Happen." *Chicago Sun-Times*, 2 March.

Ortiz, Daniel R. 1998. "The Democratic Paradox of Campaign Finance Reform." *Stanford Law Review* 50: 893–914.

Page, Benjamin. 1978. *Choices and Echoes in Presidential Elections*. Chicago: University of Chicago Press.

Palermo, B. J. 2000. "Rights Groups Latch onto *Bush v. Gore*." *National Law Journal*, 21 May.

Patterson, S. C., and G. A. Caldeira. 1983. "Getting Out the Vote: Participation in Gubernatorial Elections." *American Political Science Review* 77(3): 675–689.

Patterson, Thomas E. 1993. *Out of Order*. New York: Alfred A. Knopf.

Patterson, Thomas E. 2002. *The Vanishing Voter: Public Involvement in an Age of Uncertainty*. New York: Alfred A. Knopf.

Pennock, J. Roland. 1979. *Democratic Political Theory*. Princeton, NJ: Princeton University Press.

Peretti, Terri Jennings. 1999. *In Defense of a Political Court*. Princeton, NJ: Princeton University Press.

Pildes, Richard H. 2002. "Is Voting-Rights Law Now at War with Itself? Social Science and Voting Rights in the 2000s." *North Carolina Law Review* 80: 1517.

Plato. 1957. *The Republic*. Trans. A. D. Lindsay. New York: Dutton.

Plissner, Martin. 1999. *The Control Room: How Television Calls the Shots in Presidential Elections*. New York: Free Press.

Polsby, Nelson. 1983. *Consequences of Party Reform*. New York: Oxford University Press.

Polsbsy, Nelson, and Aaron Wildavsky. 2000. *Presidential Elections: Strategies and Structures of American Politics*. Chatham, NJ: Chatham House.

Popkin, Samuel L. 1979. *The Rational Peasant*. Berkeley: University of California Press.

———. 1991. *The Reasoning Voter*. Chicago: University of Chicago Press.

Posner, Richard A. 2001. *Breaking the Deadlock: The 2000 Election, the Constitution, and the Courts*. Princeton, NJ: Princeton University Press.

Powell, G. Bingham. 1986. "American Voter Turnout in Comparative Perspective." *American Political Science Review* 80(1): 17–43.

Powers, William. 2000. "Amending the Media Constitution." *National Journal* 15: 369.

"Progress on Election Reform" [Editorial]. *New York Times*, 15 May.

Rabinowitz, G., and S. E. Macdonald. 1986. "The Power of the States in U.S. Presidential Elections." *American Political Science Review* 80: 65–87.

"A Racial Gap in Voided Votes" [Editorial]. 2000. *Washington Post*, December 27.

Rae, Douglas. 1971. *The Political Consequences of Electoral Laws*. New Haven, CT: Yale University Press.

Rakove, Jack N. 1996. *Original Meanings: Politics and Ideas in the Making of the Constitution*. New York: A.A. Knopf.

Ralph, Julian. 1903. *The Making of a Journalist*. New York: Harper & Bros.

Rasky, Susan. 2002. "The Crusade That Ate Reform." *Los Angeles Times*, 31 March.

Reif, Karl, and Hermann Schmitt. 1980. "Nine National Second Order Elections." *European Journal of Political Research* 8: 3–44.

"Report of the NACO/NACRC Commission on Election Standards and Reform." 2001. National Association of Counties, 30 April.

Research Triangle Institute. 2001. *Evaluation of the Voter News Service's Procedures and Operations for the 2000 Presidential Election*, 22 January. Chapel Hill, NC: Research Triangle Institute.

Reynolds, Andrew, and Ben Reilly. 1997. *The International IDEA Handbook of Electoral System Design*. Stockholm, Sweden: International IDEA.

Rhine, S. L. 1995. "Registration Reform and Turnout Change in the American States." *American Politics Quarterly* 23(4): 409–426.

Richardson, L. E. J., and G. W. Neeley. 1996. "Implementation of Early Voting." *Spectrum* 69(3): 16.

Riker, William H. 1982. *Liberalism Against Populism*. San Francisco: Freeman.

Riker, William H., and P. C. Ordeshook. 1986. "A Theory of the Calculus of Voting." *American Political Science Review* 62: 25–42.

Robinson, James A., and William H. Standing. 1960. "Some Correlates of Voter Participation: The Case of Indiana." *Journal of Politics* 22(1): 96–111.

Robson, Christopher, and B. Walsh. 1974. "The Importance of Positional Voting Bias in the Irish General Election of 1973." *Political Studies* 22: 191–203.

Roeper, Richard. 2002. "In Oscar or Political Race, Smear Campaigns Reign." *Chicago Sun-Times*, 18 March.

Romans, Christine, Ali Velshi, and Deborah Marchini. 2002. "Disney Tightens Policies to Keep Independent Board More Independent." *CNNFN*, 29 April.

Rose, Richard. 2000a. "Unfree Elections." In *The International Encyclopedia of Elections*, ed. R. Rose. Washington, DC: CQ Press.

———. 2000b. *International Encyclopedia of Elections*. Washington, DC: CQ Press.

Rosenstone, S. J., and J. M. Hansen. 1993. *Mobilization, Participation, and Democracy in America*. New York: Macmillan.

Rosenstone, S. J., and R. E. Wolfinger. 1978. "The Effect of Registration Laws on Voter Turnout." *American Political Science Review* 72(1): 22–45.

———. 1980. *Who Votes?* New Haven, CT: Yale University Press.

Rule, Wilma. 2000. "Women's Enfranchisement." In *International Encyclopedia of Elections*, ed. R. Rose. Washington, DC: CQ Press.

Rusk, JG. 1970. "The Effect of Australian Ballot Reform on Split-Ticket Voting: 1876–1908." *American Political Science Review* 64(4): 1220–1238.

Sanko, John. 2001. "Bill Would Parcel State's Electoral Votes." *Rocky Mountain News*, 18 February.

Schwarz, Jerry. 2000. "One Man's Florida Mess Is Another Man's Civic Lesson." *Associated Press Wire*, 27 February.

Schwarz, Norbert, H. J. Hippler, and E. Noelle-Neumann. 1993. "A Cognitive Model of Response Order Effects in Survey Measurement. In *Autobiographical Memory and the Validity of Retrospective Reports*, ed. N. Schwarz and S. Sudman. New York: Springer-Verlag.

Scott, W. James. 1972. "California Ballot Position Statutes: An Unconstitutional Advantage to Incumbents." *Southern California Law Review* 45: 365–395.

Scripps Howard/Ohio University Poll. October 21 1-N November 15, 2001. Online. http://nationaljournal.com/members/polltrack/2000races/whitehouse/wh2000recount.htm.

Seelye, Katharine Q. 2001a. "National Awash in Ideas for Changing Voting." *New York Times*, 28 January.

————. 2001b. "Action on Voting Lags, Experts Warn." *New York Times*, 4 April.

————. 2001c. "Four Senators Seek to Revive Effort to Overhaul Balloting." *New York Times*, 15 May.

————. 2001d. "Divided Civil Rights Panel Approves Election Report." *New York Times*, 9 June.

————. 2001e. "Little Change Forecast for Election Process." *New York Times*, 26 April.

Shapiro, Walter. 1988. "Battling for the Post-Liberal Soul; For Now It's Gephardt vs. Dukakis, with Simon Scrambling to Keep Up." *Time Magazine* 131(8): 19.

Shaw, Daron, Rodolfo O. de la Garza, and Jongho Lee. 2000. "Examining Latino Turnout in 1996: A Three-State, Validated Survey Approach." *American Journal of Political Science* 44(2): 332–340.

Shaw, Gwyneth K. 2002. "Enron's Fall Resurrects Campaign-Finance Reform: Petition Forces House Vote on Donations." *Orlando Sentinel*, 25 January.

Shocket, Peter A., Neil R. Heighberger, and Clyde Brown. 1992. "The Effect of Voting Technology on Voting Behavior in a Simulated Multi-Candidate City Council Election: A Political Experiment of Ballot Transparency." *Western Political Quarterly* 45(2): 521–537.

Sidel, Robin. 2001. "Deals & Deal Makers: Web Site Draw SEC Concern in Bid Battle." *Wall Street Journal*, 7 May.

Sigelman, Lee, and Malcolm E. Jewell. 1986. "Voting in Primaries: The Impact of Intra- and Inter-Party Competition." *The Western Political Quarterly* 39: 446–454.

Sigelman, Lee, et al. 1985. "Voting and Nonvoting: A Multi-Election Perspective." *American Journal of Political Science* 29(4): 749–765.

Simon, Herbert. 1957. *Models of Man*. New York: Wiley.

Smolka, Richard G. 1977. *Election Day Registration: the Minnesota and Wisconsin Experience in 1976*. Washington, DC: American Enterprise Institute for Public Policy Research.

Smolkin, Rachel. 2001a. "Ascent into Male-Dominated Fields Requires More Than Being Qualified. A Little Help Makes Breaking Barriers Easier." *Pittsburgh Post-Gazette*, 3 June.

————. 2001b. "Equality at Work Remains Elusive." *Pittsburgh Post-Gazette*, 3 June.

Solop, F. I. 2001. "Digital Democracy Comes of Age: Internet Voting and the 2000 Arizona Democratic Primary Election." *PS, Political Science and Politics* 34(2): 289–293.

Southwell, Priscilla L., and Justin Burchett. 1997. "Survey of Vote-by-Mail Senate Election in the State of Oregon." *PS, Political Science and Politics* 30: 53–57.

————. 1997. "Survey of Vote by Mail Senate Election in the State of Oregon." *PS, Political Science and Politics*. 30: 53–7. March.

————. 2000. "The Effect of All-Mail Elections on Voter Turnout." *American Politics Quarterly* 28(1): 72–79.

Squitieri, Tom. 2000. "Proposals Hit Table on Ways to Reform Election Process." *USA Today*, 22 November.

Stanton, Frank. 1964. Letter to Dean Burch. Personal correspondence.

Steel, Michael, and Michael Posner. 2001. "Campaign 2000 Lends Urgency to Reform Bills." *National Journal*. Online: www.nationaljournal.com.

Steen, Jennifer A., and J. G. Koppell. 2001. "First Guys Finish First: The Effect of Ballot Position on Election Outcomes." Paper presented at the annual meeting of the American Political Science Association, 30 August—2 September, San Francisco, California.

Stein, R. M. 1998. "Early Voting." *Public Opinion Quarterly* 62(1): 57–69.

Stein, R. M., and P. A. Garcia-Monet. 1997. "Voting Early but Not Often." *Social Science Quarterly* 78(3): 657–671.

Steinem, Gloria. 1994. *Moving Beyond Words*. New York: Simon & Schuster.

Stern, Sydney L. 1997. *Gloria Steinem: Her Passions, Politics, & Mystique*. Secaucus, NJ: Carol Publishing Group.

Story, Joseph. [1833] 1987. *Commentaries on the Constitution of the United States*. Reprint, Durham, NC: Carolina Academic Press.

Stout, David. 2002. "Senate Overwhelmingly Passes Bipartisan Election Reform." *New York Times*, 11 April.

Straffin, P. D. 1978. "Probability Models for Power Indices." In *Game Theory and Political Science*, ed. P. Ordeshook. New York: New York University Press.

Sudman, Seymour, Norman M. Bradburn, and Norbert Schwarz. 1996. *Thinking about Answers: The Application of Cognitive Processes to Survey Methodology*. San Francisco: Jossey-Bass.

Sunstein, Cass. 1993a. *Democracy and the Problem of Free Speech*. New York: Free Press.

———. 1993b. *The Partial Constitution*. Cambridge, MA: Harvard University Press.

———. 2001. "What We'll Remember in 2050." In Bush v. Gore: *The Court Cases and the Commentary*, ed. E. J. Dionne and W. Kristol. Washington, DC: Brookings Institute Press.

Swisher, Kara. 2002. "Boom Town: Hewlett, Fiorina: Can the Marriage at H-P Be Saved?" *Wall Street Journal*, 18 March.

Taebel, Delbert A. 1975. "The Effect of Ballot Position on Electoral Success." *American Journal of Political Science* 19(3): 519–526.

Teixeira, Ruy A. 1992. "The Disappearing American Voter." Washington, DC: The Brookings Institute.

Thomas, Norman C. 1968. "Voting Machines and Voter Participation in Four Michigan Constitutional Revision Referenda." *Western Political Quarterly* 21: 409–419.

Thornton, Emily, and David Henry. 2002. "Big Guns Aim for Change." *Business Week*, 24 June.

Timmerman, Kenneth R. 2002. *Shakedown! Exposing the Real Jesse Jackson*. Washington, DC: Regnery Publishing.

Toedtman, James. 2000. "Civics Lesson Comes to Life." *Newsday*, 14 December.

Topf, Richard. 1995. "Electoral Participation." In *Citizens and the State*, ed. H. D. Klingemann and D. Fuchs. Oxford: Oxford University Press.

Traugott, Michael. 1997. "An Evaluation of Voting-by-Mail in Oregon." Washington, DC, University of Michigan and the League of Women Voters. Unpublished paper.

Traugott, Michael, and R. G. Mason. 1996. "Report on the Characteristics of the Oregon Electorate Participating in the Special General Election for the U.S. Senate on January 30, 1996." Presented at the Conference on Evaluating Vote-by-Mail Elections, Millbrae, California.

Tufte, Edward R. 1974. *Date Analysis for Politics and Policy*. Englewood Cliffs, NJ: Prentice-Hall.

Upton, G. J. G., and D. Brook. 1974. "The Importance of Positional Voting Bias in British Elections." *Political Studies* 22: 178–190.

———. 1975. "The Determination of the Optimum Position on a Ballot Paper." *Applied Statistics* 24(3): 279–287.

U.S. Census Bureau. 2001. "Profiles of General Demographic Characteristics: 2000 Census of Population and Housing, California." Washington, DC: U.S. Department of ˜merce.

———. 2001. "Statistical Abstract of the United States: The National Date Book, 2001." Washington, DC: U.S. Department of Commerce.

———. 2002. "Reported Voting and Registration by Race, Hispanic Origin, Sex and Age Groups: November 1964 to 2000." Washington, DC: U.S. Department of Commerce.

U.S. General Accounting Office, October 2001. "Statistical Analysis of Factors that Affected Uncounted Voters in the 2000 Presidential Election." Washington, DC: GAO-02-122.

U.S. House Committee on Government Reform. 2001. "Income and Racial Disparities in the Undercount in the 2000 Presidential Election." Washington, DC: U.S. House of Representatives (July).

Vanderleeuw, James W., and Richard L. Engstrom. 1987. "Race, Referendums, and Roll-Off." *Journal of Politics* 49(4): 1081–1092.

"Vindicating the Court" 2001. [Editorial]. *Wall Street Journal,* 13 November.

Vita, Matthew, and Helen Dewar. 2000. "Congress Debates Election Reform; Members' Proposals Range from Modest Changes to Abolition of the Electoral College." *Washington Post,* 17 November.

Volcansek, Mary L. 1981. "An Exploration of the Judicial Election Process." *Western Political Quarterly* 34: 572–577.

Von Sternberg, Bob. 2000. "How about Fine-Tuning the System? Minnesota Republican Legislators Argue That the Winner-Take-All Model Be Replaced by Apportioning States' Electors." *Star Tribune,* 26 November.

"Vote Counting: Fix It" [Editorial]. 2000. *Los Angeles Times,* 17 December.

Voting System Standards: A Report on the Feasibility of Developing Voluntary Standards for Voting Equipment, a report by the Federal Election Commission in consultation with the National Bureau of Standards, 1984.

Walker, Adrian. 2000. "Civics Lesson a Harsh One." *Boston Globe,* 15 December.

Walker, David M. 2001. "Elections: Issues Affecting Military and Overseas Absentee Voters." Statement of David M. Walker, Comptroller General of the United States for the Subcommittee on Military Personnel, Committee on Armed Forces, House of Representatives, 9 May.

Walker, Jack L. 1963. "Negro Voting in Atlanta: 1953–1961." *Phylon,* 379–387.

———. 1966. "Ballot Forms and Voter Fatigue: An Analysis of the Office Block and Party Column Ballots." *Midwest Journal of Political Science* 10(4): 448–463.

Walsh, Edward. 2002. "House Approves Election Reform: $3.9 Billion Bill Aims to Overhaul Federal Voting System." *Washington Post,* October 11.

Wattenberg, Martin P., and Craig Leonard Brians. 1999. "Negative Campaign Advertising: Demobilizer or Mobilizer?" *American Political Science Review* 93(4): 891–899.

Wells, Susan J. 2001. "A Female Executive Is Hard to Find." *HR Magazine* 46(6): 40.

Wertheimer, Fred, and Susan Weiss Manes. 1994. "Campaign Finance Reform: A Key to Restoring the Health of Our Democracy." *Columbia Law Review* 94: 1126–1159.

Westin, David. 2001. Testimony before U.S. House of Representatives Committee on Energy and Commerce, 14 February.

White, Howard. 1950. "Voters Plump for First on List." *National Municipal Review* 39: 110–111.

White, John P. 1960. *Voting Machines and the 1958 Defeat of Constitutional Revision in Michigan.* Ann Arbor: Institute of Public Administration, University of Michigan Press.

Wills, Garry. 2002. *James Madison.* New York: Times Books.

Wilson, Woodrow. 1910. "Hide-and-Seek Politics." *North American Review* 191: 585–601.

Wolf, Jim, and Dan Harrie. 2000. "Utahns Voice Pros, Cons of Electoral Setup." *Salt Lake Tribune,* 12 November.

Wolfinger, Raymond E., and Jonathan Hoffman. 2001. "Registering and Voting with Motor Voter." *PS, Political Science and Politics* 34: 85–92.

Wolfinger, Raymond E., David Glass, and Peverill Squire. 1990. "Predictors of Electoral Turnout: An International Comparison." *Policy Studies Review* 9: 551–574.

"Women Still Rare on Boards of Directors" [Editorial]. 1998. *San Francisco Chronicle*, 16 October.

Wood, Gordon S. 1992. *The Radicalism of the American Revolution*. New York: A.A. Knopf.

———. 2002. "Rambunctious American Democracy." *New York Review of Books* 49: 20–23.

Woodroofe, M. 1975. *Probability with Applications*. New York: McGraw Hill.

Zajonc, Robert B. 1968. "Attitudinal Effects of Mere Exposure." *Journal of Personality and Social Psychology*, 9, Monograph Supplement No. 2, Pt. 2.

Zukerman, David T. 1927. "The Voting Machine Extends Its Territory." *American Political Science Review* 21(3): 603–610.

Court Cases

Abbott Laboratories v. Gardner, 387 U.S. 136 (1967).
Alden v. Maine, 527 U.S. 706 (1999).
Allen v. Wright, 468 U.S. 737 (1984).
Andrews v. Cox, No. 1:01-cv-00318-ODE (U.S. District Court. N.D. GA, filed January 5, 2001).
Avery v. Midland County, 390 U.S. 474 (1968).
Baker v. Carr, 82 S.Ct. 691 (1962).
Black v. McGuffage, 209 F. Supp. 2d 889 (ND Ill. 2002).
Bohus v. Board of Election Commissioners, 447 F2d 821 (1971).
Bolin v. Superior Court In and For Maricopa County, 85 Ariz. 131 (1958).
Burdick v. Takushi, 504 U.S. 428 (1992).
Buckley v. Valeo, 424 U.S. 1 (1976).
Bush v. Gore, 121 S.Ct. 525 (2000).
Bush v. Palm Beach County Canvassing Board, 121 S.Ct. 471 (2000).
City of Boerne v. Flores, 521 U.S. 507 (1997).
Clough v. Guzzi, 416 F. Supp. 1057 (1976).
Cook v. Gralike, 121 S.Ct. 1029 (2001).
Common Cause v. Jones, pending in the United States District court for the Central District of California.
Culliton v. DuPage County Board of Election Commissioners, 419 F. Supp. 126 (1976).
Elliott v. Secretary of State, 294 NW 171 (1940).
Engle v. Isaac, 456 U.S. 107 (1982).
Ex parte Clarke, 100 U.S. 399, 404 (1879).
Foster v. Love, 522 U.S. 67 (1997).
Glenn v. Federal Election Commission, 822 F.2d. 1097 (1987).
Gore v. Harris, 773 So. 2d. 524 (2000).
Gould v. Grubb, 14 Cal. 3d. 661 (1975).
Graves v. McElderry, 946 F. Supp. 1569 (1996).
Harper v. Virginia Board of Elections, 383 U.S. 663 (1966).
Holtzman v. Power, 313 N.Y.S.2d. 760 (1970).
In re election of November 6, 1990 for Office of Atty. Gen. of Ohio, 569 N.E.2d. 447 (Ohio, 1997).
Kautenburger v. Jackson, 85 Ariz. 128 (1958).
Koppell v. New York State Board of Elections, 108 F. Supp. 2d. 355 (2000).
Lujan v. Defenders of Wildlife, 504 U.S. 555 (1992).
McLain v. Meier, 637 F.2d. 1159 (1980).

Munro v. Socialist Workers Party. 479 U.S. 189 (1986).

Murdock v. City of Memphis, 87 U.S. 590 (1874).

NAACP v. Harris, 567 F. Supp. 637 (1983).

New Jersey Conservative Party v. Farmer, 753 A.2d. 192 (1999).

New State Ice Co. v. Liebmann, 285 U.S. 262 (1932).

New York v. United States, 505 U.S. 144 (1992).

Nixon v. Shrink Missouri Government PAC, 528 U.S. 377 (2000).

O'Shea v. Littleton, 414 U.S. 488 (1974).

Printz v. United States, 521 U.S. 898 (1997).

Ray v. Blair, 343 U.S. 214 (1952).

Reno v. Catholic Social Services, 113 S.Ct. 2485 (1993).

Republican Party of Minnesota v. White, 2002 WL 1378604.

Reynolds v. Sims, 377 U.S. 533 (1964).

Sangmeister v. Woodard, 565 F.2d. 460 (1977).

Seminole Tribe v. Florida, 517 U.S. 44 (1996).

Shaw v. Reno, 509 U.S. 630 (1993).

Smiley v. Holm, 285 U.S. 355 (1932).

Sonneman v. State of Alaska, 969 P.2d. 632 (1998).

South Dakota v. Dole, 483 U.S. 203 (1987).

Stone v. Powell, 428 U.S. 465 (1976).

Texas v. U.S., 118 S.Ct. 1257 (1998).

Timmons v. Twin Cities Area New Party, 520 U.S. 351 (1997).

Turner v. Slagle, Supreme Court of Ohio, Case no. 72-887 (1972).

United States v. Cruikshank, 92 U.S. 542 (1875).

United States v. Gradwell, 243 U.S. 476, 483 (1917).

United States v. Lopez, 514 U.S. 549 (1995).

United States v. McCrainie, 169 F2d 723 (11th Cir. 1999).

United States v. Morrison, 529 U.S. 848 (2000).

United States v. Reese, 92 U.S. 214 (1875).

Ulland v. Growe, 262 N.W.2d. 412 (1978).

Weisburg v. Powell, 417 F.2d 388 (1969).

Surveys and Polls

ABCNews.com poll conducted by ICR (International Communications Research). November 14–19, 2000. Online. http://nationaljournal.com/members/polltrack/2000/races/whitehouse/wh2000recount.htm

ABC News/Washington Post poll. December 14–15, 2000. Online. http://nationaljournal.com/members/polltrack/2000/races/whitehouse/wh2000recount.htm

CBS News polls. November 19, 2000, and December 9–10, 2000. Online. http://national journal.com/members/polltrack/2000/races/whitehouse/wh2000recount.htm

CBS News poll. December 14–16, 2000. Online. http://nationaljournal.com/members/polltrack/2000/races/whitehouse/wh2000recount.htm

CNN/Gallup/USA Today survey. November 11–12, 2000. Online. http://national journal.com/members/polltrack/2000/races/whitehouse/wh2000recount.htm.

CNN/Gallup/USA Today poll. November 26–27, 2000. Online. http://nationaljournal.com/members/polltrack/2000/races/whitehouse/wh2000recount.htm

Fox News/Opinion Dynamics Poll. November 29–30, 2000. Online. http://national journal.com/members/polltrack/2000/races/whitehouse/wh2000recount.htm

Gallup poll. November 13–15, 2000. Online. http://nationaljournal.com/members/polltrack/2000/races/whitehouse/wh2000recount.htm

Gallup poll press release. November 16, 2000. Online. http://www.gallup.com/poll/releases/pr001116.asp

ISA/Caltech Survey. 2001. Conducted for the California Institute of Technology by the Interview Service of America, 26 March—9 April.

NBC News/Wall St. Journal poll. December 7–10, 2000. Online. http://nationaljournal.com/members/polltrack/2000/races/whitehouse/wh2000recount.htm

Newsweek/Princeton Survey Research Associates poll. December 14–15, 2000. Online. http://nationaljournal.com/members/polltrack/2000/races/whitehouse/wh2000 recount.htm

Author Index

Subject Index